LIGHT ON LIFE

Robert Svoboda has lived in India for nearly fifteen years. He graduated from the Talak Ayurveda College of the University of Poona in 1980 as the first and, until today, only Westerner ever to become a licensed Ayurvedic physician. Since then he has travelled extensively, lecturing and conducting workshops on Ayurvedic and other subjects. Among his writings on Ayurveda are three books: *Prakruti: Your Ayurvedic Constitution*, *The Hidden Secret of Ayurveda* and *Ayurveda: Life, Health and Longevity* (Arkana, 1992), and a self-study programme, *The Ayurvedic Home Study Course*. His books *Aghora: At the Left Hand of God* and *Aghora II: Kundalini* introduce some of the little-known Tantric traditions of his teacher, Vimalananda. It was Vimalananda who first set him to study Jyotish, and he has since pursued this study under the direction of various experts, including in particular Mr Hart deFouw. Dr Svoboda is on the staff of the Ayurvedic Institute in Albuquerque, New Mexico, and divides his time among North America, India and the rest of the world.

Hart deFouw has been studying and practising Vedic astrology since 1968. He trained intensively for fifteen years with his Indian Vedic astrology teacher, who also introduced him to other relevant components of classical Indian culture. Since 1988, he has travelled extensively by invitation to give lectures, seminars and consultations world-wide. He is a featured and popular speaker at international conferences. He is a visiting faculty member and a board member at the Ayurvedic Institute of New Mexico.

A cassette by Robert Svoboda, that will assist your absorption of the material in *Light on Life*, is available from:

Ayurvedic Institute   *and*   Ayurvedic Living Ltd
PO Box 23445   PO Box 188
Albuquerque   Exeter
NM87192-1445   EX4 5AB
USA   UK

LIGHT ON LIFE

An Introduction to the Astrology of India

HART DEFOUW AND
ROBERT SVOBODA

ARKANA
PENGUIN BOOKS

ARKANA

Published by the Penguin Group
Penguin Books Ltd, 27 Wrights Lane, London w8 5tz, England
Penguin Books USA Inc., 375 Hudson Street, New York, New York 10014, USA
Penguin Books Australia Ltd, Ringwood, Victoria, Australia
Penguin Books Canada Ltd, 10 Alcorn Avenue, Toronto, Ontario, Canada m4v 3b2
Penguin Books (NZ) Ltd, 182–190 Wairau Road, Auckland 10, New Zealand

Penguin Books Ltd, Registered Offices: Harmondsworth, Middlesex, England

First published 1996
3 5 7 9 10 8 6 4 2

Astrological charts drawn by Nigel Andrews

Set in 10/12.5 pt Monotype Garamond
Typeset by Datix International Limited, Bungay, Suffolk
Printed in England by Clays Ltd, St Ives plc

CONTENTS

CHAPTER THREE

ESSENTIAL ASTRONOMY FOR JYOTISH   39

CHAPTER FOUR

THE GRAHAS (PLANETS)   55

CHAPTER ELEVEN
DASHAS AND GOCHARAS

CHAPTER TWELVE
EXAMPLE CHARTS

LIST OF TABLES

LIST OF FIGURES

DEDICATION

We join a long line of jyotishis in invoking the blessings of the incomparable Ganesha, the Remover of Obstacles, the Lord of Jyotish and the Divine Patron of scribes. To the extent that Ganesha sees fit to to have this work accepted as a faithful account of the foundations of Jyotish, to that extent will it help to preserve and spread the knowledge of Jyotish.

We thank our Gurus, especially the astonishingly gifted and knowledgeable Mantriji, who planted the seed of Jyotish in us and nurtured it over many years. Although he preserves his anonymity, this work is dedicated to him. Without his guidance we would be overwhelmed by the enormity of Jyotish.

I (Hart deFouw) give tender thanks to my wife, Aletha, for being a pillar of support over the past twenty years while I pursued my dream. Without her practical support in the 'trenches' of life, I would still be dreaming!

ACKNOWLEDGEMENTS

Our publishers, who made it possible for you to hold this book in your hands.

The many who have directly contributed comments to this book, especially Fred Smith, Ph.D., for his erudite critique of the manuscript.

The many clients and sponsors over the years, too numerous to mention or even to recall. You know who you are, and we acknowledge you for your support.

NOTE

In this book we will use the following abbreviations for the twelve constellations:

AR = Aries	LE = Leo	SA = Sagittarius
TA = Taurus	VI = Virgo	CP = Capricorn
GE = Gemini	LI = Libra	AQ = Aquarius
CN = Cancer	SC = Scorpio	PI = Pisces

The abbreviations for the nine planets used in Jyotish are:

SU = Sun	ME = Mercury	SA = Saturn
MO = Moon	JU = Jupiter	RA = Rahu
MA = Mars	VE = Venus	KE = Ketu

'R' after a planet's abbreviation means that it is retrograde.

NOTE: Jyotish's Nine Planets are sometimes referred to as 'male', sometimes as 'female' in this book. This results from the conventions of the historical period in which a particular story or principle developed. At one time all the planets were referred to as 'male', a convention which continues to be followed in certain contexts by most jyotishis in India today. It is true, however, that most Indian jyotishis regard the Moon and Venus as 'female planets' for practical work.

FOREWORD

Jyotish is a Sanskrit term derived from two roots: *jyoti*, which means light, and *Isha*, which means Lord or God. Jyotish, then, literally means the Lord of light, with special reference to the Sun, Moon, stars and planets. It is a science of the study of heavenly lights and their effects on human life. *Atma Jyoti Parama Dhama* means that *atma* (the soul) or pure awareness is also the light, and that one should seek to attain that light of life with the help of Jyotish. Jyotish helps to achieve the four main goals of human life: *dharma* (religious merit), *artha* (acquiring wealth), *kama* (worldly enjoyment) and *moksha* (liberation). It governs not only individual life, but global affairs as well. The study of the influence of light on every living and non-living thing is the science of Jyotish. The word 'astrology' has the same roots: 'astro' refers to the stars (the source of light) and 'logos' science. Everything in the universe is moving and changing, and that which is moving is bound by time. Stars are luminous bodies radiating energy into space. The rays of light, then, come from the stars and planets, which are surrounded by their own magnetic and gravitational fields influencing this light. The Earth, then, receives this light. According to ancient jyotish shastra (scriptures), Saturn is the most distant planetary body influencing the Earth, and the Moon is the nearest. The Sun is considered the soul of our solar system. These light energies coming from the Sun, Moon, planets and stars all separately influence the physical, environmental, mental and spiritual status of all beings. This light also affects the dark recess of distant future. (Just consider the fact that the light from many stars began its journey millions of years ago.) The ancient science of jyotish uses accurate mathematical calculations to determine the position (past, present and future) of the heavenly bodies in order to foretell the future of individuals and the fate of nations, empires, kingdoms, wars, revolutions and other terrestrial events.

Jyotish believes that man is a creation of the cosmos. From the *Ayurvedic* standpoint, every human being has a unique body type, called *prakruti*. Jyotish also believes that everyone has a unique planetary constitution. This combination governs the entire psycho-somatic make-up of an individual. The unique combination of every individual depends entirely upon the specific time and place of physical birth. So it is very important to check in the *kundali* (astrological chart) for personal compatibility before marriage, in order to bring clarity, communication and success in marital life. People should plan well in advance for conception, building a house or beginning any auspicious work according to the most favorable planetary positions.

Just as imbalance of bodily *dosha* causes disease, likewise the undesirable effect of certain planets can become a causative factor in ill-health. According to *Ayurveda*, every individual has seven bodily tissues, and according to Jyotish they are influenced by the different planets. For instance, the Sun influences consciousness and eyes, the Moon governs the mind, Mercury the intellect, and Jupiter super-vises knowledge. Mars is related to the blood and liver, Saturn rules the neuro-muscular systems. Venus governs the reproductive system and artistic talent. Jyotish can be studied under several different aspects: astro-physiology, psychology, etiology, pathology, symp-tomatology and therapeutics. Like any other *Vedic* discipline, the study of Jyotish needs the guidance and blessings of a guru (one who has mastered the subject) in order to have the insight to read and interpret the Jyotish chart. It is a wonderful healing science which can suggest certain stones, gems, crystals and metals in order to balance the undesirable effects of the planets. Jyotish also advises fasting on certain days to lessen these negative effects. It can also recommend a proper *mantra*, aspect of God to worship, *yagya* (fire ceremony) and certain spiritual rituals in order to neutralize *karmic* and planetary effects.

In the true sense of the word, the science of Jyotish embraces the whole human being in order to bring health, happiness and harmony in personal relationships and in the business world. Mr Hart deFouw and Dr Robert Svoboda have together produced a marvelous book, as a practical guide for every reader to bring light and love into his or her life.

Dr Vasant Lad
August 1994
Director, Ayurvedic Institute
of New Mexico

INTRODUCTION

Time and space are the fundamental dimensions of existence. We forfeit our opportunities in life, be they ever so sterling, by being in the right place at the wrong time or in the wrong place at the right time. Each of us is, therefore, naturally drawn toward a greater understanding of the time and the space in which we live, that we may better know who we are, where we come from, and where we are going. One of the yardsticks that we can use to measure our time and space is divination, which is discovery of the 'unknown' by using chains of cause and effect which are not always evident to the objective observer.

Jyotish (literally, 'Light'; by extension, 'the Study of Light') is India's system of divination. Sometimes referred to, especially outside India, as Hindu or Vedic astrology, Jyotish is a model of reality which interprets the observed conditions of the cosmos at the time of an event in order to provide insight into the nature of that event. Because models merely represent the reality of an experience, they can at best guesstimate it; they can neither portray it with perfect accuracy nor infallibly predict it. The better a model, the more reliable its representation of reality. Whenever a model ceases to reflect reality adequately, it must be refined. India alone among the world's great civilizations has developed, refined and maintained many different divinatory models during its long history. Its various astrologies have over time been combined and transmuted into a fascinating and intricate, living discipline.

JYOTISH FOR EXPORT

One reason why astrology is an intrinsic part of India's religious and cultural experience is that few models of human experience describe past, present and future with such breadth of vision and variety of method as does Jyotish. Jyotish is still as integral to the lives of India's common people as are those prayers, marriages, christenings and other ceremonies whose observance it helps to time. The immense importance of Jyotish to its native land suggests to some that its utility is peculiar to Indians, and that it is fundamentally too foreign to speak meaningfully to others. On the contrary, Jyotish is a more universally applicable model than are many other forms of divination. Jyotish can easily adapt to Western conditions, just as foreign therapies such as acupuncture have adapted, provided its general principles are systematically understood.

This book will give you a sound theoretical basis in Jyotish. Experimentation can provide you with personal experience, and if your experience should draw you to the path of Jyotish as a way of life you can then begin the practical training which can be had only by apprenticing with a traditional practitioner of Jyotish. The facts of Jyotish can be transmitted through books, but the system of Jyotish must be transmitted from a teacher, a *jyotishi* (practitioner of Jyotish) who has received the needed spark from his or her own mentor, one fire igniting the next, generation after generation.

Because a thorough study of the principles of Jyotish is one essential precondition for becoming ignitable, one purpose of this book is to try to assist those many students who are frustrated by the lack of suitable expositions of Jyotish in English. This book necessarily retains much original Sanskrit terminology because some Sanskrit words and concepts simply do not translate directly into English. Jyotish has its own rigorously defined technical vocabulary which permits the quick and precise comparing of the astrological equivalents of apples and pears, and it is much easier to learn a few simple words like *graha, rashi* and *bhava* than it is constantly to invent them in English. Translators today are in some ways luckier than were translators in earlier days, for words like yoga, karma, pundit, chakra and Vedanta have now entered English. All these words are used freely in this book, and the terms *graha* (for planet), *rashi* (for constellation), and *bhava* (for house) will be used interchangeably with their English equivalents.

However, even if all the many classical Jyotish texts were to be translated into flawless contemporary English, they would still confuse the beginner more than they would elucidate because they were never intended as self-instructors. Every Indian text was written under the assumption that it would be studied under the guidance of a guru who would enliven it for the student.

The average modern reader does not have access to such a guru, therefore this book and its sequels will begin by presenting the facts of Jyotish in a way that is more easily comprehended by the modern mind than is the Indian way, while introducing, side by side, the context necessary to plant these concepts deep in the consciousness. Jyotish is a life-long study that embraces many other disciplines – philosophy, psychology, medicine, economics, astronomy, religious ritual and history, among others – and demands from its votaries an alchemical blend of logic and intuition, pragmatism and idealism, realism and imagination, and analysis and synthesis. Above all, Jyotish is a *sadhana*, a spiritual path that can transform your life.

This book tries to preserve that spark of life which makes Jyotish vital by organizing, wherever possible, its immense and scattered detail into systematic principles. While its style is tailored mainly to Western astrologers and to Indophiles, we hope that everyone who seeks self-knowledge will find it useful. Even if you do not plan a deep study of Jyotish, what you learn here will enrich your experience when you visit a jyotishi for astrological advice and should enable you to gauge the skill of those you approach for such consultations.

Were we to include all of Jyotish here in full detail, those readers who are not expert in thinking 'Jyotishically' would be lost. Were we, however, to force Jyotish into simplistic comments, its life would be lost. Too often the Western mind first simplifies a complex idea in order to grasp it, and then misidentifies that simplification with the original. We have, therefore, introduced in this book more complexity than the average novice may look for. We have blended simplicity with complexity in the way a chef marries a main course with its side dishes, to preserve that thin line between sufficient theory and sufficient particularity which keeps our material savory. From a tradition which has thrived unbroken over many thousands of years we have extracted a little taste whose seductive flavor should not alienate a foreign palate.

This study of Jyotish should remind you of a visit to your favorite ethnic restaurant: the décor reflects the cuisine's original culture, yet it is nested comfortably in your town; the food is authentic but toned down slightly and varied to accommodate the amateur palate; the menu is partially but not exclusively in a foreign language; and the waiters speak English. You leave with a minimum of culture shock, longing to return again and again . . .

CHAPTER ONE

THE ORIGINS OF JYOTISH

ORAL VERSUS WRITTEN

No authoritative history of Jyotish is ever likely to be written, for its historical origins are now thoroughly lost in the shadows of antiquity. Some maintain that Jyotish is a divine dispensation – one of God's gifts to humankind – which was revealed to us by India's sages; others see it as a hybrid of borrowings from other civilizations, a cunning cultural theft. We view Jyotish as a developing body of knowledge, an original and indigenous astronomy and astrology which, after its inspired origins, has absorbed and integrated insights from other cultures.

Some authors use the conspicuous absence of written Jyotish prior to the Greek conquest of parts of northern India to conclude that Jyotish was borrowed. Contemporary researchers, being generally suspicious of oral transmissions of knowledge, look for a culture's written records, believing that oral history deteriorates into myths and legends. Yet the possibility also exists that mythic and legendary knowledge was used by the ancients to transfer esoteric knowledge from one generation to the next. Those of us who believe the written word to be inherently superior to the spoken word should consider the following, spoken by Thamus, the god-king of Egypt, to the god Thoth, who was congratulating himself on having invented the alphabet:

this invention will produce forgetfulness in the minds of those who learn to use it, because they will not practice their memory. Their trust in writing, produced by external characters which are no part of themselves, will discourage the use of their own memory within them.

The specific which you have discovered is an aid not to memory but to reminiscence, and you give your disciples not truth, but only the semblance of truth (quoted in de Santillana, p. 348).

The written word was an afterthought, not an ideal, for many civilizations. In India, traditional authorities assert that the custodians of sacred knowledge recorded it in written form only when its transmission became endangered because fit disciples could no longer be found. Traditional training in India's classical traditions (*shastras*) to this day relies on oral transmission via memorization, prosodic recitation, and discussion. Until recently, all students were trained to develop powerful memories, and in modern India savants still perform prodigious feats of recall, effortlessly reciting chapter after chapter of the works which embody their various classical traditions, including Jyotish.

We of the twentieth century who believe in the linear progress of civilization possess an inborn bias for silent reading, an evolutionary development which is much more recent than writing. We belong to a culture which worships the visual, and this makes it difficult for us to conceive that knowledge was once transmitted orally from generation to generation with accuracy and that writing was once regarded as a crutch of little intrinsic value. It is possible that not only were our ancestors' minds comparable to our own, they may even have been superior to ours in certain ways. Most of us never fully develop our capacity to memorize; how then can we know how or what our forebears thought?

VEDA, VEDANGA, VIDYA

Oral traditions, which still abound in India, are remnants of the time when entire civilizations were organized orally. The first texts to be taught, heard and learnt in India were the *Vedas*, the sacred books of the Aryan peoples. Most non-Westernized Indians believe that the foundation of their culture was not created by ordinary humans but was cognized as *Veda* (sacred knowledge) by the ancient Seers, known as *rishis*. The four Vedas, which are generally acknowledged to be the source texts of what is usually known as Hinduism, are collections of hymns, or sacred songs, whose deep significance lies less in the literal meaning of their words than in their symbolic meaning, their rhythm and melody, and the personal power of their reciter. The printed page can transmit only a small fraction of the Veda, and an audio or video recording only a bit more. But even those who learn to recite the Veda perfectly may never gain access to its deep knowledge, which can be transmitted only from one initiated living being to another.

The Vedas themselves may be considered living beings. Those who open themselves to these entities, by being initiated into their study by a guru who has served as their receptacle for many years, become filled with this deep knowledge. Unfortunately, even though a few Vedic traditions survive in India, there is substantial doubt that anyone living today fully knows the deep knowledge contained within the Vedas, for the keys to understanding their esoteric import started being lost well before the Christian era. Lack of fit disciples dooms a tradition as surely as lack of children dooms a family, or a species.

Because even at their birth the Vedas were fully comprehensible only to the rishis, the Seers who divinely cognized them developed six auxiliary disciplines called *Vedangas* (Limbs of the Veda). These Six Vedangas must be studied before one can attempt to comprehend the Vedas themselves; they are *Vyakarana* (Grammar), *Chandas* (Meter), *Shiksha* (Intonation), *Nirukta* (Etymology), *Kalpa* (Ritual) and *Jyotish* (Astronomy/Astrology). When the Veda is personified as a living being, Vyakarana is regarded as the face, Chandas the legs, Shiksha the breath, Nirukta the ears, Kalpa the hands, and Jyotish the eyes. Each Vedanga is a living being who can be obtained only through a guru.

These beings, and others like them, which have sprouted from the Vedic corpus, are often generically termed *vidyas*, a word which is derived from the same root as the word *veda*. Every *vidya* is a goddess who must be worshipped in order that you and she may develop a personal relationship so profound that she can possess you. Jyotish is the *Jyotir Vidya* (the Lore of Light), a vidya which can be had only from jyotishis, because Jyotish is the study of all facets of the 'lords of light': the Sun, Moon, planets and stars.

THE ETERNAL FAITH

The Vedas, which have existed in their present form, unchanged, for thousands of years, represent an even older tradition, which evolved centuries earlier. As time went by, and humans became less able to be possessed by the Vedic hymns – as the 'fit' between the humans and the hymns deteriorated – new forms of sacred knowledge sprang into being from Vedic roots. The philosophical and religious ideals introduced into Indian culture by the Vedas have been amply fertilized by a wide variety of influences, both local and imported, and the immense mass of spiritual, ethical and religious vegetation which has sprung from these Vedic roots has come to be known popularly as Hinduism.

Although Jyotish is sometimes called 'Hindu astrology', this term is misleadingly sectarian, for it is also practiced by Buddhists, Sikhs, Jains, Muslims and Christians, in many countries other than India. Jyotish is 'Hindu astrology' in the sense that it is an outgrowth of 'Hinduism', which is sometimes referred to as the *Sanatana Dharma*, 'the Eternal Faith'. The Sanatana Dharma is eternal because it sprouts vigorous new growth whenever one of the saints or seers who are its inspired founders receives new inspiration from the One Absolute Reality. The Eternal Faith has grown over millennia into a broad spectrum of religious attitudes, philosophies, sects, deities, rituals, and conceptions of Supreme Beingness, many of which have only one thing in common: their acknowledgement of Reality's Ultimate Oneness. The seers of Jyotish, inspired by the Jyotir Vidya, have similarly developed many varied methods with which to examine and describe Reality, and Jyotish is the aggregate of their inspired compositions.

A religion's structure codifies inspired knowledge, and its innovators ensure that this structure remains an accurate reflection of Reality. Throughout Indian history many sects and religio-political movements have claimed that they alone have preserved 'true tradition' or possess the 'new revelation'. Such movements have generally contributed to the Eternal Faith's vitality, but when they disparage or suppress the beliefs of others they lose that broadness of vision which is the Eternal Faith's most valuable attribute. Jyotish has likewise been enhanced by those jyotishis who, inspired by the Jyotir Vidya, have codified new principles of interpretation. However, jyotishis who assert that their style alone is 'appropriate for this day and age' paradoxically prevent the Jyotir Vidya from inspiring them, for the Jyotir Vidya flowers only according to her own sweet will.

MYTH AND OBSERVATION

Although today's Jyotir Vidya is the same Jyotir Vidya who possessed and inspired the jyotishis of the Vedic era, no one today knows exactly what sort of astrology was practiced in Vedic times. Just as medieval calculation methods differ significantly from those in use in modern India, Vedic calculations may also have been different. This is likely to be true of interpretational principles too – which is one of the many reasons why the term 'Vedic astrology' is an unfortunate translation for the word 'Jyotish'.

Vedic astrology almost certainly relied much more on observational astronomy than it did on calculation. Simple positional data were augmented by evaluation of qualities, such as the observation that a full moon whose light had a bluish tinge to it exerted a different influence on the Earth from one whose tinge was reddish or blackish, or purely white. Today those who speak of, say, Venus in Scorpio rarely consider that the passage of Venus through the mouth of the Scorpion may have suggested to ancient skywatchers a far different interpretation than did Venus passing through the Scorpion's tail. Or consider the *nakshatra* (Vedic constellation) Rohini, which appears in the constellation Taurus and is said to represent a wain or cart. Many Sanskrit texts, even those which have little to do with Jyotish, report that when Saturn passes not around but through the 'wain of Rohini' immense famine and other disasters will result.

One of the Sanskrit names for Venus is *Shukra*, which means 'white', and Venus is indeed a bright, white orb, the brightest object in the night sky after the Moon. Venus is so bright that you can see it even during daylight, if you know exactly where to look. Another meaning of *shukra* is 'semen'; just as Venus is the brightest (= most potent) planet, semen is the most potent (the 'brightest') substance in the male body. People tend to be at their most amorous when Venus is shining brightly in the sky, either in the early part of the night, just after going to bed, or early in the morning, just after waking up (a man's testosterone being at its highest daily level around four a.m.).

From the mythic angle, the deity who plays the role of Venus in the cosmic drama of Jyotish enjoys a capability which no other celestial possesses: the power to bring the dead back to life. He was awarded this ability after being swallowed by Lord Shiva and spending one hundred divine years in His belly. Venus dies and is reborn in many cultures, including the Sumerian (where her name is Inanna) and the Mayan (Quetzalcoatl, the Plumed Sky Serpent). Should you plot Venus' risings and settings, you would find that he creates a serpent in the sky, the death and rebirth serpent which the Tantric tradition calls the Kundalini Shakti. This is one reason why Venus is one significator of Tantric ritual in a horoscope.

This death and rebirth myth is a product of observational astronomy. Venus, which has a 584-day cycle of visibility, appears as both the Morning Star and the Evening Star. In between these periods of visibility, each of which lasts about 263 days, come two periods of invisibility, during which Venus is conjunct with the Sun. When Venus, as the Evening Star, moves toward its solar conjunction, it 'sets' in the sky – it appears lower and lower each night until that fateful night when it fails to appear at all, swallowed up by the Sun, who may be identified here with Lord Shiva. Both the Sun and Shiva represent the Universal Soul.

When, after two weeks (or sometimes less) of invisibility, Venus reappears, he becomes the bright Morning Star, the Soul's Herald for another 263 days. Then again he sinks into conjunction, this time for about seven weeks, until finally he re-emerges as the Evening Star. When some clever observer of the heavens noted that the period of these two Stars is almost precisely the same length as the average human pregnancy (roughly 265 days) – enough time for a slain hero to die and be reborn – all the elements of the death-and-rebirth motif were in place and ready to be mythified.

Because of these many changes Venus is also regarded as an inconstant, unstable planet, as are Mercury and the Moon, the two other very changeable 'planets'. Saturn, on the other hand, is the slowest planet, since he is furthest from the Sun, and many of his principal qualities derive from this distance: being furthest away, he is the most isolated, the coldest, the darkest (in complexion) and the gloomiest (darkest in mind). Termed 'the Lame One' for being so slow, Saturn tends to produce delayed, limited results, because he displays these qualities wherever he sits in a horoscope.

TEACHING TALES

One way in which deep knowledge is imparted to students of Jyotish is through observations and interpretations like these, which are stored in planetary stories and myths. Part of the *sadhana* (spiritual path) of Jyotish is to learn these myths and their cosmological import. When well heard and digested, these stories help to integrate Jyotish's tenets into the pupil's consciousness, which makes the model of reality which is Jyotish become vividly real and solid. There is no doubt that the best way to learn Jyotish is to hear teaching stories at the feet of your guru. But because the tales themselves are also alive, they can speak softly to those who listen to them mindfully, even if they have no guru handy to amplify them.

The story of how the twelve *rashis* (constellations) of the zodiac got their lords, the planets who rule them, is a good example of such a teaching tale. It conveys the order of the rulerships of the constellations in a way that is not quickly forgotten; it relates the planets to their internal correlates; it summarizes the personalities of the planets; and it includes some astronomical knowledge – all in a package that is ear-friendly and is easier on the mind than mere memorization. So far as we know, this particular legend appears nowhere in the classical literature. It has been preserved solely by being told from one generation to the next.

In the beginning were Sun and Moon, the king and queen of heaven. Absolute monarchs of all they surveyed, they ruled from the constellations of Leo and Cancer respectively. When Mercury saw that these two owned everything, he decided to ask (since Mercury rules communication) for some land in the zodiac for himself. The Sun, being naturally magnanimous, said, 'All right, you may take possession of Virgo, the constellation that is next to mine.'

Now Mercury is well known as a dual planet, a master of duplicity who speaks with a forked tongue. He found it so easy to get land from the Sun that he waited until night (Mercury rules both day and night) and then told Moon, the Queen of the Night, 'O Queen, the Sun has given me a plot; are you going to be outdone?'

Now, Sun is the soul, and Moon is the emotional mind. Mind is insecure, knowing that it has no independent light of its own, that it only reflects the soul. Since it is insecure, mind is always trying to aggrandize itself, and so it often tries to duplicate processes which are part of the life of the soul. This, for example, is the reason why the mind frequently tries to convince itself that it might live forever. So Moon replied to Mercury, 'All right, you take Gemini, the plot next to mine.' In this way Mercury, the thinking mind, gained possession of Virgo and Gemini.

Venus (desire) saw what Mercury (thinking mind) had done, and made the same request. Sun (who is very honest, and would not gift away the same space twice) said, 'I've promised the space next to me to Mercury, but you may have the next space,' which was Libra. Venus then repeated his request to Moon, obtaining Taurus thereby. Seeing what Venus (desire) had done, Mars (action) did the same, obtaining Scorpio and Aries from Sun and Moon respectively. Requests from Jupiter (wisdom) gained him Sagittarius and Pisces, and finally even Saturn got the news – Saturn, who is slow to catch on, always the last to know. Saturn (renunciation) got what was left on both sides: Capricorn and Aquarius. Table 1.1 shows the final position of the planets as rulers of the constellations of the zodiac.

This order reflects the distances from the various planets to the Sun: Mercury is the closest planet, followed in order by Venus,

TABLE I.I

Constellation	Planetary Ruler		Constellation
Leo	Sun	Moon	Cancer
Virgo	Mercury		Gemini
Libra	Venus		Taurus
Scorpio	Mars		Aries
Sagittarius	Jupiter		Pisces
Capricorn	Saturn		Aquarius

Mars, Jupiter and finally Saturn. (Earth is not counted because she is our frame of reference.) The column led by the Sun's constellation follows the natural direction of the constellational order, while that led by the Moon follows the reverse direction.

The real beauty of the story is that this order also reflects the evolution of embodied consciousness, which arises from the soul and is experienced first in the emotional mind. As objective thought gradually develops, so does the thinking mind. The more the mind thinks, the more it desires. Desires lead to action, in order to actualize those desires; and from action comes wisdom, as one learns the beneficial and detrimental results of good and bad actions. When wisdom finally matures, renunciation becomes inevitable, because you become satisfied with what is bestowed upon you by Nature; you are happy with whatever remains (in Sanskrit, the *ucchishtha*). The same life dramas that are acted out on Earth appear symbolized in the skies; as above, so below.

JYOTISH'S LIMBS

The original Vedanga Jyotish was mainly confined to identifying and predicting the recurring astronomical phenomena which signaled occasions for ritual sacrifice. Myth may have so sufficed the Vedic jyotishis that they needed little of a system of Jyotish in order to practice divination. As the deep significations of the Vedic texts hid themselves, however, it became nearly impossible to learn Jyotish by tales alone. As time passed, greater precision of measurement made it possible to introduce a more mathematical approach to observation. Rational thought then gradually replaced intuition as the dominant form of human consciousness.

The Seers who saw these changes in human consciousness codified their observations into rational principles, which metamorphosed into systems of astrological analysis. The branches of Jyotish which grew during the Golden Age of India's astrological development are traditionally classified into either *skandhas* (parts) or *angas* (limbs). The Three Skandhas, which appear to have been an earlier classification, are listed in Table 1.2.

TABLE 1.2

The Three Skandhas and their Meanings

Ganita Skandha	astrological/astronomical calculations
Samhita Skandha	sundry observations, including celestial omens, the weather, economic cycles, earthquakes, the varying fortunes of the population at large, erotic recipes, house-construction, the manufacture of exceptional glues, and the siting of water wells
Hora Skandha	interpretation of horoscopes

There are Six Limbs to Jyotish, just as there are Six Vedangas for the Vedas. *Prashna Marga*, a text on horary astrology, lists them as shown in Table 1.3. *Prashna Marga* states that one conversant with all six branches of astrology will never err in predictions – a tall order! Such an astrologer is a true *daivajna* (roughly, 'a knower of God's intention'). Jyotishis of this quality still exist but are very rare, even in India.

TABLE I.3

The Six Limbs of Jyotish

Gola	Spherical astronomy and direct observations; observational astronomy
Ganita	Astronomical and astrological calculations
Jataka	Birth or natal astrology
Prashna	Answering questions without the use of a natal horoscope; horary astrology
Muhurta	Choosing astrologically auspicious beginnings for any endeavor; electional astrology
Nimitta	Interpretation of omens

Observational Astronomy (Gola)

Jyotish concentrates its observations on nine 'planets': Sun, Moon, Mars, Mercury, Jupiter, Venus, Saturn, Rahu and Ketu. From the scientific point of view, the word 'planets' is an obvious misnomer, for only five of them are what science today calls planets, the other four being the Sun (a star), the Moon (Earth's satellite) and Rahu and Ketu (which have no physical existence at all). Rahu is the northern intersection (the North Node) and Ketu is the southern intersection (the South Node) of the plane of the Moon's orbit around the Earth with the plane of the ecliptic. (The ecliptic is the plane of Earth's orbit around the Sun, which is perceived by observers on Earth as the Sun's orbit around the Earth.) These two orbital planes intersect because the Moon's orbital plane is inclined about five degrees from the plane of the ecliptic. The Two Nodes are the points where solar and lunar eclipses occur.

Some astrologers today, noting that science has discovered three more planets and numerous asteroids, assert that Jyotish is somehow incomplete and can be improved by adding these bodies to its repertoire. It is, however, no coincidence that the number of the planets used in Jyotish is also the number of single-digit integers in our base-ten numbering system. Jyotish needs no more than these Nine Planets to describe reality because, as we shall see, these Nine Planets are more than mere material entities. Those who seek to add new planets to Jyotish do so only because they have not yet comprehended its heart.

Astronomical and Astrological Calculations (Ganita)

Ganita dealt with observations and calculations for horoscopes as well as for computing calendars, seasons, eclipses, lunar and planetary cycles, the helical rising and setting of the stars, and other such matters. Since the ancients had no aids as sophisticated as those the modern astrologer uses for calculations, most jyotishis in the past were forced to master both mathematics and spherical astronomy in order to generate their data. Such jyotishis always took their calculations seriously; the famous authority Varahamihira cautioned that 'an error in *ganita* is as heinous a sin as the murder of a Brahmana [priest]'.

Because Jyotish originally included astronomy and astrology as two inseparable portions of one and the same study, works that discussed both *gola* and *ganita* went under the name of *siddhanta*. The most famous of these works are the *Surya Siddhanta* and the *Drik Siddhanta*. Because inaccuracies were inevitable in the early days, the *Surya Siddhanta* advises jyotishis to use regular observations to confirm the accuracy of predicted planetary motions.

Natal Astrology (Jataka)

The relating of the position of the planets at an individual's time and place of birth with the various events in that person's life (which is known as birth or natal astrology in English and as *jataka* or *janma* in Sanskrit) is what is usually meant by the term 'astrology'. Most of what appears in this book is natal astrology.

Horary Astrology (Prashna)

Horary astrology investigates the correlation of planetary phenomena at the time a question is asked with the answer to that question.

Almost all questions are answerable from a horoscope calculated at the time of the question, or determined in a variety of other ways, including: the phonetic values of the syllables uttered by the questioner, the parts of the body the questioner might touch, the compass direction in which he or she stood at the time of the question, or a random number he or she might choose.

Although the body of horary knowledge gradually grew to rival in volume that of natal astrology, little of this was written down. A few famous classical works in this genre are Varahamihira's *Daivajna Vallabha*, the *Shatpanchasika* of Prithuyashas (Varahamihira's son), *Prashna Marga*, a detailed and complex work authored by an anonymous jyotishi, and Neelakantha's famous Tajika work *Prashna Tantra*.

Electional Astrology (Muhurta)

Jyotish is the 'eye' of the Veda partly because it enabled the ancients to 'see' the astronomical moment when religious and social rituals should be performed. Actions tend to produce results according to the planetary configurations under which they are initiated. The need to gauge the efficacy of actions begun at a given moment (one *muhurta* = forty-eight minutes) may have made *muhurta* the first sector of Jyotish to have been systematically developed. The literature in this field is small compared to that of *jataka* and *prashna*, but it is relatively concise; a standard work is the *Kalaprakashika* of Narasimha. Much of this tradition remains oral and only now is being gradually committed to print.

Interpretation of Omens (Nimitta)

To read an omen is to read the Book of Nature, a tome which is written in the language of events. The texts of Samhita Skandha deal extensively with the interpretation of such non-cyclical omens as the flights of birds, the sights and sounds encountered during journeys, the burning of lamp wicks, and the appearance of meteors. Among the many varieties of natural omens, celestial omens alone are predictable.

A thorough understanding and interpretation of omens requires one's intuition to be in full bloom. It is nearly impossible to do this without direct instruction from a skilled omenologist, thus making *nimitta* the Jyotish limb most dependent on the oral tradition. Still, sections devoted to it appear in the classical works, the most famous of these being Varahamihira's *Brihat Samhita*.

STYLES OF JYOTISH

Although, properly speaking, Jyotish should involve the planets and constellations, jyotishis also often resort to three allied, non-celestial disciplines: *sankhya shastra* (numerology), *samudrika shastra* (divination through interpretation of body parts, using their shapes, relative size and markings), and *hasta samudrika shastra* (palmistry, a specialized branch of samudrika shastra). It is not unusual for a jyotishi to predict travel only from the palm of the hand, forecast a career change based on the numerology of a birthdate, or predict marital success from the size of a toe. Palmistry is used so pervasively by jyotishis that it and Jyotish are commonly known in India as 'sister' sciences.

Five principal styles of Jyotish have evolved, each of which retains its distinctive character and capabilities, though they have repeatedly cross-pollinated over the centuries. Each was originated by a famous mythical and/or historical figure who wrote, or is reputed to have written, its seminal treatise, and each has been enriched by inspired commentaries. Aspiring jyotishis in India are still taught to be as deferential to the classical authorities who authored the texts they study as those authors were to their own teachers. As *Maharshi* ('Great Rishi') Parashara, the reputed author of *Brihat Parashara Hora*, who is regarded by many as the father of Jyotish, states in the conclusion of that work:

The knowledge I have imparted to you is that same science of Jyotish that Lord Brahma [the Creator] spoke to Narada [the Divine Messenger], and that Narada spoke to Shaunaka and other sages, from whom I received it. I have narrated it to you as I learnt it from them (BPH 97:1–2a).

The lineage of a tradition of Jyotish begins when the living principles of the Jyotir Vidya become embodied via a Seer's consciousness, and these principles are then embellished, over generations, by human jyotishis who are possessed by the Jyotir Vidya, who see the Light. A tradition's Seer, who has one foot on the celestial plane and the other here on Earth, helps to maintain the bonds between deep human knowledge and its sacred origins, and those who accept students mold them mercilessly into fit receptacles for the Jyotir Vidya, that the lineage may continue unbroken. All sincere jyotishis regard themselves as custodians of their lineages, and revere all those who have come before them.

The chief styles of Jyotish are: *Nadi Jyotish, Parashari Jyotish, Jaimini Jyotish, Tantric Jyotish* and *Tajika Jyotish*.

Nadi Jyotish

No one knows when Nadi Jyotish originated. Legend has it that India's rishis became so adept at Jyotish that they were able to generate the horoscopes of people who were not yet born, and to predict salient patterns in their lives. After these rishis had produced a river of such birthcharts, the gods, alarmed at this challenge to their omniscience, sent a great fire which destroyed most of the collection. Those fragments of the Nadis that survived are handed down from parent to child in certain families of Indian astrologers who act as their custodians. These Nadi remnants are identified by their purported authors; among the best known are the *Bhrigu Nadi, Parashara Nadi, Shuka Nadi* and *Chandra Nadi*.

Each Nadi collection is reputed to contain the horoscopes of only those individuals who are destined to consult that particular collection. Our experience tends to bear this out. When complete, a Nadi reading traditionally consists of four parts: the first, known as *bhava phala*, deals with issues like career, marriage, children, health and finances. The second, *yoga khanda*, gives precise predictions, usually involving political, social or scientific attainments, based on certain planetary combinations found in that horoscope. The third part, *karma khanda*, details specific occurrences in a previous life (misdeeds for the most part), whose effects create obstructions in this life. The last section, *shanti khanda*, prescribes remedial measures to mitigate or nullify any lingering undesirable results accruing from past-life misdemeanors.

Since the methodology of a Nadi reading remains a secret which is guarded closely by those custodians for whom the Nadis are a family business, the Nadis yield their principles grudgingly to outsiders who try to research them. One curious fact: while a Nadi reading is often strikingly precise regarding one's past, predictions of the future rarely achieve the same success at detail, though they are usually broadly accurate.

Parashari Jyotish

'Parashari' refers to the tradition of Jyotish enunciated by Parashara in his great work *Brihat Parashara Hora*. In its current form this treatise contains in its 97 chapters a total of over 2,000 verses dealing with natal astrology. Other famous classical works, including *Saravali*, *Jataka Parijata* and *Phaladipika*, are elaborations of the Parashari system, which is the form of Jyotish that is most widely practiced today. This book focuses predominantly on the Parashari tradition of interpreting natal horoscopes.

We do not know when Parashari Jyotish took on its present form, or which parts of it were laid down by the Rishi Parashara and which were added by learned commentators. It is also impossible to know whether Parashari Jyotish solidified earlier or later than the time of Varahamihira, the court astrologer who, according to one tradition, served the famous Emperor Chandragupta II (probably fourth century A.D.), who was a great patron of science and art. Renowned for his erudition, wisdom and verified predictions, Varahamihira wrote voluminously on all aspects of Jyotish. Of his six principal treatises, the most widely read today are the *Brihad Jataka*, which deals with birth or natal astrology, and the *Brihat Samhita*, which is chiefly concerned with various forms of divination.

Without knowing whether the current system ascribed to Parashara preceded or followed Varahamihira, we cannot know how much one stream of information influenced the other; but it is a fact that there is no Varahamihiri tradition that is independent of the

Parashari tradition. Varahamihira is still, however, greatly respected as the author of the best-known works of Jyotish composed by a non-Seer.

Jaimini Jyotish

Maharshi Jaimini, a great Vedic Seer, is believed by some to have written the Jaimini Sutras, a work which forms the foundation for this system. Today a relatively small minority of jyotishis in India practice the Jaimini style of Jyotish, though this fascinating style of interpretation is held in high esteem by many others who, knowingly or unknowingly, utilize some of its principles to augment Parashari Jyotish. While some of the fundamental principles of Jaimini Jyotish seem to have been adopted from the Parashari system, Jaimini Jyotish so developed these that they now little resemble the system which may have been their source. Jaimini Jyotish is also filled with interpretational principles which appear nowhere in Parashara's work.

It is possible that some commentator developed Jaimini Jyotish from Parashara's system and then appended Maharshi Jaimini's name to his creation. Indian commentators or innovators in ancient times commonly ascribed authorship of their works to renowned historical or mythical figures in order to enhance their chances of acceptance by scholars. Thus, although the astrologer Kalidasa, who wrote the Jyotish text known as the *Uttara Kalamrita*, was almost certainly different from the poet and dramatist Kalidasa, who wrote some of India's greatest literature, many still adamantly believe that these two might well have been the same man.

It may also be that Jaimini's inspiration created the egg of Jaimini Jyotish, an egg which first required Parashara's fertilization before it could develop on its own. It may even be that a Parashari commentator extracted from Jaimini Jyotish those few chapters that the Parashari and Jaimini styles share and added them to the *Brihat Parashara Hora* as if they had been there from the beginning. We are unlikely ever to know for sure.

Tantric Jyotish

If the origins of the Parashari and Jaimini systems are unclear, then Tantric Jyotish's roots are utterly unknown. In fact, neither Tantric Jyotish nor *Tantra*, its parent, can be readily defined. Like Ayurveda, Tantra is said to be an offshoot of the Atharva Veda, the fourth of the four Vedas; but as yet no one has a clear idea of the origins of the Atharva Veda, a hymnal filled with occult chants and charms. In an astrological context the word 'Tantric' implies a mystical and intuitive attitude toward Jyotish. Tantra calls for 'sacrificial rites', and a practitioner of Tantric Jyotish tends to rely on internally derived information over that collected from external sources, arriving at startling correct conclusions via magical techniques.

These techniques include but are not limited to the observation and interpretation of omens; the observation and analysis of the jyotishi's breathing patterns at the moment a question is asked; the interpretation of a client's speech-patterns and actions; the encouraging of spontaneous or forced visions; clairvoyance, clairaudience, or astral travel; the use of information received from ethereal beings; the use of substances or techniques to induce such paranormal or psychic phenomena as the charming of objects or people, past-life readings, miraculous cures, and the granting of boons; and the use of intense spiritual practices to bring the powers of nature under one's direct and personal control.

Many systems of divination around the world also employ such techniques, but few who do past-life readings or trance channeling are practicing Tantric Jyotish. Tantric methods of divination are typically performed within the framework of Jyotish's model, a framework which helps to focus, enhance and structure them. It is this process of standardization and correlation which makes astrological the collection of shamanic techniques that is Tantric Jyotish. For example, while omens may be interpreted in many ways, Jyotish tends to interpret them according to time (when they happen) and space (where they happen). An omen which occurs in a westerly direction is likely to cause a jyotishi to think first of Saturn, who rules the west, and then to consider Saturn's implications on the question at hand.

Another example: people in many cultures have been able to gain control over certain classes of spirits, but most do so haphazardly, and are often unaware of what sort of spirit they have harnessed. Jyotish, however, can determine, by examination of the horoscope, whether or not a person can succeed at such an endeavor and, if so, what classes of spirit they will be able to summon, when in their lives they will be able to succeed, and at what precise moment they should begin their rituals in order to succeed.

Tajika Jyotish

Because Neelakantha Daivajna was the prime proponent of this form of Jyotish, its other common name is Neelakantha Tajika. Though this school is a relatively late development (Neelakantha states that his book was composed in A.D. 1587), it has since its introduction into India from the Arabs ('Tajika' is a Sanskrit term for an Arab) become thoroughly Indianized. This form of Jyotish often feels more familiar to the Western astrologer than do the other styles, since Arabic astrological methods also figured prominently in the West. For example, exact aspects, especially including the sextile, square, trine and opposition, are as intrinsic to this system as they are to Ptolemaic astrology (the source of Western astrology).

Probably the most famous contribution of the Tajika school to the other styles of Jyotish is the technique of the solar return, which Indian jyotishis have named Varshaphala ('the result of the year'). Though Varshaphala is not part of the Parashari tradition, it may one day succeed in becoming so if it sends its roots sufficiently deep into the Jyotir Vidya.

CHAPTER TWO

THE PHILOSOPHY OF
JYOTISH

The Jyotir Vidya actually draws to herself those people she wants to possess her, by attracting them to a guru who already possesses her. The aspirant first tests the guru for knowledge and teaching ability, then the guru tests the aspirant for fitness to study the science. Once satisfied that the aspirant is worthy to be possessed by the Jyotir Vidya, the guru initiates the long years of oral training which prepare the student for possession. The Jyotir Vidya herself directs the disciple's studies through the guru until the aspirant becomes thoroughly fit to be possessed. Then, after the mentor ignites the Jyotir Vidya within the student, the spirit of Jyotish is brought to life within that student's consciousness. The Jyotir Vidya then slowly settles into the disciple's mind, and thereafter personally guides the fledgeling through the path of divination. Disciples who follow that path sufficiently far become able to comprehend the spirit of the astrological rules on their own. Then their every use of the rules becomes a way to honor Jyotish's spirit.

Only after the student is filled with the Jyotir Vidya does he or she become ready to practice Jyotish. An eminent jyotishi used to say, 'When you can see the *jyoti* [light], then you become a jyotishi,' by which he meant both the external light of the stars and the planets and the internal light of the Jyotir Vidya.

SANSKRIT

Just as those who can communicate telepathically need not know a language, those who are perfectly clairvoyant and clairaudient need not study Jyotish, for they are already possessed by the Jyotir Vidya. The rest of us, though, require preparation in order to become fit receptacles for her. This preparation was traditionally accomplished by memorizing one of Jyotish's texts which incarnate the Jyotir Vidya. While no book can transmit the Jyotir Vidya to a reader, books can help prepare the ground in which that vidya can later be planted. Daily repetition of a text's inspired Sanskrit poetry creates within one's mind conditions into which the text's inherent spirit can be infused by a guru's commentary.

Simple linear logic, in which principles come first and deductions follow, is not very useful when it comes to comprehending a vidya, because the sages who developed these vidyas employed an entirely different mode of thinking. 'They thought rather in terms of what we might call a fugue, in which all the notes cannot be constrained into a single melodic scale, in which one is plunged directly into the midst of things and must follow the temporal order created by their thoughts' (de Santillana, p. xi). Probably the most essential condition for becoming a capable jyotishi, which happens to be the most difficult one for the average Westerner to fulfill, is to learn how to think in this holistic, non-linear way. Because it is also very difficult to write or teach non-linearly – it is simply impossible to 'square the circle' – imperfections in books on Jyotish that are written in modern languages are inevitable.

One reason why Jyotish's texts are written in Sanskrit is that Sanskrit helps facilitate holistic thought. The Seers taught that Sanskrit's very sounds are sacred, and they held that Sanskrit (when properly intoned) speaks directly to the soul of living creatures, transmitting, as does music, a universal meaning which does not depend on its composition or lyrics. Because the essence of the Vedas is believed to be transferred to the listener when Vedic hymns are recited correctly, the Vedas must be studied vocally in their original Sanskrit if they are to be truly understood. This also applies to the Vedas' satellite vidyas such as Jyotish and *Ayurveda* (India's traditional medical system). Other languages may convey the vidyas' theoretical meaning, but only Sanskrit captures and conveys their quintessence. Anyone who wishes to become a master jyotishi must eventually possess and be possessed by Sanskrit, and although theoretical or book learning can be helpful, Sanskrit, like Jyotish, can only be truly learned orally from a competent teacher.

THE SANKHYA PHILOSOPHY

No Indian vidya is a stand-alone subject; all must be comprehended together in order to create well-rounded and holistic Sanskritic knowledge. Since knowledge of one model of reality enhances the understanding of other models, Jyotish has adopted Ayurvedic principles to enrich its medical knowledge, embraced the philosophies of Sankhya, Yoga and Vedanta to enhance its psycho-dynamics, and enlisted *Niti Shastra* (political science) to teach jyotishis about secular dynamics. Sanskrit is crucial to a thorough knowledge of these ancillaries, for specific word references within a work on Jyotish (words like pitta, karma, *manas*, *buddhi* and *sattva*) are meant to trigger memories of the full implication of these terms in their original contexts. Any well-educated jyotishi who reads that '*manas* is ruled by the Moon' knows what part of the mind *manas* represents and knows that it is something other than what we commonly express in English by the word 'mind'. Such words as these cannot be understood outside the context of the Sanskritic system of knowledge, any more than similar modern technical terms can be used outside the context of the psychology to which they belong.

Some people who peruse Jyotish's ancient texts without first studying their context conclude that Indian astrology is all prediction and no psychology. But Jyotish need not present psychology explicitly in its texts because psychology is explicitly presented in those auxiliaries (like Ayurveda and Yoga) which every jyotishi is expected to study. It would violate the well-respected principle of verbal frugality to repeat such information in a work on Jyotish. Psychology is in fact central to each reading that a jyotishi performs. Jyotishis use horoscopic insights to anticipate likely developments on the concrete level of reality, and use their psychological skills to teach their clients how to cope with those potential results.

Anyone who hopes to learn Jyotish, Ayurveda, Ashtanga Yoga, or Tantra must first learn something of the Sankhya philosophy, which is their structural basis. *Sankhya* means 'number', which indicates that the philosophy is composed of a number of *tattvas* ('things') which evolve out of one another and which possess both literal and numerological significance. Only one of Sankhya's tattvas, *Purusha*, is really real and forever, changelessly true. It is the One, the Supreme Singularity, the transcendent consciousness which is beyond time, space and causation, the Reality which remains whenever the universe ceases to exist. Creation begins whenever the Purusha desires to experience Itself; that desire causes a sense of separateness to arise, which is known as *Prakriti*, or Nature, and is the womb of the manifested universe, the macrocosm. Desire is the foundation of the manifested universe. Awareness of this separateness produces *mahat*, or *buddhi*, which is transcendent, limitless awareness, and individuation of this awareness produces *ahamkara*.

Ahamkara, which means literally the 'I-creator', is the force which provides beings with their individuality. It is the power of self-identification, the force that tells an individual 'I am performing such-and-such an action'. This power to self-identify with one's actions is the basis of the Law of Karma (see below). Ahamkara's Three *Gunas* (qualities or attributes) are *Sattva*, *Rajas* and *Tamas*. In the context of the evolution of consciousness Sattva represents individuality that is relatively self-aware; Tamas, individuality that is relatively unaware of self; and Rajas, the ability to become relatively more or less self-aware.

From Sattva arises *manas* (the mind) and the ten senses: the five senses of perception – hearing, touch, sight, taste and smell – with which we import into ourselves things from the external environment; and the five senses of action with which we export things into the external environment. The five senses of action are speech, which represents all forms of communication; hands (which symbolize creative action); feet (locomotion); genitals (reproduction); and anus (elimination). From Tamas arise the five objects of the senses – sound, texture, form, flavor and odor – and from these objects arise the Five Great Elements (*Maha Bhutas*), the building-blocks of the physical universe: Ether, Air, Fire, Water and Earth. Rajas produces no evolutes.

The Srimad Bhagavata, one of India's greatest spiritual texts, likens *buddhi* to a charioteer, *manas* to the reins, the senses to the horses, and the individual soul to the experiencer who sits or stands behind the charioteer, directing his actions. The body is more Tamasic than are the senses, which are in turn comparatively more Tamasic than is *manas*. While *ahamkara* is fundamentally Rajasic, and *buddhi* (the faculty of discrimination) is predominantly Sattvic, the soul is beyond the Three Gunas.

Jyotish assigns these various functions to various planets. The Moon represents *manas*, Mercury characterizes *buddhi*, the ascendant or rising constellation indicates *ahamkara*, and the Sun stands for the *atma* or *jiva*, the individual soul. The whole horoscope is the field of *prakriti*, an individual's microcosmic expression of his or her personal reality as a part of the macrocosm (which is the cosmic Prakriti, capital P). All these factors in an individual's horoscope must therefore be analyzed if we are to analyze that individual's mind truly. We cannot, in the context of Jyotish, speak about 'quality of mind' unless we know which qualities of 'mind' are activated within the organism at any one time.

Manas, the most important of the various factors used to evaluate the average person's mind, measures your likes and dislikes, the life experiences to which you are attracted and the ones which you avoid. Because people commonly become emotional over their likes and dislikes, the Moon's condition in the horoscope usually indicates one's overall emotional state. Jyotish places so much importance on the Moon because a strong, well-placed Moon tends to produce a stable, enjoyable life, while a disturbed Moon creates imbalances, leading perhaps to addictions or obsessions. Those beings who act from the soul at all times will not of course be much affected by the lowly *manas* – but then, what need do such saints have for Jyotish?

KARMA AND JYOTISH

Since the Srimad Bhagavata teaches that all states of mind in which the feeling of 'me' and 'mine' is present are the results of permutations and combinations of the Three Gunas, in order to know *manas* we must know the Three Gunas. Sattva is the natural state of the conscious mind, and Rajas and Tamas are the two ways in which the mind can go out of balance. Although these Three Gunas can theoretically exist as pure Sattva, Rajas or Tamas, in our world all created things are innately composed of combinations of all three, just as all matter is a combination of all Five Great Elements, with one or two predominating at a time. The nine states of relative imbalance which thus originate from the permutations of Sattva, Rajas and Tamas is one more reason why Nine Planets suffice to describe all of human nature and experience. In each human life the specific proportions of the Three Gunas determine, via the Nine Planets, that individual's aptitude for the various possible actions which a living human can perform.

Though the Law of Karma is simply stated – 'as you sow, so shall you reap' – it is no simplistic, tit-for-tat theory, nor is it an arbitrary human creation. The Law of Karma is another name for Newton's Third Law of Motion: 'For every action there is an equal and opposite reaction.' As such, it is inherent in the universe's structure: 'The doctrine of *karman* and *phala*, act and fruit, is less a product of man's sense of justice, that one shall be punished for what one has done, than a necessary consequence of the doctrine of the inherent efficacy of the acts' (van Buitenen, p. 35).

Everything does not happen all at once in our world, thanks to the inherent limitations of time, space and causation. A tree and the seed from which it sprang cannot exist simultaneously; the former must develop from the latter. Events occur in our universe according to a sequence which is scheduled by the Law of Karma on the great calendar known as time.

As soon as Prakriti separates from Purusha, the Law of Karma begins to operate, for everything that happens thereafter is ultimately due to that first act. Each action inexorably causes some effect, and each effect causes further effects, like ripples spreading from a rock pitched into a pool. As a myriad actions accumulate, the cascade of effects becomes exceedingly intricate and perplexing, embroiling us in extended matrices of cause and effect which bind us and the world together into a vast, self-regulating system. As Mahatma Gandhi is reported to have said, 'After inventing the Law of Karma God was able to retire.'

In living individual beings the Law of Karma acts primarily at the level of *ahamkara*. Humans, who have much more self-awareness than do animals or plants, have a proportionately greater ability to self-identify with their actions. They thus sow more than do other sentient beings, and more do they reap. What they sow and reap depends on the relative balance of the Three Gunas in their personalities. When Sattva predominates, a person performs altruistic karmas, unattached to their results, while a predomination of Rajas causes one to act from passion, blinded by desires. Those who act without thinking act from a predominance of Tamas. Only those whose minds are fixed solely on the Absolute remain untouched by the Three Gunas.

Karmas are divided into four categories: *Sanchita* (a collection of all karmas), *Prarabdha* (the ready-to-be-experienced karmas), *Kriyamana* (current karmas) and *Agama* (approaching karmas). Classification of any action into one class of karma or another is not always easy, because the cause-and-effect relationship is essentially an inseparable unit. While the partitioning of an indivisible whole into fictitious parts makes that whole easier to comprehend, all four types of karmas overlap one another.

1. Sanchita Karma

Sanchita ('heaped together') Karma is the sum total of all past actions, known and unknown, that a being has performed and that are saved in his or her karmic account. 'Known' karma is karma you are aware of having performed, while 'unknown' karma is karma you are not conscious of having done. 'Unknown' karma is a sort of cause-and-effect relationship which is not easily known by the finite mind. The complexity of this unknown karma is exponentially increased when the notion of the transmigration of souls, commonly called reincarnation, is factored into the karmic equation.

Reincarnation assumes that actions performed in previous lives may well be the causes of effects experienced in this lifetime. Although it is not enunciated very clearly in the Vedas themselves, the doctrine of reincarnation has been an integral part of almost all Indian philosophies since Vedic times. The *Bhagavad Gita* (The Song of God), one of India's most famous and best-loved scriptures, neatly expresses this idea in an analogy: 'Just as a person casts off worn-out clothes and puts on others that are new, even so does the embodied soul cast off worn-out bodies and take on others that are new' (II: 22).

A woman who wonders why she found it so easy to earn her law degree, so difficult to find a husband, so easy to relate to her parents, and so difficult to have children wonders about these things because she has forgotten the karmas which she performed in her previous lives. It is those past karmas which cause some of her present circumstances, good or bad, to seem disproportionate to the effects expected from known causes in this lifetime. And, since every action has a result that the performer of the original action must also experience, all the actions which she performs during this life will produce their own reactions, and any anticipated results that she has not yet experienced at the time of her death will inevitably be enjoyed in a future incarnation.

If you do not believe in reincarnation, you may assume that previous actions in this lifetime, including intra-uterine influences and formative experiences in infancy, were the forgotten karmas which surface for better or worse later in life.

2. Prarabdha Karma

Prarabdha Karma, that portion of Sanchita Karma which is ready to be experienced by an individual during his or her lifetime, represents the current effect of past actions which appear as fate or destiny. A woman who is simultaneously a daughter, a wife, a mother and a lawyer does not at any particular moment simultaneously experience all the results of the previous actions which created these roles. She is instead predominantly a daughter only when with her parents, a wife only when with her husband, a mother only when with her children, and a lawyer in her professional life alone. Similarly, an entity does not experience all of its Sanchita Karma at once; only that portion which has 'become ripe' for experiencing will surface at any one time.

3. Kriyamana Karma

Kriyamana Karmas consist of the total potential effect created by current actions. People are not mere puppets, mechanically manipulated by the effects of their past actions; we can, by exerting our will, create new actions in the present. Sanchita and Prarabdha Karmas are in a sense 'destined', or 'fated', because they are the product of past actions which have matured. Our Kriyamana Karma is what we do, at any moment, with our capacity to will and to create; it is our 'free will'.

For example, a congenital condition which prevents our lawyer from having children may be said to be due to Prarabdha Karma, or destiny: a ripe effect ready to be experienced. This is also a matter of Sanchita Karma, the longer-term version of fate, for the congenital deficiency was a part of the overall results to be experienced eventually that became ripe for experiencing now. If corrective surgery is possible for this condition and if, at a particular moment in adult life, the woman chooses to undergo surgery, that decision may occur thanks to her Kriyamana Karma.

4. Agama Karma

Agama Karmas, new actions that you contemplate as a result of insight, represent your capacity to envision future actions, whether or not you choose to implement them. In the above example, Agama Karmas are being performed once the lawyer dreams of or plans for surgical correction of her infertility. It is said that for success you must plan your work and work your plan; the former is an Agama Karma, the latter a Kriyamana Karma.

KARMIC INTRICACIES

Jyotishis attempt in their analyses to interpret the varieties and intensities of a person's karmas in particular domains of life. Sanchita Karmas are assumed to form a constant karmic background that is not totally comprehensible by ordinary means, Jyotish included. It is Sanchita Karma that prompts Indians to claim that the ways of karma are unfathomable. Prarabdha, Kriyamana and Agama Karmas are, however, knowable through Jyotish.

Jyotish assumes that the human condition always arises from a dynamic interaction between fate and free will. Fate is fundamentally an expression of the Sanchita and Prarabdha Karmas, and free will the result of Kriyamana and Agama Karmas. Agama and Kriyamana Karmas eternally evolve into Sanchita and Prarabdha Karmas with the passage of time, the axle that turns the great wheel of karma. What was done by free will today acts as the cause of what is experienced as fate tomorrow. Though no one is ruled by fate alone, it may seem so until true free will emerges. Only when free will emerges can the quantity and quality of effort invested in modifying a situation equal or exceed the quantity and quality of effort that created the situation; only then can transformation, as opposed to simple change in life, be achieved. In other words, transformation can occur only when the Agama and Kriyamana Karmas neutralize the Sanchita and its currently materializing Prarabdha Karmas. The quantity and quality of effort required to alter previous karmas depends on the intensity of the Prarabdha Karma.

The three degrees of karmic intensity which may apply to one, many, or all areas of a person's life are:

1. *Dridha* (fixed) Karma
2. *Dridha-Adridha* (fixed/non-fixed) Karma
3. *Adridha* (non-fixed) Karma

Dridha Karma

Dridha Karmas give fixed results because they are so difficult to change that they are practically non-changeable. These karmas, pleasurable or painful, are destined to be experienced because of the intensity of their causes. Most people have noticed that from time to time an experience simply 'happens', despite all efforts to avoid its occurrence. If, for example, a pregnant woman who has enjoyed perfect health before and during her pregnancy and who has had the best of medical care delivers a child with a congenital deformity, a jyotishi might well find that she was experiencing Dridha Prarabdha Karma concerning children, and that her child was experiencing Dridha Prarabdha Karma concerning its body. Remember that this kind of karma may be pleasurable as well as painful; as we all know, those who seem the least deserving are often those who get ahead in life.

Dridha Karmas appear in a horoscope where *confluence* exists. Confluence occurs wherever many astrological factors converge in their indications. The greater the number of indications for good OR for bad in a particular area of a horoscope, the more obvious its results will become. Only when several indications in the horoscope of a pregnant woman concurrently suggest deformity to her child may we conclude that she possesses Dridha Prarabdha Karma concerning children. Although confluence is a particularly important interpretive principle, Jyotish's traditional texts mention it almost in passing, for they rely on the teacher's expert commentary to transmit this notion to the student.

Dridha-Adridha Karma

Dridha-Adridha Karmas occur wherever some (but not most) horoscopic factors relating to a particular area converge in their indications. These karmas, good OR bad, can be changed through the concentrated application of creative will, though considerable effort is required. They give fixed or non-fixed results according to the quantum of effort employed. If the congenital deformity in the child mentioned above is corrected or substantially alleviated through surgery, prolonged diet, intensive exercise, or some other corrective, then its Prarabdha Karma was of the Dridha-Adridha variety. If your father leaves you his hard-earned money at the end of his life, and you determinedly squander it, this would also be a case of Dridha-Adridha Karma being changed by assiduous application of free will.

Adridha Karma

Adridha Karmas are said to give non-fixed results because they are easily altered. Wherever no confluence exists in a horoscope,

Adridha Karmas are present. This state is akin to having a clean slate on which you may write what you please. When a child of normal physique exercises and her body responds with increased strength so that the gain is directly proportionate to the effort made, and no unforeseen hindrances or other unanticipated variances occur, it is a case of Adridha Prarabdha Karma in the area of her physique.

REMEDIES

Upaya (Sanskrit for 'method') refers in Jyotish to the use of Agama and Kriyamana Karmas to remedy adverse astrological combinations. Though not formally one of Jyotish's limbs, this 'phantom' limb may well be its most important and useful division. Jyotish can often diagnose the good and bad times one will encounter in life, but it is *upaya* which can help to augment the good and mitigate the bad. The existence of *upaya* shows that Jyotish is anything but fatalistic, for, if everything were totally predestined, how could remedies exist?

A well-motivated person who is given a method by which to neutralize some undesirable karmas will implement that method for whatever time and with whatever intensity is necessary, but a poorly motivated person will either lack the discipline to follow through or will find obstacles cropping up regularly to interrupt the process. Obstacles to an *upaya* occur particularly for Dridha Karmas, since the force of the karma strongly discourages a change in direction in that area of life; the karmas will themselves interfere with the person's motivation to implement the remedy.

When the karma is non-fixed, the jyotishi will expect immediate change on commencement of an *upaya*. If the karmas are fixed/non-fixed, results are anticipated after some concentrated efforts, often after a period of forty days. But even for those who do persevere, transformation of fixed karmas may not necessarily be expected during this lifetime, though a slight modification of results will perhaps be secretly anticipated. So long as the *upayas* are patiently and consistently resorted to over the course of this incarnation, however, they will act as well-planted seeds whose crop of desired results will be reaped during a future incarnation.

Remedies exist for every planet except of course Uranus, Neptune or Pluto, which were never part of traditional Jyotish. The methods of *upaya* are almost endless, but a partial list includes: *mantras* (sacred syllables, hymns, or prayers) which flow from the heart, devoid of elaborate ritual; recitation of ritually elaborate private and/or public mantras that may go on for days, months or years; the wearing of specific gemstones or other objects; the consumption of particular foods or other elaborately prepared substances; the observance of fasts and other vows; worship of the fire, the planets, and certain deities; and specific acts of charity. The tradition of *upaya* is partly oral and partly written, the *Karmathaguruh* of Pandit Mukundavallabha being one representative work which details some of the more elaborate rituals. It has been said that if all existing *upayas* were written out, their literature would greatly exceed that of all the numerous branches of Jyotish!

Just because remedies exist and are given does not mean that one is home free. Suppose you want to use a gemstone as an *upaya*; perhaps a diamond, to correct some Venusian imbalance. How well this remedy will work will depend on:

· how accurate is the diagnosis
· how appropriate is the diamond (for all diamonds are different)
· who gives the *upaya*
· how the stone is empowered
· the *muhurta* for all the above, and for the time the stone is
   obtained, set, and first worn

The above criteria apply to every remedy, including especially the use of *Bija Mantras* ('seed sounds'). *Bija* means 'seed', and a Bija Mantra is a sound which, like a seed, enters one's consciousness and sprouts into a *devata* (deity). In Jyotish, each planet has a Bija Mantra, which can create the energy of that planet in the consciousness of whoever repeats it properly. (No Bija Mantra for Uranus, Neptune or Pluto appears anywhere in classical Jyotish.) To use a Bija Mantra properly, you must first establish that the planet in question needs to be strengthened. Then you must ensure that you are using the correct mantra, which you must receive during an initiation, at an appropriate *muhurta*. You must also begin to recite the mantra at an appropriate moment. Even then you must be very careful, because Bija Mantras are very, very powerful!

THE GRAHAS

While the question of precisely how a Bija Mantra works is beyond the scope of this book, we can say that they enhance a planet's ability to influence consciousness. 'Planet' is the best of a poor crop of English synonyms for the Sanskrit word *graha*. A graha is literally a Seizer, one of a group of astral forces which can enter your organism and take control of your being. Like vidyas, the grahas grasp and possess you, but they do so in ways which are usually less pleasant and productive than are possessions by vidyas. A graha grabs hold of your being with its emanations and directs you, for better or worse, to perform particular actions that you might not otherwise perform, in pursuit of goals which may not agree with your personal dharma. The grahas, who are the agents of the Law of Karma, direct you to experience at specific moments the reactions to the actions you have previously performed. Your horoscope is a map of your karmas, drawn to the specifications of the Nine Seizers.

Generally speaking, your individual karmas are stored in the warehouse of your causal body (*vijnanamayakosha*, the 'sheath made of transcendent wisdom') and your shared karmas (the karmas you share with your family, clan and race, and with your fellow citizens in the city, region and country in which you reside) in your greater causal body (*anandamayakosha*, 'sheath made of bliss'). As these karmas ripen to fruition, they project into the subtle or astral body (*manomayakosha*, 'sheath made of mind'), the home of your self-image, where they affect the mind (particularly the *manas*). The mind thereupon directs the etheric body (*pranamayakosha*, 'sheath made of prana') to energize the physical body (*annamayakosha*, 'sheath made of food') to perform or avoid certain actions, in order that the stored karmas may thus be worked out. These five bodies (which are enumerated in the Taittiriya Upanishad) nest within one another like Russian babushka dolls. When taken together as a whole, they compose a single human being.

Physical gravity grasps the physical body; Mother Earth's gravity gathers to her all the beings who grow on her bosom. Just as human personalities reside within physical bodies, the corporeal planets act as physical bodies for the nine deities who are the Great Graspers. Except for that of the Sun and Moon, the physical gravity of the planets affects all beings on Earth to a fairly minimal degree. In our opinion, physical gravitation is the least likely field in which the causation of Jyotish operates. In fact, someone has calculated that the body of the doctor or midwife who delivers a child exerts a gravitational force on the child that is greater than any distant planet can deliver.

Instead, the subtle and causal gravities of the Nine Grahas influence the way in which we experience the results of our karmas by seizing and controlling our subtle and causal bodies. By analogy, although thought has minimal 'reality' in the physical universe, it is the cause of most physical actions that most humans perform.

THE ISHTA DEVATA

It is the nature of the karmas themselves – Dridha, Dridha-Adridha or Adridha – which determines how strongly a graha can grasp. For Dridha Karmas, the grahas seize their prey and refuse to let go, while for Adridha Karmas they can be pried loose with relative ease. Remedies are designed to prevent or to correct undesirable seizures, those which cause you to perform selfish, evil karmas. Sometimes *upayas* encourage seizure by benefic grahas which will keep your mind moving in a healthy direction. Often the best remedy of all is to worship an *ishta devata*, a personal deity, which is the remedy jyotishis themselves use to keep from being affected by the grahas in their work. While jyotishis of the earliest days relied on the Vedic deities as *ishta devatas*, today some people make one of the grahas into their *ishta devata*; others prefer to worship an *ishta devata* who can control all Nine Seizers; and a few even make the Jyotir Vidya herself into their *ishta devata*.

Because all humans (except for the finest of saints) always sit securely in the grasp of the grahas, the graha or grahas which have seized the client's mind may so perturb the jyotishi's mind that the jyotishi will proffer poor advice. This will in turn enhance the likelihood that the client will perform the action that is 'fated' by those karmas. So long as an *ishta devata* possesses the jyotishi, however, the client's grahas will be unable to do so, and this will provide the jyotishi with a bigger perspective, a greater reality from which to advise the client. An *ishta devata* makes it easier to live a life in which you act of your own volition, instead of being perpetually driven by your karmas, or by the karmas of others, to act in frequently undesirable ways.

Another reason why those who practice Jyotish must cultivate a relationship with a personal deity is that a jyotishi is always coming to crossroads in readings, at which two or more interpretations seem equally feasible. At these moments an *ishta devata* can 'jump the gap' in your model of reality and flash you the right answer. Fluctuations in the mind occur because of the continual interchange of Sattva, Rajas and Tamas. When you worship an *ishta devata*, your focus restrains those fluctuations, which permits a little spark of Reality to flow from your deity to you. It is this spark which appears in your awareness as intuition. The word most commonly used for intuition today in India is in fact *ishta bala*, which means literally 'the strength of the deity'. It was this strength that the rishis who originated Jyotish tapped into in order to collect and systematize their astrological information.

Though the worship of an *ishta devata* may seem to some an exercise in idolatry, the deities are really representatives of the One Reality. When you worship a personal deity, you indirectly worship the Absolute One, the Singularity who hides behind the mask of the deity's personality. Worship of deities really means appreciating them for the skill with which they play their roles in the cosmic drama. You can also worship the One directly, but the One is undifferentiated, unqualified and absolute, while the world a jyotishi lives in is relative, qualified and differentiated. The personal relationship you create with an *ishta devata* plugs you in to a personal relationship with the One Reality, the source of all questions and all answers.

But intuition alone is insufficient for the practice of Jyotish, for unless you are a great saint you will be unable to call on your deity for help and advice twenty-four hours a day, even if you should want to do so. And besides, in the words of our Jyotish guru, 'The *ishta devata* is busy; call on him or her only in an emergency.' The Seers systematized Jyotish for beings like you and me who have to use rational methods and intuitive powers to complement one another, and only those who become adept at both these approaches to divination can ever become fit receptacles for the Jyotir Vidya.

JYOTISH IN ACTION

Even an adept cannot predict the course of a human life from cradle to grave through examining the natal horoscope unless all the karmas indicated therein are Dridha Karmas, which is very uncommon. Natal astrology gauges Prarabdha Karma by constructing a 'snapshot' of the heavens at the time and place of a birth, which is then interpreted to predict the course of that life, a life which should evolve along a totally predictable pattern if fate is in fact immutable. But this is rarely true in practice.

A good jyotishi makes predictions about configurations in the natal horoscope which indicate the presence of fixed karmas in one or many areas of life. One fundamental error that fledgeling jyotishis commonly make is to predict dire or wonderful results from a single bad or good influence in a horoscope. Fixed karmas exist only in those areas of life in which the several different astrological factors which signify those areas all confluently suggest the same sorts of results. Since Dridha Karma is very difficult to transform, such predictions will usually be correct. Natal astrology can also indicate how long such Dridha Karma will last, when it will be most and when least active, and whether it will yield pleasurable or painful results.

Predictions in those areas of life in which the natal horoscope shows Dridha-Adridha or Adridha Karma become progressively more tenuous as life progresses, because all the actions that have been performed after birth are transforming, positively or negatively, the potential results. In these areas the jyotishi employs *prashna* (horary astrology) to gauge the potential effects inherent in the Kriyamana and Agama Karmas by casting a horoscope for the moment at which a question is asked or an event occurs. A horary horoscope thus gauges the accumulated influence of free will in one's life up to the point of the reading. The information garnered in both horoscopes, natal and horary, is then blended for the reading. A good jyotishi, like a soothsayer, composes a well-tuned story for a client, a story which creates an image of reality as it was in the past, as it is at the time of the reading, and as it may become in the future, according to the client's life goals.

If, for example, the question is about marriage, and the natal horoscope indicates Dridha-Adridha Karma, then the horoscope calculated for the moment the question is put to the astrologer will reveal what energies have been activated by the individual with regard to marriage in the time between his or her birth and the asking of the question. As it happens, when a natal horoscope shows fixed karma in one area of life, the same sort of confluence of indications will usually be present when the same area is investigated via the horary horoscope.

Once a conclusion is drawn about the nature of the karmas in the area of life under investigation, *muhurta* (electional astrology) is used to maximize the effectiveness of the Kriyamana and Agama Karmas selected for use as remedies, since *muhurta* is an astrological method for optimizing free will. *Nimitta* (omenology) spontaneously enhances natal, horary and electional astrology when they, due to karmic complexities, cannot provide the detail necessary for making effective decisions. That unforeseen developments can occur in life is accommodated philosophically through the notion of *kripa* (divine grace). In spite of all his disadvantages, a beggar can become a king if favored by grace, and kings can and do become beggars on falling from grace. Consideration of omens permits a jyotishi to take the factor of grace (or its lack) into account when making an astrological interpretation of a life.

The particular complexity of influences with which a jyotishi must juggle when attempting to make a judicious evaluation of someone's karmas explains why Jyotish cannot be scheduled. 'Every jyotishi is trying to play the game of God in aspiring to omniscience,' says our Jyotish guru. 'For God this may be easy, but for us humans with our limited brains it is not; it requires effort, experience, intuition and saintliness. If a jyotishi can attain even a drop of the ocean of God's omniscience, that jyotishi will be pursued by all, and will not have to advertise for clients.' A good jyotishi often says to a client, 'Come back tomorrow, my mind is not right today.' While a sensible client who wants a reliable reply will acquiesce, many clients today, driven by the force of their karmas, will insist that it be done there and then. If the client forces the jyotishi to read at that moment, good results cannot be guaranteed.

Mastery of all of Jyotish's limbs is thus essential for the correct and unfailing predictions that make one a *daivajna*, a knower of God's intentions. Varahamihira in his *Brihat Samhita* (2: 3) lists the qualities displayed by one who has become an expert at Jyotish: 'He must be pure, skillful, bold, eloquent, possessed of a ready wit, a knower of time and place, filled with equanimity, not timid in assembly, victorious in debate with other astrologers, expert, free from vices, well-versed in palliative, preventative magic and bathing rituals, ever engaged in worshipping deities, vows, and penances, possessed of great and unusual power as a result of his achievements, and capable of answering questions and prescribing remedies.' Mastery of Jyotish occurs when all the Nine Seizers come to life in the jyotishi's consciousness, transforming these planets from mere symbols into living beings who, when pleased, can assist in the work of Jyotish.

CHAPTER THREE

ESSENTIAL ASTRONOMY
FOR JYOTISH

Because astrology depends on astronomy, certain astronomical concepts must be understood before we can introduce the three steps of Jyotish, which are *calculation*, *representation* and *interpretation*. The first step in most astrology is to calculate a map of the heavens as seen from the time and place of an event (such as a birth). That map is then represented symbolically (as a horoscope or birth chart, in the case of a birth). Only when we have a precise map can we accurately interpret that map's meaning, for inaccurate calculations make for incorrect interpretations.

THE ZODIAC

Although objectively the Earth moves around the Sun in an elliptical orbit, we on Earth subjectively see the Sun appearing to move around the Earth. The path of this motion is called the *ecliptic*. The movements of the planets used in Jyotish are confined to a band in the heavens which extends approximately eight degrees to both the north and the south of the ecliptic, as seen from the Earth. This limited swath of sky within which the planets are constrained to wander ('planet' is Greek for 'wanderer') is the *zodiac*, which is divided into 360 degrees (°). Each degree is divided into 60 minutes (') of arc, and each minute of arc is divided into 60 seconds (") of arc.

Although there is only one ecliptic and (as a consequence) only one zodiac, the latter is given two different names to differentiate between two ways of measuring along the same circle: the *tropical zodiac* and the *sidereal zodiac*. Each circle of these zodiacs contains

360°, and each is divided by astrologers into twelve equal segments of 30 degrees each. The twelve divisions of the tropical zodiac are known as *signs*, and the twelve divisions of the sidereal zodiac are known as *constellations*.

The majority of non-Asian astrologers use the vernal equinox (the apparent position of the Sun at the commencement of spring) as their starting point for their measurements along the zodiac. Because of certain complex astronomical phenomena, the point of the vernal equinox changes slightly each year, receding against the background of the sidereal zodiac at an approximate rate of one degree every 72 years. Thus if spring began at point 'X' in relation to the sidereal zodiac in the year 1938, it will begin at a point one degree less than 'X' in the year 2010 because the vernal equinox will have moved in the opposite direction to the apparent usual direction of motion of the planets. This is called the *Precession of the Equinox*.

Because the vernal equinox moves against the background of the fixed stars in the zodiac, the astrologers of most ancient cultures, including India, favored measurement along the zodiac from a starting point that was more permanently fixed in relation to the zodiacal stars than is the vernal equinox. This zodiac is known as the fixed or sidereal zodiac (*sidereal* means 'pertaining to the stars'), while the zodiac measured from the point of the vernal equinox, which moves in relation to the fixed stars, is called the movable or tropical zodiac (*tropical* means 'pertaining to the turning', which refers to the turning of the Sun at the time of the equinoxes). Jyotishis call the former the *nirayana chakra* (loosely, 'the wheel without movement') and the latter the *sayana chakra* ('the moving wheel'). Though they have long been aware of these two ways of measuring along the zodiac, the many traditions of Jyotish have consistently rejected the tropical zodiac for astrological purposes, though it is sometimes used for calendrical design.

The sidereal zodiac uses fixed stars, singly or in groups, as markers to identify its different segments along the band of the zodiac in such a way that each 30° segment contains within it most or all of an identifiable group of fixed stars known as a *constellation*. The tropical zodiac measures its signs from the point of the vernal equinox, which changes each year with relation to the constellations.

These signs have nothing in common with the constellations after which they were named except for those names. Those with a background in Western astrology must therefore be careful not to confuse these constellations of the sidereal zodiac with the signs of the Western zodiac. The zodiac signs and constellations currently in use are (in order from the zodiac's beginning): 1 – Aries; 2 – Taurus; 3 – Gemini; 4 – Cancer; 5 – Leo; 6 – Virgo; 7 – Libra; 8 – Scorpio; 9 – Sagittarius; 10 – Capricorn; 11 – Aquarius; 12 – Pisces.

Because some of the stars which make up the twelve constellations of the zodiac actually appear outside the 30° band that each constellation is assigned, the constellations seem to have been originally created in non-standard sizes, which may imply that the constellations antedated the signs of the tropical zodiac. The 27 or 28 Vedic constellations known as *nakshatras* likewise seem to have begun life as irregular asterisms, which later became standardized as equal slices of sky. In the early days, before the institution of the uniform zodiac and the standard circle of nakshatras, jyotishis may well have made their observations using individual constellations and nakshatras as their frames of reference, just as now their frame of reference is the whole of the zodiac. If so, it would reinforce the idea that Vedic astronomical observations were based less on degree precision and more on the characteristic behavior of celestial bodies moving in that area of the sky.

THE AYANAMSHA

Once every 25,800 years or so, the starting points of the sidereal and tropical zodiacs coincide. After this coincidence, these points will separate from each other by the above-mentioned approximate one degree of arc for each subsequent 72 years. The distance between the starting points of the sidereal and tropical zodiacs at any given time is known in Sanskrit as the *ayanamsha* (roughly, 'the portion of movement').

There is some controversy over the year in which the starting points of the two zodiacs last coincided, which makes determination of the *ayanamsha* one of Jyotish's major confusions, one which is probably unresolvable. Each *ayanamsha* has its staunch proponents, and each deserves respect, since each is the work of eminent jyotishis possessing considerable experience and intuitive insight. Known ancient observations of planetary and stellar positions do not precisely correlate with modern observations. We do not know whether those ancient observations were wrong (due to less precise measuring technology) or whether there have been perturbations in stellar positions or planetary motions over time. It may even have been that the rate of the equinoxes' precession has been changing over the course of the past several thousand years. There is thus no way to be sure when the last coincidence occurred.

The most widely used year in India for this coincidence is A.D. 285 and this *ayanamsha* is known as the Lahiri or Chitra *ayanamsha*. Other *ayanamshas* widely used in India are those of Krishnamurti (A.D. 291) and Raman (A.D. 397). The majority of Indian jyotishis use and get good results from the Lahiri *ayanamsha*; since the fledgeling jyotishi should probably first acquire experience by being grounded in the most widely used of the *ayanamshas*, this book expresses all planetary positions in the sidereal zodiac using the Lahiri *ayanamsha*.

A sidereal zodiacal position is converted to a tropical zodiacal position simply by adding the *ayanamsha* for the year in question to the sidereal zodiacal position. To go from a tropical to a sidereal position, the process is reversed and the appropriate *ayanamsha* amount is subtracted from the tropical position. The *ayanamsha* to be added or subtracted is obtained by multiplying the averaged rate of the accumulated *ayanamsha* (which, according to Lahiri, is approximately 50.29 seconds of arc per year) by the number of years elapsed since the most recent year of coincidence of the tropical and sidereal zodiacs.

Table 3.1 indicates the amount of various *ayanamshas* for the twentieth century, approximated to a minute (') of arc. The *ayanamsha* for intervening years can be arrived at by simple proportion.

PLANETARY MOTION

The Earth's rotation from west to east creates the illusion that the heavens rotate around the Earth from east to west, so that the

TABLE 3.1

Ayanamsha Values of Different Authorities
(rounded to the nearest minute)

Year	Lahiri	Krishnamurti	Raman
1900	22° 28'	22° 22'	21° 01'
1910	22° 36'	22° 30'	21° 09'
1920	22° 45'	22° 38'	21° 18'
1930	22° 53'	22° 47'	21° 26'
1940	23° 01'	22° 55'	21° 34'
1950	23° 10'	23° 04'	21° 43'
1960	23° 18'	23° 12'	21° 51'
1970	23° 26'	23° 20'	22° 00'
1980	23° 35'	23° 29'	22° 08'
1990	23° 42'	23° 37'	22° 16'
2000	23° 51'	23° 45'	22° 24'

constellations in their natural order flow anti-clockwise for observers on Earth. Like the Sun, the planets daily appear to rise in the east and set in the west in a clockwise direction for an observer who is facing south. This is called *diurnal* motion. In addition to this apparent motion around the Earth once every twenty-four hours, the planets also seem to move along the zodiac, as seen from the Earth, as a result of their orbits around the Sun (and, in the Moon's case, its orbit around the Earth). This is called *proper* motion. Diurnal motion seems to take a planet east to west in the local sky of the observer, while proper motion takes it west to east through the stars of the zodiac.

Diurnal motion, which completes its cycle once daily with one complete rotation of the Earth on its axis, is always faster than proper motion. The following are the approximate proper motions of each of the planets. These are only averages; Mars, for example, can under certain conditions occupy one constellation for up to six months.

SUN – 1° per day or 30 days per constellation
MOON – 13° 58' per day or 2¼ days per constellation
MARS – 38' per day or 1½ months per constellation
MERCURY – 1° 19' per day or 30 days per constellation
JUPITER – 5' per day or 1 year per constellation
VENUS – 1° per day or 30 days per constellation
SATURN – 4' per day or 2½ years per constellation
RAHU/KETU – 3' per day or 1½ years per constellation

While diurnal motion never changes its direction, the proper motion of every planet except the Sun and Moon does. As the Earth orbits the Sun, we repeatedly seem to 'lap' the outer planets. When this happens, our frame of reference makes it appear that these planets are moving backwards against the fixed stars. This seeming backward movement is termed *retrogression*. While the averaged proper motion of Rahu and Ketu carry them backwards through the zodiac, some modern writers have pointed out that, due to complex perturbations of the orbits of the Earth and the Moon, the invisible positions of the nodes sometimes move forward. Since classical Jyotish does not mention this 'change' of motion, it is not regarded as the 'retrogression' of the nodes.

Retrogression always begins for the outer planets (Mars, Jupiter and Saturn) when Earth sits between them and the Sun. These planets are always brightest, and therefore strongest, when they are nearly opposite the Sun in the sky, because it is then that we are closest to them. Jupiter and Saturn move backwards once each year. Mars is not as cyclical in his retrogression, which is one reason we call him 'the Crooked' (*vakri*). *Vakri* also happens to be the Sanskrit word for retrograde. Because Mars was observed to be independent in the skies, he gained a reputation for causing independence in the horoscope. Here interpretation follows observation yet again.

The situation for the inner planets (Mercury and Venus) is a bit more complex. While Venus does not necessarily go retrograde each year, Mercury retrogrades several times annually. Even though Mercury's perceived motion is an average of 19' per day more than that of the Sun or Venus, Mercury goes retrograde so often that, like the Sun and Venus, it covers only one constellation every 30 days, on the average.

Sometimes the planets conjoin the Sun in the sky and are lost in the Sun's glare. In this state they are referred to as being *combust*, burned up by the Sun's rays. In Sanskrit we speak of them as being *astam*, which means 'having set', because they have become as invisible as any heavenly body becomes when it sets. The outer planets, who become combust when they are furthest from Earth, become extremely weak astrologically when obscured by the Sun's rays. The situation for the inner planets is, again, more complex: they can be combust either when nearest or furthest from the Earth, and either when retrograde or in direct motion. When either Mercury or Venus is combust while retrograde, it is weakened astrologically, but less so than when combust while in direct motion.

THE HOUSES OF A HOROSCOPE

A planet's proper motion is shown by its degree position within a constellation, while its diurnal motion is shown by its house position. The astrological houses at a locality are a permanent division of space into twelve equal sectors of 30° each, measured from the ascendant. The *ascendant* of your horoscope, which is the degree of the zodiac intersected by the eastern horizon at the place and time of your birth, establishes where a planet is within its rhythm of rising and setting in relation to your birth place. The ascendant is called the *lagna* in Jyotish because the word 'lagna' conveys a sense of being tied down; the ascendant 'ties' the position of the planets to the place and time of birth.

Although the words 'ascendant' and 'lagna' are often used synonymously, the concept of lagna in Jyotish actually encompasses all the varied methods which make the heavens specific to one's astrological purpose. The lagna which is fixed by the ascendant is known as the *Udaya Lagna*. Jyotish's most common alternative lagna is the *Chandra Lagna* (Moon Lagna), which is created by taking whatever constellation the Moon is sitting in as the first house. For the *Surya Lagna* (Sun Lagna), the Sun's constellation is taken as the first house.

For horary (*prashna*) charts, the lagna can be fixed by the *Udaya Lagna*, the *Chandra Lagna*, the *Dig Lagna* (by compass direction), the

Shabda Lagna (by the words the clients utter), the *Sparsha Lagna* (by the parts of the body they touch), the *Nama Lagna* (by the first letter of their names or the numerical value of the full name), or even by a random number the jyotishi asks them to choose. In this book, whenever the word 'lagna' is used without any modifier, it should be taken to mean the *Udaya Lagna*, the lagna fixed by the ascendant.

Jyotishis emphasize the *Udaya Lagna* because it is the one factor in astrology that greatly differentiates births that take place on the same day. For example, when Mars is in Cancer, it will be at the same degree position in Cancer for anyone born anywhere on Earth at that moment. If all we could say about that Mars was that it occupied a certain degree of Cancer, it would become a relatively meaningless factor in astrological interpretation, one which would not help us to differentiate one horoscope from another. If, however, we note that the same Mars who is rising for someone born in Chicago will be setting at that same time for someone born in Bombay, we have an important point of differentiation for the two horoscopes, since Mars rising in Cancer on the eastern horizon and Mars setting in Cancer on the western horizon have different astrological interpretations.

Most jyotishis use the method of equal house division (30° = one house), though advanced and detailed work is often accomplished through other methods of house division which are based on proportionate divisions of time or proportionate divisions of space. The method of Shripati, which is based on proportionate divisions of space, is one of the most popular of these alternative methods.

MAPPING A HOROSCOPE

Astrology's first step is to calculate a map of the heavens, an arithmetical process whose description is beyond the scope of this book. While many people, especially non-mathematically inclined students, resort to computerized astrological calculations to avoid this initially cumbersome area of astrology, we believe that anyone who wishes to pursue the study of Jyotish seriously should learn how to calculate a basic horoscope manually. No matter how you obtain them, astrological calculations should be as precise as possible.

After calculation comes astrology's second step, the presentation of the calculated results in the form of a map of the heavens as 'tied down' by the lagna. Different cultures use different ways to map the three-dimensional heavens on a two-dimensional surface. While horoscopes in the West are usually represented today in a circular form, in India they appear most often in square or rectangular form. The horoscope diagram which is primarily used in this book is one which is used by most of the astrologers of northern India. This basic representation of a natal chart is known as a *'Rashi Chart'*. It represents the houses and constellations simultaneously by dividing a rectangle into twelve segments, as shown in Figure 3.1:

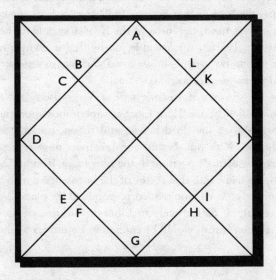

Figure 3.1

The diamond marked 'A' always represents the first house; the triangle marked 'B' adjacent and to the left of 'A' always represents the second house, and so on, the representation of the houses continuing consecutively until the twelfth house, marked 'L', completes it. The houses are fixed in the horoscope in the same way that they are fixed in each locality, with the ascendant always on the eastern horizon. We prefer the northern Indian style of horoscope mapping because it reflects astronomical reality by showing the houses as fixed in space. Since the respective houses in this type of horoscope always occur in the same places, jyotishis memorize the house positions in the diagram, counting them consecutively counter-clockwise, so that they need not identify the houses visibly.

The constellations superimposed on each of the twelve houses will, however, vary according to the ascendant at the birth time and birth place, for a total of twelve possible arrangements. The number that appears written inside each house of this type of horoscope is the number of the constellation of the zodiac superimposing itself on that house. The lord of that constellation becomes, in that horoscope, the lord of that house. While the lords of the constellations are always fixed, the lords of the houses vary from horoscope to horoscope. Jupiter, for example, may rule (or own) houses one and four in one horoscope, houses two and five in another, houses three and six in yet another, and so on.

Figure 3.2 shows a horoscope with a Virgo ascendant superimposed on the first house. Here Libra is superimposed on the second house, Scorpio on the third house, and so on, up to Leo on the twelfth house. With houses and constellations now represented in the diagram, a planet's position in the horoscope is indicated simply by writing its name into that sector of the horoscope which bears the number of the constellation that corresponds to the planet's position.

For example, if Saturn were in Libra at the time of the birth in Figure 3.2, then Saturn would be entered in Figure 3.2 as shown.

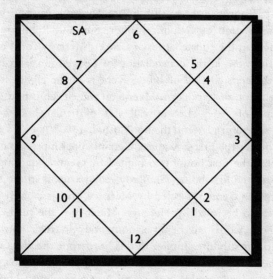

Figure 3.2

Figure 3.3 shows a horoscope with a Gemini lagna (ascendant), which puts Cancer in the second house, Leo in the third house, and so on, up to Taurus in the twelfth house. Saturn is in the first house in the constellation of Gemini. Jupiter, Sun and Rahu are in the second house in the constellation of Cancer. Mercury and Venus are in the third house in the constellation of Leo. Moon is in the fifth house in the constellation of Libra. Ketu is in the eighth house in the constellation of Capricorn. Mars is in the eleventh house in the constellation of Aries. Let us call this particular horoscope, to which we will return later in the book, Chart 1.

In Figure 3.3 the first house has Gemini superimposed on it. We may say that the first house is occupied by Gemini, or simply that Gemini is in the first house. Similarly, Sagittarius is in the seventh house. Because Gemini is ruled by Mercury, the first house is said, in this case, to be ruled by Mercury. Mercury is the ruler, lord or owner (these words all being synonymous in their astrological usage) of the first house. Jupiter in this horoscope then becomes the lord of the seventh and tenth houses, because he rules Sagittarius and Pisces, which in this horoscope are superimposed over the seventh and tenth houses respectively. Mercury becomes the ruler of the fourth house, Sun the owner of the third house, and so on.

The lordship and the occupation of the planets in the horoscope shown in Figure 3.3 can lead to statements of the following type: Saturn is in (or occupies) the first house. Mercury and Venus occupy the third house. The lord of the first house (Mercury) dwells in the third house. The ruler of the ninth house (Saturn) tenants the first house. Because each house has its own ruler, we can also express the last two statements in another way: Mercury, the first house lord (or first lord), is situated in the Sun's house (because the Sun in this horoscope rules the third house). Saturn, the ninth lord, occupies Mercury's constellation in the first house (or occupies Mercury's house). The ability to describe and analyze planetary placements in a horoscope in this way must become habitual and instinctive.

Figure 3.4 is a way of representing a horoscope which is particularly popular in southern India. In this type of diagram the constellations are always represented by the same squares, and so, once memorized,

SU RA JU
3
VE
4
2
5
SA
1
MA
ME
6
12
MO
7
11
8
10
9
KE

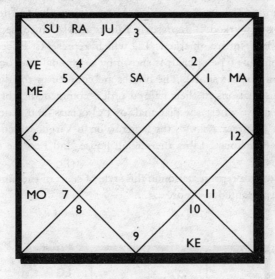

Figure 3.3

Figure 3.4

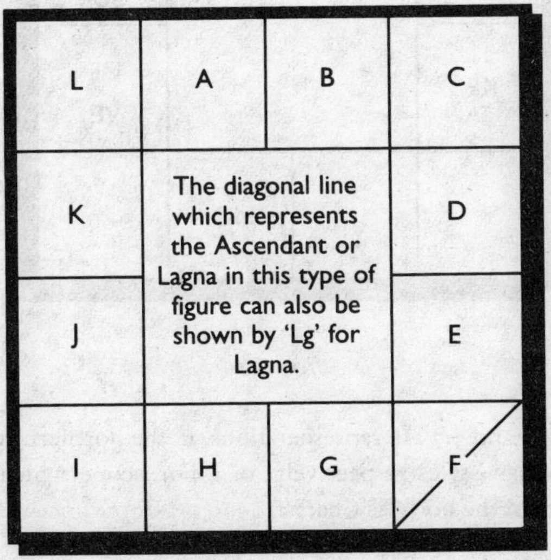

L
A
B
C
K
The diagonal line which represents the Ascendant or Lagna in this type of figure can also be shown by 'Lg' for Lagna.
D
J
E
I
H
G
F

there is no need to identify the squares with any symbols for the constellations. The square marked 'A' represents the constellation Aries, the one marked 'B' represents Taurus, and so on consecutively until the last square, marked 'L', which represents Pisces. The ascendant in this type of chart is shown by a diagonal line, or by the word lagna (Lg for short). The houses are counted in the direction of the constellations in their natural order, commencing the count from the square where the diagonal (or Lg) occurs, and proceeding clockwise. Figure 3.4 shows the lagna to be in Virgo, which makes Virgo the first house, Libra the second house, and Leo the twelfth house.

Figure 3.5 is a representation in this style of chart of the horoscope that was represented in Figure 3.3.

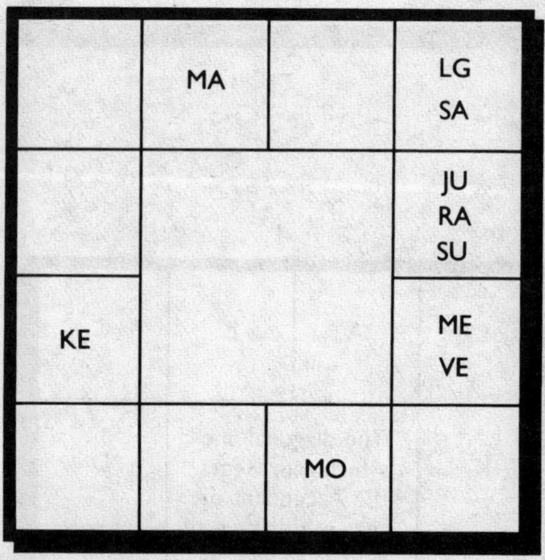

Figure 3.5

Figures 3.6 and 3.7 are representations, in the northern Indian and southern Indian styles respectively, of a horoscope which we shall refer to later in the book as Chart 2.

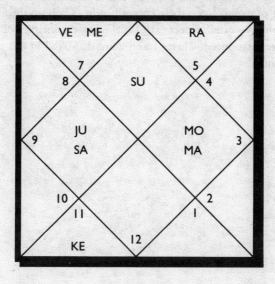

Figure 3.6

Figure 3.7

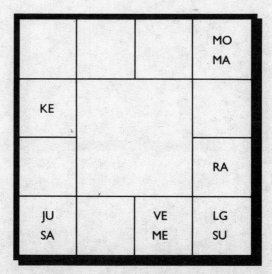

As an exercise in horoscope mapping, copy out Charts 1 and 2 on to a sheet of paper. Keep these copies handy as you go through this book so that you can inspect each for the basic principles of Jyotish as they are introduced. Charts 1 and 2 are displayed in full detail in the Appendix.

CHAPTER FOUR

THE GRAHAS (PLANETS)

THE LANGUAGE OF JYOTISH

Only the jyotishi who has augmented reasoning with experience and cultivated a sharp intuition can select the astrological principle that is most appropriate for a situation. Jyotish, which is a sort of language, offers a variety of words and a series of basic rules which dictate when, where and how those words may be used. While an effective communicator may intuitively know when logical rules of word-selection can be broken, this sort of intuition works only when the communicator is well versed in the rules of the language.

The words of the language of Jyotish are the planets, constellations and houses. Anyone who sets out to learn a new idiom must follow the tedious but unavoidable procedure of acquiring a basic vocabulary by memorizing lists of words and their meanings. The next three chapters of this book form a comprehensive vocabulary which must be memorized by anyone who hopes to become proficient in the language of Jyotish, because Jyotish is classically taught by proceeding from the specific to the abstract. First the student learns specific examples, then the mentor helps the student to see the theory from which those examples have originated. When you learn specifics first, you rarely if ever forget them; the specifics will then unfailingly remind you of their underlying principles.

Many people who study Jyotish try to take shortcuts by learning just enough of the Jyotish vocabulary they believe to be essential and then trying to fill in the gaps with their knowledge of Western astrology. Such haphazard learning cannot prepare you adequately to speak in Jyotish's idiom any more than you could carry on an intelligible conversation in grammatical French if you chose to learn only a fraction of French vocabulary and elected to substitute English words for everything you had not bothered to absorb. The result might be original, but it would also be unintelligible. Remember this Sanskrit proverb: 'Knowledge that has not been memorized is as useless in time of need as money that was lent but never repaid.'

JYOTISH IN TRANSLATION

All interpreters often face difficulties and ambiguities in interpretation, and this is particularly true of astrologers, who assume the role of interpreter for those who do not understand astrological jargon. Just as a well-trained interpreter must sometimes take liberties with language in order to preserve its meaning, a good jyotishi must become proficient at resolving astrological idiomatic expressions and ambiguities in order to translate precisely astrological statements during a consultation. To translate the French expression '*mon petit chou*' into English as 'my little cabbage' is literally correct, but such a literal rendering is absurd, for '*mon petit chou*' is an idiomatic expression which means 'my dear' or 'my darling'. 'Honey' may, however, be a good translation for '*mon petit chou*', even though 'cabbage' does not mean 'honey'.

Because of inherent ambiguities in everyday speech, even people who are not professional translators must translate within their native language much of the time. When someone tells you to 'hit the nail with the hammer', you probably will not slug away at your fingernail, because you understand that a different sort of 'nail' is indicated. When you hear the phrase 'bull's-eye', you are not likely to visualize a bovine organ of sight, because your previous experience of the phrase helps you to interpret it appropriately.

Proficiency in any language comes through experience but, by comparing the many translations of the Bible, you will discover that differences of opinion can and do arise even among experienced translators. Several English possibilities exist for each of the most vital Greek or Hebrew words in critical passages, and each variant interpretation is sanctioned by a rival group of reputable scholars. This is precisely the situation among groups of jyotishis when they debate pithy astrological statements, for, in the words of the Vedas, 'the truth is one, the learned speak of it in many ways'. On rare occasions these translations may even oppose one another.

Such differences of interpretation do not invalidate Jyotish any more than differences of interpretation invalidate biblical scholarship, for the majority of jyotishis share a consensus about their scriptures that is similar to the consensus shared by scholars of the Bible. Differences of interpretation occur in every symbolic language because the symbol itself, no matter how perfect, can never be precisely the thing it symbolizes. The words we use to describe the planets, constellations and houses are decidedly poor substitutes for the things they represent.

Even the word 'symbol' is subject to varying interpretations. The cosmic events we view in the sky are real and they are also symbolic. Although many people, particularly Westerners, take as unreal the mythic symbols which represent these events, Jyotish treats them as being real both independently and dependently. They are dependently real in that they can remain alive on the material plane only so long as humans continue to remember them, and they are independently real in that they do not require humans in order to continue to live. Those who study Indian vidyas do not *study* symbols, they create relationships with them.

Our introduction to the planets can be divided into three parts: aspects, strengths and characteristics.

PLANETARY ASSOCIATIONS AND ASPECTS

By virtue of their positions in certain constellations, planets influence certain other constellations. These special influences are known as *aspects*. The aspects discussed in this book are primarily those of the Parashari system. In Jaimini's system it is the constellations and not the planets which aspect one another, while in the Tajika system planets aspect within certain orbs of influence, much as in Western astrology. Influences in Parashari Jyotish are by association, and by full, special or partial aspects.

Association

Two or more planets influence one another by association when they occupy the same constellation. In Chart 1 Jupiter, Sun and Rahu all influence one another because they are all in association in the constellation of Cancer. Planets also influence constellations and houses by association: every planet is associated with, and consequently influences, the constellation and house it occupies. In Chart 1 both Mercury and Venus influence the third house and the constellation of Leo, which they both occupy.

Full Aspects

All planets fully aspect the seventh constellation (counted inclusively) from the constellation that they occupy. For example, any planet which occupies the constellation of Gemini automatically influences by aspect the seventh constellation from Gemini, which happens to be Sagittarius (1 – Gemini; 2 – Cancer; 3 – Leo; 4 – Virgo; 5 – Libra; 6 – Scorpio and 7 – Sagittarius). In Chart 2, Moon and Mars, who occupy Gemini, influence Sagittarius by their full seventh aspects. They also influence any planet(s) occupying Sagittarius, which in this horoscope happen to be Jupiter and Saturn. Jupiter and Saturn return the favor by aspecting Gemini and the two planets situated therein.

Special Aspects

In addition to these full seventh aspects, Mars, Jupiter and Saturn also have what are called *special aspects*. These are as strong as association and as the full seventh aspect common to all planets. Mars aspects the fourth and eighth constellations from its position; Jupiter aspects the fifth and the ninth constellations from its position; and Saturn aspects the third and tenth constellations from its position. Always count inclusively, beginning with the constellation in which the aspecting planet sits.

In Chart 1 Mars occupies the constellation of Aries. From this position it aspects Libra by its seventh aspect, Cancer by its fourth aspect and Scorpio by its eighth aspect. Jupiter, which occupies Cancer here, similarly influences Scorpio by its fifth aspect and Pisces by its ninth aspect; and Saturn, who here tenants Gemini, influences Leo by its third aspect and Pisces by its tenth aspect – all counted inclusively from the constellation where the planet resides. Any planets placed in these aspected constellations are also influenced accordingly; in this chart, Mars affects Jupiter, Sun and Rahu by its fourth aspect and Moon by its seventh aspect; Jupiter affects Ketu by its seventh aspect; and Saturn affects Mercury and Venus by its third aspect.

Rahu and Ketu are said by some jyotishis to cast a full aspect on the fifth and ninth constellations counted inclusively from their position.

Mutual and One-sided Aspects

When two planets aspect each other, this is a *mutual aspect*. This can happen by association, full aspect or special aspect. In the case of association the two planets occupy the same constellation, and in the case of full aspect they occupy the seventh constellations from each other, from which positions they 'gaze at' each other. Only one mutual special aspect can occur: between Saturn and Mars, when Mars occupies the tenth constellation from Saturn. When a planet aspects another without the latter reciprocating, this is a *one-sided* aspect. This situation always involves the special aspects of Mars, Jupiter and Saturn. For example, in Chart 2 Mars aspects the Sun, but the Sun does not aspect Mars; this is a one-sided aspect.

Partial Aspects

Besides their full and special aspects, the planets Sun through Saturn also have partial aspects. All planets except Mars have a 75 per cent aspect on the fourth and eighth constellations counted inclusively from the constellation in which they sit; all planets except Jupiter have a 50 per cent aspect on the fifth and ninth constellations so counted; and all planets except Saturn have a 25 per cent aspect on the third and tenth constellations therefrom.

Mars, Jupiter and Saturn are excepted because in these various cases they have full special aspects to the same places. While in theory these partial aspects exert some effect on the various factors of a horoscope, in practice most jyotishis usually ignore them, and this book will ignore them too.

PLANETARY STRENGTHS

The Nine Seizers do not always seize with equal force, for their ability to influence human affairs is determined by their position in the sky. Each planet can act strongly or weakly in each of the constellations. This evaluation includes exaltation/debilitation, constellation rulership, trinal strength (in Sanskrit *mulatrikona*), planetary relationship, planetary state, and directional strength.

Exaltation and Debilitation

Table 4.1 shows the strength of the planets based on exaltation and debilitation:

TABLE 4.1

Exaltation and Debilitation of the Planets

Planet	Exaltation Rashi	Exaltation Degree	Debilitation Rashi	Debilitation Degree
Sun	Aries	10°	Libra	10°
Moon	Taurus	3°	Scorpio	3°
Mars	Capricorn	28°	Cancer	28°
Mercury	Virgo	15°	Pisces	15°
Jupiter	Cancer	5°	Capricorn	5°
Venus	Pisces	27°	Virgo	27°
Saturn	Libra	20°	Aries	20°
Rahu	Scorpio	—	Taurus	—
Ketu	Scorpio	—	Taurus	—

Rahu and Ketu have no established constellations of exaltation and debilitation. The majority of jyotishis agree that Rahu is exalted in Taurus and debilitated in Scorpio, and Ketu exalted in Scorpio and debilitated in Taurus. However, a small but significant group of jyotishis take Gemini and Sagittarius to be the exaltation and debilitation constellations of Rahu, and Sagittarius and Gemini to be the exaltation and debilitation constellations respectively of Ketu.

A very small group considers both Rahu and Ketu to be exalted in Scorpio and both to be debilitated in Taurus. This approach seems to be verified both by experience and by the logic of the scheme of exaltation. In this scheme the grahas form contrasting pairs: Sun and Saturn, Moon and Rahu/Ketu (both nodes being the opposite ends of the same axis), Mercury and Venus, Mars and Jupiter. For each pair of planets, the exaltation constellation of the one becomes the debilitation constellation of the other, and vice versa. Within this framework it follows that the exaltation constellation of the Moon should be the debilitation constellation of both Rahu and Ketu, and that the debilitation constellation of the Moon should be the exaltation constellation of both Rahu and Ketu. Throughout this book it will be assumed that Rahu and Ketu are both exalted in Scorpio and both debilitated in Taurus.

A planet placed in its exaltation degree, or (practically speaking) in any other degree of its constellation of exaltation, attains its strongest placement in a horoscope and so will exhibit its energies, for good or evil, with great intensity. Exalted planets are not, however, always benevolent planets! Whether or not a graha will give good results is determined by other indicators in the horoscope. An exalted graha acting malevolently will cause exalted problems in one's life, while a planet in its debilitation degree (or, effectively, in any other degree of its debilitation constellation) will express its energies very feebly, because it has attained its weakest placement in a horoscope. It may well be desirable for one's prosperity to have certain planets debilitated (fallen) in one's chart, though certain malefic grahas may actually become, for complex reasons, more malign when fallen.

Constellational Rulership

Table 4.2 shows the strength of the planets based on constellation rulership:

TABLE 4.2

Planetary Rulership of the Constellations

Planet	Positive Constellation	Negative Constellation	Mulatrikona Constellation	Degrees of Mulatrikona
Sun	Leo		Leo	0° to 20°
Moon	Cancer		Taurus	4° to 30°
Mars	Aries	Scorpio	Aries	0° to 12°
Mercury	Gemini	Virgo	Virgo	16° to 20°
Jupiter	Sagittarius	Pisces	Sagittarius	0° to 10°
Venus	Libra	Taurus	Libra	0° to 15°
Saturn	Aquarius	Capricorn	Aquarius	0° to 20°
Rahu	Aquarius		Not specified by tradition	
Ketu	Aries			

The Two Nodes are *Chaya Grahas* ('shadow planets'); they have position but no substance, which makes them difficult to know. Jyotishis through the ages have disagreed over which constellations the nodes rule, which constellations they are strong or weak in, and so on. This confusion just goes to show how strongly Rahu and Ketu seize. Though the nodes do not have independent rulership of any constellation, Nadi Jyotish sometimes assigns them the rulership of Aquarius and Aries respectively. While we usually take this to be the case, the average traditional jyotishi does not use this principle when analyzing a horoscope.

Planets are strong and well placed when they occupy their own constellations. Unlike exalted planets, which can perform strongly for either good or bad, planets in their own constellations act only in favorable ways, all other factors being equal. With the exception of the Sun and Moon, which rule only one constellation each, there is a slight difference in the quality of effect for the placement of a planet in each of the two constellations it rules. From Mars through Saturn the grahas are said to be more favorable in their positive constellations than in their negative ones.

Trinal Strength

Almost every traditional work on Jyotish adds a further refinement to the system of exaltation and constellation rulership. A planet is strong for good or bad in the constellation where it is exalted, weak for good or bad in the constellation where it is debilitated, strong and almost always favorable when in its own positive constellation, and slightly less strong and favorable when in its own negative constellation. A planet is very strong and always favorable in its *mulatrikona*, a Sanskrit word without an English equivalent. We can tentatively translate *mulatrikona* as 'trinal strength'. A graha's *mulatrikona* is the sector or zone of a particular constellation where each planet is exceptionally strong and favorable, even more so than in its own positive constellation. The *mulatrikona* positions listed in Table 4.2 are Parashara's.

The addition of *mulatrikona* can make analysis very complex when it is compounded with rulership and with exaltation. For example, the situation of Mercury in the constellation Virgo can be analyzed as follows: when Mercury is in the first 15° of Virgo it is exalted, in the next 5° it is in its *mulatrikona*, and in the last 10° it is in its own negative constellation. In actual practice *mulatrikona* is often ignored, since most jyotishis see it only as a theoretical and pedantic consideration in the scheme of planetary strength. Here is one example of its use: suppose a planet owns two constellations, one of which falls in a bad house (see Chapter Six) and the other in a good house. If doubt arises over how to interpret the planet's behavior, the planet will most likely give the results of the house in which its *mulatrikona* constellation falls.

Friendliness and Enmity

Jyotish is often taught by assigning human attributes to the grahas, and planetary relationship is a case in point. If a planet is not exalted, debilitated, in its *mulatrikona* or in its own constellation, its strength is decided on the basis of the relationship between the planet and the ruler of the constellation in which it sits. The grahas may be friendly, inimical, or neutral towards each other, as shown in Table 4.3.

TABLE 4.3

Planetary Relationships

Planet	Friends	Neutrals	Enemies
Sun	Moon Mars Jupiter	Mercury	Venus Saturn
Moon	Sun Mercury	Venus Mars Jupiter Saturn	None
Mars	Sun Moon Jupiter	Venus Saturn	Mercury
Mercury	Sun Venus	Mars Jupiter Saturn	Moon
Jupiter	Sun Moon Mars	Saturn	Mercury Venus
Venus	Mercury Saturn	Mars Jupiter	Sun Moon
Saturn	Mercury Venus	Jupiter	Sun Moon Mars
Rahu	Not specified by tradition, although some jyotishis use the		
Ketu	friends, neutrals and enemies of Saturn for Rahu and of Mars for Ketu.		

When Mars occupies the constellation Taurus, which is ruled by Venus, he occupies the constellation of a planet who is neutral to him. Mars is there placed indifferently, neither strong nor weak. Similarly, if Mercury is in the constellation of Capricorn or Aquarius, both ruled by Saturn, then Mercury sits in a constellation whose lord is neutral to Mercury. Note though that if Saturn is in the constellation of Gemini or Virgo, both ruled by Mercury, then Saturn occupies a constellation whose lord is friendly to him, and Saturn is therefore strong for either beneficial or detrimental results. The relationship between two grahas is thus not always reciprocal, just as relationships between two humans are not always reciprocal.

In summary, planets display the following relative amounts of their potential strengths:

· An exalted planet: 87.5% to 100%
· A planet with trinal strength: 75.0% to 87.5%
· A planet in its own positive constellation: 62.5% to 75.0%
· A planet in its own negative constellation: 50.0% to 62.5%
· A planet in the constellation of a friend: 37.5% to 50.0%
· A planet in the constellation of a neutral: 25.0% to 37.5%
· A planet in the constellation of an enemy: 12.5% to 25.0%
· A debilitated planet: 0% to 12.5%

Planetary States

While most jyotishis employ the above four rules to evaluate planetary strength, several other sophisticated methods for fine-tuning planetary strength also exist, including *graha yudha* ('planetary war'). Two planets are said to be at war when their longitudes are within one degree of each other. In this situation, whichever planet has the higher *latitude* is declared the winner and is strengthened thereby, while the loser is weakened. Many modern books on Jyotish however take the planet with the lower *longitude* to be the victor. A planet's latitude can be found in tabulated form in a *Panchanga* (an Indian ephemeris; see Chapter Seven), but this is usually missing from a Western ephemeris.

Another group of methods for evaluating strength are collectively known as *graha avasthas* ('planetary states' or 'conditions'). Parashara devotes a whole chapter to the subject, as do many other classical works. Calculations for some of the five systems of avasthas mentioned in that chapter are exceedingly complex; one even requires, among other variables, the numerological value of the first Sanskrit letter of the native's name. We will consider here one set of avasthas which is particularly useful in interpretation: the *Baladi Avasthas*.

In this system, each constellation is divided into five portions: 0°–6°; 6°–12°; 12°–18°; 18°–24°; 24°–30°. For the odd constellations (Aries, Gemini, Leo, Libra, Sagittarius and Aquarius) these states are named, in order, *Bala, Kumara, Yuva, Vriddha* and *Mrita*. For the even constellations (Taurus, Cancer, Virgo, Scorpio, Capricorn and

Pisces) the order is reversed: *Mrita, Vriddha, Yuva, Kumara* and *Bala*.

All these states relate to the progressive age of maturation of a human being. *Bala* here means 'child'; a planet in Bala Avastha will have a child-like energy to it, and like a child will not be able to exhibit the full potential of its strength. In fact, a planet in Bala Avastha displays only about one-fourth of the strength that would otherwise be predicted for it. *Kumara* means 'youth' and, like a vigorous youth, a planet in Kumara Avastha gives one-half of its results since, though strength is present, the wisdom needed to direct that strength, which is derived from experience, is usually lacking. *Yuva*, which also means 'young', indicates a young adult who has had sufficient experience to gain some of life's wisdom. A planet in Yuva Avastha gives full results. *Vriddha* means 'aged' and indicates a planet which has entered its senior, retired years; it gives minimal results. *Mrita* means 'dead'; relatively speaking, dead planets produce no results, though every planet does in some way or other give some result.

Directional Strength

TABLE 4.4

Directional Strength and Weakness of the Planets

House	Planet's Strength	Planet's Weakness
First (East)	Mercury Jupiter	Saturn
Fourth (North)	Moon Venus	Sun Mars
Seventh (West)	Saturn	Jupiter Mercury
Tenth (South)	Sun Mars	Moon Venus

A horoscope's tenth house corresponds to the sector of the heavens that is highest in the sky at any particular moment, while the fourth house corresponds to the sector that is underfoot, i.e. opposite the tenth house below the earth. Just as the ascendant, or first house, corresponds to the sector of the heavens that is always on the eastern horizon, the seventh house corresponds to the sector that is always on the western horizon, opposite the first house. Because in the northern hemisphere you can see the zodiac only when you face south, the tenth house of a horoscope represents the southern direction and, by extension, the fourth house represents the northern direction.

Directional strength is another principle derived from observational astrology. Jupiter and Mercury are the planets of intelligence and wisdom, and early morning is the very best time for study and meditation, when the mind is fresh and clear. Sun and Mars, the two hottest planets, show their influence best at midday, the hottest part of the day. Saturn, the lord of shadow and darkness, the *alter ego* of the rising Sun, shows his strength best when the Sun sets. Moon and Venus, the two brightest objects in the night sky, are strongest when it is darkest.

The effect of directional strength (*dig bala*) on a planet is much the same as the effect of exaltation, except that while exaltation is determined by position in constellation, directional strength is determined by position in house. Jupiter is therefore strong to give its effects (good or bad) when located in a horoscope's first house, while a Jupiter who occupies the seventh house is weak to give the results it symbolizes (bad or good). The other planets are analyzed in a similar manner. Of course, if that Jupiter in the first house is sitting in Capricorn, its constellation of debilitation, it will be weak by constellation but strong by house placement, and the jyotishi will then face a challenging translation, in which other factors must be considered before drawing any conclusion.

The Six Strengths

Shad Bala (the 'Six Strengths') is the name given to a group of mathematical formulas which are often used in Jyotish to generate precise numerical values for each planet's overall strength. *Shad Bala* calculations, which require familiarity with many technical aspects of Jyotish, are time-consuming when done by hand; even when calculated in full, the planetary strengths obtained require interpretation. Although the modern mind leaps towards anything which promises mathematical quantification, the interpretation of *Shad*

Bala results is not precise. Consequently, many jyotishis in India accommodate the general *Shad Bala* methods without going through all the cumbersome calculations, by extracting such criteria as exaltation, debilitation and directional strength, all of which are major portions of *Shad Bala*, from their numerical matrices. Thus, while this book does not concern itself with the mechanics of *Shad Bala* mathematics, it does address *Shad Bala*'s fundamental principles.

PLANETARY CHARACTERISTICS

Jyotish's old-world approach to learning about the planets provides abundant examples of rulerships which, when taken together, create the graha's image within the student's consciousness. As you become more and more familiar with these characteristics the image becomes clearer and your relationship with that image deepens. How astute a jyotishi you may become is directly proportional to how deep a personal relationship you create with these grahas through the *sadhana* ('spiritual practice') that is Jyotish.

Keep in mind as you read the sections below that each graha may display each of its characteristics strongly or weakly, according to its strength or weakness. It is left to the discretion of each astrologer to use the rulerships which follow according to circumstances, since in Jyotish necessity often truly does become the mother of invention. Some classifications, including the appearance of the grahas and their diseases, have been deliberately omitted from this section because they are difficult to present clearly in an introductory text. Others, such as the correspondence between the grahas and the chakras, are misleading, for the chakras do not exist for everyone in exactly the same way.

Note that the meanings of Rahu and Ketu are in many respects interchangeable, and that they do not have designated rulerships in many of these categories. There is a saying in Jyotish that Rahu will usually act like Saturn and Ketu like Mars, so, when specific rulerships for Rahu and Ketu are not mentioned, those of Saturn will usually apply to Rahu and those of Mars to Ketu.

Also note that it is one of Jyotish's conventions that, unless otherwise specified, the grahas are always listed in the order of the days that they rule. According to this 'weekday' order – Sun, Moon, Mars, Mercury, Jupiter, Venus and Saturn – the Sun rules Sunday, the Moon Monday, and so on. When this book, or any classical Jyotish text, refers to the order of the grahas without listing them, it is the above sequence that is always intended. Rahu and Ketu, which have no rulership over any particular day, always grace the end of this list.

Ages

There are three types of age rulerships for the planets: *maturation*, *personification* and *duration*. These are to be applied in a general way; other timing principles often supersede them.

The *maturation* ages for the planets are: Sun – 22; Moon – 24; Mars – 28; Mercury – 32; Jupiter – 16; Venus – 25; Saturn – 36; Rahu and Ketu – 48.

The *personified* ages for the individual planets are: Sun is a mature person of 50, Moon is an old person of 70, Mars is a young child below school age, Mercury is a youth, Venus is a teenager of 16, Jupiter is a young adult of 30, and Saturn, Rahu and Ketu all represent a very old person of 100.

The *age durations* ruled by the planets are: Sun – 23 to 41; Moon – 0 to 4; Mars – 42 to 56; Mercury 5 to 14; Jupiter – 57 to 68; Venus – 15 to 22; Saturn, Rahu and Ketu – 69 to 108.

Maturation: Those people who have, for example, Saturn strongly configured with the ascendant in their horoscopes will find that their lives 'mature' in some way at 36, the age of Saturn. Often this 'maturation' occurs in one of the matters that Saturn represents in the horoscope. If in a particular chart Saturn becomes an indicator of the native's mother, then the native's relationship with her mother may 'mature' at age 36. When Jupiter is similarly configured, the matters activated by Jupiter in the chart may mature at age 16. Whether the indications ripen in progressive or regressive ways will depend on the planet's condition. Planets who occupy beneficial and strong locations in the horoscope may indicate that something desirable will ripen in the native's life, while weak planets that are afflicted may portend something undesirable manifesting itself at that planet's maturation age.

Personification: The specific ages associated with each planet for this purpose are evocative, not literal. Saturn thus represents all very old people, not just people who are 100; Jupiter represents anyone in the prime of life; Sun a mature person of middle age, and so on. This classification is frequently used in both natal and horary astrology. If, for example, Venus indicates a friend in a certain horoscope, that friend may be a teenager.

Duration: This classification is a general yardstick used to evaluate the times in one's life when the planets may present the results that they indicate in a chart. If, for example, the Sun favorably activates the marriage or partnership sectors of a horoscope, then from age 23 to age 41 these matters may operate smoothly in the native's life. If, on the other hand, Mars detrimentally influences the factors of health in a horoscope, then age 42 to age 56 may bring illness.

Animal, Vegetable and Mineral

MOON, SUN and VENUS preside over organic matter, such as
   vegetation (*Mula*)

MARS, SATURN and RAHU preside over inorganic matter, such as
   minerals (*Dhatu*)

JUPITER and MERCURY preside over living beings, such as animals
   (*Jiva*)

Dhatu (mineral) actually refers to all insentient matter, *Mula* (vegetable) to all simple sentient matter having a limited range of movement, such as plants and fungi, and *Jiva* (animal) to all complex sentient matter having a relatively wide range of movement, including humans, other animals, insects, and so on. This classification is mainly used to estimate how a person may come by gains or losses. Someone who is influenced predominantly by Saturn or Mars may come by gains or losses through inanimate matter, as, for example, if she trades in or works with metals, or marries someone who does. Gains will accrue if Saturn or Mars are strong and well placed, otherwise there will be losses.

The animal category is further classified according to this general principle: Sun, Mars, Jupiter and Venus represent creatures who walk, while Moon and Rahu represent creeping or aqueous creatures. Specifically:

ṢUN/MARS rule four-legged creatures e.g. horses

JUPITER/VENUS rule two-legged creatures e.g. humans

MOON/RAHU/KETU rule rodents, reptiles and multi-legged creatures e.g. insects

MERCURY/SATURN rule flying creatures e.g. birds

It is true that Mars rules both minerals and walking creatures, but this is merely the difference between using Mars to help classify general categories and using him to help classify a more specific category. Differentiation depends on the point of view of the rulership's application. Mars will indicate gains through animals only when it occupies certain houses, while in other houses it may indicate gains through minerals. Common sense often dictates the correct rulership: a farmer who seeks astrological advice on his prospects in livestock will obviously take Mars to apply to animals and not to inanimate matter.

Bodily Constitution

SUN governs Pitta

MOON governs Vata and Kapha

MARS governs Pitta

MERCURY governs Vata, Pitta and Kapha

JUPITER governs Kapha

VENUS governs Vata and Kapha

SATURN governs Vata

This classification, which involves the Ayurvedic theory of the three forces, or *doshas*, which control the bodies of all living beings, is used by jyotishis and *vaidyas* (Ayurvedic physicians) alike in India to diagnose disease and to determine appropriate preventive or curative measures. A living organism is maintained in a state of healthy balance through the harmonious interaction of these Three Doshas. No good translation exists for Vata, Pitta and Kapha, which are sometimes mistranslated as wind, bile and phlegm respectively. Fundamentally, Vata represents the body's Air + Ether,

Pitta its Fire + Water, and Kapha its Water + Earth. The purpose of medicine is to help Nature re-establish a harmonious relationship among the Three Doshas.

As with bodily substances and flavors (see below), this information will be useful to those who have an extensive grasp of the Ayurvedic model of reality. Here is one use: if the ascendant, which is the primary indicator of physical characteristics in a horoscope, is predominantly influenced by Pitta planets, then (all else being equal) that person may have a Pitta constitution.

One allied classification of the planets distinguishes them according to their effect on bodily fluids. Sun, Mars and Saturn are dry planets which, when configured with the ascendant, tend to dry out the body and make it thin. Moon, Jupiter and Venus are wet planets, which tend to cause the body to gain or retain water or fat when they influence the ascendant. Mercury, Rahu and Ketu have no significant effect in this respect.

Bodily Substances

SUN rules the bones

MOON rules the blood

MARS rules the marrow and muscle tissue

MERCURY rules the skin

JUPITER rules the fat tissue

VENUS rules the semen and the ovum

SATURN rules the nerve tissue

These rulerships also come from Ayurveda. Many of those who believe that Jyotish lacks psychology also maintain that its medical knowledge is severely lacking, when in fact the medical knowledge of Jyotish is contained primarily within Ayurveda. Just as a weak and afflicted Sun in a horoscope indicates conditions such as weak bones, broken bones and rickets, weakness of the other planets will indicate problems in the corresponding body tissues. Always interpret the bodily substances allotted to the planets in their broadest sense. For example, Venus, which rules semen and ova, represents by extension the whole of the male or female reproductive system. Similarly Saturn, which represents the actual nerve tissue of the body, can also represent nervous breakdowns.

Body Limbs

SUN represents the head
MOON represents the face
MARS represents the chest
MERCURY represents the hips
JUPITER represents the
abdomen

VENUS represents the pelvis and
the sexual organs
SATURN represents the thighs
RAHU represents the hands
RAHU represents the legs

If, for example, the Sun in a horoscope sits in the ascendant, which among other things represents the body, that person's head is likely to be prominent. An afflicted Sun may indicate head problems, while a strong Sun (whether or not in the ascendant) will contribute to a well-developed head. This sort of reasoning should also be applied to the other planets.

Cabinet

SUN is the king
MOON is the queen
MARS is the commander-in-chief

MERCURY is the prince
JUPITER and VENUS are the
advisors
SATURN is the servant

When the planets are personified into a celestial court, Sun and Moon are allotted noble and regal qualities. Mercury has a meaning of youthfulness, and often, like a prince, borrows its power from an external source. The meaning of the other grahas can likewise be deduced. If the Moon, say, is strong and well placed, and is influencing the factors that represent friends in a horoscope, that person will have powerful and/or regal friends.

Castes

JUPITER and VENUS are
Brahmanas
SUN and MARS are Kshatriyas

MOON and MERCURY are
Vaishyas
SATURN is a Shudra
RAHU and KETU are Mlecchas

This classification refers to the infamous caste system which is much decried in its present form – and rightly so – as a great social injustice. Originally caste was not solely determined, as it is today, by the vocation or status in life of one's parents. It seems instead to have been an attempt to classify people by their natural propensities, in the same way that people today are often classified as artistic or scientific. The natural inclination of the *Brahmana* is to be immersed in philosophy, religion and altruistic service; that of the *Kshatriya* is to concentrate on politics and rulership; the Vaishya's natural aptitude is for trade and business; and the *Shudra* naturally gravitates towards service and manual labor. The *Mleccha* was outside the pale of Vedic society, being a general misfit.

A creative approach that uses this traditional information, particularly when analyzing the horoscopes of non-Hindus, is to return to the original spirit of caste classification and use this principle to indicate a person's natural inclinations. A Brahmana is someone with a prominent and well-placed Jupiter and/or Venus, someone who would actually display the qualities of a Brahmana, and so on. In our modern context, Brahmanas are philosophers, priests, thinkers, academics, scientists, teachers, writers, artists, and people whose work involves a high degree of inspiration and altruistic service, like doctors and healers. Kshatriyas can be thought of as politicians, military commanders, police, administrators, lawyers, judges, and others who decide and enforce policy for collective and public entities like companies, municipalities, countries and the like. Vaishyas consist of the members of the business and trade communities, merchants, manufacturers, etc. Shudras are people involved in service and in manual labor, skilled or unskilled. The Mlecchas remain what they always were: the misfits of society, incapable of locating a niche for themselves.

Clothes

SUN rules clothes that are coarse or thick

MOON rules clothes that are new

MARS rules clothes that are variegated

MERCURY rules clothes that are immaculate and clean

JUPITER rules clothes that are average and ordinary

VENUS rules clothes that are
strong, durable and decorated

SATURN rules clothes that are
old and ragged

A person who has Mars in a strong relationship with the ascendant in his horoscope will consistently vary his wardrobe, while someone with Saturn similarly placed tends to be sartorially conservative. If such a Saturn is also badly placed, the affected individual may dress shabbily. Because these rulerships are usually more suggestive than they are specific, 'old' for a strong Saturn may mean by extension fashionably ultra-conservative, while for a weak Saturn it may suggest army surplus wear from World War II.

Colors

SUN rules dark red
MOON rules white
MARS rules bright red
MERCURY rules green

JUPITER rules yellow
VENUS rules white and
variegated colors
SATURN rules black

The classical scheme of rulerships provided for colors is so incomplete that it omits one of the three primary colors and most of the basic colors of the spectrum. The other schemes of color rulership that exist are esoteric and so are not commonly employed. It is, however, generally agreed that violet, indigo and blue are ruled by Saturn and orange is ruled by Sun.

While it is true that the Seizers tend to influence one's choice of clothes, so that an alert jyotishi may be able to discern which graha is ruling someone by the hue of their apparel, this principle is also used as a remedy. When the colors of clothes, gems, automobiles, walls and the like are judiciously chosen, they can produce beneficial effects for their user. For example, if you are going out to solicit a favor from someone, it is prudent to wear something yellow, because Jupiter is the enemy of no planet; wearing red, on the other hand, may generate confrontation or excitement during the meeting due to the influence of Mars.

We can extract even more information when we combine this classification with the previous one. Saturn rules all sorts of blue jeans (they are blue, and they are work clothes), but 'ragged' blue jeans for a weak Saturn may be a pair which has been patched so often that little of the original fabric remains, while a strong Saturn may instead indicate a pair of cutoff shorts which were snipped from expensive, designer jeans.

Direction

SUN rules the east	JUPITER rules the northeast
MOON rules the northwest	VENUS rules the southeast
MARS rules the south	SATURN rules the west
MERCURY rules the north	RAHU and KETU rule the southwest

This information is used in a variety of ways. For instance, a person in whose horoscope Jupiter is the most powerful and best-placed planet may live in the northeast sector of a country or city, or may have success in that direction on travels. Or, a Vedic or Tantric occultist may face the northeast when performing rituals designed to invoke Jupiter's energy.

Diseases

SUN rules overheating, fever, eye diseases, dental problems, and neuralgia

MOON rules lethargy, drowsiness, lung problems, mouth problems (including loss of taste), blood-related illnesses, digestive complaints, water retention, and disorders of the 'mind'

MARS rules overheating, fevers (particularly eruptive), liver complaints, skin rashes, ulcers, lacerations, operations, and all sorts of acute complaints

MERCURY rules disorders of the buddhi, the skin and the nerves

JUPITER rules lymphatic and circulatory congestion, tumors, liver complaints, and ear problems

VENUS rules disorders of the sex organs and the urinary tract, sexual perversions, and loss of bodily luster

SATURN rules arthritis, rheumatism, emaciation, paralysis, deformities, coldness of the body, nerve disorders, and all sorts of chronic complaints

RAHU and KETU rule epidemics, hysteria, insanity, epilepsy,
   persistent skin diseases, and conditions resulting from all sorts
   of poisons

Medical astrology requires much Ayurvedic knowledge, so here we
merely provide examples of diseases which can arise from the doshas
the grahas represent, to demonstrate how the planetary archetypes
can manifest as ill-health. Most other diseases can be similarly
classified. For example, since Moon represents blood-related disease
and Jupiter indicates circulatory congestion, a poorly placed Jupiter
which has some association with a Moon which already indicates
disease in a horoscope may create high blood-pressure. If it is
Saturn who influences the Moon instead of Jupiter, this may
indicate chronic lung problems (like asthma) or chronic digestive
complaints (like certain types of colitis). Mars (acute) influencing
Mercury (nerves) may cause acute neuralgia, while Saturn influencing Mercury may betoken chronic neuralgia.

Distances

SUN and MERCURY represent
   eight yojanas
MOON represents one yojana
MARS and KETU represent seven
   yojanas

JUPITER represents nine yojanas
VENUS represents sixteen
   yojanas
SATURN and RAHU represent
   twenty yojanas

The values given traditionally for a *yojana*, 'the distance driven at a
stretch', vary between four and eight miles. This information may
also be generalized: Moon represents very short distances; Sun,
Mars, Mercury, Jupiter and Ketu represent medium distances; and
Venus, Saturn and Rahu represent long distances. This becomes
useful when estimating the distance of journeys, transfers, and
similar phenomena, both in horary astrology and when timing
events from the natal horoscope.

Elements

SUN rules Fire
MOON rules Water
MARS rules Fire
MERCURY rules Earth

JUPITER rules Ether
VENUS rules Water
SATURN rules Air

The Sankhya philosophy claims that the whole of creation comprises five basic states of matter (Maha Bhutas). These states of matter are also called *Tattvas* ('things'), because they are the most material (the most 'thing-like') of all the Sankhya philosophy's Tattvas. These are Earth (*Prithvi*), Water (*Jala* or *Apah*), Fire (*Agni* or *Tejas*), Air (*Vayu*) and Ether (*Akasha*). Earth predominates in everything in the universe which is solid, Water in every liquid, and Air in each gas. Fire helps to change state, from solid to liquid to gas and vice versa; and Ether is the space in which all these other transformations take place.

One of the specific applications of this information is in the rectification of doubtful birth times. Another application is in *Svarodaya*, the science of Tantric breathing, which states that these Tattvas rule in a certain order during certain times of each day. There are several methods of deciding which Tattva is dominant at a particular moment; one is to analyze the qualities of your inhalation and exhalation, as noted above. Knowledgeable jyotishis use this theory to divine the success or failure of actions that their clients contemplate, since certain specific actions performed during each Tattva's period produce optimum results.

Another application for this classification is to attribute the five senses to each of the elements. Mercury rules the sense of smell, Moon and Venus rule taste, Sun and Mars rule sight, Saturn rules touch, and Jupiter rules hearing. This is only one system of sense classification, one which may owe a great deal to Tantric Jyotish. One other system maintains that, because we see by the light of the Sun and the Moon, these two luminaries rule the eyes, the Sun ruling the right eye and the Moon the left eye because right and Sun are traditionally regarded as male, and left and Moon as female. The Sun in the ascendant (which represents the head here) may result in red and/or angry eyes; the Moon when very poorly placed in a horoscope may create some deformity, injury or disease of the face, and particularly of the eyes.

Flavors

SUN governs bitter flavors
MOON governs salty flavors
MARS governs pungent flavors
MERCURY governs mixed or
    varied flavors

JUPITER governs sweet flavors
VENUS governs sour flavors
SATURN governs astringent
    flavors

This classification makes use of the Ayurvedic theory of the Six Tastes. One of the ways a jyotishi can confirm the diagnosis of illness based on a horoscope is to question the client about his or her predominant taste. If the client strongly prefers the salty taste, for example, then the chances are good that she will suffer from disturbances of both Vata and Kapha, which can lead to diseases like bronchitis. Another way in which this information is used by jyotishis is to prescribe diets rich in one or more particular tastes in an effort to help restore the equilibrium of the Three Doshas. This procedure requires much skill and should be attempted only after thorough training with a suitable expert.

Note that in this Ayurvedic classification the Sun symbolizes bitter flavors and Mars pungent ones; but the section on flowers, food and trees (see below) indicates that the Sun rules pungent flavors and Saturn bitter ones. The differences of opinion which occur occasionally in the scheme of rulerships are really instances of the overlapping symbolisms of the grahas. For example, the statement that the Sun and Mars are said to rule pungent flavors originates from the fact that both Sun and Mars are fiery planets, and fire in the realm of taste appears particularly in hot, pungent spices.

Flowers, Food and Trees

SUN rules the red lotus, wheat, and strong, massive trees
MOON rules the lily, rice, and trees with much oil or sap
MARS rules red flowers, red lentils, and strong or thorny trees
MERCURY rules leaves, mung beans, and fruitless trees
JUPITER rules the jasmine, Bengal gram, and trees bearing fruit
VENUS rules the white lotus, beans, and flowering trees
SATURN rules the violet, sesame seeds, and useless or ugly trees

Information pertaining to colors, gems, metals, clothes and the like may seem useful only for their amazement value in prediction, but there are profound reasons for the inclusion of such material in astrological works. Many of these articles are used in Vedic and Tantric religious ceremonies meant to relieve negative karmic pressures; a ritual intended to mitigate adversity symbolized by Saturn, for example, may involve the use of violets, sesame seeds, and other substances ruled by Saturn. Also, jyotishis often use astrology in reverse: if a client brings red flowers, an article ruled by Mars, to a consultation, the jyotishi may then surmise that the person is interested in advice on an issue symbolized by Mars, such as litigation, younger brothers, or courage.

The rulerships presented in this section are rather limited because they were conceived many centuries ago for a particular cultural milieu. The following is a more modern list which remains faithful to the original intent:

SUN. Mountainous trees, rare or expensive wood, pine, timber, orange trees, cedar, almond, chamomile, lavender, rosemary, saffron, medicinal herbs, large and showy flowers of yellow color, pepper of all kinds, nutmeg, various aromatic herbs, cardamom, ajowan (an Indian herb), fine wines and rare liqueurs.

MOON. Night- and water-blooming flowers and products, rice, melons, coconut, palm trees, common fruits and vegetables, cucumber, milk and milk products, corn, poppy, mild herbs, water, beer, anything that is stewed or brewed, cooked food in general, water, cold substances, most tender and very juicy fruits.

MARS. All thorny shrubs/plants and weeds, stinging-nettle, poison-ivy and oak, pungent herbs, peppers, mustard, coriander, garlic, hemp, coffee, tea, strong liquors, plants and foods with strong odors, foods heavy in protein, meat, foods which excite the passions, stimulants.

MERCURY. Small plants, wild flowers, roots of various kinds consumed as food or spice, root beer, carrot, parsnip, okra, nectarine, fruits and vegetables that are the result of grafting or of hybridization (like the tangelo).

JUPITER. Fatty but pure foods, butter, ghee, cream, gourd, pumpkin, squash, naturally sweet foods, berries, sugar cane, dates, honey, olive oil, orchard trees, sweet herbs, peppermint, spearmint, sweet wines.

VENUS. Cotton, silk, all fancy or exotic vegetables and fruits or berries, pomegranate, gooseberry, fruit juices that are naturally sweet or sour, refined sweeteners, white sugar, glucose, fragrant trees and blossoms, sandalwood, perfumes, garden flowers, creepers and vines, candy and confections, liqueurs, exotic spices, processed but essential food, flour.

SATURN. Food that is difficult to digest, legumes, alfalfa, clover, peas, peanuts, soya beans, dark-colored food, rye, coarse food, old food, impure or putrid food, junk food, bitter herbs and roots, salt, fermented foods such as pickles, vinegar, dry wines, weeds, foreign dishes.

This list is illustrative, not comprehensive. As with other planetary rulerships, you must learn the essence of the rulerships by learning the specific rulerships listed. Then you will be able to deduce as needed other specific rulerships not listed here. The general principles will automatically begin to flow through your awareness as soon as you become truly comfortable with the specifics, enabling you to classify products not specifically listed. For example, teak (being an expensive wood) is ruled by the Sun, cloves (being pungent) are ruled by Mars, and so on.

Many substances can be ruled by several planets. Ice-cream is usually a cold milk product, often comprised mostly of refined sugar, and commonly regarded as a junk food, so it could potentially be ruled by the Moon, Venus or Saturn respectively. A casual reader may find three rulerships for ice-cream to be contradictory, but a reader who understands the fundamental qualities symbolized by the grahas will see the overlapping rulership instead of the contradiction.

Geometrical Shape

SUN rules the shape of a quadrangle

MOON rules the shape of a circle

MARS rules the shape of an hourglass

MERCURY rules the shape of a triangle

JUPITER rules the shape of an ellipse

VENUS rules the shape of an octagon

SATURN rules the shape of a window with four panes

RAHU rules the shape of a line

KETU rules the shape of a flag on a pole

This information is used by jyotishis or occultists in the preparation of amulets, an ancient and now almost-forgotten art. Energies symbolized by the grahas are enhanced or modified by the preparation of rings, lockets or pendants under suitable planetary positions, accompanied by sincere and sometimes elaborate prayers. Even today, many Indians have a profound faith in amulets that have been properly prepared by an expert.

Glances

SUN, MARS and KETU glance upwards

MERCURY and VENUS glance sideways, like someone being coy

MOON and JUPITER glance straight ahead

SATURN and RAHU glance downwards

This classification is used as an aid to correcting or confirming a horoscope whose accuracy is in doubt. A person with Venus or Mercury in a particular relationship with the ascendant will constantly look to the side; one with Saturn or Rahu so placed will continually keep the eyes down; and so on. Another use is in *prashna*; if a client asks a question while glancing steadily downwards, the desired result is not likely to be achieved (since Saturn tends to rule bad results) unless that Saturn or Rahu (which behaves like Saturn) is particularly well placed in the horary chart.

Height

> SUN and VENUS are of average height
> MOON, MARS and MERCURY are short
> JUPITER, SATURN, RAHU and KETU are tall

This information is useful in determining a person's stature from the horoscope by evaluating the planets which aspect or occupy the ascendant. If many planets influence the ascendant, the strength of each must be evaluated, for only the effects of the strongest will prevail.

Metals and Gems

SUN rules copper and ruby
MOON rules bronze and pearl
MARS rules copper and coral
MERCURY rules brass and emerald
JUPITER rules gold and topaz

VENUS rules silver and diamond
SATURN rules iron and sapphire
RAHU rules lead and hessonite quartz
KETU rules lead and cat's-eye or chrysoberyl

NOTE: The rulership of gold and silver is often allocated to the Sun and Moon respectively, and Saturn is sometimes also assigned the rulership of lead. Jupiter is sometimes said to rule yellow sapphire, in which case Saturn is allotted the rulership of blue sapphire.

Jyotish subscribes strongly to the theory that metals and gems can effectively augment or minimize the effects of the energies symbolized by the grahas. Gems of a specific weight set in certain metals, or metals inscribed with certain diagrams called *yantras*, are routinely prescribed by jyotishis to augment their clients' well-being. This is a complex system, and few jyotishis retain the expertise and knowledge required for these astrological remedies to exert their full effects. Without such arcane procedures as the *prana pratishtha* (the 'establishing of life'), few gemstones will give the sort of dramatically beneficial effects that the scriptures promise. While many people have read that the use of gemstones can radically improve their lives, most of them are unaware that, when used improperly, gemstones can disrupt their lives, particularly if they are worn without consideration for their possible effects.

In particular, those who wear large, flawless diamonds or sapphires must be very wary of potential calamities unless they are sure that those particular gems suit them. Both our gurus were extremely wary of the blue sapphire. On one occasion a man desiring to wear a blue sapphire to increase his luck was told that neither he nor his mother might survive his wearing of the jewel. He insisted, however, and tied the stone on his arm for seven days (which is one approved procedure for testing such a gemstone). After his mother died suddenly within that week he promptly decided that the guru was right, and he removed the gem. Nor was this some bizarre coincidence; both authors have witnessed such events several times.

In addition to all the above caveats, remember that, in the words of our jyotish guru, 'Gemstones are the game of kings.' Since a gemstone meant for use as a remedy must be flawless, of good color and of supreme luster, and must weigh at least three carats, such baubles are very expensive. But a remedy should solve the problem, not add to it. If you suggest an expensive remedy to a poor man, he will become even more depressed for, while the promise of the remedy will tantalize him, it will remain forever outside his grasp. To solve this problem, Jyotish also provides for *uparatnas* ('substitute gemstones'). Although the *uparatnas* are substantially weaker than their precious counterparts, all the criteria of effectiveness that apply to more valuable gemstones apply equally to the *uparatnas*. Among these substitutes are:

SUN rules garnet

MOON rules moonstone

MARS rules bloodstone

MERCURY rules peridot or green tourmaline

JUPITER rules citrine

VENUS rules white sapphire

SATURN rules lapis lazuli

RAHU rules agate

KETU rules turquoise

Nature

JUPITER and VENUS are natural benefics

MARS, SATURN, RAHU and KETU are natural malefics

SUN is cruel

MOON is a natural benefic when waxing (moving from new to full), otherwise it is a natural malefic

MERCURY is a natural benefic when not associated with natural malefics, otherwise it is a natural malefic

This classification addresses planetary nature in terms of what most people identify as desirable and undesirable qualities. The *benefics* generally stand for qualities like growth, expansion and preservation, while the *malefics* represent decay, restriction and destruction. Of themselves these qualities are neutral, but from the human perspective they are frequently characterized as being positive or negative. Both sets of qualities are necessary; for one tree to grow strong and tall, many others must die in its shadow. Note that the malefic planets outnumber the benefics. This is partly due to the fact that Jyotish is a way of mapping karmas; since most people tend to perform those actions which they believe to be in their own self-interest, the strongest karmas are frequently those which are most selfish, not the most altruistic. The more selfish an action is, the less benevolent is the karma it creates.

In Sanskrit a benefic planet is a *shubha* (a 'pious being'), while a malefic is a *papi* (a 'sinner'). The malefics are 'sinners' because they encourage the people whose minds they seize to scorn Nature and Her laws. Nature favors no man or woman: if you follow Her rules, you will prosper; if you flout them, you will suffer.

Some jyotishis refer to the Sun as a natural malefic, others say it is merely 'cruel' (krura), and a few assert that it is cruel only when exalted, and malefic otherwise. Malefics are also cruel, but the Sun is less likely to cause a person to 'sin' than are the other malefics. The Sun is fierce by nature but is not deliberately cruel; anyone who has lived through a hot season in India knows precisely how cruel the Sun can be. Astrologically, the Sun is cruel because he dries up the *rasa*, the juice or nectar of life which makes life worth living.

It is the position and strength of the Moon in a horoscope which determines how much and what kind of juice that person will enjoy in life, and one of the names Jyotish uses for the Moon is *Soma* ('nectar'). Everyone can see how brightly the waxing Moon shines at night, pouring cool rays on to the Earth and its denizens. During its waning phase, though, since the Moon becomes visible early in the morning and then quickly drops out of sight, its ability to influence earthly affairs is correspondingly reduced. Because the Moon radiates the least light just before and just after the new Moon, the Moon is regarded as being relatively strong during the period extending from the fifth day after the new Moon (during its *bright fortnight*, when it waxes) until the tenth day after the full Moon (during its *dark fortnight*, when it wanes).

Nature of Birth

MERCURY, JUPITER, VENUS and RAHU are born head first
MOON and KETU are born back first
SUN, MARS and SATURN are born feet first.

A literal application for this classification may have been true thousands of years ago when most children were born without medical services. A general application would suggest that when the head-first grahas influence the ascendant, which is the main factor in the horoscope that indicates birth, a normal and easy birth is likely; the back-first grahas would indicate a stressful birth, perhaps involving medication, prolonged labor or other complications; and the feet-first grahas would suggest a birth involving great trauma for mother and child, as in a Caesarean or forceps birth. This same classification can also be extended to apply to the intra-uterine period, thus providing useful insights into birth psychology. When Jupiter, for instance, exclusively influences the factors indicating birth, both a stable and enjoyable pregnancy and a smooth and non-traumatic birth become likely.

Personification

SUN rules the soul	JUPITER rules knowledge and
MOON rules the senses and the	fortune
emotions	VENUS rules desires and
MARS rules power and strength	yearnings
MERCURY rules the rational	SATURN rules sorrows and
mind and speech	misfortunes

Our solar system is sometimes taken to be the personification of the Divine Person of Time (*Kala Purusha*). The Sun is the soul of this Kala Purusha, the Moon His senses and emotions, Mars His power and strength, etc. These provide the keynotes for the anthropomorphical nature of the planets. The Sun is royal and noble, the Moon changeable, inconstant and fickle. Mars the warrior is fiery, angry, hasty and courageous; while Mercury, the student, is a calculator and a communicator. Jupiter is the wise teacher of the gods and spiritually minded people, and Venus the teacher of sensualists, fashion plates, art lovers, and courtesans. Saturn, deformed and detached, is an ascetic and a laborious worker; and Rahu and Ketu are shady characters, troublemakers lurking invisibly in the wings of the solar system's stage.

The condition of the various component parts of Kala Purusha at the moment of birth will indicate the corresponding qualities of that individual's life. Consequently, in order to deduce the quality of a person's rational mind, jyotishis study the condition of Mercury in the horoscope. Other grahas are similarly studied. These indications are never used in isolation, however; they are always blended into the study of the horoscope as whole.

Examining this classification from the angle of positional astronomy, we find that the Sun is at the center of the solar system, just as the soul is at the center of the microcosm, your own personal universe; Mercury, Venus and Moon represent internal factors, because they are within the 'being' formed by the Earth and the Sun; Earth represents the skin of your body, the boundary between the external and the internal; Mars represents your actions, the projection of your energy; Jupiter represents the good results of those actions, and Saturn the bad results of those actions.

Persuasion Method

SUN and MARS rule punishment (*danda*)	MERCURY and SATURN rule diplomacy (*bheda*)
MOON rules temptation (*dana*)	JUPITER and VENUS rule good counsel (*sama*)

This classification refers to the four methods of persuasion employed in classical India. That person who has a particular planet strong in his or her horoscope will respond best to, or will adopt naturally, the corresponding method of persuasion. People with a prominent Moon will thus attempt to gain their own way by temptation, which is to say by incentives of various sorts, potentially including bribes. Moon people respond most readily to similar temptations.

The Sun and Mars resort to punishment or threat of punishment and are very forceful, compelling and insistent in their method of persuasion; they also respond best to these tactics. Mercury and Saturn most readily accept or use artfulness, including secret, behind-the-scenes maneuvers and the employment of spies and hearsay, and are potentially capable of unethical negotiations, like blackmail. Jupiter and Venus spontaneously work through and naturally accept appeals to reason, mild and polite but direct and honest requests, and good advice.

Places

SUN rules temples	JUPITER rules treasuries
MOON rules watery places	VENUS rules places of pleasure and amusement
MARS rules places near fire	
MERCURY rules places for sports	SATURN rules dirty places

This is a simple list from a work by Parashara, the father of Jyotish. Since life today is more complex than it was in his era, a modern list, which includes many of the places assigned rulerships by traditional authors subsequent to Parashara, is appended:

SUN. Open areas, deserts, palaces, magnificent buildings, government buildings, towers, great halls.

MOON. Aquariums, beaches, docks, rivers, seas, wells, houseboats, ships, public places, hotels, motels, nests, breweries, womens' residences, hospitals.

MARS. Kitchens, factories where fire and electricity are heavily used, machine shops, burned areas, areas where carnage has taken place, battlefields, slaughterhouses, butcher's shops, laboratories, places for aggressive and violent or physical contests, boxing and wrestling rings, karate *dojos*, football stadiums, places frequented by blue-collar workers, armories, military installations.

MERCURY. Places of business or transportation and communication, airports, post offices, telegraph stations, accounting offices, public but non-violent games and the places where they are played, parks, playgrounds, publishing places, bookstores, libraries, public assemblies, the United Nations.

JUPITER. Banks, vaults, dignified places such as courts of law, prestigious universities, altars, pompous functions, society balls, political assemblies, charitable institutions, high-level financial institutions, stock and commodity markets, monasteries, missions.

VENUS. Places of amusement, theaters, restaurants, bedrooms, brothels, places focusing on beauty, art galleries, beauty salons, elegant shops, shopping malls, places where music is featured, dance halls, clubs, opera and symphony halls.

SATURN. Slums, gutters, sewers, garbage heaps, subterranean places, basements, cellars, mines, graves, inaccessible places, hermitages, retreats, prisons, neglected and lonely or melancholy places, cemeteries, abandoned houses, ruins.

While the above planets do represent the places mentioned, the planet's condition must first be considered before trying to decide on a specific interpretation. An exalted Saturn may indicate not merely ruins or an abandoned house but rather exalted ruins (like Stonehenge) or a house that is listed on the register of historic locations, while a debilitated Saturn may indicate drafty houses, or even houses where drugs are pushed. Venus exalted may represent Carnegie Hall; Venus debilitated, the local honky-tonk. Mercury in the Bala Avastha? Maybe the library of a primary school. The Moon in Vriddha Avastha? Perhaps a nursing home for the aged, or a chronic-care facility. Though the choices may seem impossibly wide and varied at this stage, once the planets are examined from the perspective of which houses of the horoscope they activate (see Chapter Six) the choices narrow significantly.

Profession

Those people in whose horoscopes the following planets most influence the factors which indicate profession will tend to earn their livelihoods through:

SUN - Fruit trees, repetition of *mantras*, fraud, gambling, lying, working with metals, wool or medicines, or service under a ruler or other prominent person.

MOON - Trade in the products of water (such as pearls or coral, kelp or fish); agriculture and livestock; fashion and clothing; work related to or for women; travel; the food and hospitality industries; the public.

MARS - Metals (especially gold) and machinery; men, and things connected with men; fighting and confrontation; vocations involving heat and energy, such as cookery, firefighting, and jobs relating to electricity; cutting professions, like butcher or surgeon; real estate; harassing others; weapons; adventurous, dangerous or courageous acts; associations with wicked people, spies and thieves.

MERCURY - Astrology, poetry, speaking, study and learning, writing, clerical work, teaching, sacred knowledge, repetition of *mantras*, use of numbers, resort to fraud, plagiary, counterfeiting or other trickery; officiating as a priest; artisans and others who require manual dexterity.

JUPITER - Religion or religious instruction, teaching and preaching, children, advice and counseling, philosophy, judging and legislating, planning, recitation and study of scriptures, moneylending; or assistance from the wise, the gods, or the government.

VENUS - Women; cows, horses and other large animals; the arts; romance; silver; delicacies, ornaments and finery; poetry; advice or counseling; fashion design.

SATURN - Dealing in roots and fruits, physical exertion, bearing burdens, dealings with servants, rogues and other low-class people; working with spoiled food, stones or wooden materials; base avocations; sculpture; serving as a butcher, executioner or mortician; and products or activities below the earth.

RAHU / KETU — Rahu will act like Saturn and Ketu like Mars. In addition, they indicate professions involving juggling; prestidigitation; immigration and foreign lands or languages; poisons, alcohol and other intoxicants; involvement with the masses. Rahu implies some involvement with occult or psychic knowledge, and Ketu has some involvement with the pursuit of spiritual knowledge.

Psychology

SUN - Nobility, individuality, generosity, grandeur, dignity, power, authority, leadership, creativity; OR pride, egotism, self-centeredness, pompousness, ostentation, despotism.

MOON - Receptivity, sensitivity, imagination, good memory, sound habits and conditioning; OR hyper-sensitivity, over-reaction, inability to respond, difficulty getting in touch with feelings.

MARS - Goal-directed energy, strength, courage, passion, action, competitive and fighting spirit, vim and vigor; OR anger, irritability, haste, impatience, inconstancy, inconsistency, lack of drive and courage, 'all-or-nothing' attitude.

MERCURY - Rationality, intelligence, wit, cleverness, skill, dexterity, verbal and mental ability, shrewdness; OR aloofness, detachment, amorality, expediency, over-intellectualization, difficulty in thought and communication.

JUPITER - Growth and expansion, humanitarian and spiritual outlook, wisdom, optimism, faith, geniality, generosity, joviality, humor, idealism, good powers of judgement; OR overconfidence, overindulgence, extravagance, immorality, greed, materialistic attitude (in the sense of wanting the best of everything).

VENUS – Affection, friendliness, love, gentleness, sociability, harmony, balance, elegance, gracefulness, refined sensuality; OR laziness, vanity, sentimentality, vice and sensual corruption, lack of taste and refinement.

SATURN – Authoritativeness, discipline, responsibility, conservatism, practicality, realism, durability, constancy, consistency; OR anxiety, inhibition, isolation, depression, rigidity, stinginess, disappointment, loneliness, resignation, lack of adaptability, melancholy, lack of trust, suspicion.

RAHU – Originality, individuality, independence, insight, ingenuity, inspiration, imagination; OR confusion, escapism, neurosis, psychosis, deception, addiction, vagueness, illusion, delusion.

KETU – Universality, impressionability, idealism, intuition, compassion, spirituality, self-sacrifice, subtleness; OR eccentricity, fanaticism, explosiveness, violence, unconventionality, amorality, iconoclasm, impulsiveness, emotional tensions.

To assist the average modern reader, whose study of the mind is usually structured through modern psychology, this section alone among the sections in this chapter mimics the Western technique of providing 'key words' for each of the planets' psychological behaviors when they are well placed or poorly placed in a horoscope. Although this approach is not to be found in any classical text, nor is it explicitly supported by any eminent classical author, a between-the-lines reading of most treatises will disclose these qualities.

A prominent, well-placed planet in a horoscope will provide many of its positive attributes to that horoscope's owner, while a prominent but poorly placed planet will cause that planet's negative psychological attributes to dominate. As an example, consider the key words listed above for the Moon. The Moon, as noted earlier, represents *manas*, the very organ of receptivity and imagination, which means that the Moon represents an individual's overall emotional state. When the Moon is well placed, the emotions will be more or less harmonious and all the other mental faculties like memory will work well. A stressfully placed Moon however signifies unbalanced or abnormal emotional states, like hyper-sensitivity, over-reaction, inability to respond, and general difficulty experienced in getting in touch with one's feelings.

Qualities

SUN, MOON and JUPITER rule Sattva
MERCURY and VENUS rule Rajas
MARS, SATURN, RAHU and KETU rule Tamas

The Sankhya philosophy teaches that nature can be broken down into three fundamental component energies: Sattva ('equilibrium'), Rajas ('activity') and Tamas ('inertia'). Applied to human nature, Sattva inclines one toward pure and noble thoughts, which lead to virtuous and altruistic actions; Rajas inclines one toward a sensual life in which the active pursuit of money and passion is of the utmost importance, which leads to arrogant and selfish actions; and Tamas inclines one toward mental or physical inactivity, punctuated by angry, violent actions. A jyotishi who fully comprehends this system can use the horoscope to diagnose a person's preponderant quality. If in a horoscope only Sun, Moon and Jupiter affect the ascendant, the native will be primarily Sattvic in nature and actions. Similarly, when these planets alone influence the segment of a birth chart which represents a particular relative, the nature of that relative may be Sattvic.

Relations

SUN rules the father
MOON rules the mother
MARS rules the siblings
MERCURY rules the maternal
   uncles
JUPITER rules the children

VENUS rules the spouse
SATURN rules subordinates
RAHU rules the maternal
   grandparents
KETU rules the paternal
   grandparents

This information helps to decide questions regarding the health, longevity and prosperity of a person's various relatives, as for example to diagnose ill-health to the mother from her child's horoscope. There is no specified significator in classical Jyotish either for maternal aunts or for paternal uncles or aunts.

In Jaimini Jyotish the indicators for the various relations are not fixed but change from horoscope to horoscope. The seven planets (except Rahu and Ketu) are graded from highest to lowest according to how far they have advanced in the separate constellations that they occupy. For example, if someone has Mars in 27° of Aries and Venus in 25° of Pisces, Mars has advanced further in its constellation, even though Pisces as a constellation is more advanced than is Aries. Whichever planet is most advanced in any constellation in the horoscope is called the significator of soul (*Atma Karaka*). The next most advanced planet is the significator of mind (*Amatya Karaka*), and these are followed in order by the significator of siblings (*Bhratri Karaka*), the significator of mother (*Matri Karaka*), the significator of children (*Putra Karaka*), the significator of other relations (*Jnati Karaka*), and the significator of spouse (*Dara Karaka*). The significator for father is the Sun *except when* two planets have the same degree and minute position, in which case another complicated method which involves Rahu is employed.

Many of the practitioners of Parashari Jyotish who employed Jaimini's indicators are unaware that they form an integral part of the entirely different system of interpretation that is Jaimini Jyotish. Some defend this practice by saying that this method is part of the Parashari system, since it is included in *Brihat Parashara Hora*, but this does not mean that it is integral to Parashari Jyotish; it may have been a later addition. To determine the significators for relatives by the Jaimini method and then to use them in a Parashari mode to analyze relations causes inherent contradictions. It is as illogical to use Jaimini significators with Parashari aspects as it would be to use diesel fuel in a petrol engine.

Seasons

VENUS rules Vasanta (20 March to 19 May)
SUN and MARS rule Grishma (20 May to 19 July)

MOON rules Varsha (20 July to 19 September)
MERCURY rules Sharad (20 September to 19 November)
JUPITER rules Hemanta (20 November to 19 January)
SATURN rules Shishira (20 January to 19 March)

These rulerships correspond to the seasons of India, where they are known to this day by these Sanskrit names. From Vasanta to Shishira respectively they may be translated as spring, summer, rainy season, autumn, windy season, and winter. Some authorities propound different season systems, due to regional variations in India's calendars.

These rulerships help to time the events in a person's life. For example, in one horoscope Jupiter and Venus are strong and beneficial planets connected with the indicators symbolizing children, and one of this man's children was born in early January during Hemanta, which is ruled by Jupiter, and the other was born in April during Vasanta, which is ruled by Venus. In this same gentleman's horoscope, Mercury is very beneficial for profession, and during twenty years of active professional life every major beneficial change in his career has taken place in the fall during Sharad, the season ruled by Mercury.

Sex

SUN, MARS and JUPITER are masculine
MOON, VENUS and RAHU are feminine
MERCURY, SATURN and KETU are neuter

This information is used mainly to determine the gender of children and siblings. It is also useful for determining the type of qualities a person may have. For example, if masculine grahas exclusively influence the factors symbolizing the wife in a man's horoscope, his wife may well have many masculine qualities. Similarly, if the neuter grahas are very prominent in a horoscope, that person may be slow to mature sexually.

Sexual Union

SUN gives union with high-class partners
MOON, JUPITER and VENUS give union with suitable partners
MARS gives union with one deformed in some way
MERCURY gives union with artisans
SATURN gives union with older partners or sickly or ugly partners
RAHU gives union with widowed or with divorced partners

Once again, although literal interpretations are possible, this information is better applied in a broader sense. For instance, if the client wants an astrologer to elaborate on an intimate relationship, and the Moon, Jupiter or Venus happens to indicate the partner in that horoscope at the time of the reading, this would suggest a partner who is of suitable temperament, age and social standing; and so on.

Temperament

SUN is fixed and steady
MOON is fickle and changeable
MARS is violent, angry and rash
MERCURY is volatile and
  versatile
JUPITER is mild, benign and
  soft-hearted
VENUS is easy-going and
  accommodating
SATURN is harsh, hard-hearted
  and cruel
RAHU and KETU are eccentric
  and explosive

Like the section on psychology above, this classification is used to analyze a person's temperament through the influence of the horoscope's predominant planets. It can also be used to analyze the temperaments of people who are close to the native, including spouse, children, mother, father, other relatives, friends, and partners. An example: if all the factors in a horoscope that symbolize the mother are influenced by Venus, then that person's mother will be easy-going and accommodating.

The qualities of the planets listed in this – and in most of the other sections of this chapter – may seem stark and absolutist, but they are not meant to be; they simply indicate the fundamental natures of the grahas. Arsenic is fundamentally poisonous, but it is also an essential nutrient and, when properly prepared in small doses, it can be a beneficial medicine. To say that Saturn is harsh, hard-hearted and cruel does not mean that everyone who is ruled by Saturn is unrelievedly harsh, hard-hearted and cruel, for when Saturn is 'properly prepared' (i.e. strong and well placed) the native is often wise, patient, and insightful.

NOTE: Prediction from a horoscope is not the sole use for these planetary characteristics, for they are expressions of the planets in the language of the material world. If a person brings a melon or a milk product to a jyotishi (since in India it is traditional to bring a gift when approaching an astrologer for a reading), the jyotishi may use the information concerning flowers, fruit and trees to conclude either that the person must be strongly ruled by the Moon or that the question the person is about to ask is pertinent to the things ruled by the Moon in his or her horoscope. If the fruit another person brings is rotten inside, the jyotishi will know that Saturn's influence predominates and, even before hearing the petitioner's request, will know that it is likely to remain unfulfilled. Jyotish is more than mere birth charts; it is the ability to read reality like a book.

CHAPTER FIVE

THE RASHIS
(CONSTELLATIONS)

How a planet acts is determined by the nature and meaning of the constellation in which it sits. One way in which the constellations modify the planets is by establishing whether they are strong, weak or indifferent, as detailed in Chapter Two. This principle is constantly used by jyotishis and must be thoroughly known.

But constellations modify planets in other ways as well. Recall, for example, that Mercury represents the rational mind, the activity we usually call 'thinking'. An individual's thinking process will be influenced by the natural attributes of the constellation in which Mercury sits in that horoscope. Mercury also symbolizes speech and, if it is in Pisces (which is known to be a mute constellation), the person will often have difficulty with vocal patterns and speech.

Or recall that Jupiter represents or rules the fat tissue. All other factors being equal, Jupiter in Aries specifically relates to the fatty layer of tissue which, along with the skin, constitutes the scalp; when in Taurus, it represents the same layer of fat, but under the skin of the face; when in Gemini, the fat of the shoulders, arms and hands; in Cancer, that of the chest or breast; and so on. Saturn rules or represents contraction and, by extension, spasms. In Aries, it gives spasms in the muscles of the head; in Taurus, spasms of the facial muscles; in Gemini, spasms of the muscles of the shoulders, arms and hands; in Cancer, of the chest; and so on.

Please note that the above example involving Mercury truly evokes the idea of a modification of Mercury's action by the constellations, while in the examples involving Jupiter and Saturn, though the constellations modify the planets' actions, there is greater emphasis on the site of their action rather on than on how it will act. The effect of the constellations in the latter examples mimics the meanings of the houses of the horoscope. Though such overlap between the meaning of constellations and houses does occur in certain matters, in the total scheme of astrology this overlap is negligible.

CONSTELLATIONAL CHARACTERISTICS

This being an elementary book, only the essential rulerships of the constellations have been classified in the sections which follow. Remember that Aries and all the other rashis mentioned here are *constellations* and not the *signs* of Western astrology which bear the same names.

Method of Rising

GEMINI, LEO, VIRGO, LIBRA, SCORPIO and AQUARIUS rise over the eastern horizon with their beginning portion first; these are called in Sanskrit the *shirshodaya* or 'head-rising' constellations.

ARIES, TAURUS, CANCER, SAGITTARIUS and CAPRICORN rise over the eastern horizon with their ending portion first and are called in Sanskrit the *prishthodaya* or 'back-rising' constellations.

PISCES rises with both its beginning and ending portions first and is the *ubhayodaya* ('both-way-rising') constellation. According to a few authorities, Gemini is also *ubhayodaya*.

For example, because of Leo's position in the zodiac, the stars which form the lion's head will rise before the stars which form its feet. Leo is consequently called a 'head-rising' constellation. Astrologically, the 'head-rising' constellations are auspicious, the 'back-rising' ones are inauspicious and the 'both-way-rising' constellation is changeable.

When a naturally benefic graha (Jupiter, Venus, waxing Moon, or Mercury unassociated with malefics) occupies a 'head-rising' constellation, it becomes still more benefic. A naturally malefic graha (Saturn, Mars, Rahu, Ketu, waning Moon, Mercury associated with malefics) becomes more malefic when in a 'back-rising' constellation. By extension, a benefic in a 'back-rising' constellation loses some of its benefic nature, and a malefic in a 'head-rising' constellation loses some of its malefic nature. This classification is one classic example of how the constellations modify the planets.

Appearance

The twelve rashis have the following appearances:

1.	ARIES	A ram
2.	TAURUS	A bull
3.	GEMINI	A man holding a club and a woman holding a musical instrument
4.	CANCER	A crab
5.	LEO	A lion
6.	VIRGO	A young woman, often in a boat, holding wheat in one hand and fire in the other
7.	LIBRA	A man holding scales in his hand
8.	SCORPIO	A scorpion
9.	SAGITTARIUS	A centaur holding a bow from which he is about to shoot an arrow
10.	CAPRICORN	A crocodile with the upper body of a deer, or a fish with the upper body of a goat
11.	AQUARIUS	A man with a pitcher so tilted on his shoulder as to suggest that the contents are being poured out
12.	PISCES	Two fish swimming in opposite directions

The ancients saw a crab in the five stars that make up the constellation of Cancer, projected a maiden holding wheat and fire on to Virgo's fifteen stars, and so on. However, as the arrangement of the stars in the various constellations does not readily evoke the images projected on to them, we must consider the possibility that astrologers of yore were not so overwhelmed by that primitive amazement which we moderns tend to project on them that they hallucinated these pictures in the sky. Perhaps, in fact, it was quite the other way round, and the seers of antiquity first generated images infused with philosophical and astrological import, images that expressed in symbolic language the results of their observations about that particular strip of sky, and only then wrestled those images into alignment with the observed stars.

Whatever their origins, the images are now used astrologically to suggest some of the traits of their associated constellations. Many of the psychological meanings of tropical or Western astrology seem also to have evolved from these basic constellational images, even though that system applies these meanings to the signs of the same name and not to the constellations.

A person born when Leo was on the eastern horizon sidereally (technically called 'Leo rising', 'a Leo ascendant' or 'Leo lagna') would be proud and regal like a lion – provided of course that there are no other factors influencing the constellation of Leo by occupation or by aspect. Because planets are more important than constellations, the qualities of Saturn would dominate over those of Leo when Saturn occupies Leo. In this case, of all Saturn's traits the negative ones would tend to predominate, since Saturn has difficulty expressing himself positively in his enemy's rashi. The result? If unchecked, Saturnine attitudes like loneliness, lack of trust, disappointment or rigidity are likely to beset the person.

Jataka Bharanam states that when Mars occupies a horoscope's ascendant, the native will roam around. The basic interpretation here again comes from observation: Mars' movements are so erratic that it seems to 'roam' about more than do the other planets. Mars' house position will determine which areas of life are affected by this roaming, and Mars' strength will determine how beneficial or detrimental this roaming will be to the individual. A Mars which is exalted or in its own constellation may well cause roaming that produces some enjoyment or profit, while a Mars that is debilitated, combust or otherwise weakened may cause one to drift aimlessly.

Bodily Constitution

The constellations and their elements (see Elements, below) are correlated to the Ayurvedic concept of bodily constitution. Parashara correlates the Twelve Rashis and the Three Doshas in this way:

· The Watery Rashis indicate Kapha
· The Fiery Rashis indicate Pitta

· The Earthy Rashis indicate Vata
· The Airy Rashis indicate mixed (*mishra* or *sama*) doshas

These identifications are used in Ayurveda's medical astrology in much the same way as described for the planets in the last chapter. They can also be used to estimate the type of body a person may have, based on the way in which these rashis are configured with various planets in the lagna, the epitome of the body. For example, one famous combination states that if a Watery rashi rises in a lagna which is exclusively occupied and aspected by Watery planets (Jupiter, Venus and Moon), the person will be stout. This condition harmonizes well with Ayurveda's basic principles, which ascribe stoutness mainly to Kapha.

Planetary constitution is modified or enhanced according to the placement of the grahas in different rashis. When for instance Jupiter sits in its own or exaltation rashi (Pisces or Cancer respectively), its Watery/Kapha nature becomes much more pronounced than when it sits in a Fiery rashi, even when that Fiery rashi happens to be Sagittarius, which it also owns.

Bodily Parts

1.	ARIES	The top and back of the head
2.	TAURUS	The face and throat
3.	GEMINI	The neck, shoulders, arms and hands
4.	CANCER	The chest
5.	LEO	The upper portion of the abdomen down to the navel
6.	VIRGO	The middle portion of the abdomen, from the navel halfway down to the pubic bone
7.	LIBRA	The lower portion of the abdomen, from the pubic bone halfway up to the navel
8.	SCORPIO	The genitals and anus
9.	SAGITTARIUS	The thighs and hips
10.	CAPRICORN	The knees
11.	AQUARIUS	The calves
12.	PISCES	The feet

These classifications are illustrative, not exhaustive. The rulerships, especially those pertaining to the body's trunk, indicate a full anatomical cross-section of that area, not just the front of the body. Cancer can therefore be said to rule – in addition to the chest – the heart, the lungs, and the upper thoracic area of the back. The other constellations should be similarly extrapolated.

This classification is used to deduce the physical state of the body's different parts. When, for example, Jupiter is strong in its own constellation of Pisces he will give strong, well-proportioned feet with good arches, feet that will not be subjected to injuries, while Saturn in Pisces would give problems pertaining to the structure of the feet, or foot pain, or injuries, and so on. These deductions are not confined to planets in constellations but also extend to the rashi's ruler. The placement of Jupiter, the lord of Pisces, in Capricorn, where he is debilitated, would indirectly affect the feet detrimentally.

Directions

1.	ARIES	East	7.	LIBRA	West
2.	TAURUS	South	8.	SCORPIO	North
3.	GEMINI	West	9.	SAGITTARIUS	East
4.	CANCER	North	10.	CAPRICORN	South
5.	LEO	East	11.	AQUARIUS	West
6.	VIRGO	South	12.	PISCES	North

This classification is used similarly to that described under *Places or Haunts*, below. Note that the cardinal directions are assigned as indications in this way: Aries, which is the ascendant in the natural zodiac, represents east, since by definition the ascendant is whichever rashi happens to be rising in the east at a particular moment. The other Fire constellations (Leo and Sagittarius) follow Aries' lead and indicate east. Capricorn, the tenth house of the natural zodiac, sits at the zenith in the natural zodiac. Since in the Northern Hemisphere it would be seen in the south, it and the other two Earth constellations represent south. Libra in the natural zodiac is seen to be setting on the horizon in the west, so it and the other two Air constellations represent west. Cancer in the natural zodiac is below the earth in a northerly direction, so it and the other two Water constellations represent north.

Elements

ARIES, LEO and SAGITTARIUS are Fiery	GEMINI, LIBRA and AQUARIUS are Airy
TAURUS, VIRGO and CAPRICORN are Earthy	CANCER, SCORPIO and PISCES are Watery

Earth is the densest of the elements, the most difficult element to move, so when the factors in a horoscope which indicate physiology and psychology are influenced by Earth rashis, that native will be difficult to move physically and mentally. He is likely to have a strong, well-knit body, may dislike travel, and is unlikely to accept new ideas readily or easily.

When wet planets (Moon, Jupiter and Venus) predominantly influence a Water rashi in the ascendant, the native is likely to be rotund. Also, since water is the matrix of life, the element from which life originated, the Water rashis signify fertility, gestation and fecundity. When therefore the Water rashis are prominently associated with those areas of the horoscope which indicate progeny, the native is likely to produce offspring.

Fire requires new combustible materials to perpetuate its very existence. Unlike the other elements, it cannot simply just be. Planets which occupy a Fire rashi acquire some of its restless nature, and cause the native restlessly to seek change in whatever realms of life those planets indicate. Also, when dry planets (Sun, Mars and Saturn) predominantly influence a Fire rashi in the ascendant, the native is likely to be lean.

The Sun is the source of all Fire in the solar system, and its Fire (heat, light, radiation) is conveyed to the Earth by the atmosphere. Air is therefore by analogy the element which communicates. When therefore Air rashis occupy houses in the horoscope which represent communication, or when those rashis are occupied by planets which represent that ability, communication skills may be enhanced.

The inferences listed here are only examples; similar processes can be used to derive many more such indications. Ether, the fifth of Sankhya's five Maha Bhutas, has no specific constellational rulership because it is the undifferentiated field from which all the others arise, in which they all exist, and into which they all resolve.

Fruitful and Barren

CANCER, SCORPIO and PISCES (the Water rashis) are fruitful
ARIES, GEMINI, LEO and VIRGO are barren
TAURUS, LIBRA, SAGITTARIUS, CAPRICORN and AQUARIUS are
    semi-fruitful

This classification is applied predominantly to the astrological analysis of progeny. If, for example, all the factors connected with children in a person's horoscope occupy barren constellations, that individual is unlikely to have children or will have very few of them.

Height or Length

ARIES, TAURUS, AQUARIUS and PISCES are short
GEMINI, CANCER, SAGITTARIUS and CAPRICORN are average
LEO, VIRGO, LIBRA and SCORPIO are long

This classification is also taken from astronomical observation. In the Northern Hemisphere, Aries, Taurus, Aquarius and Pisces are the constellations of *short ascension*; because of the angle the observer on Earth makes with the zodiac, they take a shorter amount of time to move their 30° of space through the houses than do Leo, Virgo, Libra and Scorpio, the constellations of *long ascension*. This is similar to how your shadow changes according to the angle you make with the sun, except that the shadow is reduced or elongated in space, while the rashi is reduced or elongated in time. This classification is predominantly used to gauge the height of a person, or even the relative size of any of his or her organs or limbs, provided that the height of the grahas involved is also taken into consideration.

Odd/Even

ARIES, GEMINI, LEO, LIBRA, SAGITTARIUS and AQUARIUS are odd
  or masculine rashis

TAURUS, CANCER, VIRGO, SCORPIO, CAPRICORN and PISCES are
  even or feminine rashis

The foremost use of this classification is to help determine the sex
of children, for which purpose the odd constellations are referred to
as being male, and the even ones female. It is also used to judge a
person's character and motivation. 'Masculine' and 'feminine' here
are archetypes, and do not refer solely to gender. The odd or male
constellations are said to possess archetypal male qualities such as
aggression and logical thought, while the even or female constellations display archetypal female qualities such as nurturing and
intuition.

Places or Haunts

1.	ARIES	Forest or plateau
2.	TAURUS	Field or meadow
3.	GEMINI	Village or bedroom
4.	CANCER	Pond or well
5.	LEO	Mountains or caves
6.	VIRGO	Land that is with water and cultivated vegetation
7.	LIBRA	Busy town or marketplace
8.	SCORPIO	Hole or cavity
9.	SAGITTARIUS	Villages, cities, treasuries or military posts
10.	CAPRICORN	Forests with plenty of water
11.	AQUARIUS	Villages
12.	PISCES	Watery places

A few of the manifold uses of this classification include: to indicate
in what kind of an environment a person feels most comfortable; to
locate missing or hidden articles; and to indicate the destination of

travel. The expanded list below was compiled from rulerships listed in various astrological works subsequent to Parashara:

1 – ARIES: Newly developed lands, sandy soil or terrain, hilly, unfrequented or dangerous places, furnaces and similar heat-producing places, ceilings, roofs, the east wall of rooms or buildings, places rich in natural jewels and minerals, medium levels.

2 – TAURUS: Grazing or agricultural land, places where farmers reside, meadows, lawns, dim rooms with low ceilings, barns, closets, basements, storerooms for food and provisions, the south-east wall of a room or house, ground or below-ground levels.

3 – GEMINI: Places where entertainers reside and where games are played, areas within walking distance, the neighborhood, abutting properties, places that connect to other places, stairs, streets, escalators, schoolrooms, recreation rooms, the west wall of a room or house, high levels.

4 – CANCER: Fountains, pools, canals, rivers, plumbing, reservoirs, kitchens, laundromats, wharves, restaurants, north wall of a room or house, low level.

5 – LEO: Rocky, high and steep places and difficult of access, forts and castles, jungles, deserts, main halls, disorderly places, the east wall of a room or house, medium level.

6 – VIRGO: Places frequented by artisans, places frequented mostly by women, gardens, cornfields, granaries, pantries, rented rooms, bookshelves, medical boxes, the south wall, ground or below-ground level.

7 – LIBRA: Shops, places frequented by merchants and consumers, markets, trade shows, alcoves and public places in a house, linen closets, wardrobes, west wall, high level.

8 – SCORPIO: Places where snakes or vermin or poisonous creatures live, swamps, hidden or secret places, oil wells, stagnant and rotting places, cesspools, toilets, sewers, sinks, north-east wall, low level.

9 – SAGITTARIUS: Temples, state residences, estates and high-class acreage, high but easily accessible ground, upper and large rooms,

places where ammunition, a safe, or horses are kept, south-east wall, medium level.

10 − CAPRICORN: Slums, uncultivated fields, barren fields, mines, mountain peaks, cliffs, swampy woods, uncomfortable or neglected rooms, dark rooms, dark corners, south wall, ground or below-ground level.

11 − AQUARIUS: Unusual or unique places, areas where scientific research is done or where unique instruments are kept and stored, places where communication devices such as TVs are kept, antique shops or rooms furnished with antiques, the north-west wall, high level.

12 − PISCES: Oceans, seas, beaches, damp places, places of confinement or segregation, prisons, monasteries, hospitals, north-west wall, low places.

Qualities

ARIES, CANCER, LIBRA and CAPRICORN are movable
TAURUS, LEO, SCORPIO and AQUARIUS are fixed
GEMINI, VIRGO, SAGITTARIUS and PISCES are dual or mutable

The movable constellations (*chara rashis*) are dominated by Rajas (activity), the fixed constellations (*sthira rashis*) by Tamas (inertia), and the mutable constellations (*dvisvabhava rashis*) by Sattva (equilibrium). For more information on the Three Gunas, see Qualities in Chapter Four.

Planets occupying constellations take on in part the qualities of that constellation, so a planet in a movable rashi, which implies change, may imply travel in those matters ruled by that planet in the horoscope. Travel is much less likely when a planet that represents travel in a horoscope occupies a fixed constellation, for fixed rashis suggest fixity. The dual or mutable rashis imply a balance between motion and fixity; when they indicate travel, it may involve repeatedly leaving and returning to a home base.

All other factors being equal, planets which represent the career tend to promote frequent change of employment when they are associated with movable rashis, and discourage such change when associated with fixed rashis. When they become associated with dual rashis, a balance may be struck between stability and mobility in vocation. Similar logic can be applied to many other indications.

Vegetable, Animal and Mineral

> The MOVABLE RASHIS are mineral or insentient
> The FIXED RASHIS are vegetable or semi-sentient
> The DUAL RASHIS are animal or fully sentient

This classification and its uses parallel the classification provided for the planets on this subject in the last chapter in the section *Animal, Vegetable and Mineral*.

THE DIVISIONS OF A CONSTELLATION

Just as the basic principle of the solar system is replicated in the atom, with smaller bodies orbiting larger ones, the horoscope can be replicated in minute ways. A *rashi* (literally, a 'heap of things') is a heap of micro-zodiacs, or *amshas*. Since every *amsha*, or portion of the zodiac, is smaller than a rashi (ranging in size from 15° to 30', and, in Nadi Jyotish, to 6' of arc), they manage the rashi by delineating results for specific matters within the broad context of each rashi. They are particularly useful to differentiate between two similar horoscopes. For example, everyone born within the two and a half years that Saturn transits Libra will have Saturn in their birth charts in Libra but, because most will have a different pattern of amshas according to their specific times of birth, the differences in the amshas will suggest differences in life experience.

Parashara lists sixteen amsha charts (we can also call them subcharts). Nadi and Tajika Jyotish add the fifth, sixth, eighth and the one-hundred-and-fiftieth amshas. We will confine our comments here to the ninth subchart, or *navamsha*, which is by all accounts the most important of all the amshas. One reason for its pre-eminence is the numerological fact that there are nine grahas. Another reason is the spatial fact that since the navamsha is the ninth division, each 30° rashi is divided into nine parts of 3° 20′ each, a distance which happens to be one-fourth of a nakshatra (see Chapter Eight). Therefore nakshatras always start at the beginning point of a navamsha and end at the terminating point of a navamsha.

Calculation of Navamsha

The last portion of *Phaladipika* 3:4 states, 'The first navamsha in the several constellations from Aries onwards commences respectively with Aries, Capricorn, Libra and Cancer.' Thus, the first navamsha of Aries is Aries, of Taurus is Capricorn, of Gemini is Libra, of Cancer is Cancer, of Leo is Aries, of Virgo is Capricorn, and so on. In each rashi the rest of the navamshas then follow the natural order of the zodiac. For example, the first navamsha in Capricorn is Capricorn, followed by Aquarius, then Pisces, Aries, Taurus and so on up to Virgo.

Note that the first navamsha for the cardinal constellation (*chara rashi*) is always that constellation; the fifth navamsha for a fixed constellation (*sthira rashi*) is always that constellation; and the ninth navamsha for a mutable constellation (*dvisvabhava rashi*) is always that constellation. Note also that this table begins with Aries as the first navamsha of Aries and ends with Pisces as the final navamsha of Pisces.

The natural zodiac is therefore repeated in order nine full times over the 108 navamshas of the twelve rashis: $9 \times 12 = 108$. 108, which is regarded by many in India as a perfect number (since $1 + 8 = 9$, the complete number of material creation), is also the result obtained by multiplying the Nine Grahas by the Twelve Rashis. Also, the sun covers 10,800 minutes of arc (six rashis or 180°) in the zodiac over the span of one half of a year, and a human breathes 10,800 breaths (at the standard yogic rate of fifteen breaths per minute) over the span of twelve hours (one half of a day). For these and other reasons, 108 has been numerically significant for millennia; the *Shatapatha Brahmana*, a Vedic text, states that to achieve immortality (though not in this body) one should lay down 10,800

TABLE 5.1

Navamshas

Constellation	Degree Positions								
	0° to 3°20'	3°20' to 6°40'	6°40' to 10°00'	10°00' to 13°20'	13°20' to 16°40'	16°40' to 20°00'	20°00' to 23°20'	23°20' to 26°40'	26°40' to 30°
Aries	Ar	Ta	Ge	Ca	Le	Vi	Li	Sc	Sa
Taurus	Cp	Aq	Pi	Ar	Ta	Ge	Ca	Le	Vi
Gemini	Li	Sc	Sa	Cp	Aq	Pi	Ar	Ta	Ge
Cancer	Ca	Le	Vi	Li	Sc	Sa	Cp	Aq	Pi
Leo	Ar	Ta	Ge	Ca	Le	Vi	Li	Sc	Sa
Virgo	Cp	Aq	Pi	Ar	Ta	Ge	Ca	Le	Vi
Libra	Li	Sc	Sa	Cp	Aq	Pi	Ar	Ta	Ge
Scorpio	Ca	Le	Vi	Li	Sc	Sa	Cp	Aq	Pi
Sagittarius	Ar	Ta	Ge	Ar	Le	Vi	Li	Sc	Sa
Capricorn	Cp	Aq	Pi	Ar	Ta	Ge	Ca	Le	Vi
Aquarius	Li	Sc	Sa	Cp	Aq	Pi	Ar	Ta	Ge
Pisces	Ca	Le	Vi	Li	Sc	Sa	Cp	Aq	Pi

lokamprnna (space-filler) bricks during the course of the involved Vedic sacrifice known as Agnichayana.

To draw up the navamsha you begin by fixing its ascendant. If, for example, a horoscope's ascendant is 15° of Sagittarius, that ascendant point will fall in the fifth navamsha of Sagittarius, which happens to be Leo. The table above informs us that the navamsha chart for this horoscope will therefore have Leo as its first house. Then, each graha's navamsha is determined, and they are placed in the navamsha chart accordingly. If Jupiter in this example is located in Gemini at 22° it occupies the seventh navamsha counted from Libra, which is Aries. Consequently Jupiter in the navamsha chart for this horoscope will occupy Aries, which is the ninth house from Leo, this navamsha chart's ascendant.

Employing the Navamsha

Jyotish's primary use for the subcharts in prediction is to evaluate planetary strength by observing whether a planet is placed predominantly in the beneficial divisions (exaltation, own, or friendly rashi) or the inauspicious divisions (inimical or debilitation rashi) of the chart. A graha which occupies the same rashi in both the birth chart and the navamsha chart is said to be *vargottama* (the best division). A planet can be vargottama in any of the subcharts, but this term is usually confined to its navamsha position. One text states, 'The same effects produced by a graha which occupies its own constellation occur when that graha occupies its vargottama amsha.' Vargottama planets therefore enhance the desirable matters of the houses they occupy and own, provided of course that those planets are not devitalized in some other way, such as combustion, avastha, etc. Note that the strength of a vargottama graha will *not* be greatly enhanced if that rashi is its place of debilitation.

When the lord of the ascendant of the navamsha (the 'rising navamsha') is strong, the overall status and the life expectations of the native are substantially improved. *Jataka Parijata* observes, 'The appearance, visage and peculiar features of a person can be determined from the lord of the rising navamsha at his birth or from a powerful planet occupying the ascendant in the birth chart' (11:15a).

By implication, the lord of the rising navamsha is as influential in a person's life as is a powerful planet sitting in the first house of the birth chart, *provided that* the lord of the rising navamsha is strong in the birth chart. In the example above of a Sagittarius rising horoscope which has Leo as the rising constellation of its navamsha, if the Sun (which rules Leo) is posited, say, in its own rashi in the ninth house of the birth chart, the appearance and features of that individual would resemble those of someone whose Sun was strong in the first house.

Another use for the navamsha: *Jataka Parijata* 15:44 observes that profession can be determined through the lord of the rashi which is the navamsha occupied by the lord of the tenth house of the birth chart. For a Sagittarius ascendant, the tenth house is Virgo and the tenth lord is therefore Mercury. If Mercury is situated, say, at 9° Virgo, it will fall in Virgo's third navamsha, which happens to be Pisces. Since the lord of Pisces is Jupiter, that person would be likely to follow a Jupiterian profession, like teaching, preaching or, in this case, possibly consulting (since we must include in our interpretation the fact that the mercantile Mercury is exalted in that tenth house). There are of course other ways to determine profession, but this example does indicate the great utility of the navamsha.

The navamsha is sometimes read like a birth chart, particularly by South Indian jyotishis, to help to refine predictions in specific realms of life experience. Most standard rules of influence apply to such interpretations; for example, planets which influence the navamsha's lagna affect both the general and the specific indications of that amsha for better or worse, according to whether they are natural benefics or malefics respectively. It is said that the birth chart represents the tree of a life, and the navamsha represents its fruit. Examination of the navamsha can help to indicate what sort of fruit can be expected in life, for you cannot tell the fruit just by looking at the tree. Weak or ugly trees sometimes produce sweeter and more abundant fruit than do strong, handsome trees, and a strong navamsha can often indicate good results in an otherwise weak horoscope.

Some jyotishis follow another of Parashara's leads, however, and read the navamsha only to predict marriage and similar relationships. From this angle, natural benefics which influence, by occupation or aspect, the lagna of a navamsha chart will tend to enhance marital happiness, while natural malefics in similar positions will tend to disturb wedded bliss.

Those interested in amshas other than the navamsha should consult *Brihat Parashara Hora*, Chapter 6.

CHAPTER SIX

THE BHAVAS (HOUSES)

The houses of the horoscope define where, on what, or on whom the planetary energies act, in the manner indicated by the constellations. 'House' is a poor translation of the Sanskrit word *bhava*, a word which means both 'a state of existence' and 'a state of mind'. To refer to, say, the second house of family as the second bhava connotes not merely the mundane details of the family but also its state, its overall condition. A bhava is thus more a 'home' than it is a 'house'; it is a home to all your experiences in that segment of your life.

The twelve bhavas of your horoscope represent the totality of the external conditions of your existence as experienced by the internal states of your mind, including particularly your emotions, which influence and are influenced by those outer conditions. Internal experience is often disproportionate to external environment; being rich will not necessarily make you happy, nor will being poor doom you to being miserable. Bhavas are the cosmic looms on which the grahas weave the tapestry of your life from the yarn of your karmas. They suggest to the jyotishi what advantages or disadvantages will be available to an individual in the various arenas of life, and what he or she will do with these.

Before we describe the meanings which have over the centuries been applied to each bhava, let us examine their inherent natures, that is to say, the sorts of energies they fundamentally indicate, for it is from these inherent attributes that many of their meanings spring.

THE FOUR GOALS OF LIFE

HOUSES 1–5–9 are the *dharma* bhavas
HOUSES 2–6–10 are the *artha* bhavas
HOUSES 3–7–11 are the *kama* bhavas
HOUSES 4–8–12 are the *moksha* bhavas

Desire is equally well the ultimate foundation of both macrocosm and microcosm, of both human existence and the existence of the whole universe of name and form. Almost all human actions, subtle or gross, selfish or altruistic, are motivated by some sort of desire. Actions can be classified with the help of the Vedic concept of the *Four Purusharthas*, the four fundamental human desires. These four aims or objects of life are *dharma, artha, kama* and *moksha*. All of them are influenced by the play of the Three Gunas, which can be read from the horoscope.

Dharma

Sometimes translated 'duty', dharma is really 'doing what you are born to do', doing what best fits your individual aptitude in the context of your familial and societal responsibilities. Although vocation is an important part of one's personal dharma, many Westerners who hear this definition promptly jump to the wrong conclusion that dharma equals career or profession. Many Indians mistakenly translate *dharma* as 'religion', and render *Sanatana Dharma* as 'the eternal religion', when dharma is so much more than mere dogma and ritual.

Dharma, which comes from a Sanskrit root meaning 'to establish', is that path through life which establishes an individual as a stable, productive, satisfied human being. The Sanatana Dharma, like the Tao, is the One Way, the Infinite Path which differs for every seeker but which, when followed wholeheartedly, takes each unerringly to the goal. Dharma is an inborn faculty of existence, not an externally derived discipline: 'These activities called *dharma* are imposed as a kind of natural law on all existent beings in the universe; and a being's initiating of such activity is no moral act contingent on his disposition, but an innate characteristic, that which makes a being what it is, assigning the part it is to play in concert. It is the *dharma* of the Sun to shine, of the pole to be fixed, of the rivers to flow, of the cow to yield milk . . .' (van Buitenen, p. 36).

Because everyone's road to reality is personalized, what is dharma for one person may be non-dharmic for another. Dharma is part of destiny and cannot be ignored simply because it may be painful, boring or inconvenient. As our Jyotish guru once observed, 'Why are you Westerners so interested in changing your destiny when it is so hard to live up to it?' One of Jyotish's tasks is to teach you what your true dharma is, instead of what your ego desires it to be. Your ability accurately to perceive and act on your dharma will depend in great part on your ability to minimize the influence of Rajas and Tamas on your consciousness.

Artha

'Wealth', or more aptly, 'resources'; the acquisition of adequate means for self-support to live life fully. Money is essential for self-support, especially today, but when knowledge is used for self-support it can also be included in artha.

Kama

'Desire'; the achievement of one's aspirations. Kama is often translated as 'lust', but in this context it represents relationships in general, the innate urge to relate to others. Everyone seeks perpetual success in their relationship with the world, especially with regard to relationships with other living beings.

Moksha

'Liberation'; freedom from bondage. That happiness which comes from knowledge of the Self is Sattvic, that which is owed to the enjoyment of sense objects is Rajasic, and that which one finds in confusion and misery is Tamasic. All these forms of happiness are limited because they are conditioned. Absolute fulfillment and true happiness, which are not conditioned, do not exist within the limited realms of dharma, artha and kama; they develop only after an individual develops a clear vision of Reality. While each of India's philosophical systems champions a different definition of moksha, moksha fundamentally represents the quality of being able to free yourself from the mirage that dharma, artha or kama are able to provide enduring satisfaction. As the Aghori Vimalananda used to enjoy saying, 'Moksha is the dissolution of delusion.'

All four life-goals are important to a healthy, well-rounded life, but most people do not pursue each goal with equal enthusiasm because their own individual karmas encourage them to prefer particular courses of action. Almost all humans, however, need to achieve all four life-goals at least to some degree if they hope to achieve a life well lived. Choices of which life aims to pursue when, in what way, and for how long, so that balance and proportion in life are maintained, are all the province of Jyotish.

Because a graha tends to focus on the aim of the bhava it tenants, a planet which occupies the eighth house focuses on all things it represents in the horoscope through the lens of moksha. When, for example, the eleventh lord occupies the eighth house there will be loss (eighth house) of gains and material enjoyments in life (eleventh house). When viewed with materialist (artha) eyes, such losses may seem intolerable, but if seen from the perspective of moksha those same experiences may become so meaningful that they may help create a strongly philosophical attitude toward life.

KENDRA AND KONA HOUSES

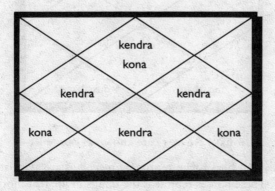

HOUSES 1–4–7–10 are the *kendra* (angular) bhavas
HOUSES 1–5–9 are the *kona* (trinal) bhavas

Because the first house is both an angular house and a trinal house, it is given the pre-eminent place among the twelve houses of a horoscope. The angular bhavas (*kendra*) indicate conscious, self-initiated actions, while the trinal (*trikona*, or simply *kona*) bhavas indicate unconscious actions. When these qualities unite in an individual there is congruence: such people act consistently in a particular direction on both the conscious and unconscious levels of their being. Congruent behavior produces maximum results in life. Certain connections between the trinal and angular houses in a horoscope are therefore extolled by the majority of jyotishis. These combinations and their formation will be explained in Chapter Ten.

DUSSTHANAS

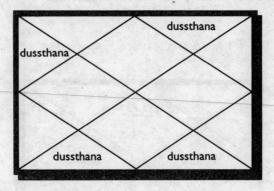

HOUSES 3–6–8–12 are known as *dussthanas*

A *dussthana* is a bhava whose primary meanings are associated with suffering. These houses represent the things in life that most people generally fear, like illness, loss and death. The third house tends to produce only slight fear, usually in relation to minor debts, which makes the other three bhavas much more malevolent than the third. These three are referred to by the special term *trik* (The Three).

UPACHAYAS

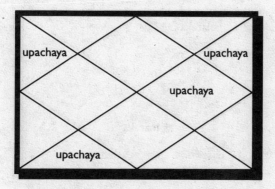

HOUSES 3–6–10–11 are known as *upachayas*

Upachaya means improvement. Certain astrological combinations involving these houses improve one's condition in life. These combinations will be considered later in the book, as will some seeming contradictions in the classifications of the bhavas (e.g., how the third and sixth houses can simultaneously be bhavas of both suffering and improvement).

MARAKAS

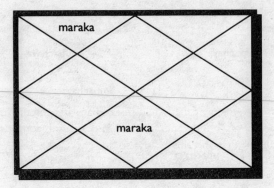

HOUSES 2 & 7 are known as *marakas*

Maraka means killer. Westerners are often surprised to learn that Jyotish estimates an individual's longevity from the horoscope. Among the foremost factors to be considered in longevity analysis are the two maraka houses, their lords, any planets occupying these two houses, and any planets conjoined with or aspected by the lords of the second and seventh houses. Certain combinations in a horoscope, such as when the lord of one maraka house occupies the other maraka house while being afflicted by malefics, can curtail life *if* the native's lifespan is already almost exhausted; otherwise that graha may simply perturb his or her health.

Often the marakas simply indicate problematic results for health and, to some extent, for prosperity. One example of the planetary combinations which can kill the native's prosperity is this (from 'Combinations for Penury', Chapter 42 of *Brihat Parashara Hora*): when the first lord occupies the twelfth house and the twelfth lord occupies the ascendant *and* that twelfth lord is conjoined with or aspected by a maraka lord. In this combination, both the first house and the first lord are afflicted by loss, in the person of the twelfth lord and the twelfth house respectively. Here the influence of the maraka guarantees loss.

DERIVATIONS OF HOUSE MEANINGS

Some of the following meanings were introduced into Jyotish by India's seers through their direct cognition, and other meanings have been developed over the centuries by inspired jyotishis through personal experimentation. There tends to be a natural parallel between the meanings of the constellations and the meanings of the houses. For example, both the first house and Aries, which is the first house in the so-called 'natural zodiac', represents the head; both the second house and Taurus, the natural zodiac's second house, rule the face and throat; and so on.

Some house meanings may be derived by astrological logic, and others are verifiable only by experience. The origins of many house meanings can be grouped into two loose categories: Astronomical Realities and Numerical Value of the Houses.

Astronomical Realities

Houses 1 through 4 are the foundation houses of the horoscope, houses 5 through 8 the development houses, and houses 9 through 12 the culmination houses. The last four houses are the epitomes, the peak achievements, of the four Vedic aims of life; this is astronomically true of houses 9, 10 and 11, which are the highest houses in the sky, and even the twelfth house is at least still ascending. While this sort of evaluation is not much used in natal interpretation, it is one way in which the zodiac reflects the progress of human endeavor.

Jyotish's texts call planets which are above the horizon strong because they are at least theoretically visible and so they can act in a more externalized way than can planets which remain unseen. Planets in kendras are strong because they are in commanding regions of the sky, namely on the eastern horizon, overhead, on the western horizon, and underfoot. The kendras represent the turning points of the sun during the perpetual succession of nights and days. The ascendant represents birth and everything associated with birth, because the sun is born as it rises. Just as when a baby is born its tiny body strongly affirms its existence and displays the qualities that are characteristic of that existence, a planet's characteristics become discernible at the time it rises. The first house rules over a person's body, characteristics, birth, infancy and youth chiefly because the first house is the house being 'born' on the horizon when a person is born.

The Sun is at its peak in the sky in the tenth house, which by extension suggests that human activity (specifically, one's career) is at its peak in the tenth house. Tenth-house activities are public activities which are performed in the bright light of the Sun, as opposed to private human activity, which happens predominantly at home, at night, when the Sun is invisible in the fourth house of home. The Sun is not as happy in the fourth house as it is in the tenth. The death of the Sun as it sets in the seventh house makes that house a maraka. This principle extends to all the planets: They are 'born', or come into visible existence, when they rise in the first house of a locality; they act most strongly in the tenth; they die in the seventh, and they are most private and home-bound in the fourth.

The rising Sun, which is by definition always in the ascendant, is impressive because of the dramatic contrast it provides between the darkness of the night now past and the promise of light of the day just dawning. An hour or two after its rising, however, the Sun is no longer so impressive, because that contrast has been lost; it has risen far enough into the sky to be merely a weak Sun, thanks to its ongoing diurnal motion. This applies to the other planets too, when the constellations in which they sit completely leave the ascendant and are replaced there by the next constellation in line. Such planets now occupy the twelfth house of the sky, a house of loss.

Another house of loss is the eighth house. Often called the house of longevity, the eighth house represents the impending awareness of the end of life for any planet sitting in it, for that planet is retreating from the visible sky as it nears the western horizon and prepares to set. Such planets are always weak, since their influence is about to disappear, which means the eighth house is almost always an undesirable placement for a planet. The seventh house is better, because the Sun is now on the horizon engaged in setting. This again enhances the contrast factor, for the mind is almost as attracted to the setting Sun as it is to the rising Sun. A planet in the seventh house has accepted its fate and is now prepared to die.

The sixth house, the first segment of the netherworld of the sky, is where planets go after setting; it is the Land of Darkness, another place of loss. Since, however, the planet has made its transition from visible to invisible and is now moving toward another angular house, the sixth is also an upachaya house, a house in which things gradually improve. One reason why the sixth is better than the eighth is that when you are about to die (eighth house) you still have fear, but after you are dead (sixth house) you gradually become accustomed to your new state, just as your eyes become accustomed to the lack of light after you enter a dark room. This 'becoming accustomed to' is what makes the sixth an upachaya house.

The second house is a special case. Though houses in similar positions in the sky – the sixth and eighth, which are immediately above and below the western horizon, and the twelfth, which is just above the eastern horizon – tend to produce undesirable results, the second is the house which is always just about to rise on the eastern horizon. Because it shows the promise of what is to come, the second is classed as a generally good house, rather on a par with the eleventh. Also, the second house is a maraka because it indicates something coming to an end: in this case, the end of the night. But because the end of the night is the beginning of the day, and since most humans welcome the light of day, the second house, though parallel in sky position to the eighth, does not carry the eighth's severe connotations, particularly since the planets within the second house are readying themselves to take birth.

Numerical Value of the Houses

Since houses 1, 5 and 9 are all dharma houses, the fifth reflects many of the same meanings of the first, somewhat changed in intention; the ninth likewise reflects some fifth-house meanings. They are harmonics of one another, the higher house an altered image of the lower one. Jyotish makes extensive use of this developmental effect when evaluating a house's derivative meanings. The third house is often said to indicate younger brothers and sisters, while the eleventh, which is a kama house like the third, represents older siblings. The first house and the planets which influence it indicate the profession you have an inclination or talent for, while the tenth house, a kendra like the first, represents the actual profession you pursue.

The seventh house to any house reflects many of the original house's meanings. While the third house rules the conscious mind, the ninth represents the wisdom of the higher mind; the tenth is a house of the public, as is the fourth to some extent. The sixth house rules sickness, and the twelfth hospitals and isolation. One reason this mirroring effect occurs may be that any planet seven houses away from a house aspects that house.

Sometimes a sort of numerological duplication of a house occurs. For example, because one of the fundamental meanings ascribed to the eighth house is longevity, the number eight is consistently associated in Jyotish with longevity. The eighth house away from any house therefore indicates a limitation to the duration of effect of the matters of that house. Counting eight houses from the eighth house gives us the third house, which becomes a sort of derivative eighth house. Similarly, since the sixth house is a house of disease, the eleventh house, being the sixth from the sixth, becomes a derivative house of disease. The ninth house, being fifth from the fifth, likewise becomes a derivative house of children.

We should also mention here the special circumstance in which the lord of a house is the same number of houses away from that house as that house is from the lagna. This situation, which is called *Bhavat Bhavam*, tends to perpetuate the good or evil results of that bhava. For example, when the sixth lord sits in the eleventh house (the sixth from the sixth) the native may suffer from one disease after another. Or, when the lord of the fourth house of education sits in the seventh house (the fourth from the fourth), the native may well study one subject after another, or obtain one degree after another. This will be particularly true for a Pisces lagna, in which the fourth lord Mercury will be exalted in the seventh house, from which it will aspect the lagna.

Since houses 6, 8 and 12 from the lagna are bad houses, and all the rest are basically good, the sixth, eighth, or twelfth house from any house often causes trouble to that house. Because the twelfth house of a horoscope is the house of loss, the twelfth house to any house indicates the loss or the end of the things that bhava indicates. Because the third and eighth houses of a horoscope are houses of longevity, the twelfth house counted from the eighth house (= the horoscope's seventh house) and the twelfth from the third house (= the horoscope's second house) become the houses of 'loss of longevity', or death. This is another reason why the second and seventh houses are marakas. Because the third house is twelve houses away from the fourth house, it may represent the end of residency or home (which means a move). It might also represent the end of the mother, or the partition of property.

The sixth house from any house also holds ominous implications for that house. When the fifth lord sits in the tenth house it occupies the sixth house away from the house it rules. Normally planets that occupy the tenth house should give good results, since the tenth is a good house; but the lord of a house in the sixth from its own house should give bad results. This contradiction can usually (but not always) be reconciled by dividing the matters indicated by the fifth house into two classes: living beings (like children) and everything else (like intelligence, or speculation). The position from the lagna (the tenth house = a good house = good results) will tend to predominate for all indications of the fifth house other than living beings, which means that those things will tend to prosper. For living beings, however, the position of the house lord vis-à-vis the house (tenth house = sixth from fifth = bad results) tends to predominate, suggesting difficulty begetting progeny, or problems with those children.

This applies to all other houses as well. When Jupiter, the lord of the second house for a Scorpio ascendant, occupies the seventh house (the sixth from the second) there is bound to be initial trouble with cash flow and other non-living second-house matters, but this trouble will dissipate as time passes. Because the second house also represents one's family, however, the individual may have difficulty with his family, or may leave home early and live far away from them. The fourth lord in, say, the eleventh house will likewise create difficulties with education or with vehicles, which will eventually be resolved but which may create a much more problematical situation with the native's mother.

Here is a general rule: When the lord of a house is in a good house as counted from the lagna and a bad house (sixth, eighth or twelfth) as counted from the house it rules, there will be a tendency for everything indicated by that house (except for living beings) to be initially obstructed and then to be rectified, while the living beings indicated by that house will tend to be more permanently disturbed.

There are of course exceptions to this rule that the living beings indicated by a bhava are adversely affected when the lord of that house is in the sixth, eighth or twelfth house from it. For a Cancer ascendant the fifth house is Scorpio, which is ruled by Mars. When Mars occupies the tenth house, it will be in the sixth from the fifth, *but* (a) it will tenant its own rashi, and (b) it will aspect the fifth bhava as its own bhava. Mars should therefore give good results for children (a fifth-house matter), unless it is severely afflicted. But even an exalted planet with no obvious afflictions which serves as the fifth lord and resides in the tenth house (as Venus can do for a Gemini ascendant) may be unable to produce a child or may give some difficulty with children, because it sits in the sixth from the fifth but does not strengthen the fifth by aspect.

When the lord of a horoscope's third house occupies the eighth house, its position is inauspicious both from the lagna and from the house (since the eighth is the sixth from the third). This position is therefore doubly bad for younger brothers and sisters. A similar situation occurs when the lord of the seventh house tenants either the twelfth house (the sixth from the seventh) or the sixth house (the twelfth from the seventh). A desirable placement occurs when the lord of a house occupies good positions both from the house and from the lagna, as it does when the lord of the ninth house resides in the fifth house, which is the ninth from the ninth (and so in this situation is also a case of Bhavat Bhavam).

All these numerical values for the houses are derivative, calculated meanings which can only be taken so far, lest they become contradictory.

HOUSE MEANINGS

The following list of house meanings was compiled from diverse classical sources. Some archaic indications (e.g. elephants and palanquins) have been restated in the modern idiom (as vehicles). The comments added are intended to show that these lists are not arbitrary but follow a certain logic, a logic which may sometimes seem peculiar to the Western mind.

'Predominant' meanings are those mentioned most often by most authorities; 'Common' meanings are mentioned somewhat less often but are still commonly accepted; and 'Rare' meanings are mentioned in one or a few texts only. Whenever a noun appears in these lists as a predominant meaning, as 'birth' does for the first house, all the many things associated with it are also indicated by that bhava. For 'birth', these include (but are not limited to) the nature of birthplace, the conditions surrounding birth, who was present at the birth and who was not, whether labor was easy or delayed, whether the delivery was normal or abnormal (breech, forceps, Caesarean) and so on.

First House

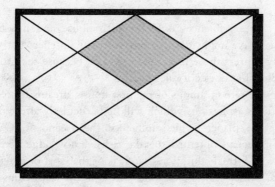

PREDOMINANT — appearance, behavior, birth, birthplace, body, complexion, constitution, dignity, fame, happiness or sorrow, head, health, honor, infancy, life, longevity, nature of a person, prestige, strength or weakness of the body and personality, victory over enemies, virtue, youth

COMMON — accidents, caste, comforts or lack thereof, hair, help obtained through relatives, illness, infamy, livelihood, loss of respect, maternal grandfather, new ventures, paternal grandmother, politics, present time, proficiency and aptitude, proportion, protection, recovery from illness, residence abroad, respect from others, skin, splendor, status in society, stigma, tendency to insult others, thinking

RARE — dreams, gambling, knowledge, old age, sleep, stomach

COMMENTS Matters which have specific houses assigned to them can also be evaluated, in a general sense, from the first house. These include (but are not limited to) honor, fame, profession and livelihood (all matters specific to the tenth house); ill-health, and victory over enemies (sixth house); gambling, and thinking with discernment (fifth house).

Because the first house as microcosm applies to everything in the horoscope, any planet that affects the ascendant (by occupying or aspecting it or, to a lesser degree, by conjoining or aspecting the first lord) will contribute its qualities to all parts of the native's life. When Mars for instance affects the ascendant, it colors all aspects of life with Martian colors, and so may give courage tinged with irritability, potentially aggressive behavior such as insulting speech, a Martian profession, Mars-related illnesses, and the like. When, however, Mars influences only the fifth house and not the first house, the native might have a sharp, sarcastic intellect but will not necessarily express those thoughts in words, because the fifth house rules intellect but does not rule speech.

Among the rare meanings of the first house, dreams relate mainly to the native's aspirations, which will be particularly affected by the nature of the planets which influence the ascendant. Gambling indicates a general potential to take risks. Knowledge here is less suggestive of formal education than it is of that sort of practical life experience which can guide one through the capricious sea of mundane existence.

Second House

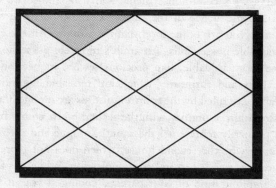

PREDOMINANT — ability to speak, accumulated money, death, drinks, eating, eyesight, face and throat, family members, food, liquid assets, mouth, movable possessions, power and quality of speech, right eye, speech, wealth

COMMON — all who are to be fed and maintained, belief in sacred traditions, ability to fulfill one's promises, clothes, education, generosity in giving, jewels, knowledge and learning (primarily oral), livelihood through the courtesy of others, luster of the face, maintenance of others, metallic wealth, finger- and toenails, the Nine Gems, the Nine Grains, the nose, people close to the native, perfumes, precious metals, robes, self-earned money, selling and buying, teeth, tongue, truth and untruth

RARE — enemies, enmity, horses, income through friends, liberality of mind, steadiness of mind

COMMENTS The second house is often taken as the extended family, in the almost undifferentiated sense of 'people close to you', an indication which is derived from the proximity of the second house to the first. More properly, though, it indicates those to whom you are related by either blood, marriage or adoption. This group, which changes over the course of a lifetime, can at various times include your parents, uncles and aunts, cousins, brothers and sisters, spouse, children and in-laws. A poorly placed Saturn in the second house can indicate a lifelong tendency to be separated or isolated from this ongoing family.

One pervasive second-house theme is that of immediate support almost as a consequence of the birth, i.e. the things that support you just after you are born: food, family, clothes. All these are an infant's movable possessions. An adult's movable possessions tend to become more valuable, like precious jewels, money, and bank accounts. Cars and furniture, which are movable but not easily transportable, are ruled by the fourth house, as are mobile homes.

The association of oratory with the second house comes from the organs it primarily represents: the mouth, tongue and throat. This is one reason why the second house, which does not represent all communication, stands for oral communication. While this includes the oral communication of your parents' cooing at you, it particularly indicates the communication of classical oral traditions, especially sacred traditions, and also the classical subjects which are part of such traditions, like Sanskrit, Jyotish, Ayurveda, and Chinese medicine. In our opinion this house does not represent more modern, secular forms of education.

Perfume is food, or wealth, for the nose, the nose being assigned to the second house under one system of anatomical rulership. Enemies and enemity may be attributable to the fact that the second is the reflection house to the eighth, which rules enemies.

Third House

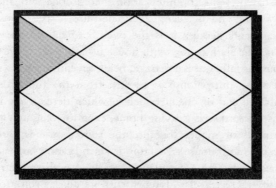

PREDOMINANT — arms, communications (especially routine), parents' death, brothers and sisters (especially younger), great prowess (physical or mental), hands, shoulders, hearing, neck, partition of property, short travels, traveling, valor, writing and written communication, the arts

COMMON — advice or learned discourse, apparel, assistants, companions, ear ornaments, education (primary or vocational), friends, neck, neighborhood, neighbors, patience and perseverance, perplexity or mental confusion, power, religion, right ear, stamina, steadiness that arises from courage, strength

RARE — edible roots and fruit, servants

COMMENTS Most authorities take the third house to mean all brothers or sisters, but one school takes the eleventh to be the indicator of older siblings. Although the former view is more classical, the latter has been so frequently presented by modern native writers on Jyotish that it is now almost universal in India. Many learned traditionalists, though, still determine the number of siblings and their attributes and experiences from an examination of the condition of the third house. Servants, who are often treated as extensions of the family, are indicated by the third house because it is the second house away from the second house.

The third house represents both the conscious mind and the arms and hands and, when the mind and hands function together coordinately, skill arises, which may become great prowess. The third house also represents communication that is done with the hands, such as writing and sign language. The third house stands for the death of parents because it is the twelfth to the fourth house of mother *and* the sixth to the tenth house of father (or, if we take the ninth house as father, it is a maraka, being seventh from the ninth).

Because the third house is twelfth from the fourth house, it represents the end of one's residence, which derivatively indicates partitions, short travels (leaving home, even to commute) and even longer travels or moves (because the third house is a reflection house to the ninth house). Religion is an indication because of this ninth-house reflection. The planets involved with the third house will modify these travels: Mercury with its quick orbit around the Sun gives shorter journeys and quick returns, while Saturn with its longer orbit gives long journeys, or moves farther away from home.

Fourth House

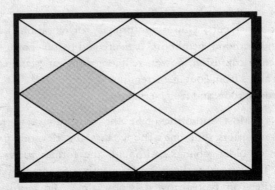

PREDOMINANT – chest, conveyances, land and water dwellings, emotions, education, happiness, houses, immovable property, mother

COMMON – undifferentiated ancestors including the parents (living or dead), agricultural property, ancestral or childhood home, anointing the body or massage, architecture, clothes, crops, end results, fields, gardens, heart, heredity, holy places, livestock, morals, rain, rental properties, shelters, sleep, spiritual efforts, treasures, water wells

RARE – divine herbs for medication, friends, leaving one's home or birthplace, maternal uncle, milk, sweet scents and perfumes

COMMENTS Some fourth-house meanings are observable astronomical derivatives because the fourth house is the point lowest beneath the earth, in terms of the sky pattern observable at the locality of birth. It is thus associated with inner matters like happiness, the satisfaction of the emotions; with the private life as opposed to the public life (the unseen sky versus the seen sky); with land, as opposed to sky; with wells (water below the earth); with one's domicile and sleeping, because at midnight most people are asleep, as natural circadian rhythms would encourage; with agriculture, things planted in (below) the earth; and with treasures of the hidden (buried) variety.

The fourth house represents that education which comes from parents and other ancestors (the formation of attitudes) and, by extension, from society in its role as parent (the educational system). While the jyotishis of South India maintain that this house indicates higher education, we prefer the approach in which the education indicated by the third house is of the basic, not-particularly-intellectual sort; that of the fourth house is formal education of the mid-level sort, which nowadays means high school and undergraduate college; and higher education is allocated to the ninth house. A well-placed fourth house may, however, in and of itself indicate a highly educated person, provided that the planets involved with it also indicate education.

Fourth-house friends are those friends who are like family. The Moon being a mobile planet as lord of the constellation Cancer, the fourth house in the natural zodiac, suggests vehicles as a fourth-house meaning. The fourth house in its role as a house of moksha indicates a spiritual education, one which forms attitudes (morality, positive emotions, contentment) essential for making that spiritual progress which eventually yields that profound understanding of the true nature of spiritual pursuits which is moksha.

Fifth House

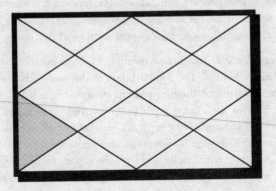

PREDOMINANT – advice and counsel, belly (upper abdomen and the organs therein, including the stomach and liver), children, discernment and discrimination

COMMON – artisans, disciples and students, education, embrace of a courtesan, ishta devata, gain through the partner (being eleventh from the seventh), heart, intelligence, intuition, mantras, memory, ministership, music, poetry, previous good karmas, yantras

RARE – books and authorship, fall from kingship or other high office, father, pilgrimage

COMMENTS One pervasive fifth-house theme is that of constructive intelligence from which good advice and counsel can flow. The accurate analysis of what is right and wrong usually characterizes those who hold the rank of government minister or statesperson. Such a person is called in Sanskrit a *mantri* (both 'someone who uses mantras' and 'an advisor'). North Indian jyotishis take this to be the house of formal education, since strong intelligence is often necessary for higher education; but many people obtain advanced degrees from venerable institutions without actually learning anything, and many well-educated people may lack formal education. Though education and intelligence often do correlate, it seems better to take the fourth house for education and the fifth for intelligence. The fifth house also rules teaching, the ability to educate, which is why it is associated with disciples and students.

Another pervasive fifth-house theme is that of creativity, be it procreation (creation of children) or creation of art, poetry or music, for both children and artists value spontaneity, amusement and fun. The fifth house being a house of dharma, it is associated with spirituality in its religious context (yantras, ishta devatas, previous karmas, and so on). Being ninth from the ninth, the fifth house represents the father; being eighth from the tenth, a fall from kingship or other high office; and, being eleventh from the seventh, gain through the partner.

Sixth House

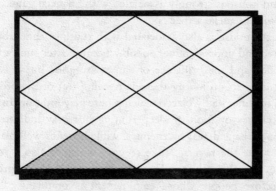

PREDOMINANT—accidents, anxieties, debt, diseases, enemies, lawsuits, maternal aunt or uncle, middle abdomen (and the organs therein, including the small intestine), service (especially routine), theft

COMMON — blame, combat, credit, cruel deeds, dejection, dishonor, doubt, fear of calamities and enemies, grief, injuries (due to assaults, falls, etc.), imprisonment, loss, miserliness, misunderstandings, orphans, outcasts, pain, poison, receiving charity and welfare, severe reproach, swelling in the body, trouble through servants and employees, untimely death, untimely meals, vices, vicious habits, victories or defeats, wicked deeds, worries, wounds

RARE — gain, stepmother, disagreements with cousins

COMMENTS Although the sixth house is not directly connected with healing as such, its association with disease means that planets which are beneficially placed in the sixth house may indicate individuals who benefit from ill-health, like healers, doctors, massage therapists, dietitians, rehabilitation therapists and the like. The sixth house rules debt because it is eight houses away from the eleventh house, and because it is a reflection house of the twelfth house of expenditure, which can drive one into debt. The sixth is, however, both an upachaya house and an artha house, so, though planets that have crossed the horizon have lost their power for a considerable time to come, planets in the sixth promise gradual fiscal improvement after initial setbacks. Planets in the second house, another artha house, are about to rise into sight again, which perhaps is why the second house is strongly associated with financial gains and only slightly with financial setbacks.

The sixth house is also associated with routines and habits, both productive and unproductive, possibly because after sunset both the light of day and the brilliance of sunset are gone but it is not yet time for bed, so ordinarily there is nothing out-of-the-ordinary to do; all is routine. Badly placed malefics here may indicate disruptions to daily chores or food or sleep routines, or may indicate vicious habits, or perhaps defeat by enemies, while benefics well placed here could indicate the reverse. Like service, which is also a routine, a humdrum life, this house indicates routines of career or profession, and therefore people whose employment is mundane. The sixth represents the maternal uncle because it is third (the brother) from the fourth house (the mother).

Seventh House

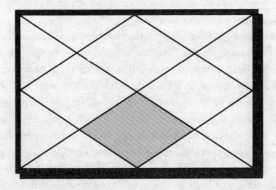

PREDOMINANT – courtship, death, enjoyment of men or women, partners in business, spouse, lower abdomen (and the organs therein)

COMMON – adultery, commercial business, controversies, desires in general, moral conduct, extramarital connections, foreign places, journey, journey within a journey, kidneys, litigation, roads, sexual desires

RARE – conveyances, lost wealth, aimless wandering, bed, adopted daughter or son, expenditure at night, gambling, one's house, losing one's way

COMMENTS The seventh house, the house farthest from the first, signifies 'the other' and, because it is also the reflection house of the first, it signifies 'significant others' (other than blood relations). Any person who is not ruled by some other house can at a pinch be classified as belonging to the seventh house. In adult life the most significant of others is probably the spouse, who is the other self (in the archetypal male–female mold). Business partners can also be significant others.

The seventh house is particularly linked to business partnerships because the seventh house of partnerships is ten houses away from the tenth house of business. Libra is the seventh house in the natural zodiac, and Libra's symbol, the merchant's scales, also links the seventh house to trade and commerce. A badly afflicted seventh house may lead to secret affairs, sexual perversions and other activities disapproved of by society, in which case 'the other' may bring litigation or conflict in his or her wake.

Because the first house indicates the birthplace and the seventh house is furthest from the first, the seventh indicates places far away from the birthplace, which leads Parashara to say that when the lord of the first house is in the seventh, the person will have his prosperity far away from home, all other factors being equal. Of course, the seventh also represents one's own home to some extent, being as it is the fourth house away from the fourth house. The seventh can also represent roads or paths, both literally and figuratively, in the sense of one's way through life. Maybe this explains the rare meaning of 'losing one's way', the aimless wandering which can occur if the seventh is badly afflicted by malefics. The reverse would likely be the case if the seventh was influenced solely by benefics.

Eighth House

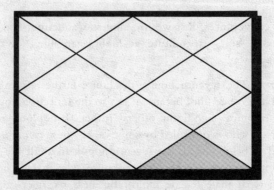

PREDOMINANT – accidents, bankruptcy, death, excretory organs (including the colon), external sexual organs, inheritance, litigation, mystery, occult, plots, poison, theft

COMMON – agonies, anger, annihilation, assassination, breaking of partnerships or friendships, cancer, crossing large bodies of water, dangerous/obstructed/fruitless journeys, decapitation, deep psychotherapy, deep and wild forests, defeat, disputes, enemy's fort or position, evil news, expenditure, fall from a height, fatigue, fear, grief, making loans (traditionally a dishonorable profession), a hole or cavity, imprisonment, insults, isolated/uncivilized/remote places, long-lasting diseases, longevity, long-standing property, loss in general, loss of a limb, *mangalasutra* (wedding necklace), mental distress, monetary loss, money in general, mountainous regions, a nose for ferreting out secrets, partner's money, permanent investments, profitless straying, punishment from authority, receiving charity, religious properties, research, robbery, ruthlessness, scandal or infamy, servitude, sidetrips, sorrow, sudden unexpected gain of money, taxes, total destruction, trouble to spouse, unchastity, war, weapons, wife, witchcraft and black magic, wounds

RARE – afflictions to the face, son, success in love affairs

COMMENTS Many eighth-house meanings are the same as or similar to sixth-house meanings (disease, enemies) and, to some degree, seventh-house meanings (death, litigation), but the eighth typically indicates longer duration and greater virulence. While a sixth-house disease is usually acute, eighth-house maladies tend to be chronic and often terminal. The sixth house indicates debt, while the eighth usually indicates bankruptcy. Both the sixth and seventh houses also represent litigation, but eighth-house litigation often involves severe legal difficulties that may destroy your life through long-term imprisonment, financial ruin, or humiliation by scandal.

The symbol of the eighth house of the natural zodiac is the scorpion, a creature whose venom is deadly to some. Death by scorpion sting comes primarily from neurologic shock, which may be one reason why the black arts (which attack an individual's mind and nerves) are represented by this house. When surprised, the scorpion retreats into its home, a hole in the ground, which recalls how a planet in the eighth house recedes almost voluntarily from view and influence, as if entering a deep cave.

One well-known modern jyotishi associates the eighth house with *patha*, traditional recitation of India's sacred or classical Sanskritic knowledge; we have found this to be an accurate attribution, and perhaps yet another indication of the reflection meaning of the second house, which governs oral forms of knowledge. Another reflection meaning of the second house may also be the *mangalasutra*, the wedding necklace which is given to a bride instead of a wedding ring at most Hindu weddings. It is not at all certain why the eighth house rules the mangalasutra, but we can speculate that, just as the second house is the house of immediate support for a child, the eighth house (by being both the second house to the seventh house and a reflection of the horoscope's second house) may represent immediate support to a newly married woman.

Ninth House

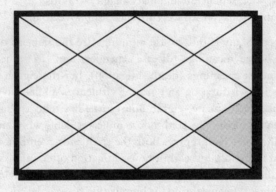

PREDOMINANT – affluence, good fortune, devotion to divine beings, pursuit of transcendental wisdom, father, foreign travel, guru, higher studies, pilgrimage, previous good karmas, thighs and hips
COMMON – baptisms, brother's wife, charity, conduct, counselor, donations, grandsons, legs, penance, piety, politics, preceptors, progeny, purity of mind, religion, respect to elders, *satsanga*, splendor, vehicles, virtue, wife's brothers, worship
RARE – fall from kingship or high office, loss of or change in career

COMMENTS Many desirable meanings associated with elevated things apply to the ninth, tenth and eleventh houses of the horoscope, the highest points in the heavens as seen at the moment of birth. They represent crowning achievement, the acme of perfection. The ninth house is generally associated with good luck and fortune, an association which is compounded by its being a house of dharma. The ninth house yields elegant and rightful prosperity and success that seem aptly bestowed awards for previous efforts. The rare meaning of loss of or change in career seems to arise from its position as twelfth house from the tenth house, and should be assumed to be likely only when the ninth is severely afflicted.

The ninth is the most important, by being the most advanced, of the dharma houses, so here dharma is applied in a purer, more spiritual way. Being a reflection of the third house, but higher in the zodiac and in the sky, the ninth house stands both for purity of mind and for religion, which is supposed to purify the soul. This higher reflection of third-house matters also applies to travel for, the ninth house being further along in the zodiac, it represents more and further travel, and travel which is undertaken for higher purposes, like *satsanga* ('contact with the true').

When you expose yourself to people who are saintly, some of their saintly qualities tend to rub off on you, making you a better person thereby; this is *satsanga*. The noted proverb, 'Live with a pig and you learn to grunt', is an apt expression of *kusanga*, the opposite of *satsanga*. The ninth house represents the guru because it represents the beings with whom you will have opportunities to enjoy *satsanga*; a severely afflicted ninth house may give you a false or fallen guru, with whom you will enjoy *kusanga*. The ninth house represents the father for South Indian jyotishis, perhaps because in that society the ideal to this day is that the father is the guru to his children. The ninth can also indicate progeny (being fifth from the fifth) and the spouse's brothers (being third from the seventh).

Tenth House

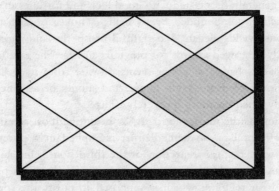

PREDOMINANT – authority, business, commerce, fame, government, knees, profession

COMMON – backbone, command, good and bad deeds, elders, fall from high position, father, governmental honors, great projects, great achievements, high position with government, honors, kingdoms, prestige, rain, rank, renunciation and asceticism, science, sky, status, trade, vehicles

RARE – adopted daughter or son, agriculture, debts, doctor, droughts, gait, living in foreign countries, mother, pilgrim rest-houses, sleep, sports

COMMENTS The tenth house, the highest point in the heavens visible to an observer, the place where planets reach their zenith, represents the zenith of human experience. Just as ninth represents the peak experience of dharma, the tenth is the peak of artha, and the eleventh the peak of kama. The tenth house, therefore, often indicates the professions, which are generally regarded as being superior to employment and other careers as ways to earn money. People normally secure any fame, honor or status indicated by the tenth house in their horoscopes via their careers or as a result of their authority. The tenth house, the strongest of the kendra houses, is a house of action, and when it is associated with certain planetary combinations it can cause the native to renounce career, and often action in general, for religious reasons.

Among the rare meanings of the tenth house, debt may be indicated if you are jobless or are unsuccessful at your profession due to an afflicted tenth house. The mother and agriculture are attributes of the tenth house as a reflection to the fourth house. The tenth represents adopted children by being the sixth from the fifth, since the sixth house mainly indicates relatives who lack clan or blood ties to the native. Rain and droughts are a likely tenth-house matter because the tenth rules the sky and because the tenth is the house farthest away from the primary house of usable water, the fourth. This distance from the fourth also indicates life in foreign countries. The organ represented by the tenth house, the legs, is probably why the tenth indicates gait.

Eleventh House

PREDOMINANT – calves, shins and ankles, desires, easy money, elder brother or sister, gains, income from career, things received (like gifts), wealth, wishes

COMMON – child's wife, decoration, employer's wealth, enemy's enemy, regaining things lost, enjoying many spouses, gain through education, relief of duress, hopes, longevity of mother, ministership, ornaments, jewelry, the paraphernalia of luxury, paternal uncle, playful sexual acts, vehicles

RARE – beautiful paintings, brother-in-law, skill in practical arts, worship of deities

COMMENTS The natural zodiac's eleventh house is Aquarius, whose symbol in Jyotish is a pot, a thing which stores that which has been attained. The pot also implies the free flow of what it stores, and so a strong eleventh house, which is a kama house, indicates the acquisition in plenty of one's desires, including beautiful ornaments and the paraphernalia of luxury. Because the eleventh is twelve houses from the twelfth house, it represents the end of expense and, when expenses end, only gains remain. When gains are profuse, what is extra can be stored and utilized in dalliance, including especially the enjoying of playful sexual acts with many partners. This is because the eleventh is the highest of the relationship houses, and because as a reflection to the fifth house it represents playfulness.

Examination of the eleventh house is most important when there is a question of recovery from illness, particularly a long-standing one. This is because (a) it is the sixth house from the sixth house and so is a derivative house of disease; (b) it is the twelfth house to the twelfth house, the house of hospitalization, and so it indicates the end of hospitalization; and (c) it is the reflection of the fifth house which, being the twelfth to the sixth house of disease, indicates the end of disease.

The eleventh house also represents: your paternal uncle (being third from the ninth); your child's wife (seventh from the fifth); your mother's longevity (eighth from the fourth); your employer's wealth (second from the tenth); your enemy's enemy (being sixth from the sixth; your enemy's enemy is your friend); and being a government minister (being a reflection of the fifth).

Twelfth House

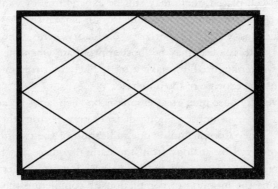

PREDOMINANT – comforts of the bed (like sleep and sex), convalescence, confinement, the end of anything, expenditures (including financial), feet, foreign residency, immigration, imprisonment, loss (including bodily vigor), moksha

COMMON – affliction of the limbs, arrest, charity, destination of soul after death, enemies, falls (physical, social or professional), hidden or secret things, misfortune, punishment, purchase of luxury items, sins, wandering far from home

RARE – acceptance of spouse in marriage, news about enemies

COMMENTS The twelfth house of the horoscope represents losses of all kinds to the native. The twelfth house represents bed comforts because sleep is a loss of consciousness, and because sex is a loss of semen and other bodily fluids. It stands for enemies and imprisonment because it reflects the sixth house.

The twelfth can represent charity, financial loss, or speculative investments which involve a short-term loss but may result in a long-term gain. To differentiate between these possibilities, jyotishis look to see how the twelfth house is placed and what is the nature of the grahas activating the twelfth house. A well-placed Jupiter in the twelfth house may indicate losses due to charity, which may however produce gains from the religious point of view. A poorly placed Jupiter in the twelfth, though, may indicate donations to a potentially fraudulent religious cause. Venus in the twelfth may indicate loss through the opposite sex (not just financial) if poorly placed; if well placed, there may still be expenditure of vitality and money in this direction, but commensurate enjoyment (*bhoga*) will be obtained as well. The purchase of luxury items, one of the meanings of this house, may be most appropriate when the twelfth house is well configured, to make it more likely that enjoyment will accompany the expense of the purchase.

The twelfth house puts great emphasis on alien lands because it is the ninth house (a house of long-distance travel) from the fourth house of home. 'Completion' is one indication of the twelfth house which is derived by analogy from the natural zodiac, in which the twelfth rashi, the last rashi in the natural forward order of the rashis, gains the meaning of completion by completing the zodiac. Completion of this existence implies the beginning of a new existence, so the twelfth also indicates the destination of the soul after death, be it heaven, hell, or the various other worlds. Since the twelfth is the last of moksha houses, this after-death state may be moksha, that release from manifested existence which is freedom from the need to exist. Sleep is a kind of mini-moksha; so is sex, for some people. The moksha principle also creates isolation or segregation, particularly if it involves life in an ashram or monastery, since the twelfth house being the fourth house (home) to the ninth house (guru) represents the home of one's preceptor.

SPECIAL CONSIDERATIONS

While each house has its own specific indications, every indication can also be analyzed according to house. To learn how a horoscope's owner may be able to obtain wealth, you can consider the first house as denoting wealth derived from one's charisma (modeling, acting) or physical prowess (athletics, dance), and the second house as indicating wealth obtained from one's family, from the interest on deposits or other liquid investments, or through speaking or oratory. The third house indicates wealth from siblings or through writings, and the fourth house wealth acquired from one's mother, or from land, vehicles or agriculture. Gambling or one's children are potential sources of wealth gained through the fifth house, while that wealth procured through disease, litigation or moneylending is sixth-house wealth.

The seventh house yields wealth through partnerships or one's spouse, and the eighth house through legacies or bequests, through such dealings with death as life insurance, through accident liability cases, or even through prostitution or pimping. Ninth-house wealth arrives through long-distance travel, higher education, teaching, or philosophy, and tenth-house wealth from the professions, government positions, the government, or one's superiors. While friends, societies, associates and elder siblings are primary sources of eleventh-house wealth, the eleventh indicates easy money of any sort (free-flowing prosperity) as well as money obtained through the realization of one's hopes, goals or aspirations. The wealth of the twelfth house commonly comes from foreign lands, such as through foreign trade (import/export) or emigration, or from other twelfth-house indications, such as the feet (e.g. podiatry). Every life experience can be similarly analyzed.

None of the principles below is an ironclad rule which works every time, though they are all often productive. Sometimes, as with anatomical rulerships, there are so many alternative interpretations possible that unwary students may run around in circles chasing their tails (tails are ruled by the eighth house); and from time to time every jyotishi faces the opposite problem: of having to determine a recently created thing's house, constellation, and planetary indicators. Jyotish being an idiom for which one requires a knack, a good jyotishi finds his way through such difficulties by relying on his ishta devata and on his guru's teachings to stay aligned with the Jyotir Vidya. While the hints in the discussion below can help you address the material presented in the far-from-exhaustive list of house meanings above, thinking through these meanings is up to you.

Anatomical Rulerships

Jyotish has more than one system for assigning anatomical rulerships. While the most common allocation parallels the constellations of the natural zodiac, an almost equally common method is to assign to the right side of the body the span from the precise degree of the ascendant to the point 180° opposite the lagna point (i.e. from the first house to the seventh house), and to the left side of the body the span from the seventh house to the first house. Then, starting from the first house as the head, the body parts are allocated sequentially to the right and left of the lagna.

In this system, that portion of the first house which follows the lagna point is taken to represent the right side of the head, and the portion which precedes the lagna point represents the head's left side. The right eye and nostril are signified by the second house, and the left eye and nostril by the twelfth house. The third and eleventh houses respectively represent the right and left ears, shoulders, hands and arms; the fourth and tenth houses stand for the chest, lungs, upper body, trunk and back; the fifth and ninth houses account for the heart and the organs of the upper abdomen, including the stomach; the sixth and eighth houses indicate the lower abdomen and pelvic organs, including the internal sex and urinary organs, and also the legs; and the seventh house represents the external genitals. Although the left/right principle is not applied with complete consistency (the fifth house for example rules the stomach and heart more than does the ninth), this method may make it possible to discover which side of an afflicted stomach or heart is more affected.

While the jyotishis who follow this system take the fifth house to indicate the heart, those who swear by the other approach insist that the heart be read from the fourth house. A third well-known method of anatomical allocation depends on the amshas known as the *drekkanas* (the third divisions of a rashi). There are yet other methods, just as there are many different systems of medicine. These methods do not agree with one another on every detail – nor do homeopathy, Ayurveda, or Chinese medicine – but they can all be useful, in well-trained hands, because they are all consistent within themselves.

In every system of anatomical allocation, the aspect and occupation of natural benefics affect for the better the body part ruled by that bhava, while natural malefics similarly placed affect that part for the worse. Mars, for example, who is known as 'the Crooked' (*Vakri*) because he moves irregularly across the sky, making crooked the body parts ruled by the houses he affects. A Mars in the second house could therefore cause a condition like squint, which is a crookedness of the eye. Mars in the twelfth house is likely to affect the feet; if he is well placed, he might cause only mild irregularities, like bunions; while when heavily afflicted, he may well inflict serious afflictions, like fractures.

Bhava Karakas

The meanings of any house are principally influenced by two planets: its ruler and its *karaka*. While a *karaka* (significator) is the planet which rules the matter under consideration, a *bhava karaka* is a planet that has great natural affinity with many of the primary matters ruled by whatever house is under consideration. For instance, because both Jupiter and the fifth house rule children, Jupiter becomes the bhava karaka of the fifth house. Similarly, since both the ninth house and the Sun rule the father, the Sun is a significator of the ninth house. Everything a human being can experience is ruled by one or other of the planets and, because a planet becomes the karaka of what it rules, each planet may be the significator for a wide variety of things. Many of the rulerships assigned to the planets in Chapter Four are in fact statements of planetary significations.

The most common house significators (bhava karakas) include:

FIRST HOUSE: Sun (health and vitality)
SECOND HOUSE: Jupiter (wealth and family)
THIRD HOUSE: Mars (younger siblings, courage, enterprise)
FOURTH HOUSE: Moon (the mother, emotions), Venus (vehicles), Mercury (education), Mars (property)
FIFTH HOUSE: Jupiter (children, speculation, statecraft, advice, intuition, condition of previous karmas, discernment)
SIXTH HOUSE: Mars (acute disease, litigation, bodily afflictions) and Saturn (debt, chronic disease)
SEVENTH HOUSE: Venus (marriage, other relationships, passion)

EIGHTH HOUSE: Saturn (unnatural desires, death/longevity, wills
and legacies, accidents, bankruptcies, sudden unexpected torment
and loss, chronic disease)

NINTH HOUSE: Jupiter (preceptors, higher education, spiritual
quests, charity, good or bad fortune) and Sun (the father, the
soul)

TENTH HOUSE: Mercury (commerce), Sun (government, authority,
fame), Saturn (tradition, employment), Jupiter (professions)

ELEVENTH HOUSE: Jupiter (elder siblings, friends, gains)

TWELFTH HOUSE: Saturn (segregation, solitude, losses)

Rotating the Chart

Some jyotishis value rotating the horoscope, and can tell a great
deal about a native's relatives simply by rotating the birth chart to
the appropriate bhava and taking it to be the lagna. To learn about
the native's mother, the native's fourth house is taken as her lagna.
The ninth from that fourth house (= the native's twelfth house)
then represents her travels, the tenth from the fourth (= the
native's own first house) her career, the sixth from the fourth (=
the native's ninth house) her illnesses, etc. This principle can also
be used to differentiate among brothers and sisters, by taking the
native's third house to represent the first younger sibling, the fifth
(third from the third) to represent the second younger co-born,
and so on; and by taking the eleventh house to represent the
brother or sister born immediately before the native, the ninth
(eleventh from eleventh) to represent the next older sibling, and
so on.

Children can be differentiated by a similar process: examine the
native's first child from his or her fifth house, but then rotate
the chart so that the fifth house becomes the lagna, and examine the
second child, which will be the first child's brother or sister, from
the third house away from that fifth house (which makes it the
native's seventh house). The next child, who will be a younger sibling of that second child, can be seen from the native's ninth house
(the third from the seventh), and further children accordingly.

Phaladipika suggests that there are two good ways to rotate the chart:

I. 'Whenever the results of any house are to be determined for a horoscope that house should be taken as the lagna and the results of the twelve houses thus formed (as counted from that house), such as the first house of appearance and the second house of wealth, should be analyzed accordingly' (25:20).

II. 'In the same way the results of the father, mother, brother, maternal uncle, son, husband and servant should be determined by treating the constellations occupied in the horoscope by their significators, viz. the Sun, Moon, etc., as their lagnas' (25:21).

Method I is exemplified above. Method II lists the relatives for whom the significators (karakas) are the planets listed in weekday order: Sun signifies father, Moon signifies mother, and so on. To study the horoscope of the husband (or wife), one would take the constellation in which Venus sits as the lagna; to examine servants (or subordinates), one would rotate the chart so that Saturn is in the lagna. In the case of Saturn, this principle also suggests that, all else being equal, those who have Saturn in the lagna will tend to serve other people in some way or other.

LAGNAS

While Western astrology assigns pre-eminence to the Sun sign, Jyotish awards that position to the ascendant, which gives greater insight into a native's life particulars than does any other factor in the horoscope. Observations of the intrinsic attributes of the various lagnas have aggregated over the centuries into a form of analysis. We have extracted from this aggregate a few salient, reliable principles:

· the symbolism of the constellation and its ruler
· the strength of the planets in the various houses
· the relationship of the lagna lord with the owners of various houses

· the house the Sun rules in that lagna
· the ownerships of the other houses in the lagna

Theoretical statements such as those that follow traditionally served to initiate dialogues between teacher and student, in which the mentor's exposition would increase the student's theoretical understanding into fully formed interpretive observations. Students who lack Jyotish gurus should themselves expand these statements as a guru would expand them, drawing them out into new statements by using these as a model, remembering all the while that these statements are only generally true. They are likely indications which will be modified by specific planetary positions.

Aries Lagna

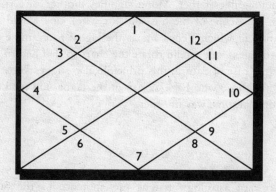

The ram, the symbol of Aries, is famous for eagerly running, headfirst, into obstacles. This may indicate a person who is prone to head injuries and who attempts to surmount his or her problems by excessive thinking. This emphasis on the head is compounded by Aries being the first house in the natural zodiac, and because Mars is known for its retrogression, which gives Arians a tendency for displaying idiosyncratic behavior. These behaviors may be extroverted, because Mars is extroverted. Mars, which indicates a general predisposition to violence, be it through an accident or an argument, is a natural significator of accidents. This tendency for accidents is reinforced by Mars's simultaneous rulership of the eighth house, which also rules accidents. This reinforcement is further enhanced if we take the violent, accident-prone Ketu to be the co-ruler of Aries.

Most of the characteristics of Mars also characterize Pitta, the impatient dosha which Mars rules and which is therefore often predominant in Arians, particularly because the fiery Sun is exalted in the ascendant of an Aries lagna. This dedication to intensity is compounded by the fact that the Sun, a friend of the first-house lord, is exalted in the first house as lord of the fifth house. The rapid, powerful insight which the fiery Mars and Sun together create may fuel innate Aries impatience toward those who do not share their rapidity. Unchecked, this impatience may develop into frustration, and then into anger at being held back.

Mars, the ascendant lord, is exalted in Capricorn, which is the tenth house here. The Aries native therefore innately enjoys great motivation and ambition, and tends to pioneer things well. Capricorn's ruler, Saturn, is debilitated in the first house and, since Mars represents bursts of energy and Saturn represents stamina, Arians often do not strategize well for the longer term. This is why Aries natives often need to be reminded that they will enjoy maximum success in life when they slow down and consolidate their gains.

The fact that Mars, the lord of the lagna, is debilitated in Cancer, which here is the fourth house of home, militates toward a life lived away from one's homeland, and a disinclination to settle down. Another reason why Aries natives are said to roam around like rams is that Jupiter is a mutually good friend of Mars, which causes the matters of the houses that Jupiter rules (houses nine and twelve) to tend to come to the forefront of an Arian's life.

The inherent fourth-house weakness in an Aries lagna also promotes disagreements with the mother, particularly if the Moon, the fourth lord and significator of the mother, is afflicted. The potential for differences with and/or separations from siblings is enhanced because Mercury, the lord of the third and sixth houses, is the enemy of Mars, the significator of the third and sixth houses. This blends together in an unattractive way the sixth-house indication of suffering and the third-house indication of siblings. Since the Sun rules the fifth house of progeny, and is a mutual friend of Mars,

Aries natives may be very interested in offspring. They do not, however, usually produce a large brood because the Sun does not signify children. Also the natural fieriness of the Sun and Mars tends to reduce fertility because Pitta 'burns' the sperm or ovum.

Taurus Lagna

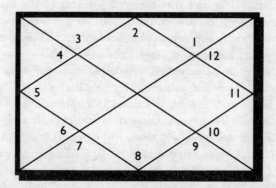

Taurus's symbol is the bull, an animal known for its strength. Like bulls, Taurus people often exhibit physical or mental strength and rise to anger slowly but, once irked, they become irresistible forces. Taurus may also give the native a bull neck, since it is lord of the second house in natural zodiac.

When Taurus rises in a horoscope, Mercury (a planet of discernment and intellect who is a mutual friend of the lagna lord Venus) rules both the second house of money and the fifth house of discernment. Mercury's double bearing on mental functions in this lagna often results in a sharp intellect, which tends to make Taureans good writers (since both Mercury and the fifth house indicate writing) and often makes them use their minds to acquire money (since both Mercury and the second house rule commerce). This tendency is reinforced by the fact that Taurus's ruler Venus is a materialistic, Rajasic graha, which is exalted in the eleventh house of gain as one of the significators for gains. Saturn's rulership of the ninth and tenth houses promotes the pursuits of knowledge and of career, particularly since Saturn is friendly to Venus.

Taurus natives rarely have many children, since Virgo (the fifth house for a Taurus lagna) is a barren constellation. The fact that lagna lord Venus is debilitated in the fifth house also indicates trouble with children, or perhaps with general artistic creativity. But discernment will not be affected, because fifth lord Mercury is exalted in the fifth house. Since the luxury-loving Venus rules the sixth house (food, diet) as well as the lagna, Mercury's rulership of the second house tends to create a strong interest in, and a loving relationship with, food. Whether Taureans become good cooks or simply overeaters will depend on the strengths and positions of the grahas in the actual horoscope.

Mars is simultaneously the lord of the seventh and twelfth houses, and Venus the lord of the first and sixth houses. This situation tends to disturb relationships because the twelfth house is the negation house to the ascendant, and the sixth house is the negation house to the seventh (being twelve houses away from the sixth). Our jyotish guru says, 'Venus, the lord of the first house for a Taurus lagna, is a very passive graha, a conciliator, while Mars, the seventh lord, is very assertive and bossy. White is the color of Venus, and red the color of Mars. When you mix red and white together only red will remain, which means that Taureans tend to submerge their own individuality in order to make their relationships work. Because this approach does not work in the long run, marriage for a Taurus native is often unsuccessful.' That Jupiter simultaneously rules houses eight and eleven implies that the one affects the other, and may indicate a general tendency to trouble through older siblings or friends, or trouble to them.

Gemini Lagna

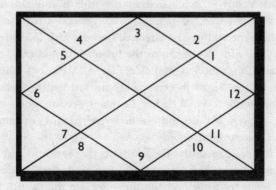

Gemini's symbol, the twins, proclaims it to be the most dual of the four dual rashis. Since these twins are a male and a female, Gemini natives tend to blend both male and female energies within themselves. This blending does not promote happiness through progeny, though, because Venus is lord of both the fifth house of children and the twelfth house of loss, which implies expenditures through children. This conjoining of houses five and twelve does, however, encourage enjoyment, since the twelfth house rules enjoyment, the fifth rules play, and Venus is the significator for pleasure. This combination particularly suggests sexual enjoyment because *maithuna*, one of the Sanskrit words for sexual intercourse, is derived from *mithuna*, the word for 'couple', which happens to be the Sanskrit name for the constellation Gemini.

Because all the kendras in a Gemini lagna are controlled by dual rashis, Geminians tend to be dual-minded about relationships and residence. This is particularly true of career, since the lagna lord, the dual planet Mercury, is debilitated in the tenth house of profession. Geminis are frequently attracted to the arts as a profession because Venus, the lord of the creative fifth house and significator of the creative arts, is exalted in the tenth house. They may not succeed at this aim, though, because Venus is also lord of the twelfth house of loss. Gemini natives are credited with loquacity, presumably both because the Moon, who is renowned for its fluctuations, rules the second house of speech, and because Mercury, who rules speech, also rules the lagna. Speech may not always serve Geminis well, however, for the Moon is Mercury's enemy.

Because Gemini is the third house of intellect in the natural zodiac, and because the Sun rules the third house of a Gemini lagna, Gemini natives tend to rely on their intellects, particularly because Mercury is the planet of intellect. This reliance may however create difficulties for those Geminis who set out to pursue a spiritual path, especially since Saturn, the lord of the ninth house of spirituality, is a materialist graha who also happens to be lord of the eighth house, the negation house to the ninth. This tendency is compounded by the fact that Mercury is the enemy of Jupiter, the natural significator of spirituality. Geminis usually prefer philosophy to devotional practices when they do go for spirituality,

Gemini people tend to have unstable health because Mercury is the enemy of Mars. Mars being the lord of the sixth and the eleventh (sixth from the sixth) houses and also the significator of the sixth house is for Gemini triply potentiated to cause disease. This situation may also indicate ill-health to friends or older siblings, who are ruled by the eleventh house.

Cancer Lagna

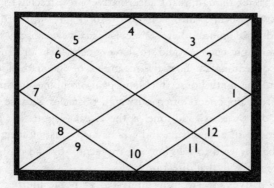

Like its symbol, the crab, whose hard carapace covers a soft underbelly, a Cancerian's formidable intellect sits atop a pool of emotions. One reason why these emotions tend to emerge to cloud thought-processes in times of crisis is that Mercury, the planet of the mind and lord of the third house of intellect, is also the lord of the twelfth house of loss. Another reason is the profound influence of the emotional grahas on this lagna: the Moon rules the first house, Cancer is the fourth house of emotion in the natural zodiac, and Venus rules the fourth house. A third reason is that while the Moon, the significator of emotions, is debilitated in the fifth house of discernment, the fifth lord Mars, who signifies a piercing intellect, is debilitated in the first house.

The reciprocal debilitation of the first and fifth lords, which makes it doubly difficult for the discriminating intellect to prevail over the emotions, often also creates a lack of or disappointment with children, including even the loss of a child. The friendship of the Moon with Mars makes the Cancer native strongly attracted to the ideals of intellect and progeny, but the reciprocal debility tends to prevent them from readily developing and sustaining these two areas of life. The friendship of the Moon with the dynamic tenth lord Mars does, however, create a dynamic interest in career.

The Moon being exalted as lagna lord in the eleventh house makes friends and associates important to a Cancer native, though those friendships may be as varied and as fluctuating as the Moon. It also happens, though, that Cancer natives are attracted to, or tend to attract, opponents, since lagna lord Moon and sixth lord Jupiter are friendly to one another. There is usually a capacity both to benefit through enemies and to have one's luck obstructed by enemies, depending on how the meanings of the sixth house (enemies) and the ninth house (luck and gain) combine. In this lagna, benefits from opponents often outweigh obstacles because Jupiter, the ruler of houses six and nine, is the Great Negotiator. Jupiter's dual rulership of a dussthana and a kona also causes Cancer natives both to be attracted to religion and frequently to find obstructions to their progress in that direction.

Cancer natives are strongly interested in home life because the Moon, Cancer's ruler, is a domestic graha who is the significator of the fourth house of home; because Venus, the planet of pleasure and enjoyment, rules the fourth house; and because the Sun rules the second house of family. Since Saturn, a secretive graha, owns both the seventh and eighth houses, and since the eighth house indicates secrets, Cancer natives often keep their partnerships and marriages private. The blending of houses seven and eight also suggests obstacles or delays to marriage, or obstacles in married life. There may be some tragedy associated with death, like chronic disease or an unnatural death, because both Saturn and the eighth house suggest tragedy, and because the seventh is a maraka house which is ruled by Saturn.

Leo Lagna

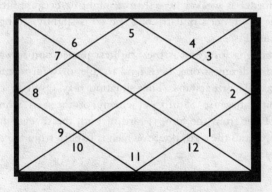

Leo natives often possess a striking, singular appearance, a regal manner, and an inclination to be served, as a king is served by his court or a lion by his pride, because the lion, Leo's symbol, is the king of beasts, and because the Sun, the lord of Leo, is the royal planet, the center around which all the other planets revolve. An Indian proverb mandates 'One jungle, one lion', and indeed the fact that the Sun is debilitated in the third house suggests that Leo natives neglect to make room for their younger siblings, who must find their own jungles in which to roar. It also suggests that the average Leo often displays more bluster than courage.

That the Sun is both the lord of Leo lagna and the significator of the first house creates a strong sense of self-interest for Leo natives, which may manifest as involvement in politics or government (since Leo is the fifth house of ministry formation in the natural zodiac). Leos are often lucky with, or are attracted to investing in, property, because Mars, the Sun's friend, is simultaneously lord of the fourth house (property) and the ninth house (luck, gains).

The fact that the Sun, which represents the *atma* or soul, signifies both the father and spiritual life, is exalted in the ninth house of father and spiritual life may cause an interest in spirituality, and may indicate that the native's father is an important man. Jupiter, the significator for children, is for Leo lord of both the fifth house of offspring and the eighth house of death, which either limits the number of progeny or affects those children adversely. The eighth-house influence is weaker here than it might be because fifth-house Sagittarius is Jupiter's mulatrikona and so is slightly stronger than eighth-house Pisces.

Because lagna lord Sun is the brightest planet, and seventh lord Saturn is the dimmest one, Leos tend to rule, or want to rule, their marriages and partnerships. This situation may result in troubled relationships, because Saturn, an enemy of the Sun who is the furthest planet from the Sun, is lord of both the seventh house of relationships and the sixth house (which is twelfth from the seventh) of enemies.

Virgo Lagna

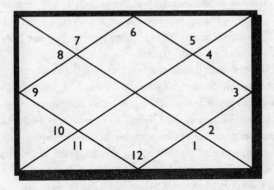

Virgo's symbol is a maiden, indicating shyness, an interest in purity, and a certain lack of skill in worldly matters, even if worldly-wise. The maiden holds a sheaf of grain in one hand and fire in the other, which may imply food (e.g. the service and hospitality industries) but does not suggest progeny, for she is a maiden. Since Virgo is the sixth house of the natural zodiac and so indicates disease, and since the Sun rules the twelfth house of hospitals, Virgos tend to be very interested in hygienics and health care, which is one sort of service industry.

Venus, a mutual friend of lagna lord Mercury, rules both the ninth house of higher learning and the second house of classical learning. Virgo natives tend therefore to love classical culture and education, particularly since Jupiter, who signifies education, rules the fourth house of education. Virgos are often interested in developing skill at a trade, especially one centered around detail (Mercury being the lagna lord, the lord of detail, and the lord of the tenth house of profession) because Virgo as the sixth house in the natural zodiac also represents the trades.

Mercury, an analytical and calculating planet, is exalted in the ascendant, which when (coupled with the fact that the incisive Mars is lord of the third house of intelligence) gives Virgo natives a propensity for analysis and calculation. Aries, which represents the head, is a Virgo ascendant's eighth house, and Mars, the ruler of Aries, owns for a Virgo lagna both the eighth and the third house. This connection of the head with the eighth house causes a Virgo native always to think unusual thoughts. Virgos will also resist following normal procedures, particularly because Mars ('the Crooked') has a contrarian nature.

These factors, combined with Mercury's debilitation in the seventh house, promote marital difficulties for Virgos. Also, since the fifth house and sixth house are both ruled by Saturn, a graha who does not indicate children and, being old himself, is against children, Virgos may experience difficulties with their children. Venus, the lord of the second and ninth houses, is debilitated in the first house, which makes Virgos fastidious about food (second house). Like natives of Gemini, Mercury's other rashi, Virgos are also inclined in religious matters (ninth house) to be ruled more by their heads than by their hearts, particularly because Venus, who is debilitated in the lagna, signifies emotions.

Mars, who is the enemy of the lagna lord Mercury, is the worst graha for a Virgo ascendant because it rules both the third and eighth houses, houses of longevity and death which are both dussthanas. The eighth house rules both accidents and surgery, and Mars is the significator of violence (both by accident and by cutting); since both these houses are tinged by the influence of Mars, Virgo natives have a distinct propensity for mishaps and surgery.

Libra Lagna

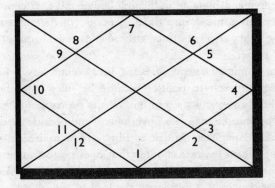

Libra's symbol, the scales (a shopkeeper's weighing scales, not the scales of justice), makes natives of this mercantile rashi less likely to be lawyers than retailers or merchants, a predilection which is reinforced by Libra's position as the natural zodiac's seventh house. Librans do, however, particularly like public professions because the Moon, a public planet, is the lord of the tenth house, which indicates both the public and one's profession. Since Venus is debilitated in the twelfth house of a Libra lagna, Librans often have difficulty controlling expenditures and tend to waste their resources, both physical and financial. This debility may lead them into sexual escapades which they may live to regret.

Because Venus is Jupiter's enemy, Venus is disinclined to accept any well-intended advice from Jupiter, the lord of wisdom and intuition, and Librans have difficulty accepting wise counsel. When coupled with Jupiter's ownership of two dussthanas in this lagna, this tendency causes a Libran's wisdom to become somewhat clouded. This is partially true for Taurus natives too, who are stubborn bulls, but is less pronounced for them because in a Taurus lagna Jupiter owns the eleventh house of friends. Also Libra is a fierce, active rashi which ignores advice actively, while Taureans are merely passive ignorers of good counsel.

The Sun rules the eleventh house for this lagna and, because lagna lord Venus is a social planet, friends, clubs and societies are important to Librans. But they are often led astray by bad company, since the Sun is debilitated in the first house, and over concern with their social lives may cause them to permit their friends to waste their time. They also tend to be fashion conscious, because Venus is a 'flashy' planet.

Saturn, a mutual friend of lagna lord Venus, gives Librans a pronounced interest in politics because he rules both the fourth house (the masses) and the fifth house (the formation of governing bodies); because he indicates government; and because he is exalted in the ascendant. That Saturn as fifth lord is exalted in the first house might also indicate children, but does not do so here to any great degree because Saturn does not indicate children. As for the Aries ascendant, in a Libra lagna the lord of the seventh house of relationship is identical with the lord of the second house of family. This situation makes marriage more likely to endure for Arians and Librans than for natives of Taurus or Scorpio lagnas. That Libra is the seventh house of the natural zodiac reinforces this likelihood.

Scorpio Lagna

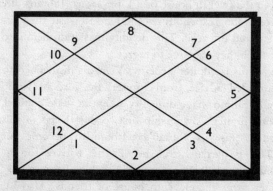

Scorpios, who prefer to avoid following normal procedures, are natural troublemakers who are as rigid as the scorpion's shiny, solid exoskeleton. Sage advice from our Jyotish guru to a Scorpio student: 'Compromise with yourself or you'll be digging your own grave.' One reason for the peculiarities of the Scorpionic personality is that Aries, which rules the head, occupies the sixth house of disease. The scorpion's tail, which is filled with poison, symbolizes an interest in chemistry, drugs, pharmacology and the like, all of which are sixth-house indications. Natives of Scorpio lagna are usually interested in medicine, with a particular penchant for surgery, because lagna lord Mars ('the Cutter') represents the scalpel. Mars is also lord and significator of the sixth house of acute illnesses, those which may need emergency surgery.

Being the eighth house in the natural zodiac, Scorpio also suggests such eighth-house medical indications as poison, surgery, chronic illness and death. Scorpios are renowned for their interest in death (which the scorpion also symbolizes), and in the occult (another eighth-house matter). Scorpios like to penetrate secrets (since lagna lord Mars likes to penetrate, and since the eighth house rules secrets) and like to get the goods on other people.

Scorpio natives usually have a strong interest in sex, since Scorpio is ruled by the virile Mars, Scorpio's twelfth house of bed pleasures is ruled by the sexy Venus, and sex is yet another indication of the eighth house. Unfortunately, as for Taurus lagna, in a Scorpio ascendant the lord of the seventh house (Venus here) is also the twelfth lord, and the ascendant lord (Mars here) is also the sixth lord. Since the twelfth house is sixth from the seventh and the sixth house is twelfth from the seventh (and so the negation house to the twelfth house), relationships tend to be lost, particularly since Venus is also the significator for marriage. Also, as for Taurus, the passive conciliator Venus must marry the assertive, bossy Mars, and the admixture of the white of Venus with the red of Mars will yield only red. Scorpios thus tend to try to submerge their partners' individuality, which is a poor prescription for a healthy relationship.

Scorpios often dispute with their parents, since Saturn, Mars's mutual enemy, rules the fourth house of parents (the mother in particular), and because Mars is debilitated in the ninth house of father. Saturn represents dearth, is old (not young), and is the mutual enemy of lagna lord Mars; these factors may cause Saturn, the third lord, to limit the number of younger siblings, or to promote disagreements with them due to the wide divergence of the native's opinions from those of his juniors.

Being a lagna of Mars, the individualist planet, Scorpios may have exceedingly heterodox views on religion and philosophy, and may have difficult relationships with their mentors, because the lagna lord is debilitated in the ninth house of spirituality. This situation is compounded because the Moon, lord of the ninth house, is debilitated in the first house of personality. Scorpios often follow teachings without deeply personalizing them and may, particularly if one or both of those grahas is afflicted, speak out against gurus, vidyas or religion.

Scorpio natives usually have strong ambitions, since the Sun rules and is the significator for the tenth house of fame, and are often brave, for Mars is exalted in the third house of courage. Scorpios are hardly ever satisfied in their own birthplace or dwelling place because Saturn as lord of the fourth house is inimical to Mars, the lord of the lagna, and because the changeable Moon is lord of the ninth house of travel. Scorpios frequently run into difficulties while on the road, though, because of Mars's debility in the ninth house.

Sagittarius Lagna

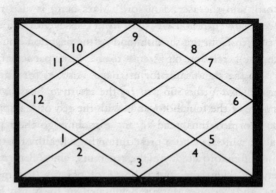

Sagittarius appears in Jyotish as a bow, an image which suggests an ability to prevail over enemies, for Sagittarians aim high. This competitiveness is often displayed in the sports arena. Since lagna lord Jupiter is the enemy of no graha (though it does have enemies), natives of Sagittarius tend to be able to prevail over their enemies by winning them over, in an active way (since it is a fierce, action-oriented, masculine sign). This tendency is reinforced because Venus is simultaneously lord of the sixth house of enemies and the eleventh house of friends. Because Venus is Jupiter's enemy, friends may become enemies and enemies friends in a Sagittarian's life.

Sagittarians are often blunt speakers because Capricorn (which is ruled by the blunt Saturn) occupies the second house of speech, where Jupiter is debilitated. The second house also rules finances, which may indicate problems controlling money because of being inappropriately generous (Jupiter represents money and, as ruler of the lagna, makes the native charitable). Mercury, as the lord of both the seventh and tenth houses, often makes for an intellectual or mental career and suggests the possibility of dual careers, since the intellectual, dual Mercury is (like Jupiter) a tenth-house significator. Mars here is lord of both Aries, the fifth house of children, and Scorpio, the twelfth house of loss, but this situation does not necessarily prevent progeny because Aries is Mars's *mulatrikona*. Since the *mulatrikona* is stronger than the other constellation that a planet rules, fifth-house indications supersede those of the twelfth house here.

Many factors give Sagittarians a strong interest in spiritual matters: Sagittarius is the ninth house of the natural zodiac; the Sun (which represents the soul) is both lord and significator of the ninth house in a Sagittarius ascendant; Jupiter, a significator for spirituality, is lagna lord; and the Sun and Jupiter are mutual friends. Also, Jupiter is lord of the fourth house of happiness, which implies that Sagittarians can derive happiness from spiritual pursuits. Sagittarius is a lucky lagna, because the Sun rules the ninth house of good fortune and lagna lord Jupiter is exalted in the eighth house (which protects against the loss of that good luck).

Capricorn Lagna

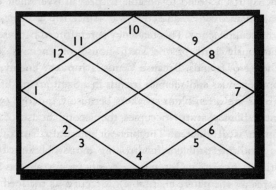

Capricorn's symbol in Jyotish is the *makara*, a word which is usually translated 'crocodile' but also indicates a sort of generic sea-monster. The *makara* symbolizes ambition, both by the ferocity of its bite into its prey (its goal) and by its amphibious nature, which betokens its aspiration to master two elements (Earth and Water). This ambition is particularly strong because Capricorn is the tenth house of the natural zodiac, because Venus is the lord of the fifth house of speculation and the tenth house of career, and because Saturn is exalted in the tenth house of a Capricorn ascendant. Mars for Aries lagna is also exalted in the tenth house, but Mars frenetically pursues fast progress, while Saturn stands for the slow, steady, behind-the-scenes, gradual sort of progress that often comes later in life. Slow progress in career becomes particularly pronounced for Capricorn because Saturn is the slowest of the planets, and because Capricorn is both a passive rashi and an Earth rashi.

As with Aries, the lord of a Capricorn lagna is debilitated in the fourth house, which often presages a dissatisfaction with family life, ancestors, roots and property. Because Venus is the lord of the fifth house of offspring, however, Capricorns are famous for doting on their children. Mars, the significator for property, is exalted in the first house of this ascendant as lord of the fourth house of property and the eleventh house of gain; this betokens gain through property.

The native may be concurrently dissatisfied with any property gained, since Saturn, another of the property significators, is debilitated in the fourth house. Capricornians tend to be money-minded because people who have been seized by Saturn, the lord of the first and second houses here, tend to become miserly and stingy.

Saturn, who (being dry) is the Vata significator, promotes a Vata constitution for Capricornians, inclining them to long slender bodies, sometimes to the point of gauntness. Arthritis may also be indicated, because Capricorn is an Earth sign, and Earth is opposed to movement. Some texts state that Capricornians are religious hypocrites because Jupiter, the significator of spirituality, rules two dussthanas (the third and twelfth houses) and is debilitated in the first house of a Capricorn ascendant. We have also observed that people who have an interest in India often have major placements in Capricorn, particularly because its lord Saturn represents conservative, old things like tradition, and because Saturn enables people to plod toward their goals patiently.

Aquarius Lagna

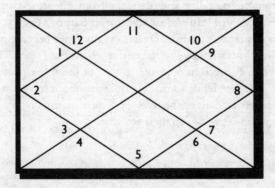

Jyotish's symbol for Aquarius is a pot which contains things (like water) that have been gathered together and stored. Aquarians thus enjoy gathering knowledge, because Venus is lord of two education houses (four and nine) and Saturn is exalted in the ninth house.

However, Aquarians are more often interested in material and scientific expertise than in spiritual wisdom, because both Venus and Saturn are materialists. Gains alternate with losses in the lives of Aquarians, for Saturn, the significator of the twelfth house of loss, rules both the first and twelfth houses of this lagna. As with Capricorn, progress in career is slow (Saturn being the slowest planet). This tendency is less pronounced for Aquarius than for Capricorn because Aquarius is a masculine (and hence archetypally active) rashi.

Aquarius being the eleventh house of the natural zodiac, and Jupiter being the lord of the eleventh house for an Aquarius lagna, Aquarians show interest in friends and in clubs and societies. They are, however, usually not overly excited by money (another eleventh-house matter) because Jupiter, the lord and significator of two materialistic houses, does not feel at home in either and because Saturn does not indicate money. Saturn does not indicate friends either, but for Aquarius the eleventh house is Sagittarius which, though it has little affinity for money (see above), is ruled by Jupiter, who has great affinity for social obligations and for friends. Saturn's debilitation occurs in the third house of an Aquarius lagna, which promotes timidity and detracts from siblings, particularly since Mars, the third lord and significator, is Saturn's enemy.

Rahu as Aquarius's co-ruler creates (as for Aries because of Ketu) a certain idiosyncratic tinge to the native's behavior, since Rahu and Ketu move in a direction opposite to that of the other planets. The Saturnian influence tends to make Aquarians more introverted than the Martian Aries natives. Natives of Aquarius usually try to hide their idiosyncrasies and keep their activities secret.

Pisces Lagna

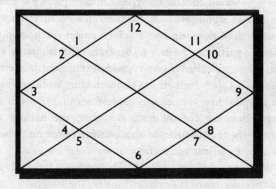

The symbol for Pisces, two fish swimming in opposite directions, reflects the native's contradictory ambitions and ideals. It may also indicate two marriages, because Mercury, the lord of the seventh house, is a dual planet which is debilitated in Pisces, a mutable rashi which is second only to Gemini in its dual nature. Mercury being also the fourth lord, instability in education (Mercury = intellect) or at home is possible. That Jupiter is exalted in the fifth house of advice, though, makes Pisceans love to teach, because Jupiter is simultaneously the lagna lord, the significator for the fifth house, and lord of the tenth house of public activities.

Venus is the worst graha for a Pisces ascendant, just as Mars is for a Virgo lagna, because Venus, who is an enemy of lagna lord Jupiter, rules both the third and eighth houses. Venus is exalted in the first house of a Pisces ascendant, which multiplies its malevolence, particularly for marriage, since it is the marriage significator. The Pisces lagna is however good for children, for lagna lord Jupiter is exalted in the fifth house of children, and fifth lord Moon is Jupiter's friend. Jupiter's exaltation in the fifth may give exalted children, or exalted relationships with children.

Because lagna lord Jupiter has no enemies, Pisces wins over its enemies passively (being a gentle, archetypally feminine rashi) but, because Pisceans tend to be benignly inclined toward others, many people take advantage of them. The native may feel or may actually be let down by friends, older siblings, clubs or societies, since Jupiter is debilitated in the eleventh house. Jupiter's fifth-house exaltation as the significator of wisdom creates an interest in the development of wisdom, and also a fascination for poetry (a fifth-house matter), particularly since Cancer, the fifth house, is ruled by the Moon, the significator of poetry, which represents the emotional mind. The Sun as sixth lord effects an interest in medicine, especially if there is hospital involvement, because Pisces is the twelfth house (segregation, hospitals) of the natural zodiac, and because the isolated Saturn, the significator of the twelfth house, is lord of the twelfth house of a Pisces ascendant.

CHAPTER SEVEN

THE PANCHANGA

SOLI-LUNAR JYOTISH

It seems inevitable that the Sun and the Moon, the two most striking objects in the sky, should have evolved into time markers. The advent of the Sun against certain fixed stars heralded the return of the seasons of the year, and the changing phases of the Moon served to segment this lengthy period into more wieldy portions (the word 'month' is derived from the word 'moon', which is related to a Sanskrit word meaning 'to measure'). Lunar calendars likely predated solar ones, particularly because marking time's passage by watching the Moon's movement through the star-sprinkled vault of the night sky is easier than following the Sun's motion through the invisible stars of the blue sky of day. Many ancient cultures besides that of India, including those of Babylon, China, Israel and Arabia, incorporated the Moon into their calendars.

When timing certain events in Jyotish, it is essential to do so in the context of an Indian calendar. While some of modern India's many regional calendars are based on the Sun and others on the Moon, almost all employ the five measurements which are collectively known as the *panchanga* ('five limbs'). These measurements – the *varana, nakshatra, tithi, karana,* and *yoga* – are central to Jyotish, for they effectively define an Indian calendar. Despite the common misconception that Jyotish is a purely lunar astrology, it was the Sun's movement which inspired jyotishis to use the twelve rashis, the twelve bhavas, and the time-unit day (*varana*). The Moon's movement along its path in the heavens inspired the use of the twenty-seven *bhas* or *nakshatras* (lunar asterisms). The thirty *tithis* (phases or days of a lunar month), their halves (the *karanas*), and the twenty-seven soli-lunar *yogas* (combinations) are all generated from the positions of the Sun and Moon relative to one another.

Days can be either *lunar* or *solar*. A *lunar day* is the time it takes the Moon to traverse either one tithi or one nakshatra, and a *solar day* is the time between one sunrise and the next. The *solar year* is either the time it takes the Sun to pass from one vernal equinox to the next (a period of 365.2422 days, known as a *tropical year*) or the time it takes the Sun to pass through all the twelve constellations of the zodiac (a period of 365.2564 days, known as a *sidereal year*). The sidereal year is some twenty minutes longer than the tropical year, a time variance which is central to one of the major differences between Jyotish and Western astrology, the *ayanamsha*.

A *lunar month* is either the time it takes the Moon to pass through all the twelve constellations of the zodiac (a period of 27.3217 days, known as a *sidereal month*) or the time it takes the Moon to go from one new Moon to the next (a period of 29.5306 days, known as the *synodic month*). It may well be that the zodiac was divided into twelve constellations because a year consisting of twelve synodic months averages 354.3672 days, which is only 10.9 days less than a year measured by the Sun. Calendar makers realized that the lunar and solar years could be synchronized, for the cumulative difference between 36 synodic months and three solar years amounts to roughly 29 days, or approximately one synodic month.

In the same way that the Gregorian calendar is synchronized with other observed celestial cycles by making every fourth year a leap year, Indian jyotishis add one additional or *intercalary* lunar month (a month which was originally dedicated to spiritual practices) every two and two-third years or so to synchronize the cycles of the Sun and Moon. This elegant modification makes Jyotish irrevocably *soli-lunar*, rather than either entirely solar or entirely lunar.

SVARODAYA

In the world of Tantra, where male and female tend to mirror one other, the Sun represents the universal male or Shiva principle, and the Moon the universal female or Shakti principle. The new and full Moons represent to the month roughly what the solstices mean to the year, for during one synodic month the Moon covers the same 360° of sky that the Sun covers during one sidereal year. However, while the Sun's 360° cycle is divided into 12 months of 30° each, the Moon's cycle is divided into 30 days of 12°. This makes the lunar month a sort of mirror image of the solar year.

Tantric Jyotish contributes yet another important alignment of the solar and lunar cycles in the form of a system of breathing patterns called *Svarodaya*. Like most of Tantric Jyotish's unique methods, Svarodaya, which has been preserved principally by oral transmission from a guru to an initiated disciple, provides some fascinating insights into the profundity of Tantric thought; Svarodaya was disclosed by Lord Shiva, one of India's principal deities, to his divine spouse Parvati, intending that she keep it secret. The great yogi Matsyendra Nath, the first head of the Nath lineage of immortal yogis, took the form of a fish and, listening carefully, stealthily absorbed that vidya into himself. He then taught it to his disciple Gorakh Nath, who taught it to his disciples. Thus, it was transferred era by era, until today.

Svarodaya's basic principles make use of the difference of effect between the functioning of the *Lunar Nadi* (the left nostril) and the *Solar Nadi* (the right nostril). Healthy humans do not normally breathe out of both nostrils simultaneously. Instead, one nostril alone breathes at a time, usually for ninety minutes; then the other nostril takes over, again for about ninety minutes. Only occasionally, particularly around sunrise and sunset, do both nostrils work together.

One of the most fundamental and widespread tenets of the Indian world view is that everything which exists outside the human body in the cosmos (the macrocosm) also exists, in altered form, within it (the microcosm). This principle, known as the Law of the Macrocosm and Microcosm, is India's statement of the old Hermetic doctrine: 'As above, so below'. Svarodaya implies that, among other things, those who know the movements of the Sun, the Moon and the other planets can use this knowledge to predict the nature of the movement of the breath in their bodies, or in other bodies. Likewise the movements of breath in the microcosm can be used to determine the positions of the planets in the macrocosm.

One way in which this can be done is to use the time unit *nadi* (literally, 'a channel, tube, or hollow stem') to correlate the movements of the breath, the pulse, and the *prana* (the life force). The *nadi*, which represents 24 minutes of time (half of one *muhurta*), is also defined in the *Surya Siddhanta* to be equal to 360 respirations (also called *prana*), each respiration being defined as the time it takes clearly to enunciate ten long syllables.

24 minutes of time is 1/60 of a day, and during one day (of approximately 24 hours) the entire 360° of the zodiac pass over the horizon. This same *nadi* which measures time, breathing and cadence therefore also measures space: one *nadi* = 1/60 × 360° = 6° = 360 minutes of arc. Since one *nadi* = 360 respirations, one respiration (or ten long syllables) covers a distance in the sky equal to one minute of arc. By standardizing the internal time-units of recitation and breathing in terms of the external time-unit day, the seers of old succeeded in transplanting external time into the internal cosmos of the jyotishi. Such a 'standardized' jyotishi functions as a sort of living clock whose breathing patterns can be used for divination.

Modern science creates new words to represent new units of measurement, and as this new terminology proliferates the awareness of how to relate these units together often recedes. Sanskritic science, which concentrates on relationships, prefers to re-use the same word to represent similar units in different contexts. That the rishis chose the word '*nadi*' when they named their science Nadi Jyotish also suggests that Svarodaya assisted them in that work.

THE YARDSTICK OF JYOTISH

Jyotish began as the eye of the Veda, the means through which one 'sees to' the correct performance of Vedic ritual. While those seers who were living calendars could 'see to' their rituals without external aids, those ritualists who lacked such knacks relied on Jyotish for scheduling assistance. Accordingly, ever since the Vedic era (or before) Jyotish's chief function in society has been to construct and maintain the calendar, the time schedule which enables prediction of cyclical celestial phenomena for ritual purposes.

Calendrical material, including especially the five measurements known as the *panchanga*, has for ages in India been compiled into a type of astrological almanac that is also called *Panchanga*. Almanacs have a venerable history, the earliest yet discovered being, it seems, a set of markings recorded on mammoth bones about 30,000 years ago which appear to chronicle the phases of the Moon. Written almanacs may have originated in the eighth century B.C. in the form of Babylonian clay tablets which list equinoxes, solstices, eclipses and lunar phases. Most learned jyotishis of today, who still need to be well versed in calendrical matters in order to select appropriate times for religious and social functions, continue to rely on the *Panchanga* as their source of celestial data.

In addition to providing precise planetary positions, the *Panchanga* predicts the weather, as well as the local, national and global political, economic and social climate. It combines detailed information on religious holidays and how to observe them with advice on how to select auspicious moments and avoid inauspicious times for any action, from marriage to the commencement of journeys according to direction. A *Panchanga*'s pages may also list mantras meant to ward off the undesirable effects of each graha, together with the prescribed number of recitations of each and a short description of the rituals involved in their recitation. Ordinary Hindus revere the *Panchanga* as a verbal embodiment or sourcebook of the sacred Jyotish, and many people literally worship it accordingly.

The essence of the *Panchanga* remains however the basic astronomical information codified into its 'five limbs'. A *Panchanga* is a *Panchanga* only if it lists the daily starting and ending times of all five of these soli-lunar limbs, which reflect the Panchanga's role as juxtaposer of the rhythms of the two luminaries. It performs this role by applying appropriate correctional factors (like the intercalary lunar month) to keep the solar and lunar cycles properly aligned with each other.

Jyotishis, who typically use the *Panchanga* in the context of electional astrology, do not rely heavily on the meanings of the days, tithis, karanas and yogas in the practice of natal astrology because, unless these factors are clearly supported by the greater

context of the whole chart, they tend to be too general. Examples of
some uses of these factors appear in Chapter Twelve.

THE VARANAS (WEEKDAYS)

The Origin of the Seven Days of the Week

While the Chaldaeans are usually credited with originating our
seven-day week, India has for many centuries had its own seven-day
week. 28 = 7 × 4, 7 being the number of visible grahas and 4
being the four phases of the Moon (the new Moon, the full Moon,
and the two quarters). The number 28 is particularly important here
because the average of the lengths of the synodic month of 29.5
days and the sidereal month of 27.3 days is approximately 28.4 days,
a number which is not too far from the 30 days of the solar month.
Because each of the seven visible planets can own one day of a
seven-day week, the system of rulerships thus formed can correlate
the grahas with the 28 nakshatras. The system of 28 *Yogas* in
Shripati's *Ratnamala*, which connects the nakshatras with the days
of the week to determine auspicious moments for activity, is evidence of just this sort of astrological thinking.

The question of how the grahas, the bright gods of the heavens,
divided these seven days among themselves is the subject of another
teaching tale. After the twelve constellations of the zodiac had been
assigned their lords, the time came to distribute the lordship of the
days of the week. The life-giving Sun, the most important body in
the heavens, naturally took the first unit, which became Sunday.
The Moon accordingly took possession of the next unit, which
became Monday. The two regents then turned their attention to
apportioning the remaining weekdays to their 'followers'. After
pondering over the problem, the Sun and Moon agreed that while
the constellations are divisions of *space*, days are divisions of *time*.
Day rulerships were then allocated according to the speed at which
the planets move. Based on their averaged rate of daily proper
motion, as seen from the Earth, the Moon is the fastest planet,
followed in descending order by Mercury, Venus, Sun, Mars,
Jupiter and Saturn. The Sun therefore awarded rulership of the next

day (Tuesday) to Mars, the planet next in order of decreasing speed from his regal self. Moon then bestowed Wednesday on Mercury, the planet next in order of decreasing speed from the Moon. Jupiter, the planet next fastest after Mars, was assigned Thursday, and Venus, the next fastest after Mercury, obtained Friday. Finally, when the Sun gifted Saturday to Saturn, the scheme was complete.

The Hours of the Day (Horas)

A day is divided in Jyotish into twenty-four units called *horas* (our modern hours). An interesting comparison exists between this system and the other system that is commonly used for time division in Jyotish. Just as the day can be divided into twenty-four hours of sixty minutes each, it is also divisible into sixty *nadis* (which are often called *ghatikas*) of twenty-four minutes each. These two systems complement each other in the same sort of way that the 30 tithis of 12° each complement the 12 rashis of 30° each.

The first hora (hour) of each day is ruled by that day's planetary ruler. Since the day in India is taken to start from sunrise, the first hour after sunrise on a Sunday is ruled by the Sun, the first hour after sunrise on a Monday belongs to the Moon, Mars rules Tuesday's first hour after sunrise, and so on. After the ruler enjoys his hour, the other planets then rule in the sequence of their *increasing* averaged rate of daily proper motion. After each planet has ruled an hour, the process begins again from the day lord. Thus on Sunday the order is: Sun, Venus, Mercury, Moon, Saturn, Jupiter and Mars; on Monday it is Moon, Saturn, Jupiter, Mars, Sun, Venus and Mercury; and so on. Note also that the cycles flow uninterruptedly from one day to the next, creating thereby the rulerships shown in Table 7.1.

An approximation of the time of sunrise can be obtained from the weather section of a big-city newspaper. While the hora is commonly taken to be one hour long, it is precisely one hour long only at the equator, or on equinoctial days (when day and night are of equal length). Most of India is sufficiently near to the equator that its days and nights are nearly equally long; but in very northerly regions,

TABLE 7.1

Planetary Hours (Horas)

Su = *Sun* Mo = *Moon* Ma = *Mars* Me = *Mercury* Ju = *Jupiter* Ve = *Venus* Sa = *Saturn*

Hour	*Sunday*	*Monday*	*Tuesday*	*Wednesday*	*Thursday*	*Friday*	*Saturday*
1	Su	Mo	Ma	Me	Ju	Ve	Sa
2	Ve	Sa	Su	Mo	Ma	Me	Ju
3	Me	Ju	Ve	Sa	Su	Mo	Ma
4	Mo	Ma	Me	Ju	Ve	Sa	Su
5	Sa	Su	Mo	Ma	Me	Ju	Ve
6	Ju	Ve	Sa	Su	Mo	Ma	Me
7	Ma	Me	Ju	Ve	Sa	Su	Mo
8	Su	Mo	Ma	Me	Ju	Ve	Sa
9	Ve	Sa	Su	Mo	Ma	Me	Ju
10	Me	Ju	Ve	Sa	Su	Mo	Ma
11	Mo	Ma	Me	Ju	Ve	Sa	Su
12	Sa	Su	Mo	Ma	Me	Ju	Ve
13	Ju	Ve	Sa	Su	Mo	Ma	Me
14	Ma	Me	Ju	Ve	Sa	Su	Mo
15	Su	Mo	Ma	Me	Ju	Ve	Sa
16	Ve	Sa	Su	Mo	Ma	Me	Ju
17	Me	Ju	Ve	Sa	Su	Mo	Ma
18	Mo	Ma	Me	Ju	Ve	Sa	Su
19	Sa	Su	Mo	Ma	Me	Ju	Ve
20	Ju	Ve	Sa	Su	Mo	Ma	Me
21	Ma	Me	Ju	Ve	Sa	Su	Mo
22	Su	Mo	Ma	Me	Ju	Ve	Sa
23	Ve	Sa	Su	Mo	Ma	Me	Ju
24	Me	Ju	Ve	Sa	Su	Mo	Ma

---

such as Canada and northern Europe, the difference may be significant. In Toronto, for example, a winter's day may last less than nine hours. It is more precise to calculate separate horas for day and for night by dividing the length of the day (the span of time from sunrise to sunset) by 12 and the length of the night (from sunset to sunrise) by 12 respectively. Horas in Toronto will thus be less than forty-five minutes long on some short winter days, and more than seventy-five minutes long on some long winter nights. A good jyotishi relies on intuition to determine whether to use the uniform or the precise hora on any particular occasion.

How to Use the Seven Days and the Planetary Hours

The seven days of the week are used calendrically, of course, but Jyotish also uses them to help select appropriate days on which to commence actions for maximum effect; to aid in deciphering the outcome of questions; to enhance understanding of omens; and to predict results from the natal chart. The most useful astrological principle involving the days is this: *Each day's nature is akin to that of its ruler.* Jupiter infuses Thursday, its day, with many of the qualities and rulerships assigned to it in Chapter Two. This makes Thursday a generally benefic day (since Jupiter is a generally benefic graha), a day which is good for prayer, children, money, meeting gurus, and all the other things which Jupiter rules. Saturday, the day of Saturn, is similarly imbued with Saturn's qualities. This makes it generally malefic in nature, like its ruler, a day that brings delays, obstacles and disappointments to almost everyone.

Although these generic traits are subject to modification by every other astrological factor influencing a situation, since Jyotish eternally strives to reach a holistic reading of reality, this does not make them any less true. Our Jyotish guru said one day, in all seriousness, 'No wonder everyone in this country gets divorced. They all marry on Saturday!' Most Indians try to avoid choosing Saturday for any sort of auspicious function, because of its association with disappointment. Many religious Indians prefer to commence their journeys only on Thursday because its ruler, Jupiter, is a benefic who resonates with their values and purposes. Journeys on Tuesdays are often ill-starred, because Tuesday is ruled by the troublesome Mars.

Here is one example of how days are used in Jyotish: a woman who presided over board meetings held once a month on a Tuesday complained of how confrontational and stressful these meetings became. The participants were consistently uncooperative, quarrelsome, dictatorial and vengeful (all Martian qualities). Shouting matches would break out and people would frequently be reduced to tears or to rage. Absenteeism grew, which interfered with the board's functioning. While many companies are of course able to hold peaceful Tuesday board meetings, this woman's experience of Tuesdays was particularly painful because her Mars was debilitated in Cancer in her eighth house and was subject to a number of afflictions. Because her natal horoscope had a Sagittarius ascendant with a well-placed Jupiter, it was recommended that she move the board meetings to Thursdays. Since then she has reported a colossal and lasting improvement in the flow of the meetings and the attitude of the participants over two years of Thursday board meetings.

The above example of an astrological judgment uses the days of the week for a selection (*muhurta*) in the context of a person's natal chart. For an example in which the days are used in the context of Svarodaya, horary astrology (*prashna*) and omenology (*nimitta*), consider that a jyotishi may choose an answer to a question based on the nostril which dominates on a particular day. If a woman asks a question regarding pregnancy on the day of a benefic (Monday, Wednesday, Thursday or Friday), *and* if the jyotishi's breath is active predominantly in his left nostril, *and* if the questioner is standing on the jyotishi's left, then she is indeed pregnant. The same will be the case if on a malefic's day (Sunday, Tuesday or Saturday) the questioner is standing on the jyotishi's right side *and* the jyotishi's breath flows more freely in his right nostril.

Here is one application of day lordship which correlates muhurta with the birth chart:

'The good results of a bhava are more plentifully experienced if a work is started in an ascendant ruled by the lord of that bhava, or when the lord thereof is in an upachaya house, or on the weekday, hour, year or month ruled by that bhava lord. The desirable effects will be 25 per cent by year-lord, 50 per cent by month-lord, 75 per cent by the lord of the weekday and 100 per cent by the lord of the hour' (*Saravali* 7:5–7).

Horas (hour-lords) are used in much the same ways as day-lords are, except that horas are more specific. One popular principle involving horas which combines horary with natal astrology states that: *the matters that are activated in the natal chart by the planet that rules the hora that operates at the time a natal chart is read will be the matters of greatest interest to that chart's owner at that time*. If, for example, the hora at such a time is ruled by the Sun, the houses occupied and ruled by the Sun will be the primary reasons that the horoscope's owner requested the reading. Another method widely used in *prashna* is this: a question asked implies a favorable outcome when the lord of the hora is the same as (or is friendly to) the lord of the day; but if the hour-lord is an enemy of the day-lord, the outcome will be unfavorable. Both of these principles have been elaborated by jyotishis into detailed systems.

THE TITHIS

Watchers of the Moon, the ruler of the night, see his garb and splendor change dramatically over the space of a month. Sometimes full-bodied and sometimes thin, the Moon was allotted 30 different phases (*tithis*) to the 29.5 days of his synodic month by the Indian astronomers of yore: 15 for his waxing cycle, the *Shukla Paksha* or 'bright portion', which extends from the new Moon to the full Moon, and 15 for his waning cycle, the *Krishna Paksha* or 'dark portion', which extends from the full Moon back to the new Moon.

The Law of the Macrocosm and Microcosm permits us to draw a correspondence between human breathing and the two 'portions' (*pakshas*) of the Moon. The functioning of the Lunar Nadi (the left nostril) mentioned in Svarodaya corresponds to the Shukla Paksha, which is ruled by the Moon. The functioning of the Solar Nadi (the right nostril) corresponds to the Krishna Paksha, when the Sun's influence predominates. The new and full Moons are analogous to sunset and sunrise, when both nostrils work together.

The 1st to the 14th tithis of the waxing and waning moon are known by the names of their Sanskrit ordinal numbers, and they are differentiated by affixing the words *shukla* or *krishna* respectively to the names of the tithis of the waxing and waning cycles. The 15th tithi of each series has a special name: that of the waxing cycle is called *purnima*, the full Moon, and that of the waning cycle is *amavasya*, the new Moon. Table 7.2 gives the names of the tithis.

TABLE 7.2

The Names of the Tithis
(Waxing or Waning Moon)

1st = Pratipat	9th = Navami
2nd = Dvitiya	10th = Dashami
3rd = Tritiya	11th = Ekadashi
4th = Chaturthi	12th = Dvadashi
5th = Panchami	13th = Trayodashi
6th = Shashti	14th = Chaturdashi
7th = Saptami	15th = Purnima
8th = Ashtami	30th = Amavasya

How to Calculate the Tithis

1. Find the longitudinal difference between the Sun and Moon by subtracting the Sun's longitude from that of the Moon, measuring from the Sun to the Moon in the natural order of the zodiac. If the Moon's longitude is less than that of the Sun, add 360°.
2. Divide this distance by 12°, and drop the remainder.
3. The quotient plus 1 will be the number of the tithi of Shukla Paksha, if it is 15 or less; if it is more than 15, subtract 15, and the result will be the number of the tithi in Krishna Paksha.

To determine the tithi for the birth represented in Chart 1 (see p. 415), note that because the Moon is at 7° 49′ of Libra it has traveled six full rashis from the beginning of Aries (6 × 30° = 180°). The Moon's longitude is therefore 180° + 7° 49′ = 187° 49′. The Sun is at 21° 32′ Cancer, having covered three full rashis from the beginning of Aries (3 × 30° = 90°), so the Sun's longitude is

90° + 21° 32′ = 111° 32′. To find the longitudinal difference between the two luminaries, subtract the Sun's longitude from that of the Moon: 187° 49′ − 111° 32′ = 76° 17′. Dividing this distance by 12° gives us 6 + a remainder, which we drop; 6 + 1 = 7. This gentleman was therefore born on *saptami*, the seventh tithi, and since this result is less than 15, it was during the Shukla Paksha.

Tithis in Jyotish

Jyotish uses tithis in varied ways. Their most fundamental use is in the complex procedure of calendar creation. Since the lunar calendar regulates the religious life of the average Hindu, all sorts of social and personal annual celebrations, including (but not limited to) high holidays, initiations, marriages and christenings, depend on accurate knowledge of tithis. Every tithi has a presiding deity who is to be worshipped on that particular tithi, and sometimes the ritual worship of the deity of your tithi at birth can help align you with the world at large.

Detailed knowledge of tithis can also help prevent potential problems, as in Parashara's postulate that a child born in the final 48 minutes (*muhurta*, in its sense as a unit of time) of the fifth, tenth or fifteenth tithis of either the Shukla or Krishna Pakshas needs to have specific religious rites done on its behalf, to ameliorate what will otherwise become lifelong inauspicious effects. Although Jyotish computer programs frequently mention the tithi of birth many fail to indicate the portion of the tithi in which the person was born, which must then be either calculated manually by the jyotishi or taken from a *Panchanga*.

How important it is to know the various portions of a tithi is also obvious from Parashara's axiom that, while birth during the first sixth of the fourteenth tithi of the Krishna Paksha is auspicious, birth during the rest of that tithi will require remedial measures. Birth during the second sixth may lead to destruction of the father; during the third sixth to early demise of the mother; during the fourth sixth to early death of the maternal uncle; and during the fifth sixth to destruction, discontinuance and suffering for the entire family. Birth in the final sixth of that tithi causes that native's early death or, should he live, loss of wealth over the course of his life. These highly specific predictions are more suggestive than literal, for they must be interpreted in the context of the whole horoscope.

Meanings of the Tithis

The simplest way to use tithis when reading a natal horoscope is to employ the meanings of the birth tithi, which are given in several classical works on Jyotish. The descriptions given below, which were extracted from the text called *Manasagari*, have been partly modernized and elaborated in order to elicit some of the meanings implied in the original Sanskrit. The information in the following sketches cannot always be employed literally, although you will frequently find that one or two of the interpretations will apply very precisely to whatever chart is under examination. You should neither despair if you were born on a tithi whose indications seem dire, nor should you rejoice if you were born on a good tithi. Predictions by tithi meaning come true only when there is a clear confluence of the other factors in the horoscope which relate to these matters.

Note that although the tithis, excepting purnima and amavasya, have the same names in both the Shukla and Krishna Pakshas, the waxing tithis generally imply growth, preservation and plenty, while the waning tithis suggest stagnation, diminution and dearth. Indications for those born during the bright fortnight are, all else being equal, more likely to improve as time goes by than they are for those born during the dark fortnight, since the waxing Moon implies growth, preservation and plenty.

Pratipada (First Tithi)

People born on *pratipada* are bereft of enjoyment and often lack the capacity to enjoy life. They may cause reproach or scandal by their association with rascals, scoundrels and mischief makers, or perhaps in their lineage, community or professional group some disgraced person will surface through whom they will suffer a good deal.

You should be able to find examples of these admittedly unpleasant interpretations in any thick stack of horoscopes. One person born in this tithi has associated with troublesome friends throughout her life (school dropouts, drug users, alcoholics, sexoholics, thieves and their ilk), associations which have created great embarrassment for her conservative family members. Another *pratipada* person created a stir in his family by joining a religious cult and now lives a very frugal life, lacking many enjoyments and amenities. Yet another first-tithi child suffered terribly when his father was involved in a well-publicized scandal.

Dvitiya (Second Tithi)

Those born on *dvitiya* find romantic interest in partners other than their own. They may be untruthful, or incapable of understanding truth, and often distort their understanding of situations. They lack purity and cleanliness, and tend to ignore the aesthetics of their environment. They often lack love, affection and friendship, and may be plagued by people who take an irrational dislike to them.

Tritiya (Third Tithi)

Those born on *tritiya* may be unmotivated and lethargic, lacking action, spirit, gesture, demeanor, exercise or desire. Hesitant to attempt new activities, they are often agitated, confused and restless, and feel incomplete and without resources. They tend to be disliked by others.

One person born on this tithi displays several of these characteristics: she loathes exercise, tends to be overweight and, when tempted to act on some matter, habitually finds reasons to procrastinate. In spite of this, she is very well liked, because the strong placement of Venus in her horoscope overpowers the tithi's influence.

Chaturthi (Fourth Tithi)

Chaturthi people are fond of sensory enjoyments like eating, drinking and sex, but they are also liberal and generous benefactors. They love their friends, and their friends love them. They tend to be educated and to enjoy good resources and children.

Panchami (Fifth Tithi)

These people possess good qualities and attainments. They often become wealthy, and sometimes become sensualists. They enjoy either a good profession or expertise in some desirable field of endeavor. One special characteristic of *panchami* people is that, although they are devoted to and love their parents, they often get little love from them, or from others.

Shashti (Sixth Tithi)

People born during this tithi will roam around, in their native lands or in foreign countries. They can be contentious, disputatious, obstreperous, oppressive, quarrelsome and pugnacious. They love to steal the spotlight, and resist giving others their chance therein. They may experience many painful diseases. The owner of Chart 2 (see p. 418) was born on a *shashti*, and he regularly travels the world over in pursuit of international business success. Because he is aggressively argumentative, a real mental brawler, some find him oppressive.

Saptami (Seventh Tithi)

Saptami natives have little contentment. They usually aspire to be magnificent, glorious and illustrious, but may simply succeed in seeming pompous. They are generally fortunate with children and wealth, being sufficiently opportunistic to develop useful career skills. One unique feature that *saptami* people often display is a certain brightness or luster of face or body.

Ashtami (Eighth Tithi)

Ashtami people tend to be religious, unless there are strong indications to the contrary in the horoscope. They like to speak the truth, and to understand the truth. They are sensually inclined, merciful, compassionate, skillful, and expert in whatever they do.

Navami (Ninth Tithi)

Navami natives are fond of the gods and their worship. They enjoy children and wealth, and they are especially fond of and are fascinated by the opposite sex. They are learned, and like to pursue knowledge.

Dashami (Tenth Tithi)

Because of their good powers of discrimination, *dashami* people know the difference between right and wrong. They love their country, community, or home. They like to participate in religious rituals, like fire sacrifices. Like *saptami* people, they often have a certain brightness or luster on their faces or bodies and, also like *saptamis*, they usually aspire to be magnificent, glorious and illustrious, which may make them seem pompous. They are generally happy.

Ekadashi (Eleventh Tithi)

People born during this tithi typically have very little contentment in life, though they are often honored by the government or by other ruling powers (such as corporate boards or their heads). They are intelligent, aspire to be holy, saintly and pure, and are usually fortunate with wealth and children.

Dvadashi (Twelfth Tithi)

These natives, whose bodies are often thin, are usually fickle and restless, agile and voluble. They love to roam in other countries, and display a certain unsteadiness in life. They tend to have a fidgety, humorous, giddy, lively manner about them. Their inconstant, unsteady minds often inhibit their ability to concentrate.

Trayodashi (Thirteenth Tithi)

People born in this tithi desire perfection and may be inspired to become greatly perfected beings. They are knowledgeable, for their drive for perfection compels them to pursue knowledge. They enjoy a natural ability to control their senses, and are hospitable, kind, benevolent and charitable.

Chaturdashi (Fourteenth Tithi)

Such people may be simultaneously wealthy and religious. Valiant, bold, daring and gallant, they often have an innate ability to speak supportively and encouragingly. They easily obtain honor from or through the government or other powerful institutions, and may become famous.

Purnima (Fifteenth Tithi as Full Moon)

Natives of this tithi may be wealthy, wise and bright. They are energetic, industrious and hard working, and these qualities enable them to rise in life. They are usually very fond of food, and develop romantic attractions to partners other than their own.

Amavasya (Fifteenth Tithi as New Moon)

Birth on *amavasya* makes people somehow crooked, either mentally or physically. They may be hostile, inimical, venomous or obnoxious to others, and can be bitter, perverse, sly, cruel, mischievous, deceptive, ruthless, foolish, witless, insensitive, inconsiderate or rude. Despite these troublesome qualities, they are often courageous, and are fond of maxims and precepts. Many of them are interested in secret and mysterious knowledge, and they may be quite learned, though often not academically.

THE KARANAS

Just as the solar day is divided into two portions (day and night), the lunar day (tithi) is similarly divided into two *karanas*, of 6° each. Eleven different karanas are permuted to make up the sixty-karana monthly cycle. These eleven are: 1 – *Bava*; 2 – *Balava*; 3 – *Kaulava*; 4 – *Taitila*; 5 – *Gara*; 6 – *Vanija*; 7 – *Vishti* (also known as *Bhadra*); 8 – *Shakuni*; 9 – *Chatushpada*; 10 – *Naga*; 11 – *Kinstughna*. Table 7.3 shows how the karanas are distributed among the tithis.

TABLE 7.3

	Karanas			
Tithi	Waxing Phase of the Moon		Waning Phase of the Moon	
	1st Karana	*2nd Karana*	*1st Karana*	*2nd Karana*
1	Kinstughna	Bava	Balava	Kaulava
2	Balava	Kaulava	Taitila	Gara
3	Taitila	Gara	Vanija	Vishti
4	Vanija	Vishti	Bava	Balava
5	Bava	Balava	Kaulava	Taitila
6	Kaulava	Taitila	Gara	Vanija
7	Gara	Vanija	Vishti	Bava
8	Vishti	Bava	Balava	Kaulava
9	Balava	Kaulava	Taitila	Gara
10	Taitila	Gara	Vanija	Vishti
11	Vanija	Vishti	Bava	Balava
12	Bava	Balava	Kaulava	Taitila
13	Kaulava	Taitila	Gara	Vanija
14	Gara	Vanija	Vishti	Shakuni
15 Purnima	Vishti	Bava	—	—
30 Amavasya	—	—	Chatushpada	Naga

Note that most of the karanas of Krishna Paksha are identical to those of the Shukla Paksha *except that* the consecutive cycles of the first seven karanas for the waning phase are always one tithi behind those of the waxing phase. This occurs because:

· *Kinstughna* occupies the first half of the first tithi in the waxing phase;
· *Shakuni* occupies the second half of the fourteenth tithi of the waning phase; and
· *Chatushpada* and *Naga* are the first and second karanas of the thirtieth tithi.

Shakuni, Chatushpada, Naga and *Kinstughna* are known as fixed (*sthira*) karanas, while the other seven karanas are movable (*chara*). The four fixed karanas, and *Vishti* of the movable karanas, are inauspicious. Because the karanas, which have a relatively wide application in electional astrology, are infrequently brought to bear on natal charts, which is the primary focus of this book, for now we will leave them untranslated and without further comment.

THE YOGAS

From one perspective, the Sun and Moon are rivals as regents of the day and night, for the Sun is brighter and more consistent, while the Moon is cooler and, because of its changing appearance tithi by tithi, more alluring. In spite of their differences – or, perhaps, because of them – the two monarchs complement each other, in the same way that day and night, the realms they rule, complement one another. The 27 soli-lunar yogas, which were created to reflect the nature and effect of the interactions of Sun and Moon, are calculated by adding together their degree positions (*yoga* comes from a root meaning 'to join'). Their numbers, Sanskrit names with English translations, and brief descriptions of people born during each are listed in Table 7.4.

TABLE 7.4

The 27 Yogas (Soli-Lunar Combinations)

Number & Name	English Translation	Number & Name	English Translation
1. Vishkambha	Supported	15. Vajra	Diamond
2. Priti	Fondness	16. Siddhi	Success
3. Ayushman	Long-lived	17. Vyatipata	Calamity
4. Saubhagya	Good Fortune	18. Variyana	Comfort
5. Shobhana	Splendor	19. Parigha	Obstruction
6. Atiganda	Large-cheeked	Shiva	Auspicious
7. Sukarma	Virtuous	21. Siddha	Accomplished
8. Dhriti	Determination	22. Sadhya	Amenable
9. Shula	Spear	23. Shubha	Auspicious
10. Ganda	Cheek	24. Shukla	Bright White
11. Vriddhi	Growth	25. Brahma	Priest or God
12. Dhruva	Constant	26. Indra	Chief
13. Vyaghata	Beating	27. Vaidhriti	Poor support
14. Harshana	Thrilling	—	

How to Calculate the Soli-Lunar Yogas

1. Add together the longitudes of the Sun and Moon.
2. Subtract 360° if possible.
3. Divide the result by 13° 20', and drop the remainder.
4. The quotient + 1 will be the number of the yoga.

To determine the yoga for the birth represented in Chart 2, the Sun is at 24° 25' Virgo (= [5 × 30°] + 24° 25' = 174° 25') and Moon is at 06° 15' Gemini (= [2 × 30°] + 06° 15' = 66° 15'). Adding them together gives us 240° 40', from which 360° cannot be subtracted. To divide this sum by 13° 20', first convert both numbers into minutes of arc: 240° 40' = {240° × 60'} + 40' = 14,840', and 13° 20' = {13 × 60'} + 20' = 800'. 14,840' divided by 800' = 18, plus a remainder which is dropped. 18 + 1 is therefore the number of the yoga, which is *Parigha*, the nineteenth yoga.

Meanings of the Soli-Lunar Yogas

1. *Vishkambha* (Supported) – prevails over others, victorious over enemies, obtains property, wealthy
2. *Priti* (Fondness) – well-liked, attracted to the opposite sex, enjoys life with contentment
3. *Ayushman* (Long-lived) – good health and longevity, energetic
4. *Saubhagya* (Good Fortune) – enjoys a comfortable life full of opportunities, happy
5. *Shobhana* (Splendor) – lustrous body and demeanor, sensualist, obsessed with sex
6. *Atiganda* (Large-cheeked) – difficult life due to numerous obstacles and accidents; revengeful and angry
7. *Sukarma* (Virtuous) – performs noble deeds, magnanimous and charitable, wealthy
8. *Dhriti* (Determination) – enjoys the wealth, goods and spouses of others; indulges in the hospitality of others
9. *Shula* (Spear, Pain) – confrontational and contrary, quarrelsome, angry
10. *Ganda* (Cheek) – flawed morals or ethics, troublesome personality
11. *Vriddhi* (Growth) – intelligent, opportunistic and discerning; life constantly improves with age
12. *Dhruva* (Constant) – steady character, able to concentrate and persist, wealthy
13. *Vyaghata* (Beating) – cruel, intent on harming others
14. *Harshana* (Thrilling) – intelligent, delights in merriment and humor
15. *Vajra* (Diamond, Thunderbolt) – well-off, lecherous, unpredictable, forceful
16. *Siddhi* (Success) – skillful and accomplished in several areas; protector and supporter of others
17. *Vyatipata* (Calamity) – prone to sudden mishaps and reversals, fickle and unreliable

18. *Variyana* (Comfort) – loves ease and luxury, lazy, lascivious
19. *Parigha* (Obstruction) – encounters many obstacles to progress in life; irritable and meddlesome
20. *Shiva* (Auspicious) – honored by superiors and government, placid, learned and religious, wealthy
21. *Siddha* (Accomplished) – accommodating personality, pleasant nature, interest in ritual and spirituality
22. *Sadhya* (Amenable) – well behaved, accomplished manners and etiquette
23. *Shubha* (Auspicious) – lustrous body and personality, but problems with health; wealthy, irritable
24. *Shukla* (Bright White) – garrulous and flighty, impatient and impulsive; unsteady and changeable mind
25. *Brahma* (Priest, God) – trustworthy and confidential, ambitious, good discernment and judgment
26. *Indra* (Chief) – interest in education and knowledge; helpful, well-off
27. *Vaidhriti* (Poor Support) – critical, scheming nature; powerful and overwhelming (mentally or physically)

Like the karanas, the yogas are used more in electional astrology than in natal astrology. As with the tithis, predictions by a yoga's meaning come true only when there is a clear confluence of the other factors in the horoscope which relate to these matters.

CHAPTER EIGHT

THE NAKSHATRAS

The 27 or 28 Vedic constellations called *nakshatras* are mentioned, in order, with their presiding lords, in both the *Krishna Yajur Veda* (Kanda IV, Prasna IV), and the *Taittireya Brahmana* (another Vedic text). The nakshatras, which seem to be uniquely Indian in origin, seem to have been an important part of 'Vedic' culture, for they have been in continuous use in India since Vedic times. The nakshatras are much used in Jyotish even today, particularly in order to determine, via electional astrology, the appropriate ritual to perform or mantra to recite on a particular day. For example, jyotishis who wish to achieve success at palmistry will often begin worship of the goddess *Panchanguli* ('Five Fingers') when the Moon occupies the nakshatra Hasta (which means 'the hand'). One vital use for the nakshatras in natal astrology is in timing the events that a horoscope may promise; this is considered in detail in Chapter Eleven.

The nakshatras are regarded in Indian mythology as the Moon's brides, for each night the Moon appears to move from the mansion of one wife to the next. That there were either 27 or 28 nakshatras is likely a consequence of the fact that a sidereal month lasts 27.3217 days, which can either be rounded up to 28 or rounded down to 27. The number 28 (7 days times 4 weeks) was once more meaningful to Jyotish than is 27, probably in the era before the number of grahas became standardized at nine. 27 divides evenly into 360° to create an arc of 13° 20′ per nakshatra, while 360° divided by 28 nakshatras yields cumbersome arcs of about 12° 51′ 26″.

Four rashis cover precisely the same amount of space (120°) as do nine nakshatras, a relationship which helps to integrate the zodiac with the cycle of the nakshatras and may have helped fix the number of nakshatras at 27. In addition, the rulership of 27 nakshatras can be evenly distributed among the Nine Grahas (27/9 = 3). The system of 27 nakshatras became so evidently superior for calculation that it is now used almost universally in Jyotish, odd exceptions occurring mainly in the realm of *muhurta*.

Table 8.1 lists the Sanskrit names of the nakshatras with their English translations, modern astronomical names, zodiacal placement and astrological rulers.

Single-phrase translation of the Sanskrit names of the nakshatras into English unfortunately sometimes sounds nonsensical. For example, 'front good feet' and 'back good feet' are used for the nakshatras of Purva Bhadrapada and Uttara Bhadrapada respectively because these two nakshatras are said to resemble the legs of a cot, the stars of Purva Bhadrapada being the cot's front legs and those of Uttara Bhadrapada its back legs. Anuradha, translated as 'following Radha', refers to the fact that this nakshatra follows 'Radha', which is another name for Vishakha.

The bracketed names in the 'Astronomical Name' column are the popular names of some well-known stars. For a few nakshatras, slight differences of opinion exist over precisely which star constitutes its *yogatara* (the principal and sometimes only star of a nakshatra). Several nakshatras have alternate Sanskrit names; those given are the most common. An entirely separate list of astrological rulers is used for Vedic sacrifices (and the correlation between these two systems of rulerships is far too involved to consider here). The ancient rulers are listed below in the section on the individual nakshatras, for it is from the symbolism of these rulers that many of the meanings of the nakshatras have been derived.

Since the 27 nakshatras can be conveniently divided into three groups of nine, and since nine times 13° 20′ equals 120°, which equals three full rashis (4 × 30° = 120°), the first nine nakshatras, from Ashvini to Ashlesha, cover the same slice of the zodiac as do the constellations Aries to Cancer; the second group, from Magha to Jyeshtha, fall precisely within the constellations Leo to Scorpio; and the last group, from Mula to Revati, exactly span Sagittarius to Pisces. Each of these groupings begins with the beginning of one of the Fire rashis (Aries, Leo and Sagittarius) and ends with the end of one of the Water rashis (Cancer, Scorpio and Pisces).

TABLE 8.1

Lunar Nakshatras

Ar = *Aries* Ta = *Taurus* Ge = *Gemini* Ca = *Cancer* Le = *Leo* Vi = *Virgo*
Li = *Libra* Sc = *Scorpio* Sa = *Sagittarius* Cp = *Capricorn* Aq = *Aquarius* Pi = *Pisces*

Number & Name	Translation of Name	Astronomical Name (Modern)	Zodiacal Position	Span	Ruler or Lord
1. Ashvini	Horse-owner	α or β Arietis	00°Ar00′–13°Ar20′	13°20′	Ketu
2. Bharani	Bearer	γ Arietis	13°Ar20′–26°Ar40′	13°20′	Venus
3. Krittika	Cutter	η Tauri (Alcyone)	26°Ar40′–10°Ta00′	13°20′	Sun
4. Rohini	Growing or Red	α Tauri (Aldebaran)	10°Ta00′–23°Ta20′	13°20′	Moon
5. Mrigashirsha	Deer's Head	λ Orionis	23°Ta20′–06°Ge40′	13°20′	Mars

6. Ardra	Moist	α Orionis	06°Ge40'–20°Ge00'	13°20'	Rahu
7. Punarvasu	Prosperity	β Geminorum	20°Ge00'–03°Ca20'	13°20'	Jupiter
8. Pushya	Flower	δ Cancri	03°Ca20'–16°Ca40'	13°20'	Saturn
9. Ashlesha	Embrace	ε Hydrae	16°Ca40'–30°Ca00'	13°20'	Mercury
10. Magha	Mighty	α Leonis (Regulus)	00°Leo0'–13°Le20'	13°20'	Ketu
11. Purva Phalguni	Former Red One	δ Leonis	13°Le20'–26°Le40'	13°20'	Venus
12. Uttara Phalguni	Latter Red One	β Leonis (Denebola)	26°Le40'–10°Vi00'	13°20'	Sun
13. Hasta	Hand	δ Corvi	10°Vi00'–23°Vi20'	13°20'	Moon
14. Chitra	Bright	α Virginis (Spica)	23°Vi20'–06°Li40'	13°20'	Mars
15. Swati	Independent	α Bootis (Arcturus)	06°Li40'–20°Li00'	13°20'	Rahu
16. Vishakha	Branched/Forked	α Librae	20°Li00'–03°Sc20'	13°20'	Jupiter
17. Anuradha	Following Radha	δ Scorpii	03°Sc20'–16°Sc40'	13°20'	Saturn
18. Jyeshtha	Eldest	α Scorpii (Antares)	16°Sc40'–30°Sc00'	13°20'	Mercury
19. Mula	Root	λ Scorpii	00°Sa00'–13°Sa20'	13°20'	Ketu
20. Purva Ashadha	Former Victor	δ Sagittarii	13°Sa20'–26°Sa40'	13°20'	Venus
21. Uttara Ashadha	Latter Victor	σ Sagittarii	26°Sa40'–10°Cp00'	13°20'	Sun
22. Shravana	Ear	α Aquilae (Altair)	10°Cp00'–23°Cp20'	13°20'	Moon
23. Dhanishtha	Abundance	β Delphini	23°Cp20'–06°Aq40'	13°20'	Mars
24. Shatabhisha	100 Physicians	λ Aquari	06°Aq40'–20°Aq00'	13°20'	Rahu
25. Purva Bhadrapada	Front Good Feet	α Pegasi	20°Aq00'–03°Pi20'	13°20'	Jupiter
26. Uttara Bhadrapada	Back Good Feet	γ Pegasi	03°Pi20'–16°Pi40'	13°20'	Saturn
27. Revati	Rich	ζ Piscium	16°Pi40'–30°Pi00'	13°20'	Mercury

TABLE 8.2

Relationship of Months and Nakshatras	
Full Moon in Nakshatra of:	*Name of Lunar Month*
Chitra	Chaitra
Vishakha	Vaishakha
Jyeshtha	Jyaishtha
Purva Ashadha	Ashadha
Shravana	Shravana
Purva Bhadrapada	Bhadrapada
Ashvini	Ashvina
Krittika	Karttika
Ardra	Margashirsha (known in western India as *Agrahayana*)
Pushya	Pausha
Magha	Magha
Purva Phalguni	Phalguna

Many of India's regional calendars name their months after the nakshatra in which the Moon will sit (or, sometimes, will be near to) when it is full. The first month of one group of lunar calendars corresponds to the spring month when the full Moon occurs in Chitra and is known as Chaitra. The other group of lunar calendars begins its year with the month Karttika, in which the Moon is full in or near Krittika. Almost all the religious holidays in regions using these calendars are tied to the lunar cycle, not to the Gregorian calendar. Table 8.2 shows the relationship of these lunar months with the nakshatras.

The procession of the nakshatras possibly began with Krittika long ago because it then marked the vernal equinox. Ashvini became the leader of the nakshatra pack only after the lunar zodiac was correlated with the solar zodiac, when the initial point of Aries became identical with the initial point of Ashvini. Rahu and Ketu probably became fully planetized at the time that nine equal-sized nakshatras were made equal to three rashis, since each of the Nine Planets could then be assigned three nakshatras to rule. Perhaps it was then that the number of nakshatras became standardized at 27, and their width became standardized at 13° 20'. When the twenty-eighth nakshatra, *Abhijit*, is used, it is inserted between Uttara Ashadha and Shravana, but its insertion ruins the symmetrical distribution of the nakshatras over the zodiac and among the grahas. Since Jyotish currently uses Abhijit only occasionally, in electional astrology, we do not include it here.

GANDANTA

When using the principles of Jyotish in interpretation, it is always very important that apples be compared with apples alone, not with oranges. Once a Westerner approached a seasoned jyotishi to select an auspicious date for a marriage. After the jyotishi made his calculations and recommended a date and time, the woman objected, for she had read somewhere that marriage at the end of a month is inauspicious. This is in fact quite a common principle in Jyotish, which assumes that the strength of a juncture-point (*sandhi*) is weakened and ill-defined due to the forced intermingling of two differing energies. A *sangama* (the junction of two rivers) is auspicious, because the two energies merge completely on meeting, but a *sandhi* (literally, a 'joint') is merely a zone of transition between two energies which retain their own individual characteristics.

While most *sandhis* are inauspicious for worldly matters, because the free flow of prosperity becomes obstructed at such zones of transition, they are often auspicious for certain spiritual endeavors. In this case the jyotishi was forced to point out to the woman gently that the time recommended was at the end of a month of the *Western* calendar, while in the *Indian* calendar this date fell well within the month's midsection, and so was not a *sandhi* of Jyotish.

The *Gandanta* ('End-of-the-Cheek') portions of the nakshatras form another class of *sandhi* which Jyotish finds inauspicious. These portions are the last 3° 20′ of Ashlesha, Jyeshtha and Revati and the first 3° 20′ of Ashvini, Magha and Mula. *Ganda* means 'cheek' and/ or 'the whole side of the face including the temple', which makes the *Gandanta* segments the 'junctures' of the celestial faces that look down upon us. *Gandanta* is particularly inopportune because it is a double *sandhi*, a juncture of two rashis as well as two nakshatras. Grahas located at these points are very weak, and indicate major problems in the native's life unless the grahas involved are strengthened by appropriate remedies.

NAKSHATRA CLASSIFICATIONS

When they examine a birth chart, most jyotishis commonly examine the nature of the nakshatras occupied by the ascendant (since it is the foundation of the individual's personality) and the Moon (since it represents the individual's mental and emotional proclivities and tendencies – and since the Moon is the *raison d'être* for the nakshatras). Sometimes they also examine the Sun's nakshatra, to inspect the individual's overall spiritual nature. Many jyotishis also make predictions from the nature of the nakshatra occupied by a planet which 'rules' a person during a particular period of life (see Chapter Eleven). Some other specific uses of the nakshatras are noted below.

Activity

The Active Nakshatras are KRITTIKA, ASHLESHA, MAGHA, CHITRA, VISHAKHA, JYESHTHA, MULA, DHANISHTHA and SHATABHISHA.

The Passive Nakshatras are ASHVINI, MRIGASHIRSHA, PUNARVASU, PUSHYA, HASTA, SWATI, ANURADHA, SHRAVANA and PURVA BHADRAPADA.

The Balanced Nakshatras are BHARANI, ROHINI, ARDRA, PURVA PHALGUNI, UTTARA PHALGUNI, PURVA ASHADHA, UTTARA ASHADHA, UTTARA BHADRAPADA and REVATI.

For example, two people who are equally adept at a subject may have dramatically different learning and teaching styles. When (all other factors being equal) the lord of the ninth house (higher knowledge) occupies an active nakshatra, the native may eagerly and dynamically pursue higher knowledge. If that ninth lord is well placed, that individual may also be inclined to spread that knowledge energetically, and to do so successfully. Another person in whose chart the ninth lord occupies a passive nakshatra may in their pursuit of higher knowledge maintain that 'when the student is ready the teacher appears'. Such people when teachers would be more likely to pick one qualified student to instruct than actively to collect acolytes, though if that ninth lord is well placed they may be very successful at research behind the scenes. When the ninth lord occupies a balanced nakshatra, both behaviors are likely to occur in more equal proportions. This sort of analysis can be applied to the other houses in a similar manner.

An active, dynamic planet like Mars will find these qualities enhanced when it tenants an active nakshatra, just as a passive planet like Saturn will become even less dynamic when in a passive nakshatra. While the active nakshatras when afflicted can indicate qualities like aggression, excessive zeal, dogmatism, quarrels, disputes, instability, foolishness, self-centeredness, impulsiveness, impatience, and fast starts but poor follow-through, under favorable circumstances they indicate the resourcefulness of a willpower actively applied to the achievement of valued goals in acceptable ways.

Passive nakshatras when afflicted can indicate a listless approach to life and life goals, procrastination, excessive and paralyzing idealism, irresoluteness and lack of courage, while under favorable circumstances they signify strong awareness of others, compassion, and an ability to accept reality appropriately, to 'let Thy will be done'.

The balanced nakshatras when afflicted make for the sanctimonious finding of fault with others, an unwillingness to do anything except in a 'by-the-book' fashion, ultra-conservatism, reluctance to accept reality, and an exaggerated desire to live life with the least disturbance and adventure possible. When favorably influenced, however, the balanced nakshatras indicate that propitious sense of balance in all things expressed in the prayer, 'Grant me the power to change what I can change, the patience to accept what I cannot change, and the wisdom to know the difference between the two.'

Caste

The *Brahmana* nakshatras are KRITTIKA, PURVA PHALGUNI, PURVA ASHADHA and PURVA BHADRAPADA.

The *Kshatriya* nakshatras are PUSHYA, UTTARA PHALGUNI, UTTARA ASHADHA and UTTARA BHADRAPADA.

The *Vaishya* nakshatras are ASHVINI, PUNARVASU and HASTA.

The *Shudra* nakshatras are ROHINI, MAGHA, ANURADHA and REVATI.

The nakshatras of the Servant class are MRIGASHIRSHA, CHITRA, JYESHTHA and DHANISHTHA.

The nakshatras of the Butcher class are ARDRA, MULA, SWATI and SHATABHISHA.

The *Mleccha* nakshatras are BHARANI, ASHLESHA, VISHAKHA and SHRAVANA.

This classification is akin to that of the castes of the planets, which appears in Chapter Four, and its use is similar. It is primarily an attempt to classify people by their natural propensities. The natural inclination of the *Brahmana* is to be immersed in philosophy, religion, and altruistic service; that of the *Kshatriya* is to concentrate on politics and rulership; the *Vaishya*'s natural aptitude is for trade and business; and the *Shudra* naturally gravitates toward service and manual labor. Manual labor need not be unskilled; in the modern context, tradespeople might also well be classified as *Shudras*. The *Mleccha* (outcast) represents those who are misfits in society. The Butcher and Servant classes of nakshatras naturally gravitate to the various forms of butchery and servitude respectively.

Creation, Maintenance and Dissolution

The Creation (*shrishti*) nakshatras are ASHVINI, ROHINI, PUNARVASU, MAGHA, HASTA, VISHAKHA, MULA, SHRAVANA and PURVA BHADRAPADA.

The Maintenance (*sthithi*) nakshatras are BHARANI, MRIGASHIRSHA, PUSHYA, PURVA PHALGUNI, CHITRA, ANURADHA, PURVA ASHADHA, DHANISHTHA and UTTARA BHADRAPADA.

The Dissolution (*laya* or *samhara*) nakshatras are KRITTIKA, ARDRA, ASHLESHA, UTTARA PHALGUNI, SWATI, JYESHTHA, UTTARA ASHADHA, SHATABHISHA and REVATI.

Creation nakshatras imply the beginnings of things, maintenance nakshatras suggest their preservation, and dissolution nakshatras indicate their destruction, discontinuance or dismantling. A visionary executive brimming with initiative and with the courage to inaugurate new plans may well have significant factors of her horoscope placed in creation nakshatras. Her assistant, a nickle-and-dime-counting plodder, may be instrumental in maintaining what is established through the executive's enterprise if the assistant's chart has significant placements in the maintenance nakshatras. Dissolution nakshatras may predominate in the chart of the man who clears away things that have become useless or superfluous, whether he dismantles cars or corporations.

Direction

The 'upward' nakshatras are ROHINI, ARDRA, PUSHYA, PURVA PHALGUNI, UTTARA ASHADHA, SHRAVANA, DHANISHTHA and UTTARA BHADRAPADA.

The 'downward' nakshatras are BHARANI, KRITTIKA, ASHLESHA, MAGHA, UTTARA PHALGUNI, VISHAKHA, MULA, PURVA ASHADHA and PURVA BHADRAPADA.

The 'level' (sideways) nakshatras are ASHVINI, MRIGASHIRSHA,

PUNARVASU, HASTA, CHITRA, SWATI, ANURADHA, JYESHTHA and REVATI.

'Upward' nakshatras are auspicious for things that 'grow' upward, that take place above the ground. They are good for the construction of structures such as towers or buildings, especially multi-tiered ones; the planting of trees and other plants; aerial or above-ground means of transportation; and activities such as mountain climbing. Because these nakshatras also signify increase and expansion, when malefics occupy them without the company or aspect of benefics, it may indicate major illness or a bodily defect, particularly in the parts of the body ruled by the afflicted nakshatra.

The 'downward' nakshatras are the opposite of the 'upward' nakshatras in the sense that the downward nakshatras represent contraction or containment. Malefics placed in these nakshatras may not indicate illness at all, because the effect of the malefics is contained and contracted. Since they also indicate deep penetration, these nakshatras are auspicious for any sort of digging, including drilling for oil or water wells, mines, tunnels and archaeological excavations. They stand for below-the-surface activities and means of transportation, like diving, cave explorations, subways and submarines, and connote deep research of any kind. They are associated with gambling.

The 'level' nakshatras represent the midpoint between expansion and contraction, and malefics placed here without the company or aspect of benefics may indicate minor illnesses or bodily defects. These nakshatras are useful for leveling things like floors, pictures, door frames, buildings scheduled for demolition, or landfill sites waiting to be filled. They are also associated with the purchase and sale of animals.

Gender

The male nakshatras are ASHVINI, PUNARVASU, PUSHYA, HASTA, ANURADHA, SHRAVANA, PURVA BHADRAPADA and UTTARA BHADRAPADA.

The female nakshatras are BHARANI, KRITTIKA, ROHINI, ARDRA,

ASHLESHA, MAGHA, PURVA PHALGUNI, UTTARA PHALGUNI,
CHITRA, SWATI, VISHAKHA, JYESHTHA, PURVA ASHADHA,
UTTARA ASHADHA, DHANISHTHA and REVATI.

The neuter nakshatras are MRIGASHIRSHA, MULA and
SHATABHISHA.

This classification is mainly used to help determine the sex of a child,
although it can also be used to estimate archetypal masculine and
feminine qualities, irrespective of the native's physical sex (i.e., anyone
in whose chart female nakshatras dominate may have strong archetypal feminine qualities, even if male, and vice versa). To estimate the
sex of children, siblings, father's siblings, and the rest, note whether
the indicators of the relative in question occupy male or female
nakshatras. If, for instance, the lord of the fifth house (children) is
Jupiter (a male graha) and is in a male nakshatra, one would expect
the birth of a boy – provided of course that the chart promises a birth.

An interesting dilemma can arise when using grahas, rashis and
nakshatras in this context. No problem arises if the graha, rashi and
nakshatra all agree in gender; but if one is neutral, the next male, and
the last female, then a major difficulty exists, which can best be solved
by deciding the strongest of the factors under consideration. To do
this, use the standard methods for determining planetary strength to
evaluate the strength of the graha, the ruler of the rashi, and the
nakshatra lord involved. If the lord of the fifth house in a horoscope
is the neutral graha Mercury who sits in the male rashi of Aries (ruled
by Mars) and in the female nakshatra of Bharani (ruled by Venus), the
strongest among Mercury, Mars and Venus would then indicate the
most likely outcome. In this example, Mercury is neutral in strength,
since Mars is neutral to Mercury. If Mars were in its own rashi and
Venus were exalted, then Venus would be strongest (all other factors
being equal), and a girl would be indicated; if the relative strengths of
Mars and Venus were reversed, a boy would be more likely.

Nadi

The Kapha nakshatras are KRITTIKA, ROHINI, ASHLESHA, MAGHA,
SWATI, VISHAKHA, UTTARA ASHADHA, SHRAVANA and REVATI.

The Pitta nakshatras are BHARANI, MRIGASHIRSHA, PUSHYA, PURVA PHALGUNI, CHITRA, ANURADHA, PURVA ASHADHA, DHANISHTHA and UTTARA BHADRAPADA.

The Vata nakshatras are ASHVINI, ARDRA, PUNARVASU, UTTARA PHALGUNI, HASTA, JYESHTHA, MULA, SHATABHISHA and PURVA BHADRAPADA.

The *nadi* (which here means 'pulse') of the nakshatras is a classification used both for marital horoscope comparison and for medical astrology. Planets which occupy a nakshatra have their nature influenced by that nakshatra's pulse, which is its Ayurvedic constitution. Malefics, especially those not modified by the influence of benefics, will disturb the dosha indicated by the nakshatra, while benefics which are not influenced by malefics will favorably strengthen the dosha of the nakshatra they occupy.

For example, those natives in whose horoscopes an afflicted Jupiter (which indicates Kapha) occupies the second house (throat, eyes) in Cancer (Kapha) in Ashlesha (Kapha) may constantly have to clear mucus from their throats, may have excessive mucus draining from their eyes when they arise in the morning, or may have fleshy throats or double chins. If, however, the malefic Saturn occupies this position instead of Jupiter, then the individual's Kapha may be disturbed in some Saturnine way. Since Saturn represents Vata, one of whose qualities is dryness, Saturn may dry up the innate moistness of Cancer and Ashlesha in the area of the body represented by the second bhava, resulting in dry mouth, throat or eyes. This symptom will be particularly noticeable when that Saturn is activated during certain periods of that native's life (see Chapter Eleven).

Nature

The Fixed or Permanent (*dhruva*) nakshatras are ROHINI, UTTARA PHALGUNI, UTTARA ASHADHA and UTTARA BHADRAPADA.

The Movable or Ephemeral (*chara*) nakshatras are PUNARVASU, SWATI, SHRAVANA, DHANISHTHA and SHATABHISHA.

The Sharp or Dreadful (*tikshna*) nakshatras are ARDRA, ASHLESHA, JYESHTHA and MULA. These are also known as Hard (*daruna*) nakshatras.

The Soft, Mild or Tender (*mridu*) nakshatras are MRIGASHIRSHA, CHITRA, ANURADHA and REVATI.

The Sharp and Soft (i.e. mixed) nakshatras are KRITTIKA and VISHAKHA.

The Fierce or Severe (*ugra*) nakshatras are BHARANI, MAGHA, PURVA PHALGUNI, PURVA ASHADHA and PURVA BHADRAPADA.

The Light (*laghu* = not heavy) or Swift (*kshipra*) nakshatras are ASHVINI, PUSHYA and HASTA.

Planets occupying movable nakshatras incline one to movement, be it travel, a career change, a change of residence, or something else entirely. Fixed nakshatras conversely indicate stability, permanence, or little movement. According to Chapter 98 of Varahamihira's *Brihat Samhita*, sharp nakshatras suggest 'success in attacks, acts of torture, punishment, mesmerism, exorcism, and acts of separation or alliance', implying strong, well-defined, impassioned, focused, arduous activities. Because the soft, mild, or tender nakshatras are good for 'making friends, sexual union, enjoyment of garments and ornaments, performance of auspicious ceremonies like marriage, and music', we conclude that they are easy-going, pleasure-loving nakshatras.

The light or swift nakshatras 'are beneficial in trade, sales, sensual activities, acquisition of knowledge, the making of ornaments and other fine arts, skilled labor (like carpentry or plumbing), medical treatment, and for acquisition or repayment of money'. They are also auspicious for administering medicine, and for the acquisition and repayment of debt, perhaps because their swiftness makes the medicines work quickly and the loans be speedily repaid.

The fierce nakshatras live up to their name by being effective for 'ruining enemies, destruction, disgrace, deceit, imprisoning, poisoning, burning, striking with weapons, murders, and the like'. These nakshatras can indicate terrorists, assassins, and those who pursue lawsuits. One man, now deceased, who burned down a factory for the insurance money was born with the Moon, the lord of the second house of money, in the eleventh house of gain, occupying the Ugra nakshatra of Bharani. The severe nakshatras are not of course wholly despicable, for when they are prominent in a chart the native may be a good student of the martial arts.

Qualities

The Sattvic nakshatras are PUNARVASU, ASHLESHA, VISHAKHA, JYESHTHA, PURVA BHADRAPADA and REVATI.

The Rajasic nakshatras are BHARANI, KRITTIKA, ROHINI, PURVA PHALGUNI, UTTARA PHALGUNI, HASTA, PURVA ASHADHA, UTTARA ASHADHA and SHRAVANA.

The Tamasic nakshatras are ASHVINI, MRIGASHIRSHA, ARDRA, PUSHYA, MAGHA, CHITRA, SWATI, ANURADHA, MULA, DHANISHTHA, SHATABHISHA and UTTARA BHADRAPADA.

These qualities will be influenced by the nature of the planets which occupy the appropriate nakshatra. Pushya's Tamasic side will be displayed more readily when it is occupied by Mars than by Jupiter, both because Mars is inherently Tamasic and Jupiter is inherently Sattvic, and because Pushya appears in the constellation of Cancer, in which Mars is debilitated and Jupiter is exalted. Jupiter is particularly likely to enhance Pushya's divine propensities (see Species, below) because the ruling deity of Pushya is Brihaspati (Jupiter).

Sexual type

The nakshatras, in order, possess the sexual organs (*yoni*) and sexual habits of the following creatures:

1 – Horse; 2 – Elephant; 3 – Sheep; 4 – Serpent; 5 – Serpent; 6 – Dog; 7 – Cat; 8 – Sheep; 9 – Cat; 10 – Rat; 11 – Rat; 12 – Cow; 13 – Buffalo; 14 – Tiger; 15 – Buffalo; 16 – Tiger; 17 – Deer; 18 – Deer;

19 – Dog; 20 – Monkey; 21 – Cow; 22 – Monkey; 23 – Lion; 24 – Horse; 25 – Lion; 26 – Cow; 27 – Elephant.

This classification is mainly used for the comparison of horoscopes for marriage compatibility, in particular the couple's sexual compatibility. For this evaluation, which is always performed in the context of other factors, creatures of a similar type will have greater sexual compatibility than will those which are radically dissimilar, or which are naturally inimical to each other; common sense suggests that a rat would not be happy married to a cat, or a deer to a tiger or lion. Someone born with the Moon in, say, Bharani obviously will not literally possess the sexual organ of an elephant, but should he or she choose to marry a monkey it may seem that way.

Species

ASHVINI, MRIGASHIRSHA, PUNARVASU, PUSHYA, HASTA, SWATI, ANURADHA, SHRAVANA and REVATI are divine (*devata*) nakshatras.

BHARANI, ROHINI, ARDRA, PURVA PHALGUNI, UTTARA PHALGUNI, PURVA ASHADHA, UTTARA ASHADHA, PURVA BHADRAPADA and UTTARA BHADRAPADA are human (*manushya*) nakshatras.

KRITTIKA, ASHLESHA, MAGHA, CHITRA, VISHAKHA, JYESHTHA, MULA, DHANISHTHA and SHATABHISHA are demonic (*rakshasa*) nakshatras.

The nakshatra of the Moon is used to determine species. Like the previous classification, a nakshatra's species (*gana*) is largely used in the comparison of horoscopes for marriage compatibility, a detailed subject reserved for a future publication.

Tattvas

The Earth nakshatras are ASHVINI, BHARANI, KRITTIKA, ROHINI and MRIGASHIRSHA.

The Water nakshatras are ARDRA, PUNARVASU, PUSHYA, ASHLESHA, MAGHA and PURVA PHALGUNI.

The Fire nakshatras are UTTARA PHALGUNI, HASTA, CHITRA, SWATI, VISHAKHA and ANURADHA.

The Air nakshatras are JYESHTHA, MULA, PURVA ASHADHA, UTTARA ASHADHA and SHRAVANA.

The Ether nakshatras are DHANISHTHA, SHATABHISHA, PURVA BHADRAPADA, UTTARA BHADRAPADA and REVATI.

The rules to follow here include:

· Fire and Air cooperate with each other.
· Earth and Water cooperate with each other.
· Ether indiscriminately cooperates with all the other tattvas.
· Earth does not cooperate with Fire, and especially not with Air.
· Water does not cooperate with Air, and especially not with Fire.
· Fire does not cooperate with Earth, and especially not with Water.
· Air does not cooperate with Water, and especially not with Earth.

Tattva relationships, which are used in Western astrology as they apply to the signs of the tropical zodiac, have been part of Jyotish's tradition for many centuries. When, for example, the lord of a person's seventh house is in a nakshatra whose tattva is uncooperative with the tattva of that seventh house lord (see Elements, Chapter Four), then marriage or its happiness is obstructed. In a real-life example from our files, a Leo ascendant, the lord of the seventh house Saturn (Air tattva), occupies the twelfth house in the nakshatra of Pushya (Water tattva). Air and Water do not cooperate, and neither did this woman's spouse. She has spent a good deal of her adult life unmarried, all the while wishing for relationships. Note that here Saturn in the twelfth house, a detrimental position for the lord of the seventh house of marriage, reinforces the prediction.

THE INDIVIDUAL NAKSHATRAS

None of the rules of Jyotish are sacrosanct, for all jyotishis must develop their own rules over time. There is no use in becoming attached to the rules, but there is also no way to develop your own system without first knowing the rules. Although some assert that it is possible to know quite a lot about 'Vedic astrology' without knowing much about the nakshatras, other eminent jyotishis, including our gurus, maintain that nakshatras are among the most important of all the principles in Jyotish; we will therefore pay close attention to the nakshatras. Listed below are some elementary but representative hints concerning the traditional uses of the nakshatras in the interpretation of natal horoscopes. Varahamihira's descriptions of the Moon's predictions are literal translations from his *Brihad Jataka*.

All problems associated with the body part listed for a nakshatra are understood to be ruled by that asterism. Afflictions to a nakshatra (such as when it is occupied by a malefic whose force is not attenuated by the influence of any benefic) may create diseases in the part of the body which that nakshatra rules. Such ailments are often characterized by the nature of the graha(s) involved. For example, one person with Mars (cutting) in Shravana (the sexual organ) underwent surgery on the sexual organ. Another with Mars (inflammation) in Ardra (eyes) has had many eye infections. Yet another with Rahu (spasms) in Chitra (the neck) suffers from recurring neck-muscle spasms. While these combinations sometimes show up in isolation, they must usually be read in the context of the whole chart to become evident. At what age a person will experience the anticipated difficulty can be determined only by timing techniques (see below, Chapter Eleven).

No encyclopedically comprehensive list of nakshatra meanings exists, for they vary in different contexts. After you have digested the material provided and develop a feel for some of the major themes associated with each nakshatra, your own research and observations should enable you to complement this knowledge. Be wary, however, of the many modern authors who recount the

meanings of the nakshatras by simply parroting the indications of
the rashis in which the nakshatras fall. One book lists, under the
heading of Ashvini, cerebral hemorrhage, encephalitis and headache,
all of which are readily attributable to Aries by virtue of the latter's
rulership of the head. Careers like accountant, writer, and communicator, which are often attributed to Ardra (which falls in Gemini),
are really all attributable to Gemini and its ruler Mercury, and not
necessarily to Ardra. One classical indication for Ardra is 'those
who deal in "dead" things', which includes butchers, and could
include the canned and frozen food and junk food industries, things
which Gemini certainly does not rule. Because the nakshatras are
not simply a redundant version of the better-known twelve constellations of the zodiac, we have made every attempt to purge such
indications from the information given below.

1. *Ashvini* (00° 00' Aries to 13° 20' Aries)

Varahamihira: A person whose Moon sits in Ashvini is of fine
appearance and amiable manners, fond of ornaments, skilled in
work, and intelligent.

General Indications: Ashvini's symbol is a horse's head, and its
presiding deity are the Ashvini Kumaras, the heroic, golden-
armored, horse-headed twins of ancient Vedic lore who as physicians
to the celestial gods performed many medical miracles.

When the indicator of a relative occupies Ashvini, it may indicate
that he or she is a twin (e.g. having the ninth lord in Ashvini may
imply that the father is a twin, etc.). Ashvini's horse symbolism
often indicates an interest in things equine; Ashvini also rules all
means of transportation, and suggests a great need for movement
and speed. It inclines toward quickness of movement, acquisition,
and comprehension, and indicates both the power to initiate activities and the motivation necessary for such action. This quickness
may retard efficiency, as when speech becomes indistinct because it
is too rapid, when stuttering results from an intense desire to get
the words out, or when haste in action makes waste.

When the ascendant or the Moon occupies Ashvini, it often

indicates a happy-go-lucky disposition combined with lively intelligence. Ashvini's association with the Ashvini Kumaras may indicate medicine, healing, or ministering to people's needs, or perhaps engagement in miraculous or heroic pursuits. The personal splendor of the Ashvini Kumaras generates personal charm, elegance, love of jewelry, and popularity, but also implies a certain extravagance. There may be concerns over property, black magic, or the absence of children if Ashvini is occupied by the fourth lord, the sixth lord or the fifth lord respectively.

Physiology & Diseases: The knees; the upper part of the feet.

Professions, People & Places: Physically courageous people, like law enforcement officers, army personnel, and athletes. Physicians, and people skilled as chemists or druggists. Equestrians, horse-trainers, cavalry officers, people dealing in metals and heavy machinery, people involved in transportation. Factories, copper and steel manufacturing and mining, mechanical engineers, stables, race tracks, transportation depots, criminal courts, hospitals.

2. *Bharani* (13° 20' Aries to 26° 40' Aries)

Varahamihira: The Moon in Bharani suggests a person who is successful in work, capable, truthful, and free from diseases and grief.

General Indications: The symbol of this nakshatra is a vulva. The presiding deity is Yama, the god of death, who is regarded in India as the King of Dharma.

Bharani's womb symbolism indicates changes that occur within, often growing imperceptibly until they are suddenly born and take on a life of their own. As such, Bharani suggests personal breakthroughs that are often preceded by struggles and must be nurtured by self-control, willpower, and discipline. This nakshatra implies idealistic or moralistic revolutions and social transformations, or may merely suggest morals which are overly adaptable. The womb achieves self-purification through menstruation, and Bharani rules similar processes, including such ultimate expressions of purity as individual saintliness or societal utopia. Constructive resoluteness may permit Bharani people to overcome great odds in order to triumph over some adversity, for example major illness. Still, a tendency toward jealousy, or to being plagued by the jealousy of others, often occurs in the lives of those born with the ascendant or Moon in Bharani.

Being a symbol of birth, Bharani indicates support in life, particularly maternal love and nurturing, and rules food and hospitality. As a significator of development it governs increase, mass, bulk and large quantities; but, being a vulva, its association with the womb also signifies confinement and restraint. A new life growing within a womb is subordinate to the larger system that supports its growth. According to the placement of Bharani or the planets in it, this nakshatra rules either dependants and subordinates *or* people in position or power. It also indicates the struggle and trauma that often accompany birth, and sometimes indicates a physical injury below the waist. Every birth is a death, and every death is a birth; these two forces are paradoxically complementary and antagonistic, as are the nakshatra itself and its deity Yama (death). When birth and death complement one another, they produce gentle and progressive change; but when their interplay becomes antagonistic, the results include violent revolutions and wars.

Physiology & Diseases: The head; the bottom part of the feet.

Professions, People & Places: Professions involving creativity. Livelihood through the arts, entertainment, sports or other amusements. The film industry. Anything to do with children and childbirth. The hospitality industry, including caterers, cooks and hotel staff. People associated with the production, processing or distribution of food. The tobacco, coffee and tea industries. Slaughterhouses. Knowledge of law, politics and other secular matters. People of power and high position, such as judges and ministers.

3. *Krittika* (26° 40′ Aries to 10° 00′ Taurus)

Varahamihira: When the Moon occupies Krittika, the person may be a glutton, is fond of the spouses of others, has a bright appearance, and possesses widespread fame.

General Indications: Krittika's symbol is a sharp razor-like instrument, and its deity is Agni, the sacred fire. Mythologically, Krittika (the Pleiades) is the collective foster-mother of Karttikeya, one of the sons of Shiva.

Krittika people are sharp, cutting and penetrating by nature. The symbolism of the razor also points to sharp or pointed implements and the work done with them, such as the skinning of animals for leather and fur production. Sharp writing and sewing implements and sharp tools like drills are all ruled by Krittika. The handsome Karttikeya's role as the general of the celestial army expresses Krittika's rulership over war, battles, armies and disputes, and Kartikkeya's renown for his monumentally heroic deeds suggests for Krittika fame and larger-than-life endeavors and projects. Since Karttikeya's personal bodily luster and armor was said to shine like the golden Sun, Krittika also rules gold, and has some association with wealth. Its mythology also indicates adoption, foster care, and the assumption of responsibility for protecting others.

The full symbolism of the ruling deity, Agni, is exceedingly intricate. Physiologically it relates primarily to the body's digestive fire, which enables the digestion and assimilation of food. Therefore Krittika rules appetite, cooking, digestion and the like. Agni also indicates the mental 'fire' which enables the digestion and assimilation of information and knowledge. Just as the fire flares up and dies away, Krittika people tend to experience frequent ups and downs in their private lives. When either the lagna or the Moon occupies Krittika, ambition, pride and self-motivated qualities often appear in the native's personality.

Physiology & Diseases: The hips and loins; the upper and back portions of the head.

Professions, People & Places: Inventors, discoverers and excavators. Heads of state or other big organizations. Military, police and fire department personnel. Performers of fire sacrifices. Barbers, butchers and tailors. Makers of weaponry, including explosives; makers of sharp utensils and cooking devices. All those who live by fire, such as potters and blacksmiths. Makers and users of trade tools.

Carpenters and building contractors. Skilled magicians, metaphysicians and astronomers.

4. *Rohini* (10° 00′ Taurus to 23° 20′ Taurus)

Varahamihira: The Moon in Rohini makes for a person who is truthful, not covetous, clean in habits, sweet of speech, firm of views, and comely in appearance.

General Indications: Rohini's symbol is a cart, and its deity is the god Brahma, the creator. Because Brahma rules creation and origins, especially of the material world, Rohini governs sowing and planting, sprouting and growing. Since Rohini's cart is pulled by oxen, this nakshatra also rules both cattle and conveyances. Being very growth-oriented, it connotes rising, climbing, or being lifted to a great height, and also all sorts of promotion and development. Rohini imperceptibly but surely eludes obstacles and disengages from anything that comes in its way, but its association with materiality does create a potential for vulgarity.

One ancient Indian myth makes Rohini, the red star Aldebaran in Taurus, the favorite of the Moon's 27 nakshatra-wives, because of her beauty, charm and culture, her expertise in art and music, and her skill in the conjugal arts. The word 'Rohini' is etymologically linked with a Sanskrit term for red, a color which symbolizes passion and sensuality and is the color of its principal star. Classically feminine qualities and articles, including physical beauty, love, romance, perfumes, scents and fragrances are all associated with Rohini.

When the Moon or Venus appears in this nakshatra, their qualities become mutually enhanced, unless they are somehow afflicted. While the ascendant or the Moon occupying Rohini often indicates a critical or fault-finding nature, a slim physique, and a fondness for the opposite sex, people with the Moon or Venus in Rohini rising in the lagna often have great charm, beauty and charisma, as well as ability or strong attraction for the arts. A famous example of this is Lord Krishna, who is said to have been born with Taurus rising and the Moon in the first house in Rohini. The position of the

Moon in Rohini in the lagna admirably reflects Krishna's alluring character as master of the flute and as winner of all hearts through his beauty and charm. Similar results may occur when Moon or Venus appears well-placed in Rohini as the lagna lord.

We can extend this principle to other relatives in the horoscope. When the Moon and/or Venus occupies the fourth house in Rohini, the native may have an attractive, fashionable and/or artistic mother; someone with Moon as the lord of the seventh house occupying Rohini in the fifth house may have a spouse with similar attributes; and so on.

Physiology & Diseases: The shins and calves of the legs, and the ankles; the forehead.

Professions, People & Places: Dignified, able people. Agriculture and related subjects. People who grow, process or handle food. Herbalists. The fashion, beauty and pleasure or leisure industries. The automotive and oil industries. Bars, restaurants and hotels. Dealers in aquatic products. The navy and the shipping industry.

5. *Mrigashirsha* (23° 20' Taurus to 6° 40' Gemini)

Varahamihira: Those whose Moon resides in this nakshatra lack firm or fixed views, are capable yet timid, have good speech and active habits, are rich, and indulge in sexual pleasures.

General Indications: Mrigashirsha's symbol is a deer, and its ruling deity is the Moon. Mrigashirsha literally means 'deer's head'. Once it happened that the Creator, Brahma, lusted after his own daughter. The frightened girl took the form of a doe (the previous nakshatra, Rohini, 'the red doe', ruled by Brahma) and fled into the sky, but her lecherous father took on a stag's form and pursued her. In order to protect the girl from possible cosmic incest, Shiva cooled Brahma's passion by snipping off the stag's head, which remained in the sky as the nakshatra Mrigashirsha. When Saturn as the lord of the seventh house occupies this nakshatra, it often indicates marital unhappiness or strife through ill-considered romantic alliances, as illustrated through this mythology.

Because deer are timid, shy and nervous creatures given to quick fidgety movements in their constant search for food and safety, searching and seeking things out are primary qualities of Mrigashirsha, which also signifies the tenderness that a deer evokes. In that half of the nakshatra which falls in the Earth rashi of Taurus, the search takes place on the physical plane, and on the mental plane in the half which falls in the Air rashi of Gemini. Since deer roam around on predictable trails, this asterism is associated with journeys, moves, roads and paths. Mrigashirsha also suggests hunting, which is one form of search. Because the Moon, its deity, is an enchanting, changeable, inconstant, fickle body, Mrigashirsha indicates a clever, persuasive person who is sensual and fickle. Other traditional associations include marriage, gems, leadership, investigation, and grandeur. When the lagna or the Moon occupies Mrigashirsha, the native is often suspicious and prone to wander, and espouses rigid attitudes.

Physiology & Diseases: The eyes and eyebrows.

Professions, People & Places: Those significantly involved in sales. All those who gain through textiles and garments. Gem producers and dealers. Foresters and those associated with animals and other creatures, like veterinarians, pet shop owners and animal trainers. Poets and lovers. Administrators. Great thinkers and seekers.

6. *Ardra* (6° 40′ Gemini to 20° 00′ Gemini)

Varahmihira: The Moon in Ardra indicates an irritable, ungrateful, troublesome person who is prone to insincerity and addicted to wicked deeds.

General Indications: Ardra's symbol is a teardrop, and its presiding deity is Rudra, a storm god who controls destruction and dissolution.

Ardra (literally 'wet' or 'moist') is associated with wetness, dampness, vapors and liquids, and with their movement or flow. The watery teardrop implies loss or disappointment, as does the deity, Rudra, whose name is etymologically associated with weeping, and also with roaring and howling, which are storm sounds. Ardra thus connotes the processes through which loss and disappointment may take place. Lack of gratitude and a certain malice are traditionally associated with this nakshatra, which may create a tendency to treachery and deception concerning business or finance. Ardra also rules diplomacy, people who are critical by nature, cruelty, lawlessness, perversity, self-centered attitudes, lying and cheating. When the lagna or the Moon occupies Ardra, the native may have strong feelings which may be overwhelming.

Planets positioned in Ardra, and the matters indicated by the houses they rule, may be a source of sorrow and disappointment. If Mars, one significator for siblings, happens to be lord of the third house of siblings (as it is for Virgo and Aquarius lagnas) and happens to occupy Ardra, the native may have no siblings or may have a difficult relationship with them, or a brother or sister may die or be seriously distressed. Ardra being feminine, when the lord of a horoscope's fifth house is associated with Ardra, the first child is expected to be female, though another opinion is that any graha connected with children becomes mostly barren when occupying this nakshatra.

If Ardra figures prominently in your horoscope, you can take heart (though its significations seem undesirable) from the thought that loss may lead to new growth and that your tears may be the moisture which will make your world fecund yet again. If nothing in the world ever ceased, eventually there would be no room left for anything new and different. Rudra, who is Shiva in another guise, is really the remover of misery, because he removes everything which has outlived its usefulness. Those who endure the trials and tribulations of Ardra gain the pride and satisfaction of conscious worth, a knowledge of how much it costs to accomplish one's goals.

Physiology & Diseases: The top and back of the head; the eyes.

Professions, People & Places: Those who deal in 'dead' things like canned, frozen and junk food. Butchers. Those who are expert at misrepresentation and double-talk: meddlesome politicians and dishonorable salespeople, liars and cheats, rogues and thieves. Those who deal with primal energies, like atomic researchers. Those who actively encourage the destruction of living entities: cruel persons, murderers, makers of chemical formulas intended to kill viruses, bacteria and diseases, chemotherapists, drug-pushers, etc.

7. *Punarvasu* (20° 00′ Gemini to 3° 20′ Cancer)

Varahamihira: When the Moon tenants Punarvasu, the native is good-natured, quiet, patient and devout, lives in comfort, and is sickly, thirsty, pleased with trifles, and possessed of contrary views.

General Indications: Punarvasu's symbol is a quiver of arrows, and its deity is Aditi, a feminine goddess of the Vedas who is frequently associated with infinity and unboundedness. Aditi represents true freedom and plenty, which is the product of an amiable, adaptive, understanding and reasonable character, one who is capable of being happy with little when necessary. Aditi is also associated with virtues and, by extension, the striving to act nobly, which links Punarvasu to philosophy, religion, yoga, and similar means to enhanced self-understanding. When the lagna or the Moon occupies Punarvasu, the native often enjoys a profound and inspired imagination, accompanied by a fondness for poetry. The Moon or Jupiter posited in the fourth quarter of this nakshatra (which falls in the first part of the constellation Cancer) gives strong spiritual yearnings, and may also indicate archetypally feminine virtues and graces.

Punarvasu's quiver symbolizes potential energy and resources, the arrows being ready for use as appropriate. As the arrow's abode, the quiver suggests something that is returned to its appropriate resting place, and so represents one's home or a homecoming and, by extension, any residence or dwelling. Those in whose horoscopes Punarvasu is prominent may pursue endeavors which compel them to lead lives of relative retirement from the world, living in the intimacy of family or friends away from heavy public involvements, greatly attached to the home but, like the arrow in the quiver, always prepared for travel. This may result in a simultaneous preference for travel and a dislike for changing residence. Since an arrow may be taken from its quiver, used, and then returned to its quiver, Punarvasu also suggests repetition, recycling, and regaining that which was lost or used. The arrow also suggests flight, and a capacity to penetrate its target, no matter how distant mentally or physically.

Physiology & Diseases: The fingers; the nose.

Professions, People and Places: Philosophers, imaginative or innovative thinkers or doers, churches and temples. Teachers of virtue and self-enhancement. Psychologists and gurus. Artisans and trade people involved in the construction and maintenance of dwellings. Architects, civil engineers, scientists, and the like.

8. *Pushya* (3° 20′ Cancer to 16° 40′ Cancer)

Varahamihira: Moon in Pushya produces people who are able to control their passions, who are generally well-liked, who are learned in various lore, rich, and fond of doing charitable acts.

General Indications: Pushya ('nourishing') has for a symbol the milk-yielding udder of a cow, and its deity is Brihaspati, the planet Jupiter, who is the priest and preceptor of the gods. Pushya's old name is *Tishya* ('auspicious'), and another synonym is *Sidhya* ('prosperous'), all indications of its ability to nourish on all planes, including the physical, emotional, mental, material and spiritual. Pushya is associated with abundance, growth, opulence, and with the best of everything, which means it can also indicate plumpness or fat. Pushya promotes renown and popularity, but also ensures selflessness and philanthropy, just as the cow is famed for willingly giving its milk to others as well as to its own calf.

Because the Moon is by nature a nurturing planet, Moon in Pushya may indicate very strong tendencies to nurture, physically, emotionally or mentally. Other planets in Pushya often indicate a sense of nourishing or being nurtured in the matters they activate in that horoscope by house rulership. Natural benefics here find their positive supportive meanings enhanced; natural malefics in Pushya are softened so that, though their exteriors may still be hard, their interiors become nurturing. When the lord of the seventh house tenants Pushya, it may indicate a nurturing spouse; the fifth lord there may indicate nurturing children, and so on.

Pushya's association with Brihaspati gives it rulership over speech, oratory, eloquence, wisdom, luck and aristocracy, and over religious and priestly inclinations. Devotion and prayer, virtuous conduct, peace of mind, purity, truth, honesty and philosophy all appear in Pushya's portfolio, though it can also represent excessive orthodoxy, traditionalism or non-creativity. When the lagna or the Moon occupies Pushya, the native is often philosophical, religious or wise, and may benefit from superiors and from powerful organizations like governments.

Physiology & Diseases: The mouth, face, and facial expression.

Professions, People & Places: Aristocrats and highly-placed people like rulers, ministers and exalted (managing) directors. Food merchants and grain dealers. The dairy industry. The clergy and others associated with self-enhancement teachings, like gurus, transpersonal psychologists and priests.

9. *Ashlesha* (16° 40′ Cancer to 30° 00′ Cancer)

Varahamihira: Those with Moon in Ashlesha are inattentive to the work of other people, promiscuous eaters, sinful and ungrateful, and skilled in deceiving others.

General Indications: Ashlesha's symbol is a coiled serpent, and its presiding deity is Sarpas, the divinized serpent. Ashlesha stands for everything associated with snakes.

Indians think of snakes as wily, creepy creatures which hypnotize their prey with their movements and their eyes before entwining themselves around their victims. Snakes, which enjoy secrecy and are often misunderstood, like to operate out of sight. They are proverbial for insincerity, avarice, deception, cold-bloodedness, and for poisonous, painful, fanged bites. Yet they are also credited with great wisdom, cunning, insight, powers of concentration, and primordial energy and power, particularly sexual power. Ashlesha, therefore, represents intertwining, coiling, torment, deception, secret sexual unions, searing pain and other serpent-like qualities, as well as the insight and wisdom that are associated with this asterism.

Insight encourages holistic understanding, but this understanding often provokes misunderstandings, painful separations and other serious troubles in life.

Lagna or Moon in Ashlesha often indicates a blunt character which, when otherwise afflicted, may make the native contentious and disliked by others. The boxer Mohammed Ali, a blunt character who hypnotized opponents and fans alike while enraging his detractors, was born with Ashlesha rising. Former President Lyndon Johnson, who was also born with Ashlesha rising, amply displayed Ashlesha's profound deviousness.

Ashlesha may disrupt the significations of any grahas which occupy it. Mahatma Gandhi's Moon, which was lord of his tenth house of career, sat in Ashlesha, and his career was certainly disrupted many times. One unique claim for Ashlesha is that favorable results occur when Ketu occupies this nakshatra and Ashlesha is aspected by Jupiter.

Physiology & Diseases: The joints and the nails; the ears.

Professions, People and Places: People who deal with poisons, like chemical engineers, druggists and junkies. All who deal with reptiles, like zoologists and owners of pet snakes. People who are very self-serving, like robbers, behind-the-scenes manipulators and greedy, cunning, miserly politicians and business people. Those who deal in or gain through sex. Controversial but insightful people. Primordial energy.

10. *Magha* (00° 00′ Leo to 13° 20′ Leo)

Varahamihira: The Moon in Magha gives numerous servants, an inclination to worship the gods and ancestors, and engagement in important works.

General Indications: Magha's symbol is that of a royal throne-room, and its presiding deities are the Pitris, the ancestors of one's family who are still regularly worshipped in traditional Hindu families. The bright royal star Regulus is its principal star.

The throne-room, a place of diplomacy, tact and ceremony,

evokes images of splendor and regality, of noble and eminent persons, and of important endeavors, though Magha may also be associated with the restlessness that arises from personal ambitions. Lagna or Moon here often indicates a regal manner, and a weakness for the opposite sex. All other factors being equal, the royal planets Sun and Mars thrive in Magha, but the servant planets (Saturn, Rahu and Ketu) are very obstructed there.

The ancestors, who are the shoulders of the previous generations on which the current one stands, evoke notions of old traditions and patrician and matrician lineages. Our ancestors give us our precious lives, a gift often given in the natural biological procreative impulse without expectation of return. In this context Magha represents gifts freely given or bestowed without expectation of return, and so suggests support. In which fields of life these gifts will be given is often keyed to the planets who occupy Magha and the houses they rule or occupy in the horoscope. Sometimes the house in which Magha falls indicates the field of opportunity; when for example Magha falls within the tenth house, career opportunities may be bountiful. This principle may also be applied to the lord of a house; a tenth lord which occupies Magha may bestow abundant career opportunities.

Physiology & Diseases: The nose, lips and chin.

Professions, People & Places: Those who are involved with big concerns or companies, like government employees and heads of state or of big businesses. Lawyers and judges. High courts. People involved in the study of lineages, including historians, archaeologists, and birth registry officials. Maintainers and users of tradition, such as well-established universities, societies and clubs, and those associated with them.

11. *Purva Phalguni* (13° 20′ Leo to 26° 40′ Leo)

Varahamihira: When in Purva Phalguni, the Moon grants sweet speech, generosity in bestowing liberal gifts, a habit of wandering, and government service.

General Indications: Purva Phalguni's symbol is a bed or hammock, and its deity is Bhaga, one of the Adityas, the gods responsible for protecting and maintaining conjugal bliss and wealth. Its alternate deity is the Shiva Lingam, a symbol of Shiva.

Hammocks symbolize rest, relaxation and enjoyment, and Bhaga adds love, affection between the sexes, sexual passion and pleasure to this nakshatra's symbolism. Natives of Purva Phalguni tend to be carefree, are disinclined to worry and like to rely on their luck. Such attitudes benefit health but foster impetuousness and a lack of forethought and planning. The hammock also suggests a certain inertia, an inability to remain in motion or stay motivated for very long, which may create an ongoing craving for stimulation.

The Shiva Lingam adds a more spiritual dimension, endowing the act of creation with a sacred meaning. This potential surfaces when the nakshatra itself, or the planets within it, are well placed (as when Jupiter occupies Purva Phalguni in a kendra or kona). Such a person is likely to understand something of the process of creation. Through this association with the act of creation, Purva Phalguni also indicates the creative arts. It is traditionally said to promote fame, renown and the acquisition of wealth through personal merit or charisma. Lagna or Moon here often indicates a healthy body but an impulsive mind which leads to regrettable actions. Possible accidents occur through fire or heat.

Physiology & Diseases: The lips, the sex organs, and the right hand.

Professions, People & Places: Music, musicians, actors and other creative artists. Things, places and people associated with rest and relaxation, vacations, and entertainment (especially theater, cinema and classical music). Dressing up and going out. Professions connected with marriage: wedding planners, marriage counselors, sex therapists, etc.

12. *Uttara Phalguni* (26° 40′ Leo to 10° 00′ Virgo)

Varahamihira: When in Uttara Phalguni, the Moon makes natives earn money by their learning, be generally liked by all, and live a life in comfort and luxury.

General Indications: Uttara Phalguni's symbol is a bed or hammock, and its deity is Aryaman, another of the Adityas. In the divine scheme of things, Aryaman rules patronage, favors and kindness, and is often invoked jointly with Bhaga, the Aditya who is the presiding deity of Purva Phalguni and who is responsible for marital love, sensuality, and wealth acquired through personal merit. Purva Phalguni and Uttara Phalguni being in many ways similar, their general indications are to a great extent interchangeable and complementary; even their deities are often worshipped together. Uttara Phalguni, through its association with Aryaman, has however an additional connotation of eagerness to help others and alleviate suffering through kindness and generosity. It also indicates the people one approaches for favors and boons, the patronage one is likely to receive in life, and one's intimates and very close friends. While benefics well placed in this nakshatra may enhance intimate relationships, malefics that are poorly placed there will disturb them.

When Uttara Phalguni is somehow prominent in a birth chart, there may be gain or scandal or both through amorous adventures. Lagna or Moon here often couples good intelligence with a tendency toward indiscreet behavior and a capacity for enjoying life. Warren Beatty, an actor famed for his sexual escapades, was born with this nakshatra rising. Jack Nicholson, Beatty's reputed friend and fellow marauder, was born with a Cancer ascendant and the Moon in this nakshatra, thus creating a double influence, first on the Moon in its role as lord of the ascendant, and next on the Moon as the indicator of the mind.

Physiology & Diseases: The lips, the sex organs, and the left hand.

Professions, People & Places: People of high position with wealth who are held in esteem by others, like media or sports superstars or sex symbols. People interested in helping their fellow beings, like social workers and philanthropists. Many of the indications of Purva Phalguni.

13. *Hasta* (10° 00′ Virgo to 23° 20′ Virgo)

Varahamihira: When the Moon is in Hasta, the person has active habits, is full of resources, is shameless and merciless, and is a thief and drunkard.

General Indications: Hasta's symbol is a hand, usually with the fingers closed as if grasping something or forming a fist. The presiding deity is Savitri or Surya, the Sun.

The hand suggests skilled activities, and also indicates both a grasping nature and an ability to grab and hold on to all sorts of things, be they material, spiritual, mental, emotional or physical. Hasta's image is of daily repetitive work and achievement (e.g. as an artisan) rather than leadership, though it does enhance industry, enterprise, invention and subtle thought. It gives the potential for a questionable moral orientation and a pliable conscience. The closed fist symbolizes determination and a tendency to wish to control through any means, honorable or dishonorable. The hand also provides Hasta an association with palmistry and, by extension, with Jyotish.

The Sun, who spreads light all around, is responsible for Hasta's illuminating intelligence, especially as it applies to counseling and advising. One of Hasta's traditional associations not readily apparent from its symbolism or deity is that of jesting, merriment, laughter and ridicule. Lagna or Moon in Hasta often indicates a clever, witty and entertaining person who is somewhat flighty and not very dependable. One unique attribute of this nakshatra is that when Hasta is associated with the lord of the fifth house it may deny children, or create problems with them.

Physiology & Diseases: The hands and the fingers.

Professions, People & Places: Advisers, ministers, authors, counselors, educators and priests. Thieves, rascals and rogues. People who are skilled with their hands, like artisans, handcrafters, pickpockets, and stage magicians. People attracted to comedy: comedians, pranksters, jesters, mime artists, etc. Palmists and astrologers, and those interested in such subjects.

14. *Chitra* (23° 20′ Virgo to 6° 40′ Libra)

Varahamihira: Those who have Moon in Chitra enjoy wearing variegated clothes and flowers, and have attractive eyes and limbs.

General Indications: Chitra's symbol is a shining jewel. Its deity is usually considered to be Tvashtri (later known as Vishvakarma), the celestial architect.

Jewels dazzle, fascinate and are valuable, and Chitra is usually associated with elegance, charisma, personal charm, bright and variegated colors, and anything that is different, new or unusual. Chitra people are conspicuous; they stand out and aspire to shine in life. They have a gift for narration and well-ordered conversation, and are indefatigable and unconquerable. Mahatma Gandhi was born with Chitra rising and the lord of the lagna in the ascendant conjoined with Mars, making him very hard to defeat, and most energetic. Lagna or Moon here often indicates a serious and profound student with a fondness for books, a privately exuberant and sexy character who hides behind a publicly contained persona.

Since Vishvakarma is credited with having designed the universe and its contents, Chitra rules creation, the arts, and an ability to arrange things in orderly ways. Similar to the interaction between form and function which creates the beauty and utility of an architectural design, Chitra likes to weigh form against function, and vice versa, making Chitra people cogent, balanced thinkers and analyzers. Independent business skills are usually very strong.

Physiology & Diseases: The forehead; the neck.

Professions, People & Places: Able persons. Versatile geniuses and expert business people. Capital cities, riches, and valuable things. The arts, in particular painting, photography, design, music, and imaginative or unusual writing. Medicine, in particular a knowledge of unusual herbs and other medicinal substances. Anything to do with construction, from jewelry making, embroidery, frame making and engraving to industrial engineering and manufacturing. Machinery, its invention, organization and use.

15. *Swati* (6° 40′ Libra to 20° 00′ Libra)

Varahamihira: The Moon in Swati shows a person of mild and quiet nature who controls his or her passions and desires, is skilled in trade, merciful, able to bear thirst, sweet of speech, and charitable.

General Indications: Swati's symbol is a young sprout quivering in the wind, and its deity is Vayu, the wind.

Swati suggests new beginnings and the growth that follows them, and implies adaptability, the capacity to go with the flow in the interest of survival. The delicate Swati always strives for greater growth and independence in the same way that a plant's young shoot self-individuates on its way to maturity in spite of being vulnerable and fragile. Lagna or Moon here often indicates a person who is philosophical, thoughtful, spiritual or religious, one who tends to need time to digest his or her understanding. Swati has a special association with Saraswati, the goddess of learning who is invoked particularly for progress in literature and music. It is auspicious to begin worshipping Saraswati when the Moon occupies Swati.

Swati also symbolizes purification, restlessness and a tendency to sway back and forth or experience some instability. These tendencies may be keyed to the house that Swati occupies or to the planets which occupy Swati. That Swati's deity is Vayu reinforces its proclivity to restlessness and roaming, and alludes to the possibility that the body's wind (its Vata, Ayurvedically-speaking) may be disturbed. Vata disturbance can cause all sorts of illnesses, in particular flatulence and gastric distress due to gas, if Swati is afflicted, as it would be if Rahu occupied it in a horoscope's sixth house. When Rahu occupies the lagna in Swati, however, it can give great strength and endurance, because Rahu, Venus and Saturn become especially powerful in Swati.

Physiology & Diseases: The intestines; the chest.

Professions, People & Places: People with an independent spirit and mental strength. Merchants and others who are good at buying and selling. Those who establish independent businesses and professional practices. Ascetics and others engaged in strong devotional practices. Students of profound subjects.

16. *Vishakha* (20° 00′ Libra to 3° 20′ Scorpio)

Varahamihira: The Moon in Vishakha makes one jealous of the prosperity of others, stingy, bright in appearance, distinct in speaking, skilled at making money, and inclined to create quarrels between people.

General Indications: Vishakha's symbol is a triumphal gateway decorated with leaves, and its deity is Indragni, a pair of deities, one of which is the chief of the gods and the other fire deified.

Both the symbol and the deity invoke notions of success, triumph and concentrated power. Vishakha is the conqueror, fixated on defeating rivals. Goals form one of the primary meanings of this nakshatra but, when the only objective in life becomes attainment of a goal, the individual may begin to believe that the desired end justifies the use of questionable means. Vishakha people may become dictators (either benevolent or malevolent, depending on their values). Such people are often impelled to develop and perfect logical proofs for their dogmas, so that they delve, but obsessively, into their chosen subjects. They tend to present their findings so aggressively that they alienate their audiences.

Lagna or Moon in Vishakha often gives profound courage, and a capacity to exert Herculean efforts in the direction of the goal but, if obstructions impede achievement of those goals, courage can mutate into frustrated and impatient anger. Vishakha's firm resolve can cause the mind to force the body to perform to its ambitious expectations. Inordinate ambition can lead Vishakha to become spread too thinly in trying to fulfill too many aspirations, which can result in an egocentric life which has little time for anything but the pursuit of self-interests. Vishakha often represents a lack of intimate social involvement, especially friends, and a tendency to use people as means to an end. Vishakha people are therefore usually well advised to cultivate a greater awareness of the rights of others.

Physiology & Diseases: The arms; the breasts.

Professions, People & Places: People engaged in politics or ambassadorial acts. Those who enjoy professional versatility and many-sided activities. Those engaged in literature. People with steel wills, like dictators, leaders and conquerors. Strained victory celebrations. Those who immerse themselves in subjects and develop ideologies and dogmas.

17. *Anuradha* (3° 20′ Scorpio to 16° 40′ Scorpio)

Varahamihira: The Moon when in Anuradha inclines one to be rich, to live in foreign countries, to be unable to bear hunger, and to be inclined to move from place to place.

General Indications: Anuradha's symbol – a triumphal gateway decorated with leaves – is identical with that of Vishakha. The deity is Mitra, another of the Adityas, who is responsible for friendship and partnership.

Many of Anuradha's indications are the same as for Vishakha, as their sharing of a symbol would suggest. Mitra as deity suggests one important exception: Anuradha's decided propensity for making and maintaining friendships even while remaining fixedly devoted to a goal. Mitra also implies an ability to lead and organize, to form alliances for the cooperative attainment of goals, and Anuradha people often found, manage or lead organizations.

Lagna or Moon here often indicates robust physical or mental health, and a capacity to accommodate a variety of people and attitudes. Anuradha people have numerous opportunities in life, travel frequently, and often live their lives far from their birthplaces, for Anuradha is rarely satisfied with its place of residence. Often they have strong appetites, little luck in speculation or gambling, and a strong respect for numbers. This may range from an interest in occult numerology to scientific number theory to accounting or statistics, depending on the indications in the rest of the horoscope.

Physiology & Diseases: The breasts, stomach, womb and bowels.

Professions, People & Places: Brave and courageous people who are sweet in speech. Mass leaders who inspire love and loyalty. Those who are clever in earning money and who dote on their friends. Pork-barreling, nepotism and other forms of inappropriate patronage. Joyous victory celebrations. Travelers, and people who reside in far-off places.

18. *Jyeshtha* (16° 40′ Scorpio to 30° 00′ Scorpio)

Varahamihira: Those with the Moon in Jyeshtha have very few friends but are cheerful, virtuous and irascible.

General Indications: Jyeshtha's symbol is a round protective talisman, and its presiding deity is Indra, the king of the gods.

The talisman is a physical expression of an understanding of occult or hidden forces. It can indicate either providing or receiving protection from some danger or adversity, as well as a capacity for subtle, inventive and imaginative design. Many hymns of the Veda honor Indra for his daring deeds, power, fame, glory and praise-worthiness, all qualities associated with this nakshatra. When Jyeshtha connotes gain, it may be through supernatural, occult or extraordinary means but, when afflicted, Jyeshtha betokens hard times and poverty. Saturn in Jyeshtha in, for example, the second house of money may reflect a decided lack of money, all other factors being equal. Lagna or Moon here often indicates two-faced, hypocritical and secretive behavior.

Jyeshtha means 'the eldest', particularly in social contexts, in which it represents 'the most important', 'the founder' or 'the preferred'. Seniority or pre-eminence based on preference or merit is equated here with protection because the eldest in a Hindu family is often perceived as the family's protector. The Jyeshtha person may be the patriarch or matriarch of a family, the oldest brother, sister or child, or possibly a favored paramour. When, for example, the lord of the seventh house of marriage occupies Jyeshtha, it inclines to marriage with an older person, or with a person who is senior in his or her family, all other factors being equal. The same principle may be extended to the other houses.

Physiology & Diseases: The neck; the right side of the trunk.

Professions, People & Places: The valorous, energetic and famous. Arsenals, mines and engineering firms. People who protect or are granted protection, including police, U.N. personnel, and refugees. Nepotism, pork-barreling, and other inappropriate forms of patronage. Shamans and others involved in the supernatural.

19. *Mula* (00° 00′ Sagittarius to 13° 20′ Sagittarius)

Varahamihira: Those who have the Moon in Mula are haughty, rich, happy, and not inclined to injure others. They have firm and fixed opinions, and live in luxury.

General Indications: Mula's symbol consists of some roots bunched together and tied. Its deity is Nirriti ('calamity'), the goddess of dissolution who personifies evil and corruption and is sometimes known as Alakshmi, the opposite of Lakshmi, the goddess of prosperity. Nirriti either directly induces material privation or causes prosperity to deteriorate after it is attained.

Because roots penetrate deep into unseen realms, Mula is associated with getting to the bottom of things, literally or figuratively, by scientific, philosophical and other forms of deep inquiry. Though an individual often goes deeply into a matter ruled by a planet posited in Mula, that deep inquiry may not yield affluence, particularly if the planet is otherwise afflicted, because Nirriti and Mula are opposed to abundance. For example, when the lord of the tenth house of profession occupies Mula, the individual may not prosper from his profession in a worldly sense, though he may delve deeply into it. The late Martin Luther King, whose horoscope had this combination, was a man whose level of worldly prosperity was not commensurate with his depth of professional achievement. Since Nirriti connotes opposites, reverses and losses, Mula is associated with contrariness and with borrowing and lending to one's detriment. As such, it is against the rules of electional astrology to lend or borrow during Mula, for the debt may go bad or prove to be very vexatious.

Lagna or Moon in Mula often indicates a skilled and clever individual with good oratorical abilities who can enthrall an audience. Mula also stands for the unseen origins of visible conditions, like the germs which are the roots of some diseases. Roots are also foundations, beginnings and sources. Roots being much used for medicinal purposes, Mula is associated with medicines. The fact that Mula's roots are tied adds a certain sense of restraint, bondage or limited mobility, all meanings that accompany this nakshatra.

There may be a marked tendency to be betrayed by one's colleagues.

Physiology & Diseases: The feet; the left side of the trunk.

Professions, People & Places: Medicine. Doctors and healers. People engaged in selling roots, flowers and fruits. Ministers, officers and judges (sometimes). Big courts of justice or big institutions. Investigators and researchers of all sorts. Contrarians and others who delight in presenting opposite points of view. Debaters, orators and politicians.

20. *Purva Ashadha* (13° 20′ Sagittarius to 26° 40′ Sagittarius)

Varahamihira: The Moon in Purva Ashadha gives an agreeable spouse, a proud nature, and strong attachment to friends.

General Indications: Purva Ashadha's symbol is a fan or a winnowing basket (which is used to separate grain from its husk). Its presiding deity is Apah, or water deified as a god.

Since another name for this nakshatra is Aparajita, 'the Undefeated', it connotes victory in struggles and confrontations. Purva Ashadha enables one to be patient, to wait for obstacles or unpleasant circumstances to subside in the way that a fan enables one patiently to tolerate uncomfortable heat. Fanning is actually an act of aggression on heat, just as winnowing grain is an act of aggression on the grain. These may be the reasons why Purva Ashadha is also associated with declarations of war and other aggressions. The fan and the winnowing basket being implements of culture that improve life and comfort, Purva Ashadha tends to produce strong desires to improve one's circumstances. If the planets activating this nakshatra are poorly placed, this often occurs in a self-indulgent way.

Purva Ashadha strongly suggests invincibility and, when the lagna or the Moon appears in this nakshatra, it often indicates a good debater, whose formal education may have been interrupted. Apah or water is pervasive and universal, two qualities readily associated with Purva Ashadha, which also promotes journeys by rivers and seas, sexual excesses, and watery diseases like water retention or abnormal kidney or bladder function.

Physiology & Diseases: The thighs; the back portion of the trunk.

Professions, People & Places: All professions, people and places associated with water in its various forms: shipping, sailing, navy, marine life, water utilities, etc. People who process raw materials, like manufacturers or refiners.

21. *Uttara Ashadha* (26° 40′ Sagittarius to 10° 00′ Capricorn)

Varahamihira: Whoever has the Moon in Uttara Ashadha will be obedient and learned in the rules of virtue, and will be grateful, will have many friends, will return favors received, and will generally be liked.

General Indications: Uttara Ashadha's symbol is the tusk of an elephant, and its deities are the ten Vishvadevas, the sons of the god Dharma (righteousness) and the Goddess Vishva (universality, the all). Their names, in loose translation, are Goodness, Truth, Willpower, Skillfulness, Time, Desire, Firmness, Ancestors, Brightness and Peak (or Acme), all attributes which are associated with Uttara Ashadha.

The qualities of Purva Ashadha also apply to this nakshatra, as one is the former (*purva*) part and the other the latter (*uttara*) part of the same nakshatra. One difference between them is that Uttara Ashadha is more introspective and possesses greater permanence and durability than does Purva Ashadha. It is also less aggressive than its mate. When the lagna or Moon occupies Uttara Ashadha, it often indicates honest, sincere people who are respected and valued for their advice and who are inclined to be conciliators.

The elephant-tusk symbol leads some to associate this nakshatra with Ganesha, the one-tusked elephant-headed god who is invoked to bless new beginnings and to remove obstacles from one's path. Because Uttara Ashadha connotes new beginnings and endeavors which become successful and permanent, this nakshatra when well placed gives its natives a talent for commencing new enterprises and then seeing them through to their natural conclusions. When poorly placed, the native may start new projects helter-skelter, and then fail to complete them. An elephant's tusk is sharp, and so can penetrate.

Physical penetration may imply penetration of the body (as in hunting or surgery), or causing the body to move (penetrate) into new environments (such as new lands). Mental penetration may imply great insight.

Physiology & Diseases: The thighs; the waist.

Professions, People & Places: Gracious, elegant and well-mannered people. People who embody desirable qualities. Military men and women. Hunters and people with hunting instincts. Fighters and wrestlers. Horse owners and stables. Famous doctors. Government workers. People with high ambition and a sense of responsibility or organizing capacity. Pioneers.

22. *Shravana* (10° 00′ Capricorn to 23° 20′ Capricorn)

Varahamihira: The Moon in Shravana makes a person prosperous and learned, and gives him or her a liberal-minded spouse, riches, and wide fame.

General Indications: Shravana's symbol is three footprints in an uneven row, and its deity is Vishnu, the Preserver of the cosmos.

Shravana is etymologically related to the Sanskrit verb 'to hear'. Both its etymology and its emblem, which alludes to the goddess Saraswati, the patroness of learning and wisdom, indicate profound erudition and sagacity, particularly in the realm of orally transmitted knowledge ('hearing'), which forms one of Shravana's foremost traits. All oral transmissions, including the study of languages and even the practice of gossiping, are included here; Mohammed Ali, who has the Moon as ruler of his Ashlesha/Cancer ascendant in Shravana, used words (Shravana) to hypnotize (Ashlesha) his opponents and audience.

Shravana's deity is Vishnu, the Preserver, who combines with Saraswati to cause this nakshatra chiefly to rule sacred oral traditions which are preserved in a more or less pristine state, like the Vedas and Vedangas. By extension, it also rules teaching and instruction, particularly that which preserves the knowledge of previous generations. Lagna or Moon in Shravana often indicates a person who is kind, charitable and humanistic. Shravana also governs one's gait, and limping or lameness in particular when the lords of the ninth (hips), tenth (knees), eleventh (ankles) or twelfth (feet) bhavas are afflicted in this nakshatra. Shravana also indicates travels, and sometimes creates urinary difficulties.

Physiology & Diseases: The ear; the sex organs.

Professions, People & Places: People interested in truth and religion. Learned persons and religious teachers. Scholars, savants, students, educators. Preservers of (sacred) traditions. Universities. Classical studies. Languages and linguists. Gossip columnists and news broadcasters. The recording industry. Recitals. Story-tellers.

23. *Dhanishtha* (23° 20' Capricorn to 6° 40' Aquarius)

Varahamihira: The Moon in Dhanishtha implies a liberal, rich person, brave and fond of music.

General Indications: Dhanishtha's symbol is a drum, and its deities are the eight Vedic gods known as Vasus.

Vasu can be translated both as 'good, superb, or beneficent' and as 'wealthy or possessing property'. All these qualities are associated with Dhanishtha, which rules valuable items, including gems and precious metals. Other meanings include charity, and an innate capacity to control or command others. Lagna or Moon here often indicates a person who is optimistic and ambitious. The drum suggests sound, especially musical and rhythmical sound.

One peculiarity which is consistently ascribed to Dhanishtha is marital discord and/or sexual difficulties. When Saturn occupies this nakshatra, it aggravates this tendency, particularly when it is lord of the seventh house in the horoscope. Marriage sometimes is simply delayed, but at other times it is totally denied. Men who are strongly under Dhanishtha's influence often tend toward misogyny. As always, such tendencies must be judged in the context of the entire birth chart.

Physiology & Diseases: The back; the anus.

Professions, People and Places: Medicine and surgery. Charitable institutions. Real estate. Music, especially the rhythm sections of bands and orchestras. Drummers. Military bands and other marching bands. Reciters of rhythmical incantations, prayers, poetry, etc.

24. *Shatabhisha* (6° 40′ Aquarius to 20° 00′ Aquarius)

Varahamihira: Those who have the Moon in Shatabhisha will be harsh in their speech but truthful, will suffer grief but conquer their enemies, will thoughtlessly engage in works, and will have independent ways.

General Indications: Shatabhisha's symbol is an empty circle, and its deity is Varuna, the Vedic god of the cosmic and terrestrial waters.

The circle suggests separation and containment, its circumference dividing space into inner and outer. The circumferential fence simultaneously protects the inner being from any outer danger and prevents it from joining the greater whole by segregating it, holding it captive. A shoreline confines a body of water in the same way that the horizon, the limit of our vision, encloses the sky. Shatabhisha rules reservoirs, tanks, lakes, armor and shields, outer garments and cloaks. Shatabhisha is commonly assumed to cloak or veil things, to keep them secret or hidden from view. This asterism also rules traps and paralysis, both literal and symbolic. The empty circle may also indicate 'zero', a sophisticated mathematical concept which is used in some philosophical systems to indicate the Void behind all creation. Alcoholic beverages are also ruled by Shatabhisha, perhaps because of its deity (one variety of wine in classical India was named Varuni).

When the lagna or the Moon occupies Shatabhisha, it often indicates a person who prefers solitude, is visionary and meditative, and is inclined to eat little food. Many born in Shatabhisha are scientific, philosophical or mystical. Major reversals in business during certain stages of life are likely, sometimes because of undue ambitions or rough manners that make enemies and alienate well-wishers. Illnesses whose genesis occurs in Shatabhisha are very difficult to remedy, and may require 'one hundred physicians' (a plausible translation of *shata-bhisha*) to cure. Sometimes only the Ashvini Kumaras (see Ashvini, above) can heal diseases that arise in Shatabhisha which tend to become grave and chronic.

Physiology & Diseases: The jaw; the right thigh.

Professions, People & Places: All who deal with the sky: astronomers, astrologers, aircraft industries, rocket scientists, etc. Observatories and planetariums. Those involved in advanced medical treatment of complicated and difficult-to-cure illnesses, like AIDS researchers and chemotherapists. Institutions connected with the welfare of the masses. Killers, cruel people, those who hunt for leisure, those who set traps. People connected with electricity and other modern forms of energy: electricians, nuclear scientists, experts in gravitation, etc.

25. *Purva Bhadrapada* (20° 00′ Aquarius to 3° 20′ Pisces)

Varahamihira: Those who have the Moon in Purva Bhadrapada will suffer from grief, place their wealth at the disposal of their partners, and speak distinctly; they are skilled at earning money, and are stingy.

General Indications: Purva Bhadrapada's symbol is the front part of a funeral cot (sometimes it is a man with two faces), and its presiding deity is Ajaikapada, an obscure deity whose name may mean 'the one-footed unborn one' (or, possibly, 'the one-footed goat'). Ajaika-pada seems to be a form of Rudra, whom we encountered under Ardra.

Purva Bhadrapada is traditionally associated, both physically and metaphorically, with fire and heat, combustion, and catabolic activi-ties. Perhaps this is because of its association with Rudra, a deity of destruction who rules fire and heat, especially (considering the funeral cot imagery) the fire and heat produced by the funeral pyres which cremate dead bodies. The two-faced man may symbolize the time of death, when one faces both this world, to review the past, and the other world, to peer into the realm of death; or it may simply indicate 'two-faced' behavior, a person who has another side which he does not always show.

When the lagna or Moon occupy Purva Bhadrapada, it often indicates an overly serious, fearful, high-strung, nervous person who may nevertheless be a skillful speaker. Passion, impetuousness and anger are all strongly associated with Purva Bhadrapada, which rules cynicism, harsh words, greediness, and a fascination for the ecstasy of evil and the darker side of life. It rules searing pains, falls, and injuries from accidents or attacks. Punishment and penance are under its sway, for actions carried out under its influence often produce painful and anxious circumstances which are accompanied by remorse, sadness and difficulty.

Physiology & Diseases: The sides of the body, including the ribs, the sides of the legs, the left thigh, and the soles of the feet.

Professions, People & Places: Those associated with death or dying: morticians, murderers, etc. People who are cruel in deed or word. Very excitable or anger-prone people, like radicals, fanatics and terrorists. Those, like ascetics, who self-torment and self-mortify. Black magicians. Geriatric and terminal-illness wards.

26. *Uttara Bhadrapada* (3° 20′ Pisces to 16° 40′ Pisces)

Varahamihira: When the Moon is in Uttara Bhadrapada, it indicates happy people who are able speakers, who have children and grand-children, who conquer their enemies, and who are virtuous.

General Indications: Uttara Bhadrapada's symbol is the back legs of a funeral cot, and its deity is Ahirbudhnya, the 'Serpent of the Deep'.

As with the two other Purva–Uttara pairs, many of the meanings of the previous nakshatra also apply to this one, although it is usually easier to control the anger of Uttara Bhadrapada than it is to control that of its predecessor, and there is less emphasis on cruelty, deformity and depravity. Also, while detrimental actions are actually carried out by those who are strongly influenced by Purva Bhadra-pada, Uttara Bhadrapada displays greater restraint, and planned evil actions are usually controlled or sublimated. Lagna or Moon here often indicates a benevolent, self-sacrificing person who may benefit through gifts, donations, inheritance, and the like.

The serpent of the primeval depths (which may refer to the depths of the sky) suggests both movement and seclusion, or perhaps movement in seclusion or secrecy, and also implies solitude and retirement. Like Ajaikapada, Ahirbudhnya may well be a reference to the power that the Tantrics call the Kundalini Shakti, an energy which once activated initiates a process of spiritual evolution which climaxes in supreme wisdom, knowledge, enlightenment, and sometimes extraordinary abilities or awareness.

Physiology & Diseases: The sides of the body, including the ribs, the sides of the legs, the shins, and the soles of the feet.

Professions, People & Places: Great devotees, those who renounce the world, people who are indifferent to life. Those who enjoy extraordinary insight, erudition, intellect, or awareness. Charitable institutions. Practitioners of Tantra. Graveyards and cremation grounds. Many of the same meanings of Purva Bhadrapada.

27. *Revati* (16° 40′ Pisces to 30° 00′ Pisces)

Varahamihira: The Moon in Revati gives perfect limbs, genial manners, deep learning, riches, and no desire to covet the property of others.

General Indications: Revati's symbol is a drum used to mark time, and its deity is Pushan, who is responsible for nurturance and for safe travel.

Like the drum, Revati rules all sorts of increments, including time. Sometimes activities influenced by this nakshatra develop by leaps and bounds with considerable fanfare and noise. Anything to do with roads is related to Revati, as are protection, shelter and hospitality while traveling. Lagna or Moon here often indicates a person who is a good host and a dependable and responsible friend, who may be a socialite because of her or his love of society.

Pushan, who is also associated with finding lost creatures and articles, is the keeper of the cows of the gods, and his nurturing signifies breeding and foster-care. When on one occasion a student announced that a certain woman's horoscope had the Moon placed in the fourth house in Revati, our Jyotish guru (or his ishta devata) immediately and emphatically announced, 'Then she must have two mothers!' She did – her natural mother and a stepmother. Note the convergence of factors: the fourth house and the Moon, which both rule the mother, were both in the dual rashi of Pisces and in the nakshatra of Revati! Other influences enhanced this effect, including a serious affliction of the Moon by Saturn. Revati is frequently associated with pediatric diseases.

Physiology & Diseases: The abdomen and groin; the ankles.

Professions, People and Places: Anyone or anything dealing with time: clocks and watches, calendar makers, etc. People having work to do with roads: planners, travelers, maintenance crews, etc. Foster-parents, siblings, and other such relations.

NAKSHATRAS IN INTERPRETATION

Nakshatras are not much used in modern interpretation because few modern books emphasize their use. We are not trying here to introduce a nakshatra-based system of Jyotish, but we do suggest that nakshatras be employed more often in Jyotish than they are today. Here are a few broad hints for using nakshatra material effectively when examining a natal horoscope:

· Nakshatras, when well placed, display their more positive indications and, when afflicted, display their more negative indications. For example, if Revati is afflicted, its indications of safe travel will be greatly reduced, whereas if it is well placed, those same indications will be greatly enhanced.

· Nakshatras are well placed if occupied by a natural benefic, and are exceptionally well placed if this tenanting benefic is conjoined with or aspected by another natural benefic.

· Nakshatras are afflicted if occupied by a natural malefic, and are exceptionally afflicted if this tenanting malefic is conjoined with or aspected by another natural malefic.

· When the ruler of a nakshatra occupies a kendra *or* a kona *or* its own nakshatra or rashi *or* its exaltation rashi, that nakshatra is well placed. When the ruler of a nakshatra occupies houses 6, 8 or 12, or is debilitated, that nakshatra is afflicted.

· The lords of houses will be influenced by the nature of the nakshatras in which they are placed. For example, a man whose tenth lord occupies Ardra, which is ruled by Rudra, may shed tears over his profession.

CHAPTER NINE

INTERPRETATION OF
THE HOROSCOPE

INTERPRETATION – SIMPLE AND COMPLEX

If Saturn is in Aries at birth the person will be a fool, always on his legs, deceitful, and without friends. 'If Saturn is in Libra the person will be famous, will be the head of his clan, a leader of a town, commander of a force or the headman of a village, and will be wealthy.' These two observations, made by Varahamihira in Chapter 18 of his *Brihad Jataka*, are uncomplicated examples of the type of interpretive statements called *graha yogas* ('planetary combinations').

Simple graha yogas (which differ from the soli-lunar yogas of the *Panchanga* given above) involve only one or two astrological factors, such as the effects of each planet occupying each of the constellations and each of the houses, or the effects of the various planets when associated with or aspected by other planets. The classical works on Jyotish, in which graha yogas abound, unfortunately synthesize neither the various possible combinations that can result from a planet's position by house, by constellation and by the aspects it receives, nor the complex web of relationships that the astrological factors spin when concepts more advanced than graha, rashi, bhava and aspect are factored into the interpretation.

As a result, though the textually described effects of particular planetary positions in a horoscope are sometimes dramatically correct, at other times they land far from the mark. This is only to be expected, since every person born on Earth during the two and a half years that Saturn sits in Aries is not a friendless, deceitful fool, nor is everyone born during Saturn's thirty-month sojourn in Libra a famous, wealthy ruler. Clearly, further principles of differentiation are necessary for simple graha yogas if they are to have any utility.

One solution to this problem is to create more complex graha yogas. Look at this example from Chapter 16 of *Phaladipika*: 'If at birth the lord of the fourth house as well as the Moon occupy the sixth, the eighth or the twelfth house, and be without the association or aspect of benefic planets, and be also conjoined with or aspected by malefic planets, and/or have malefic planets flanking it, the result would be the death of the mother. But should the above two planets be strong and associated with or aspected by benefic planets, and if benefic planets occupy the fourth house, the planetary combination will be conducive to the happiness of the mother.'

Literally thousands of such statements pack the authoritative texts on Jyotish in Sanskrit. Their number and complexity require a phenomenal memory, and colossal awareness, for their effective implementation. Because any given horoscope commonly has but a few of these elaborate combinations, it is neither practical nor productive mechanically to catalogue and literally interpret them; when contradictory combinations which are not reconciled by the texts also exist in the same horoscope, the jyotishi may be in a dilemma over which interpretation to apply. No amount of bookish study can teach a student how to reconcile all these multifarious influences, any more than any other art can be learnt from a book. Books can provide only information; the reader must learn how to judge the many factors which do not admit of easy quantification, such as the fact that Saturn is such an important graha that, even when debilitated, it does not become completely without energy.

While it is certainly desirable, despite these difficulties, to become familiar with the multitude of graha yogas stored in the various texts, it is perhaps even more profitable to understand the principles of interpretation which underlie them. With good comprehension, and after mature reflection and experience, a good jyotishi can create a multitude of combinations and predict their potential effects. When, for example, you understand that malefic grahas obstruct the indications of the houses they contact, and that a confluence of similar factors will guarantee such obstruction, you can then create the statement that three or more malefics aspecting the ascendant will create health problems (since the first house represents a person's physical well-being), or that three or more malefics aspecting the second house will create family disharmony, or perhaps eye problems (because the second house represents the family and the eyes).

Malefics in or aspecting the second house may also affect one's speech. Maybe such natives speak at inappropriate times, or in inappropriate ways, or without thinking; or perhaps they simply foul up their lives by habitually using foul language. The horoscope's bhavas are the arenas of life in which one performs karmas. Because humans perform their karmas mainly via mind, speech and activities, malefics affecting the second, the fifth or the tenth bhavas of a horoscope tend to cause people to get themselves into trouble through their speech, their thoughts, or their activities respectively.

All the rules presented in texts cannot be taken at face value. Varahamihira, for example, describes the effects of Mercury when it sits in the fourth, seventh or tenth houses from the Sun, positions which are astronomically impossible. Did Mercury once occupy such places in the sky? Did Varahamihira mistake Mercury for another planet when he made this observation? Or was this a wholly theoretical exercise on his part ('If Mercury could sit in these houses from the Sun, these would be the results . . .')? Since Varahamihira is not around any longer to resolve this difficulty, only intuition or a teacher's commentary can fill the gap between confusion and conclusion.

Therefore, instead of simply piling up lists of astrological combinations and their meanings, this chapter will attempt, by following the traditional teaching method of introducing pivotal individual verses from the standard texts and then developing them through extensive commentary, to translate a few important combinations into their underlying generic principles. Since this sort of commentary is usually provided by a teacher, we will try to parallel this oral tradition in writing, hoping to convey some of its original spirit.

PRELIMINARY CONSIDERATIONS

A graha will blend the meanings of its natural indications (those matters of which it is the significator, as described above) with the meanings of the house, the rashi and the grahas with which it combines by occupation, association or aspect. The confluence of predominantly good or bad indications gives the jyotishi an idea of what to predict. If equal testimonies for good and bad indications exist, jyotishis pray for guidance before using their experience and intuition to render a judicious judgement. Results are often more predictable in a very narrow domain than in a broader field which involves more variables.

While looking for confluence, remember that life is usually not an all-or-nothing matter, and Jyotish, which tries to be a reliable model of life, tries to reflect this. Good and bad indications in a horoscope usually do not cancel each other; if a house shows very good results, the lord of the house shows very bad results and the significator shows neutral results, then both good and bad results will happen. If such conditions apply in a horoscope to the fifth house, which predominantly indicates children, the person may have beautiful children in whom they delight, but may also suffer the heartbreak of losing a child. If, on the other hand, both the fifth bhava and its lord indicate good results and the karaka indicates bad ones, then only the occasional fly will disturb the otherwise pleasing ointment of one's children.

Remember that these principles are abstractions which gain form and substance only from your own personal experience. It is one thing to say to a person whose horoscope you are interpreting, 'There will be both happiness and unhappiness pertaining to children,' and it is quite another to say, 'One of your children may cause you great concern on account of a marked tendency to ill-health, but your other two kids will most likely be healthy, highly educated, and respected in their professions.' It is something else entirely to grasp the confluence of factors well enough to be able confidently to apply upaya (remedies), Jyotish's 'phantom limb', and to recommend strategies to modify or prevent the possibility of ill-health to the child in question.

While searching for confluence, be sure to limit yourself to the principles of Jyotish. Many Westerners and some Indians are nowadays compromising the tradition of Jyotish by assuming that principles derived from Western astrology must also hold true for Jyotish. We have attempted to include in this treatise principles which are classically accepted, for beginners at Jyotish expect and deserve to discover Jyotish's realities, not someone's presumptions about those realities, when they open an introductory book on Jyotish.

BASICS OF INTERPRETATION

First, a review of some definitions.

Grahas can be:

· natural benefics or natural malefics (*naisargika shubha grahas* and *naisargika papa grahas* respectively)
· natural significators (*naisargika karaka grahas*)
· house significators (*bhava karaka grahas*)
· temporary benefics or temporary malefics (*tatkalika shubha grahas* and *tatkalika papa grahas* respectively)

Shubha means auspicious, and *papa* means inauspicious. The natural benefic or auspicious grahas (Jupiter, Venus, the bright Moon, and Mercury when unafflicted by malefics) tend to enhance desirable life experiences, while the natural malefic or inauspicious grahas (Saturn, Mars, Rahu, Ketu, the dark Moon, Mercury when afflicted by malefics, and, to a slight extent, the Sun) tend to enhance undesirable life experiences.

A graha which rules a certain thing (see the lists in Chapter Four) is the natural significator (*graha karaka*) for that thing. Grahas can also serve as natural *house* significators (*bhava karakas*), meaning that they rule, in part, the matters indicated by the house that they signify, as detailed in Chapter Six.

Houses can be:

· kendras (1, 4, 7, 10)
· konas (1, 5, 9)
· neutrals (2, 11)
· dussthanas (3, 6, 8, 12)

· trik (6, 8, 12)
· upachayas (3, 6, 10, 11)

One of Parashara's systems of analysis classes the eleventh lord as malefic, but deems planets in the eleventh house to be well placed. It also opines that the lords of the second and twelfth houses can give either good or bad results according to which bhavas they occupy and which house lords they associate with, and states that benefics and malefics who own the fourth, seventh or tenth houses but not the first house become malefic and benefic respectively. Although this complicated system holds its own ground when fully implemented, it is too confusing for an introductory text. We will, therefore, in the balance of this book ignore these criteria.

Planetary States are Determined by:

· residence in exaltation, own, friend, neutral, enemy, or debilitation rashi
· residence in a benefic or malefic rashi (*benefic rashis* are those owned by the natural benefics; *malefic rashis* are those owned by the natural malefics)
· retrogression and combustion
· the vargottama position
· the avasthas
· directional strength (dig bala)

THE GOLDEN KEY

Verse One

To illustrate the process of explication we shall begin with a golden key to horoscope interpretation: the first verse of Chapter Fifteen of Mantreshwara's *Phaladipika*. All thirty verses of this chapter shed light on how to predict the results of the various matters represented by the twelve houses, but all require the guidance of a teacher's commentary to yield their gold.

The chapter's first verse is:

'All bhavas will give rise to exclusively good results if occupied or aspected by benefics or their own lords, or by planets owning benefic houses, provided such houses are without the aspect or association of malefics. This will be so even if malefics own the houses concerned. This good effect of the houses will be certain if the planets involved are strong, that is, not in their debilitation constellation, not combust, and not in an enemy's constellation.'

Before beginning to examine these lines, we must first note that they appear at the very beginning of a chapter entitled 'Method for Studying the Effects of the Bhavas'. In a language like Sanskrit where punctuation is virtually non-existent and diacritical devices like italics are conspicuously absent, one way to emphasize information is to open a chapter with it, for the rules of Sanskrit prosody generally equate prominence of place with importance. English translations of Jyotish texts generally fail to provide such vital rules as this to the reader, which is another good reason to read these texts under the guidance of an experienced teacher.

'All bhavas will give rise to exclusively good results . . .'

Each of the verse's words and phrases must be carefully inspected. The first phrase delivers the promise that every bhava in a horoscope can give good results, but only under certain conditions. That the so-called good bhavas, which tend to represent desirable parts of the human experience, should give good results should be self-evident.

Even the dussthanas (houses 3, 6, 8 and 12), which indicate things that most people would like to minimize in their personal lives – misfortunes like ill-health, operations, enemies, litigation, debts, bankruptcy, accidents and death – can also give good results. Consider the sixth house, which represents enemies, debt and litigation. One sort of good that may come from this house is a lack of affliction from enemies, diseases, debt or litigation. Or, such initially negative experiences may contribute somehow to your overall success. One reason why Pandit Jawaharlal Nehru (independent India's first Prime Minister) became famous was the strength of his sixth house. It did give him a powerful enemy (the British Raj), but its positive placement (the sixth lord occupies the sixth house) enabled him to overcome that enemy. Or, you may prosper from someone else's enemies, diseases or debts, as do lawyers, doctors and moneylenders respectively. This type of reasoning can be applied to the other houses of suffering as well.

'. . . if occupied or aspected by benefics . . .'

Remember that all grahas aspect the seventh house from their positions, and that Mars, Jupiter and Saturn also aspect the fourth and eighth, fifth and ninth, and third and tenth houses from themselves respectively. *Always count aspects inclusively!* When we look at the second house of Chart 2 (see p. 418), we note that Venus and Mercury alone occupy that house, and no other planet aspects it, either by a direct (full) or a special aspect. Therefore, this man's second house suggests to us that his life experiences pertaining to money, speech and family, which are some of the primary meanings of the second house, will be enjoyable.

Now look at the eighth house of this same horoscope. It is unoccupied by any planet, and the only planets which aspect it are Mercury and Venus, by their direct seventh aspects, and Jupiter, by its special fifth aspect. Since all three of these planets are natural benefics, the indications of the eighth house will throughout all life be enjoyable, productive and desirable. The owner of this chart will be benefited by inheritance, and he is unlikely to be plagued by bankruptcy or vexatious litigation; if he is involved in litigation, he will in fact benefit through it. He will be protected from accidents and from chronic illness, and will enjoy a painless death at the end of a long, full life.

'. . . if occupied or aspected by . . . their own lords . . .'

In the horoscope under study, Venus, the lord of the second house, occupies its own house (because it rules and occupies the constellation of Libra which here falls in the second house). Jupiter, who is in his own constellation of Sagittarius in the fourth house, also occupies his own house. Finally, Saturn aspects by its special third aspect the sixth house, which it happens to rule because it rules

Aquarius, the constellation which falls there. Based on this portion of the verse, the native may therefore expect desirable experiences in the things represented by the second, fourth and sixth houses, subject of course to other factors yet to be considered. Note that two of the principles listed in this verse have already applied to the second house.

'. . . if occupied or aspected by . . . planets owning benefic houses . . .'

Of the benefic houses, the lords of 9 and 5 (the konas), and of 1, 10, 4 and 7 (the kendras) are powerful for this purpose, in order of decreasing power. In the chart under consideration, the second house is occupied by Venus and Mercury, who are, for this and for every other chart that has a Virgo ascendant, the lords of houses 2 and 9 and of houses 1 and 4 respectively. The second house is therefore strong even from this point of view, as is the eighth house, which is aspected by Venus, Mercury and Jupiter, all of whom are lords of benefic houses, none of whom are lords of malefic houses.

'. . . provided such houses are without the aspect or association of malefics . . .'

'Association of a planet' means either 'occupation of a house by a planet' or 'sharing a constellation with another planet'. Up to this point in our examination of this horoscope we have seen that houses 2, 4, 6 and 8 are likely to produce good results. We now see that, while neither the second nor the eighth bhavas has the aspect or association of any malefic, the fourth house has the association of Saturn and the full aspect of Mars, and the sixth house has the association of Ketu. (It also has the full aspect of Rahu but, because Rahu and Ketu are always in constellations opposite to one other, we consider the occupation of a house by only the one *or* the aspect of that house by the other.) Mantreshwara's principle therefore so far applies *in toto* only to the second and eighth bhavas, since among the four houses which are likely to produce good results they alone lack the aspect or association of malefics.

'. . . This will be so even if malefics own the houses concerned.'

Like any good jyotishi, Mantreshwara must carefully resolve any potential contradictions. When a malefic aspects or occupies its own bhava, is its lordship of the house more important, or does its status as a natural malefic win out? Here he states clearly that lordship is more important, and that a malefic which aspects or occupies its own bhava is bound to give good results for that bhava. Since in this horoscope Saturn, a natural malefic, aspects the sixth house, where lies Aquarius, one of the two constellations that Saturn rules, the sixth house is bound to be benefited thereby.

'. . . This good effect of the houses will be certain if the planets involved are strong, that is, not in their debilitation constellation, not combust and not in the constellation of their enemy.'

This is the last criterion to be applied to determine whether or not a bhava will produce exclusively good effects. Even if all the above conditions are fulfilled, good results become certain only if the planets involved are strong, as specified here. Since in Chart 2 none of the planets that favorably influence the second house (Venus and Mercury) or the eighth house (Venus, Mercury and Jupiter) is debilitated, combust or in the constellation of an enemy, we are compelled to conclude that in this horoscope Mantreshwara's principle applies *in toto* to the second and eighth bhavas, so we must predict these houses to give desirable results in abundance.

The native is in fact a millionaire who sings and speaks well, has a handsome face and good eyes, deals in precious gems, is fascinated by and supports classical lore, and enjoys the comforts of a close-knit extended family (all these being primary second-house meanings). Similarly, he will gain significantly through inheritance upon the death of his parents; has been (and will be) protected from accidents and chronic illness; has not been damaged by (and may yet gain through) litigation; and is likely to undergo a comfortable and painless death (all of which are eighth-house matters).

Once you begin to apply this principle to the horoscopes in your collection, you will find that, though it is rare to find this combination of beneficial influences to be present *in toto*, often much of it will apply to a few of a horoscope's houses. In Chart 2, most of these influences apply to the fourth house: Jupiter occupies it as a natural benefic; Jupiter occupies it as its lord; Jupiter is the lord of good houses; and Jupiter is strong (because it is not debilitated, combust, or in an enemy's sign). The one criterion missing is that the house not be occupied or aspected by malefics, which it is (by Saturn and Mars). The result: This man does, and will, experience predominantly good effects pertaining to fourth-house matters, enjoying luxurious vehicles, good property, and a long-lived mother with whom he has a good relationship. Those malefic aspects may, however, cause the odd dark cloud to pass through this area of his life.

Here is another hint for those who wish to read Jyotish's original texts: Any clearly stated principle like the one above also implies its converse. Here, for purposes of contrast, is the reverse of Verse One:

All bhavas will give rise to exclusively bad results if occupied or aspected by malefics or by planets owning malefic houses, provided such houses are without the aspect or association of their own lords or benefics. Bad results will be certain if the planets involved are weak, that is, in their debilitation constellation, combust, or in the constellation of an enemy.

Verse Six

At this point the average reader of *Phaladipika* would continue on logically to verse two, and would promptly lose the threads of the principle Mantreshwara is trying to develop. Only an experienced, well-trained teacher will know to refer the student to the appropriate verses, which are elsewhere in the book, for in the interest of brevity and in honor of its oral tradition, the book itself does not give cross-references. A good teacher would have us skip down at this point to the sixth verse of this same Chapter Fifteen:

'A bhava suffers destruction when the bhava itself, its lord and its significator (*karaka*) are devoid of strength and are hemmed in between malefics, or are associated with or aspected by malefics or unfriendly planets and not by others; or if the fourth, the eighth and the twelfth houses or the fifth and ninth houses from them are occupied by malefics. These results will be very evident and apparent when several of the conditions mentioned occur at the same time.'

We know that this is another cornerstone principle of Jyotish because those teachers who are steeped in the oral tradition of Jyotish emphasize it; because verses of similar import appear prominently in other major Jyotish texts; and because the experience of generations of jyotishis has validated it. Let us therefore examine it carefully.

'A bhava suffers destruction when . . .'

Every bhava, good or bad, may give adverse or undesirable results under certain circumstances. If the first house has malefic planets influencing it, the person's birth, infancy or youth may be traumatic, difficult or unhappy. The body and the personality may be obscured, disfigured or problematic. The physical and psychological health of the person may suffer. In this way the benefic houses, which typically represent desirable things, may give bad results and become a source of dissatisfaction to the person. The same is true of the malefic houses, the dussthanas. Their affliction in the ways mentioned by Mantreshwara will enhance suffering in the already undesirable matters that they rule, like debt, litigation and accidents.

'. . . the bhava itself, its lord and its karaka (significator) are devoid of strength . . .'

Remember that the *karaka* is the planet that has some natural affinity with the matters ruled by a particular house. The conditions of the house, its lord and its significator must all be evaluated in order to estimate the effects of that portion of a person's life which is represented by any particular bhava. For example, to estimate the experience of birth, infancy and youth, the first house, the lord of the first house, and the bhava karaka of the first house (which in this context will always be the Sun) must be analyzed.

Mantreshwara's verses provide us with the criteria we need to establish whether or not a bhava, its lord or its significator is devoid of strength. A HOUSE is devoid of strength when:

· it is occupied or aspected by malefics or by planets owning
  malefic houses

· it lacks the aspect or association of its own lord or benefics
· the planets involved are weak (debilitated, combust, or in an
   enemy's rashi)
· it is hemmed in between malefics
· it is associated with or aspected by malefics or unfriendly planets
   and not by others
· the fourth, the eighth and the twelfth houses *or* the fifth and ninth
   houses from it are occupied by malefics

Be it house lord or significator, a GRAHA is devoid of strength when:

· debilitated, combust, or occupying its enemy's rashi
· hemmed in between malefics
· associated with or aspected by malefics or unfriendly planets and
   not by others
· the fourth, the eighth and the twelfth houses *or* the fifth and ninth
   houses from it are occupied by malefics
· it occupies houses 6, 8 or 12. (This also implies that any house
   ruled by a planet which occupies houses 6, 8 or 12 is weak,
   unless it occupies its own constellation.)

Now that we have summarized the main conditions under which
bhavas, their lords and karakas are powerless, we must consider the
converse to Mantreshwara's verse six, which as before is implied in
the verse itself:

A bhava prospers and gives desirable results when the bhava itself, its lord
and its karaka are strong, and are flanked by benefics, or are associated with
or aspected by benefics or friendly planets and not by others.

Only verse six's final line remains to be considered:

'... These results will be very evident and apparent when several of the
conditions mentioned occur at the same time.'

This is how Mantreshwara introduces the notion of confluence.
When we apply this axiom to Chart 1, we note the following:

· The seventh house is exclusively aspected by the malefic Saturn
   and not by any benefics or by its lord.
· The lord of the seventh house, Jupiter, is devoid of strength

(being combust), is associated with malefics (Sun and Rahu), is aspected by a malefic (Mars), and has no association with or aspect from any benefics.

The significator of the seventh house, Venus, who is without strength (being in the rashi of its enemy, the Sun), is aspected by a malefic (Saturn), but is not aspected by benefics.

Since all three factors involving the seventh house here – the house, its lord and its significator – are afflicted in more than one way, the result is a clear confluence of effect. And in fact this man's marital history (marriage being the primary indication of the seventh house) was significantly troubled. Because he married, against his parents' wishes, someone from another culture and religion, his marriage, from the very day of the wedding, created serious family dishar-mony. Later the marriage itself became tension-filled, leading to several separations and great unhappiness. His wife, who was prey to chronic illness throughout all their years together, died suddenly after a decade of marital misery.

Discerning readers will complain that Jupiter was exalted, and so should have been strong; but here exaltation is Jupiter's only strength, a strength which hardly equals his many weaknesses (being combust, conjoined with malefics, aspected by a malefic, and without the association or aspect of benefics). It may be that Jupiter's exaltation accounts for his staying in this tumultuous marriage instead of divorcing his partner early on. While a totally precise analysis becomes possible only when you couple much experience with the insight provided by an ishta devata, even a novice who followed Mantreshwara's principles should have been able easily to predict troublesome karma in the area of marriage in this horoscope.

EIGHTEEN CRITERIA

The approach to house analysis that we have just extracted from *Phaladipika* forms one part of the generic set of principles that most modern jyotishis use while analyzing a horoscope. While each jyotishi develops a personal set of principles, many of the same rules appear in most sets, and it is from this common heap of methods that the eighteen criteria below have been extracted. These are not the only interpretive principles available, nor are they necessarily the best; but an understanding of these methods will definitely provide a firm foundation from which to proceed to an understanding of some of the equally valid but more intricate of Jyotish's styles. If these criteria, which have been extracted from various classical texts, seem at first to overwhelm you, remember that they must be re-read and studied many times before they will find a home for themselves in your memory.

Eighteen Basic Principles of Interpretation

1. Natural benefics enhance the desirable indications and suppress the undesirable indications of a *house* by:

    1. Occupying or aspecting that house, especially if they own it.
    2. Conjoining or aspecting the lord of that house.
    3. Conjoining or aspecting the significator of that house.

2. Natural benefics enhance the desirable indications and suppress the undesirable indications of any *planet* they conjoin or aspect.
3. Natural malefics enhance the undesirable indications and suppress the desirable indications of a *house* by:

    1. Occupying or aspecting that house (unless one of them owns that house, in which case it will enhance it, though less than it would were it a benefic).
    2. Conjoining or aspecting the lord of that house.
    3. Conjoining or aspecting the significator of that house.

4. Natural malefics enhance the undesirable indications and suppress the desirable indications of any *planet* they conjoin or aspect.
5. Natural house significators increase the results of the *houses* they signify when they aspect those houses. This is also true when they inhabit those houses, *except* that:

· Mars in the third house is detrimental to younger siblings and to the native's relationship with them.

· Waning Moon in the fourth house is detrimental to mother and to the native's relationship with her.

· Jupiter in the fifth house is detrimental to children and to the native's relationship with them.

· Venus in the seventh house is detrimental to spouse and to the native's relationship with him or her.

· Sun in the ninth house is detrimental to father and to the native's relationship with him.

· Jupiter in the eleventh house is detrimental to older siblings and to the native's relationship with them.

These detriments usually do not occur when the planet occupies its own constellation.

6. A planet which occupies its own house will typically give strong and beneficial results for that bhava. Such planets when natural benefics will usually strongly benefit the houses they aspect. A natural malefic which occupies its own house will not however enhance the good results of a house it aspects (except in the special case when Mars occupies Aries from which it aspects Scorpio, which is its own house). Saturn in Capricorn will aspect deleteriously, but less deleteriously than a debilitated Saturn, or one posited in an enemy's constellation.

7. When a planet occupies a kendra or kona, all the matters that it naturally signifies become enhanced. Residence in a dussthana is detrimental to the natural significations of any planet *unless* that planet is situated in its own constellation, in which case its significations will be only slightly impaired. Because the third house is only marginally malignant, it is less disturbing than are the other dussthanas. The results of planets which occupy upachaya houses will improve over time. Significations for planets in houses 3 and 6 are impaired at first and then become ameliorated, while the significations of planets in houses 10 and 11 are good from the outset and go on to become even better.

8. The lords of the konas will enhance the desirable matters of any house in which they sit or aspect *unless* they simultaneously rule a

trik house (in which case this principle does not apply). This will be especially true if this kona lord is influenced by a natural benefic without any influence from a natural malefic.

9. The lords of the trik houses will disturb the desirable matters of any house in which they sit or aspect *unless* (a) they also own a kona or a kendra, *or* (b) they occupy their own houses. This will be especially true if the trik lord is influenced by a natural malefic without any influence from a natural benefic. If, for example, the eighth lord in a horoscope being a natural malefic does not own a kona or a kendra, tenants the lagna which is not its own sign, and is conjunct a malefic and aspected by another malefic without any sort of benefic influence, then all desirable matters of the first house will be strongly impaired.

10. When the lords of kendras, konas or neutral houses occupy other kendras or konas, the desirable indications of the houses owned by those lords will be enhanced and the undesirable indications of those houses will be suppressed. When, for instance, the ninth lord is domiciled in the fifth house, we should predict successful and relatively effortless travel, since undesirable events during journeys would be suppressed. When the lords of kendras, konas or neutral houses sit in neutral houses, they will usually give rise to average, everyday results (with certain salient exceptions, such as when the eleventh lord sits in the second house or vice versa, which may promote financial gain). When the lords of kendras, konas or neutral houses are posited in trik houses, the indications of the good houses will be disturbed (and if these good lords sit in the third house they will be slightly disturbed).

11. When a trik lord occupies a kona, a kendra or a neutral house (in descending order of magnitude) the beneficial implications of that trik house will be enhanced, though the malefic implications may not be suppressed. When, all other things being equal, the twelfth lord inhabits the lagna, the native will enjoy plenty of bed pleasures, but expenses will still be bothersome. When a trik lord occupies a trik house, some of its implications will be suppressed, while others may be enhanced. Since a trik lord who makes his home in a good house will damage that house, and a trik lord who abides instead in a bad house will cause any house he owns to

suffer, trik lords are to some extent troublesome, no matter where they sit – unless they occupy their own rashis. In the words of our Jyotish guru, 'Even a brigand will look after his own house.'

12. Exalted planets will greatly increase whatever they indicate, subject to the above principles. When Venus, the lord of the eighth house for a Pisces ascendant, is exalted, it occupies the lagna, which may in some cases greatly impair the native's physical well-being (based on principle 9, above). All the auspicious indications of debilitated planets are disturbed, and all their inauspicious indications are enhanced.

13. A planet which is situated in a rashi owned by a natural benefic which is its friend will produce results that are more pleasant or tolerable than will a planet situated in a rashi owned by a natural benefic which is its enemy. A planet which is situated in a rashi owned by a natural malefic which is its enemy will produce results that are less tolerable than will a planet situated in a rashi owned by a natural malefic which is its friend.

14. Planets who are mutual friends will, when participating together in a desirable horoscopic combination, cooperate together to enhance beneficial results or to reduce detrimental results. Conversely, planets who are enemies to each other will be reluctant, even when they participate together in a desirable horoscopic combination, to cooperate with each other for these purposes.

15. A planet or a house is strengthened when it is flanked on both sides by constellations containing natural benefics, and a planet or a house is weakened when it is flanked (hemmed in) on both sides by constellations containing natural malefics. When Mars is in the fourth house and Saturn is in the sixth, the fifth house and any occupant will be weakened; while when Venus is in the eighth house and Jupiter in the tenth, the ninth house and any occupant(s) are strengthened thereby.

16. When the lord of one house aspects or occupies another house, the meanings of those two houses usually become blended. Sometimes the aspecting or occupying lord becomes the cause for the effect promised by the house that is aspected or occupied. For example, when the lord of the seventh occupies the second, money (second house) may be accumulated through one's spouse or business

partner (seventh house). At other times the relationship is not causative; the presence of the lord of the eleventh in the twelfth may mean either the loss (twelfth) of an elder brother (eleventh) *or* an elder brother living abroad (since the twelfth house also governs emigration).

17. When planets associate with or aspect each other, the meanings of those planets as natural significators and as lords of the houses they own usually become blended.

18. Planets act on the constellations in much the same manner as they affect the houses, with certain exceptions. For example, a rashi is strong when flanked by a benefic or when aspected or occupied by a benefic *unless* that benefic is debilitated, in which case the planet may actually disturb the rashi under consideration.

STRENGTH VERSUS INFLUENCE

A graha's strength or weakness is a measure of its ability to exert energy, not its intentions. Exalted grahas and those in their own rashis display their prowess freely, while debilitated or otherwise weak grahas cannot unobstructedly display the energy they possess. A graha's energy, weak or strong, can promote either a peaceful, fulfilling life or a life disrupted by confrontation, depending on the natural benefic or malefic natures of the graha itself and the grahas that influence it, and on the houses that graha rules in the horoscope.

One of the most significant ways in which one graha can influence another in a horoscope is by acting as its *dispositor*, the lord of the rashi in which it sits. In Nadi Jyotish a graha is said to possess both a *deha* (body) and a *jiva* (soul). This theory has gradually metamorphosed to mean, in the context of a bhava, that the graha itself is only the body, while the graha's dispositor represents its soul. According to this approach, one should never simply judge an individual (graha) by its body alone but should also consider its soul, which is in many ways more significant than its body. An ugly body tenanted by a beautiful soul will eventually attract the attention of those others who so value that soul that they will ignore its misshapen vessel; but an ugly soul in a beautiful body will eventually cause others to flee from it in disgust.

The dispositor principle is one of the bases on which Jyotish stands. One portion of Mantreshwara's verse that is quoted above reads: 'All bhavas will give rise to exclusively good results if occupied or aspected by ... their own lords.' When the lord of a house supports (by occupation or aspect) his own house, the soul in effect invigorates, protects and directs the body, and whenever body and soul work together harmoniously success is certain, for individual grahas, or humans. A bhava is a state of being or consciousness, and every graha takes on the state of being of the bhava it occupies. When therefore the soul of a house is tormented (by malefics, debilitation and the like), the bhava itself is bound to be tormented (because the body is secondary to, and dependent upon, the soul), and any graha therein will share in the torment.

It is particularly useful when trying to understand this thorny matter to think of the grahas in anthropomorphic forms. Indian philosophy recognizes two fundamental types of humans: those who are straightforward (*rju*) and those whose are crooked (*kutila*). Benefics resemble the straightforward, those people who are fundamentally good at heart, who try to follow the laws of the land and to live unselfishly. Malefics resemble the crooked, self-centered people of society. Just as someone who is a crook by nature will always do things the illegal way if he has the choice, a malefic always tends to cause some difficulties, no matter what other sorts of benefits he may promise.

Being straightforward, benefics are relatively predictable: a debilitated benefic is weak, and an exalted benefic powerful. Exalted benefics are strong, and have strength of character. Though debilitated benefics try to be strong, they have weak personalities; when put under stress, their morality tends to crumble and they may begin to behave like malefics. Stress arises from bad placement: the aspect of or conjunction with malefics, occupation of the trik houses, bad avasthas, and so on.

Being crooked, malefics are less predictable. An exalted malefic is a sort of elegant rogue, an iron fist in a velvet glove. Should this rogue be exposed to the influence of good people (*satsanga*), as he would be when aspected by or conjunct with benefics, his tendency to give good results will certainly be enhanced; still, on occasion, when stressed he will behave like a malefic, though a refined one. A debilitated malefic on the other hand is a truly low-life sort of being, and when this thug is egged on by other malefics (by aspect, conjunction and the like) he will display destructive tendencies at all times. An exalted malefic, whose strength gives him a sense of security, feels he can afford to act more or less benignly; but debilitated malefics, who are low in self-esteem, lash out at everyone and cause lots of trouble, sometimes destroying in a matter of moments things which may have taken much time, energy and care to build.

A natural malefic when weak needs only to remove the supports which are propping up certain areas of life to have them come crashing down on the native's head; it need not attack the poor soul directly to wreak havoc. When the lord of the eighth house is debilitated, for example, it will both reduce the native's longevity and increase the likelihood of accidents, so that when the native is in dire need of just a little bit of survival luck, that luck may be denied. Should that debilitated malefic be somehow strengthened – by being retrograde, having directional strength, being involved in a good yoga (like Parivartana Yoga; see Chapter Ten), being vargottama, having a good avastha, and so on – its good indications (by house rulership) will be enhanced, but its bad indications may not be reduced.

A debilitated graha may also obtain some energy from its dispositor if that dispositor is strong, and this may curtail its reign of terror. But when a debilitated graha's dispositor is itself debilitated, one must predict the worst sorts of results, because that graha will be tortured body and soul. Exalted grahas are much more likely to give good results when their dispositors are exalted or otherwise strong than when those dispositors are weak; when an exalted graha's dispositor is debilitated, none of the good promised by that exaltation is likely to pan out, since there is nothing to back it up. An exalted Jupiter (in Cancer) in a horoscope where its dispositor the Moon is debilitated in Scorpio would be considerably weakened; the same would happen to a Saturn in Libra if Venus tenanted Virgo.

COMBUSTION, RETROGRESSION
AND GRAHA AVASTHA

Of the myriad difficult-to-reckon factors in Jyotish, three require particular attention: *combustion*, *retrogression* and the *graha avasthas* (planetary states or conditions). All are central to interpretation, and all are frequently misunderstood.

Combustion – Combust planets move so close to the Sun that they become invisible to us. Being thus eclipsed, and because when combust they are farthest from the earth (using the analogy, which is not necessarily causative, of an object becoming less able to influence another object the further it recedes from that other object), the jyotishis of India concluded that the influence of combust planets becomes exceedingly weak, particularly regarding the houses they own. Mercury, which cannot be further than one rashi from the Sun, is frequently combust, and perceptible problems often afflict the houses a combust Mercury rules in a birth chart.

One useful rule for interpreting combustion is that *while the externalized meanings (including the various body parts) of a house are often damaged when the ruler of that house is combust, the inner meanings (including particularly the psychic or mental functions) are usually not spoiled.* On the contrary, when the Sun, who represents the soul, comes into contact with a planet, the inner or astral qualities of that graha will become illumined and enlivened. Sun + Mercury often causes the native to become intellectually brilliant (see Budhaditya Yoga in the next chapter), and Sun + Venus tends to enliven the quality of beauty. How these results materialize will of course depend on the various other influences that affect such combinations, for every person with Sun conjunct Mercury does not enjoy a lively intellect.

The external qualities of the planets differ from person to person according to their natural significations and the houses they control. Jupiter, for example, rules the seventh and tenth houses in a Gemini ascendant. Marriage being one external indication of the seventh house and career being an external indication of the tenth house,

Jupiter's combustion in such a chart may impair satisfaction in these two vital areas of life. Because Jupiter is also the natural significator of children, which form another external object of an individual's experience, the native's children may also be affected by the combustion. Jupiter's inner qualities (like generosity, wisdom, love of knowledge, and intuition) may however become more apparent in such a person, enlivened by the proximity of the Sun.

Natural benefics when combust lose ability to influence beneficently, proportionate to the closeness of the combustion. Natural malefics when combust gain ability to influence maleficently, proportionate to the closeness of the combustion. While the implications of combustion may seem harsh, remember that many of Jyotish's precepts display quite different effects in different contexts, so much so that sometimes the detrimental effect of combustion on certain house meanings may be desirable. A person whose sixth lord is combust may under certain circumstances have very weak enemies. Or, when the indicators for brothers and sisters are combust in the horoscope of someone who is disputing with his siblings over a will, the combustion will both suggest the problems with the siblings *and* weaken the ability of those siblings to pursue their lawsuit.

The closer a planet is to the Sun, the more severely combust it is, and the more severe its results will be. Also, keep in mind that a planet is weaker when approaching its exact conjunction with the Sun than it is when leaving that conjunction. A combust planet which also occupies its own rashi or is vargottama or exalted is certainly better off than is a combust planet which is debilitated or in an enemy's rashi. One very important exception to the implication of combustion occurs when the Sun signifies great prosperity in a chart. What would be combustion in another horoscope would then become a planetary combination indicating affluence in one area of life or another. Table 9.1 gives the range of degrees within which a planet is combust.

Retrogression – Remember that Mars, Mercury, Jupiter, Venus and Saturn sometimes appear to move backwards against the background of the fixed stars. This seeming backward movement is *retrogression*. While combust planets are farthest from Earth, retro-

TABLE 9.1

Combustion of the Planets

Planet	Degrees on either side of the Sun within which the planet is in Combustion when Direct in its Motion	Degrees on either side of the Sun within which the planet is in Combustion when Retrograde in its Motion
Mercury	14°	12°
Venus	10°	8°
Mars	17°	Same
Jupiter	11°	Same
Saturn	15°	Same

grade planets are nearest to us, and so are said to be strong, on the analogy of the nearby being more influential than the faraway. This is also the case for the two inner planets, which alone among the grahas can be simultaneously retrograde and combust; Mercury and Venus when retrograde and combust are not as weak as they are when direct and combust. While it has become popular for Western astrologers to say that retrograde planets indicate 'karma', in Jyotish every planet in the horoscope indicates past karmas, because the entire horoscope is a map of the native's karmas. When a retrograde planet shows a particularly strong karmic influence, it does so simply because it is strong.

Natural benefics when retrograde gain ability to influence beneficently, while natural malefics when retrograde gain ability to influence maleficently. Although a very few statements in the classical works imply that a retrograde planet carries a weakening effect, there are many more statements which insist that retrograde planets are strong, though *not* necessarily good or beneficial; they simply strengthen whatever they indicate by house ownership and by natural signification in the horoscope, be it good or bad. Saturn as the eighth lord when retrograde thus affects other planets and houses by its aspect and occupation in a much more malefic way than does Saturn as the eighth lord when it is merely direct.

Because planetary effects are cumulative in Jyotish, a retrograde planet loses a certain amount of strength when it is debilitated. Such a planet can still give some desirable results if it owns good houses, though these good results will be less than if it were retrograde and exalted. A debilitated and retrograde planet which owns bad houses is likely to give adverse results. *Phaladipika* states that a debilitated but retrograde planet is equivalent to an exalted planet, a statement which is often misunderstood to be literal truth. Our Jyotish guru taught us that Mantreshwara may have meant this to illustrate that retrograde planets, while strong (like exalted planets), still need to be evaluated in the overall context of the entire horoscope. This seems to be borne out by experience.

Mantreshwara also says that exalted planets when retrograde act like debilitated planets, which is likely to be a cautionary statement for situations like this one: a retrograde malefic who owns detrimental houses may create detrimental results even when exalted because of the cumulative results due to the combination of exaltation and retrogression. That Mantreshwara's statement is not true of all retrograde exalted planets becomes clear when we examine the horoscope of Ramakrishna Paramahamsa (see Chapter Twelve). Like other texts written to be taught by a guru who would elucidate matters for the student, *Phaladipika* often does not bother to make clear, unambiguous statements. Because this sort of interpretation can be had only from a guru, try as the uninitiated may to guess the meaning of such passages they will never be able to do so, for they lack that interpretive guide which the guru holds.

Avasthas – The avasthas introduced in Chapter Four are secondary sources of meaning which temper interpretations rather than reverse them. Take Parashara's statement that planets in Mrita Avastha (the last 6° of an odd-numbered rashi or the first 6° of an even-numbered rashi) impair the benefic results of its benefic combinations. A planet in Mrita Avastha which is otherwise very strong (as by being exalted or in its own rashi) is severely weakened, no doubt, but is still better placed than a debilitated planet in Mrita Avastha.

It is usually best to interpret the results of the avasthas metaphorically. A Saturn posited in the late degrees of Aries in the fifth house of children in a Sagittarius ascendant is both debilitated and in Mrita Avastha; if that Saturn is further afflicted by other malefics, and/or other fifth-house indicators are stressed, one of the native's children may actually die. But an exalted Venus who occupies the fifth house of a Scorpio lagna in the early degrees of Pisces (and so in Mrita Avastha) may indicate, rather than the literal death of a child, that the native may treat his children 'as if dead' – disown them, keep them at a distance, live at a great distance from them, or the like. A Mercury exalted in Virgo in the fifth house of a Taurus lagna but in Bala Avastha may create a formidable intelligence which is, however, rather exuberant and untempered by experience, since children and infants are not very experienced.

Keep in mind when evaluating avasthas that sometimes a planet at the very beginning or end of a constellation may be in its *vargottama navamsha*, which will greatly modify its condition of being either in Mrita Avastha or in Bala Avastha (the first 6° of an odd-numbered rashi or the last 6° of an even-numbered rashi). Although a Saturn at the tail end of Virgo (between 26° 40' and 30°) is in Bala Avastha, a position of weakness, it occupies Virgo in the navamsha as well, a position of strength which cancels and would sometimes override the avastha position.

To introduce yet another complexity, the star Spica, the *yogatara* (principal star) of Chitra nakshatra, is located at approximately 29° 59' of Virgo (according to Lahiri). Spica is regarded, in both the East and the West, as one of the most auspicious stars in the zodiac. Since Jyotish regards as good the conjunction of a planet with a fixed star (particularly if within an orb of one degree), the conjunction of Saturn with this most auspicious star also overrides its being in Bala Avastha. Judgement in Jyotish is never simple, but with experience and an ishta devata all these factors eventually and spontaneously find their own applications.

APPLIED INTERPRETATIONS

The eighteen principles above are general abstractions of specific rules of interpretation which may be applied to particular cases. Other methodologies also exist in Jyotish, but the method presented above is a fair restatement of the most basic fundamentals of interpretation with which neophyte jyotishis are expected to become familiar and fluent. The balance of this book will build on these fundamentals by adding additional methods that can help smooth the way to more difficult judgements.

With the help of these principles you can confidently conclude that when all the three factors – house, house lord and significator – under consideration for a particular matter are strong in a horoscope, they will enhance that matter. Similarly, when all three factors are weak, the corresponding matter will be weakened, which will create some problem or difficulty. Any condition in between these two extremes will require greater skill and experience to interpret. Regular practice with these principles of interpretation on every horoscope that comes your way will help this mode of thought to become integrated into your own way of thinking, and will prepare you for more sophisticated techniques of interpretation.

An uncomplicated example will illustrate just how much information is contained in these rules. Most works on Jyotish, including the works of modern authors, consider it obligatory to describe the effects of the planets in the various houses. *Saravali* comments, in Chapter 30, on Jupiter in the first house: '. . . (a) attractive appearance (b) energetic (c) long-lived (d) will act after assessing consequences (e) will be learned . . .' Each of these statements, which are based on a synthesis of the attributes of Jupiter with the attributes of the first house, can also be derived by using the principles enunciated above.

The first four statements are expressions of the effect of a natural benefic sited in a house, namely on the attribute of Jupiter as a benefic modifying the body, its longevity, its vitality, and one's personality, which are four first-house indications. All of these meanings are based on Principle 1. Statement (e) is derived somewhat differently, since the first house does not rule education. It exemplifies instead the sort of effect produced when a planet as *graha karaka* (significator) is situated in a beneficial house. Here Jupiter is taken in its representative capacity as the significator of education, and its position in the first house, a beneficial house, means that education will be benefited.

Phaladipika adds for Jupiter in the first house 'blessed with children', a different statement based on the same reasoning: Jupiter as the significator of children in a good house. *Saravali* and *Phaladipika* make an additional subtle point with these last two interpretations, which are based on Principle 7. When Jupiter sits in the first house, he aspects the ninth and the fifth houses, which are respectively the houses of higher education and children, in the capacity of a natural benefic. This is a good influence, again according to both Principles 1 and 5, and, since three principles of interpretation lead to the same result, this is a case of good confluence.

To summarize the effects of grahas in bhavas:

· take the graha as a benefic or malefic, and combine its benefic or malefic impact with the meanings of the house it occupies; and
· take the graha as a *graha karata*, and combine its significations with the auspicious and/or inauspicious nature of the house it occupies.

In this way you can compose many more statements concerning the effects of planets in houses. Regarding Jupiter in the first house, you can also predict marital happiness, because Jupiter is a benefic aspecting the seventh house of marriage (1); the person may speak well, because Jupiter is the significator of oratory in the good first house (7); and so on. Such composed statements will sometimes be strikingly true; but more often they will be modified by the 'texture' or 'grain' of the particular horoscope under consideration. Factors such as whether a planet is exalted, debilitated, or in its own sign, and which planets aspect or conjoin it, are bound to change its effects.

As an exercise in astrological thought, take some time to write out the interpretations you consider possible for the Nine Grahas as a result of their position in each of the twelve houses, according to the model presented for Jupiter in the first house. The multitude of influences which affect the grahas means it is impossible to be completely accurate, but if you make an honest effort to arrive at viable and probable interpretations based on the general principles enunciated above, you will markedly improve your skills as a fledgling jyotishi. In fact, when you compare your results with some textbook on Jyotish you may discover that you have learned much already. If you become diligent in this exercise, you will be well on your way to developing an ability to think astrologically. Always bear in mind though that astrological interpretation is a sophisticated and subtle process which requires the synthesis of many often-perplexing factors, and do not fall in love with your theoretical creations unless and until you find that your practical experience overwhelmingly confirms them.

As you strive to interpret a horoscope, conflicts will sometimes arise, conundrums which will usually hinge on some disparity between the natural benefics who favorably influence one sector of the horoscope and the temporary malefics (rulers of bad houses and/or rulers of good houses that are badly placed) who influence the same matter. In such cases *the natural indications typically prevail on the subjective level and the temporary indications typically prevail on the objective level* (in the person's environment).

For instance, for a Pisces lagna Venus rules the third and the eighth houses (two bad houses). Based on Principle 11, if Venus as lord of the eighth house occupies the lagna, where it is exalted, the beneficial indications of the eighth house (such as longevity) may be enhanced *but* the malefic indications of the eighth house (such as accidents) may not be suppressed. While Venus as a natural benefic in the lagna should protect the body (Principle 1), Principle 16 warns us that someone whose eighth lord of accidents is extremely strongly placed in the first house of the body may experience serious accidents. This enigma is resolved by noting that, while accidents are likely to occur (the objective level), the native is not likely to be disheartened by them (the subjective level).

To practice further the principles advanced thus far, start a collection of horoscopes which are notable in some respect, e.g. horoscopes from people who are talented musicians, or who are rich and powerful, or poor but intelligent, or plagued by chronic illness, physically beautiful, academically gifted, or whatever. Analyze the appropriate factors in these horoscopes to hone your astrological judgement, and search for those areas in which the factors become confluent. Continue to add horoscopes until you have several in each of the various categories. You may wish to create a notebook in which to record horoscopes, classifying them as notable for some first-house matter, some second-house matter, some third-house matter, and so on. This method of study will help you to gain systematic experience, which will give you the confidence to handle the horoscopes of people about whose lives you know nothing.

Discuss horoscopes with practitioners of Jyotish whenever you can and, if at all possible, discuss them with a Jyotish guru. Those who rely solely on the written word, devoid as it is of tonality, cadence, rhythm and expression, risk failing to see the forest for the trees. A single word from a teacher discussing horoscope analysis orally with a small group of students is the equivalent of a thousand written words, for a good teacher slants the information to accommodate each student's conceptual background. When Jyotish is taught in the traditional Indian context, where teacher and disciple get to know each other over a period of time, they come to speak a common language, as the student gradually learns the teacher's mode of expression. So it was that one day, after five years of intense association, our Jyotish guru said to one of us: 'Finally you are able to understand my ways, and now you will be able to understand what I am trying to teach you.'

Once you begin to understand your guru, knowledge begins to flow freely, and as soon as you learn a new principle it will often be demonstrated for you, immediately and automatically. For example, after one of us was told one day by our Jyotish guru that Saturn in Sagittarius gives problems with the right leg, the next half-dozen people whose horoscopes he read had Saturn in Sagittarius *and* also had problems with their right legs. Since Saturn stays in Sagittarius for two and a half years at a time, it is obvious that not all of the millions of people born with this combination will have right-leg problems, and this is very much the point: the Jyotir Vidya directs to the student those cases which fit the principle she wishes to illustrate at that moment.

As you begin your studies in Jyotish, however, there are bound to be times when you will feel yourself completely out of your depth, times when success seems utterly out of the question. When such hopelessness strikes, remember that the ultimate purpose behind the study of Jyotish is self-knowledge, a goal that is worth all the difficult effort necessary to achieve it. Know thyself, and all will be known! At such moments this quotation from the *Bhagavad Gita* (18:37–9) may inspire you:

that joy which is like poison at first and like nectar at the end, which springs from a clear understanding of the Self, is said to be Sattvic. That joy which arises from the contact of the senses and their objects, and which is like nectar at first but like poison in the end, is said to be Rajasic. That happiness which deludes the soul both at the beginning and at the end, and which arises from sleep, sloth and negligence, is said to be Tamasic.

Substitute 'knowledge' for 'joy' in the above quotation and you will realize that the pain and difficulty you experience as you begin to work with horoscopes will lead to the long-term Sattvic joy of fluent interpretation. Many jyotishis, beginners and advanced students alike, tend Rajasically to oversimplify their analyses, which may lead to pleasure in the beginning but pain in the end when their conclusions go awry. Little need be said of those who, inspired by Tamas, invent delusions that are foreign to Jyotish's spirit and then vigorously defend those delusions as truth. It is better to submit humbly to the ministrations of the Jyotir Vidya and suffer first, that later you may laugh.

CHAPTER TEN

GRAHA YOGAS

The novice astrologer's greatest problem is how to synthesize several astrological factors. Neophyte jyotishis tend to take one symbol and, because it is manageable, work it to death. One example is to take Jupiter as a benefic, and to wax eloquent concerning its wonderful effect over everything it influences in the horoscope. While in certain horoscopes this may well be the case, such a blanket interpretation ignores the possibility that Jupiter, in the chart under consideration, may be disadvantaged in some way. A Jupiter which is debilitated, rules bad houses, occupies a detrimental house, is aspected by Mars and Saturn, and is associated with Rahu will often create results quite the opposite of wonderful. Though such undesirable effects may build character, most people would nevertheless prefer to avoid them.

Classical textbooks on Jyotish try to avoid this difficulty by forcing the novice from the very start to work with those complicated combinations called *graha yogas*. This approach cultivates the necessary and constructive habit of taking many influences into consideration when coming to an astrological conclusion. While its initial intricacy may easily discourage students, a little discouragement can actually be healthy, as long as it does not deepen into despondency. Healthy discouragement eliminates overconfidence and engenders humility and circumspection. Good Indian gurus regularly discourage their disciples as one method of ego control.

The general rules underlying graha yogas apply equally to planets in houses, to planets in constellations, and to planets that combine with each other. Let us return to the graha yoga mentioned at the beginning of Chapter Nine. Saturn as a malefic posited in Aries will clearly influence adversely the various matters ruled by Aries. Since

Aries rules the head, the native may have some physical problem pertaining to the head; since Aries rules activity, the person may be disinclined to activity, and so on. Saturn being debilitated in Aries as the natural significator of subordinates, the person may also experience great difficulty with underlings; being the natural indicator of nerves, a debilitated Saturn may create symptoms like nervousness and irritability, and so on.

Now consider how the qualities of Saturn may blend into the qualities of Aries. Varahamihira dubs the person with Saturn in Aries 'a fool' on account of the natural malefic Saturn occupying the constellation which represents the brain; 'deceitful', because a fallen Saturn displays its worst qualities; 'always on his legs', because Saturn rules Capricorn and Aquarius, the constellations which indicate the legs, so that a weak Saturn will be detrimental to the legs; and 'without friends', because Saturn rules the eleventh house of the natural zodiac and as such cannot give good friends when he is debilitated.

Similar rules of interpretation apply for planets in combination with one another. When Mercury is associated with or aspected by Mars, all matters ruled by Mercury will be weakened, because Mars is a malefic; because Mercury rules speech, such a person may well speak badly, or tell lies. On the other hand, the things which Mars represents will be blended in with Mercurial matters. Since Mars rules aggression and fighting, and Mercury rules great dexterity and nimbleness, several works on Jyotish suggest that a Mercury–Mars association indicates a potential boxer. Mars and Mercury combined in the second house are likely to affect the individual's speaking ability, which both the second house and Mercury rule. Some traditional astrological works suggest that such a combination will indicate a logician who is skilled in debate. Since the second house relates more to speaking than to athletics, this seems a more logical indication than boxing.

But suppose this association of Mars and Mercury takes place in the second house in the constellation of Cancer, where Mars is debilitated and Mercury is in the constellation of its enemy. Such a native is less likely to be a great logician and debater than an impulsive and illogical speaker whose hasty words cause antagonism.

Contrast this with the same combination in the second house but this time in Capricorn, where Mars is exalted and Mercury is in the rashi of a friend, a situation which is more likely to create skill in debate, all other factors being equal. Similarly, Jupiter (who rules oratory) in the second house in the first half of Sagittarius (a constellation of voice) will indicate through confluence a far better speaker than would Saturn (a mute planet) in the second house in Pisces (a mute constellation).

Only a combination of experience and intuition can establish whether a Mercury–Mars combination will make the owner of the horoscope a poor speaker, a great debater, a liar and cheat, a karate expert, or all of them wrapped into one. The key to deciding which line of interpretation to follow in any particular instance lies in evaluating all factors of the combination simultaneously: the house and constellation in which the combination lies, the natures and rulerships of the grahas that compose it, the effect of other grahas on the combination, and the native's environment and cultural context.

While this style of interpretation is relatively straightforward in theory, it becomes very involved in practice. Mistakes occur because it is not always humanly possible to consider every pertinent influence in the chart. The seers who gave us Jyotish tried to simplify things for us by emphasizing graha yogas. While thus far we have used the term 'graha yoga' to refer generically to the combination of two or more grahas in a house, from now on we will use it to refer to outstanding planetary combinations which indicate specific results. A few of the many classes of such yogas are *Raja Yogas* (which indicate leadership, power and fame); *Dhana Yogas* (which suggest wealth) and *Daridra Yogas* (which promise poverty); *Pravrajya Yogas* (which lead to renunciation of the world); and *Balarishta Yogas* (which indicate death in childhood).

Many of these yogas are well known to most jyotishis, who often look for them on first glancing at a horoscope. Some jyotishis even focus exclusively on these yogas, and on the indications given for them in the traditional texts, for the more auspicious yogas there are in a horoscope, the more likely it will be for the person to become someone of note who will rise through life to be powerful and prosperous. Sometimes, though, in spite of a multitude of promising yogas, the native never rises to the expected level of success. The most important reason for this failure is that the *dashas* (planetary periods; see Chapter Eleven) of the grahas involved do not occur at the appropriate periods of life. Another reason is that the grahas involved in the yogas may be weak (because of combustion, placement in unfriendly rashis or inauspicious avasthas, or weakness in subcharts). Yet another reason is that under certain circumstances, which are described at the end of this chapter, a horoscope's benevolent yogas can be canceled or broken (in Sanskrit *bhanga*).

Except when noted, graha yogas are calculated from the ascendant. Jyotishis often seek confirmation of a combination shown from the ascendant by reading the horoscope from the constellation occupied by the Moon, using the latter as if it were the ascendant, since after the ascendant the Moon is the fastest-moving factor in a horoscope. This sort of 'tying down' of the chart is the *Chandra Lagna* (Moon Lagna), which is frequently used when the birthtime is very imprecise. When known, however, the ascendant is always pre-eminent. Many graha yogas can be counted either from the Moon (*Chandra Yogas*) or from the ascendant (*Lagna Yogas*) and, on occasion, also from the Sun lagna (*Surya Lagna*).

Every student of Jyotish should practice locating the several graha yogas below in many horoscopes in order to be able to recognize them readily, and to get a headstart on understanding Jyotish's many other yogas. As you scrutinize the horoscopes in your possession, find out to what degree the yogas therein correlate with the life experiences of the owners of the charts. Where the correlation is weak, try to find out what has weakened the planets which comprise the yoga.

THE PANCHA MAHAPURUSHA YOGAS

Experience suggests that the effects given in numerous texts for the various yogas should be read more as general statements of interpretive principle than as utterly specific applications. With this in mind, we will now consider a few of the more prominent of the many thousands of graha yogas, attempting to dissect from them their inherent operational tenets. The first of these combinations are the *Pancha Mahapurusha Yogas*, the 'five combinations of a great being', which exist when Mars, Mercury, Jupiter, Venus or Saturn in a horoscope occupies its own or exaltation constellation while in an angular or trinal house. The yogas formed by each graha are called *Ruchaka* ('luster, splendor, desire, taste'), *Bhadra* ('auspicious'), *Hamsa* ('goose' or 'swan'), *Malavya* ('a resident of the region of India known as Malava') and *Shasha* ('hare') *Yogas* respectively.

Here is a summary of the effects of the five Pancha Mahapurusha Yogas (extracted from *Phaladipika* 6:2–4):

The person born in Ruchaka Yoga will have a long face, will acquire wealth by doing many daring deeds, will be brave, will overcome his [sic] enemies, and will be powerful and arrogant. He [sic] will become renowned for his merits, will be a leader of an army, and will emerge victorious in all his attempts.

The person born in Bhadra Yoga will be gifted with long life and keen intellect (*buddhi*), will be clean, will be praised by the learned, will lead men, will be very rich, and will be clever in addressing an assembly.

The person born in Hamsa Yoga will be a king extolled by the good . . . He will possess a beautiful body, will eat sumptuous food, and will be of a righteous disposition.

The person born in Malavya Yoga will have strong limbs, will be resolute, wealthy and endowed with wife, children and good fortune, will be prosperous, will eat good food, enjoy pleasures and command good vehicles, and will become famous and learned. He will possess unperturbed senses.

The person born in Shasha Yoga will be extolled by all, will have good servants, will be strong, will be a king or the headman of a village, will be wicked in disposition, will have intrigues with women not his own, will usurp others' wealth, and will be happy.

These and other yogas occur fairly frequently, but everyone who has them does not enjoy their effects in full, and some do not enjoy their effects at all, except perhaps in their dreams. It all depends on the strength and position of the yogas. The less such a yoga is interfered with by the impact of other grahas, particularly malefics, the more the native will experience its energies. A Ruchaka Yoga, for example, is one thing when Mars is aspected by its friend Jupiter alone, and quite another when it is aspected by its enemy Saturn, and is conjoined with Rahu.

Note that the indications for these yogas are mainly the significations for the grahas involved, because a Pancha Mahapurusha Yoga allows a graha to express its inherent nature freely and strongly. The description of Ruchaka Yoga is clearly a glorified listing of the astrological attributes of Mars. Mantreshwara might as well have gone on to say that someone with Ruchaka Yoga will be fond of confrontations, will be a 'victory-at-any-cost' competitor, may be accident-prone, will serve in executive and independent positions, may be a crusader for various causes, may have powerful younger siblings, may be athletic, may be a lawyer, and so on.

Many people with strong Ruchaka Yogas do end up becoming lawyers, but this potential will be actualized only in those horoscopes in which the fourth house of education (because law requires formal education) and Jupiter (because law requires good judgement) are both strong. Similarly, a person with an unblemished Ruchaka Yoga may become an athlete if the first house is very strong, because athletes require strong bodies.

One way to gauge the magnitude of a Pancha Mahapurusha Yoga is to see whether or not it recurs from all three lagnas (the ascendant, the Chandra Lagna and the Surya Lagna), which is a sort of confluence. That yoga which does so is very strong, all other factors remaining equal. A yoga which recurs from two lagnas is better than average, while a yoga which can be counted only from the ascendant is only average. In Chart 2 (see p. 418) a Hamsa Yoga exists in the fourth house of the lagna, the fourth house of the Surya Lagna, and the seventh house of the Chandra Lagna. As we might expect, this Hamsa Yoga has created in the person concerned many Jupiterian qualities. Because this yoga is specific to the bhavas that Jupiter owns, we may conclude that this person will own expensive or valuable vehicles and houses (fourth house) and will have a noble and educated spouse (seventh house) – which, in fact, he does.

The classical texts mention other indications for these yogas which cannot be derived as easily as we have derived these general conclusions. For example, *Brihat Parashara Hora* says that a person with Hamsa Yoga will be fond of playing games and of watery places. Chart 2's owner does indeed live on a property with a pond, and very much enjoys amusements. The same text also states that such an individual will have full cheeks and a round forehead, two characteristics which this person does possess.

Simply because a graha occupies its own or its exaltation constellation does not create a Pancha Mahapurusha Yoga. Venus, which occupies Libra in Chart 2, is conjoined with the benefic Mercury. This is an auspicious placement, but it is no Malavya Yoga because it sits in the second house, which is neither a kendra nor a kona. Likewise, in Chart 1 (see p. 415) Jupiter is exalted but is in the second house, so that no Hamsa Yoga is formed. Anyway, this Jupiter is combust and is conjoined with Rahu, which spoils many of its indications. Mars does occupy Aries, its own constellation, but being in the eleventh house it does not form Ruchaka Yoga. It is, however, likely to give good results, since Mars is aspected here only by the benefic waxing Moon.

An exalted planet which occupies a kendra or kona will create a Pancha Mahapurusha Yoga *only if* its dispositor is strong. When a graha occupies its own house, it serves as its own dispositor, and is by definition strong in both body and soul. An exalted graha whose dispositor is afflicted by malefics, is combust or debilitated is highly unlikely to be able to deliver the promised goods for, though its body (*deha*) is powerful, its soul (*jiva*) is feeble.

THE DHARMA KARMA ADHIPATI YOGAS

Another class of yogas for which jyotishis always look are the *Dharma Karma Adhipati Yogas*, the 'Combinations of the Lords of Fortune and Action'. This yoga is formed when the lords of a dharma house (a kona) and a karma house (a kendra) combine in a horoscope, either by aspect or by association. 'Karma' means action, and 'dharma' indicates fortune, in the sense that those people who dedicatedly follow their own individual dharmas find that luck begins to follow them around. Real success in life appears whenever there is a felicitous conjunction of effort with luck. Enterprise alone is no guarantee of achievement, nor can chance alone be relied upon; but when both combine, the whole truly becomes greater than the sum of its parts. Whenever Napoleon was considering elevating one of his generals to the rank of marshal, his final question, after hearing a litany of the man's achievements and qualifications, would reportedly be: 'Yes, but is he lucky?'

Dharma Karma Adhipati Yogas are examples of Raja Yogas, combinations which promise success, wealth, influence and celebrity. A strong Dharma Karma Adhipati Yoga enables a person to rise to a position of great prominence in society. Although, technically speaking, a Raja Yoga is a combination for political success (a *raja* is a ruler), over the years it has come to promise success, wealth, influence and/or celebrity. While in the old days the king had the power to support and influence all others, today non-political people like writers, actors, musicians and media moguls are often more influential, wealthy and famous than most of our rulers.

The source of good fortune is the Law of Karma: The total of your past karmas determines what sort of assistance the world will give you. The kendras represent, in a certain sense, your present actions, your Kriyamana and Agama Karmas, while the konas indicate the overall positivity or negativity of your past actions, your Prarabdha and Sanchita Karmas. Parashara explains (*Brihat Parashara Hora* 41:28) that the kendras are bhavas of Vishnu, the Surmounter of Difficulties, while the konas are bhavas of Lakshmi, His wife, the Goddess of Prosperity. The lagna is particularly important because it is simultaneously a kona and a kendra. Whenever the lord of a kendra (the husband) and the lord of a kona (his wife) unite, opportunity combines with real fortune to create enduring prosperity: a Raja Yoga.

Here is another way to look at this combination: The kendra houses are sometimes called houses of environment (your objective surroundings) and the trinal houses, houses of merit (your subjective attitudes). When the objective and subjective factors in a horoscope combine harmoniously, they create by their confluence a powerful current, for then conscious (subjective) attitudes become aligned with the unconscious (objective) influences. If subjectively you happen to be academically gifted and inclined to study, and objectively you happen to live a stone's throw from Harvard Yard, then *voilà*! environment and merit have combined, and success becomes almost inevitable.

A Dharma Karma Adhipati Yoga which involves either the lords of the ninth and tenth houses or the lords of the fourth and fifth houses is particularly valuable. The combination of the ninth and tenth lords is the strongest Dharma Karma Adhipati Yoga, for the ninth is the strongest of the konas and the tenth the strongest of the kendras. Although a Dharma Karma Adhipati Yoga is defined as a combination by association or mutual aspect between a kona lord and a kendra lord, it is also said to be formed when: (a) the lord of the ninth house occupies the ninth house *and* the tenth lord occupies the tenth house, *or* when the fourth lord occupies the fourth *and* the fifth lord tenants the fifth. (In these cases, two Pancha Mahapurusha Yogas are often formed.) (b) the lord of the ninth occupies the tenth *and* the tenth lord dwells in the ninth, *or* the fourth lord appears in the fifth and the fifth lord resides in the fourth. (This is a type of *Parivartana Yoga* – see below.)

In certain lagnas a single graha owns both a kendra and a kona. Such a planet becomes a *Raja Yoga Karaka* ('Raja Yoga Significator'), a single-graha Dharma Karma Adhipati Yoga, which, if well placed in the horoscope, will produce very desirable results. Listed below are the planets which can act as Raja Yoga Karakas, and the lagnas for which they so act. Note that each of the Raja Yoga Karakas is a friend to the lord of the lagna in which they own the kendra and the kona:

For Taurus lagna:	Saturn (lord of houses 9 & 10)
For Cancer lagna:	Mars (lord of houses 5 & 10)
For Leo lagna:	Mars (lord of houses 4 & 9)
For Libra lagna:	Saturn (lord of houses 4 & 5)
For Capricorn lagna:	Venus (lord of houses 5 & 10)
For Aquarius lagna:	Venus (lord of houses 4 & 9)

Although Raja Yoga Karakas when well placed can singly create Raja Yoga, they should ideally be supported by benefics or by the rulers of beneficial houses. This is particularly true for Cancer lagna, because Mars, the Raja Yoga Karaka, is debilitated in the first house. It is sometimes said that Mars forms Raja Yoga for a Cancer ascendant only when it is supported by benefics.

Saturn acts as Raja Yoga Karaka for the ascendants of Venus, and Venus returns the favor for Saturn. Symmetry suggests that the Moon and Sun, lords of Cancer and Leo respectively, should, when conjoined, form a Raja Yoga for the two ascendants of Mars (Aries, in which the luminaries own houses 4 and 5, and Scorpio, in which they rule 9 and 10). Because whenever the Sun and Moon occupy the same house the Moon's inherent light is exceedingly dim, the Raja Yoga formed when the Sun and Moon aspect one another (as they do when the Moon is full or near full) is much stronger than is the yoga formed when they conjoin, at the time of the new Moon.

Like any other beneficial yoga, a Raja Yoga gives good results when it appears in a good house and is without affliction. Consider a Saturn at 29° in the first house of a Libra ascendant in the horoscope of a person about to enter a period where Saturn will be very influential in her life. For Saturn as the Raja Yoga Karaka to be exalted in Libra is very desirable, for it also creates a Shasha Yoga in the first house, and Saturn is a friend of Venus, the lord of the lagna. But – because Saturn occupies its Mrita Avastha there may be danger to health (since Saturn = ill health and the first house = the body), danger of bankruptcy (because Saturn is the natural house significator of the three evil trik houses; this is one reason why Saturn is the significator of misery) and danger to profession (because Saturn aspects the tenth house as a significator of the tenth house).

In Chart 2 (see p. 418) the lords of the ninth and tenth houses (Mercury and Venus) both occupy the second house, and the lords of the fourth and fifth houses (Jupiter and Saturn) tenant the fourth house. The grahas involved are all strong, being in their own, in friendly or at the very least in neutral rashis, and are simultaneously in good houses (that is, the non-dussthanas). The two pairs of planets involved – Mercury/Venus and Jupiter/Saturn – are not inimical to each other, nor are they enemies of the lord of the lagna. These yogas will therefore strongly influence those areas of life indicated by the houses in which they occur; and we have already seen that this man is a millionaire (second house) and enjoys good, profitable property (fourth house). After handling many birth charts you will begin to realize how unusual it is to find two such strong Dharma Karma Adhipati Yogas in one and the same horoscope.

Experience will also teach you that these and other yogas occur in horoscopes with some frequency but with very different strengths. Be mindful of Mantreshwara's axiom that the results of good yogas become certain when the grahas involved are strong and when there is a confluence of good influences to the participant planets. Contrast now the condition of the combination of the lords of the fourth and fifth houses in Chart 2 with the same combination in Chart 1. In Chart 1, the two planets involved (Mercury and Venus) sit together in the third house, a dussthana; Venus is in the constellation of its enemy; and both Mercury and Venus are aspected by the malefic Saturn, who is also acting as eighth lord.

Saturn as the fifth lord joins with Jupiter in Chart 2 to form the yoga, so we cannot say that the yoga there is marred by the malefic Saturn. There *is* a drawback in Chart 2 in the aspect of the malefic Mars, who also owns the eighth house, on the Jupiter–Saturn combination, but this, as your experience will eventually enable you to conclude, is a minor blemish on an otherwise strong yoga. Some slight imperfection always occurs, alas, in even the best of horoscopes; such is the nature of embodied life.

We must also examine a Dharma Karma Adhipati Yoga from the Moon and Sun Lagnas. Recall the five human bodies, the *annamayakosha* (physical body), *pranamayakosha* (etheric body), *manomayakosha* (subtle body), *vijnanamayakosha* (causal body) and *anandamayakosha* (greater causal body). The ascendant (Birth Lagna) represents the physical body, the Moon Lagna the subtle body (and hence desire manifestation), and the Sun Lagna the causal body (and hence thought manifestation). Congruence of thoughts and desires with actions, which leads to integrated activity, occurs when yogas and planetary combinations recur from all three lagnas; this is yet another form of confluence.

In Chart 2 the many Raja Yogas all recur from the Sun Lagna. Moreover, when we count from the Moon we see that the fourth and fifth house lords are conjoined in the fifth house, that the ninth and tenth house lords are conjoined in the seventh house, and that all the same grahas that were involved in the yogas in the other two lagnas (namely, Mercury–Venus and Jupiter–Saturn) are involved here. This is a clear case of confluence. Contrast this situation with that in Chart 1 where the already feeble yoga counted from the lagna (the fourth and fifth lords combined in the third house) does not recur from the other lagnas. Such a yoga is unlikely to yield anywhere near the bounty which those yogas in Chart 2 will afford.

OTHER GRAHA YOGAS

A partial list of yogas commonly cited in various Jyotish texts appears below. Specific meanings are provided for some; the reader should analyze the others with the help of the basic interpretive method explained in the last chapter. Always blend together the significations of the grahas, rashis and bhavas to arrive at an interpretation. Examples of ways in which to interpret yogas can be found in Chapter Twelve. One general rule: *The more yogas in which a graha participates, the greater its importance.*

ADHI YOGA: *Benefics occupying simultaneously the sixth, the seventh and the eighth houses, counted from either the Moon or the ascendant.* In Adhi Yoga benefics in the sixth and eighth houses flank the seventh house, which strengthens that house, and any planet therein. The aspect on the first house of such a strengthened benefic in the seventh house will then produce most favorable effects. This yoga is particularly good for raising one to a position of leadership (*adhi* means 'to add, to receive').

AMALA YOGA: *An unafflicted benefic occupying the tenth house from the Moon or the Lagna (amala means 'stainless').* Planets in the tenth house from the lagna, the zenith of the horoscope, shine there brilliantly. Amala Yoga tends to make the native's actions (tenth house) stainless (virtuous, pious, etc.). Such a person will be revered by the sovereign, which is one way in which a benefic in the tenth house enhances tenth-house meanings.

ASHUBHA MALA YOGA: *When all the benefic grahas tenant houses six, eight and twelve.* This very undesirable combination (*Ashubha Mala* means 'the necklace of inauspiciousness') indicates great difficulties in life, just as the albatross around the neck of the Ancient Mariner betokened his ruination. If there are benefics in houses six and eight alone, the beneficial influence is reduced somewhat, but is not canceled. That situation is therefore also a sort of Adhi Yoga (benefics in the sixth, seventh and eighth houses) and *not* an example of Ashubha Mala Yoga. Ashubha Mala Yoga occurs *only when* all benefics lie in the sixth house alone, in the eighth house alone, in the sixth and twelfth houses only, or in the eighth and twelfth houses only. In these cases all the power of the benefics is completely eclipsed, robbing the native of all good influences.

BUDHADITYA YOGA: *When the Sun and Mercury occupy the same constellation.* This famous yoga, which is prevalent (because Mercury can never be more than one rashi away from the Sun), confuses many who try to interpret it. While a Budhaditya Yoga is supposed to illumine one's intellect, every jyotishi finds it in the horoscopes of dullards and geniuses alike. Some people attempt to use this fact to undermine the theory of combustion, since a combust Mercury should (if combust planets are weak) give such natives uniformly weak intellects. But, as we noted in the previous chapter, an individual's inner qualities such as intellect are not necessarily impaired when their significators are combust. When intelligence is impaired in someone who has a Budhaditya Yoga, it is often due to other influences.

However, for a Budhaditya Yoga to be really effective in a horoscope it must above all be somehow configured with either the ascendant (the chief indicator of the individual) or the fifth house (intellect), with the first house being preferred. When this is so, the following criteria must then be met: (a) If either the Sun or Mercury owns either the first or the fifth houses, the yoga must appear in a good house. (b) If neither graha owns either house, the yoga must occur in either the ascendant, the seventh house (from which it aspects the ascendant), the fifth house or the eleventh house (from which it aspects the fifth). (c) Under all circumstances the grahas should be strong and not otherwise afflicted, and the first and fifth houses must be strong.

CHANDRA MANGALA YOGA: *When the Moon and Mars occupy the same constellation.* By extension (though this is not a classical precept), the Yoga is also formed when Moon and Mars mutually aspect. If the Yoga happens in good houses, particularly the elevated houses of the horoscope (nine, ten, eleven), and the Moon is bright and powerful, this Yoga can contribute considerably to the native's financial status, more especially if it is a night birth.

In a male horoscope Chandra Mangala Yoga also connotes gains through women, or through such industries as hospitality (hotels, food, and the like) and the personal beautification industry (exercise, dieting, hairdressing, and so on). If the Yoga is afflicted (if it occurs in houses six, eight or twelve, is aspected by malefics and/or there is no aspect of benefics), it may mean exploitation of women.

DUR YOGA: *When the trik lords are strongly positioned in kendras or konas, and the lords of houses one, four, nine and ten are weak or combust and occupy the trik houses.* This yoga (mentioned in *Phaladipika* 6:70) should not be confused with the yoga of the same name included in the group of twenty-four Yogas below. The results, while similar, are more pervasive, rendering difficult the entire horoscope instead of only the tenth house. If Dur (difficult) Yoga is reversed (with the trik lords weak or combust and the lords of houses one, four, nine and ten strong in kendras or konas), the native will be wealthy, happy, virtuous and powerful.

Whole systems of interpretation have been built on the principle which lies at Dur Yoga's root: the lords of dussthanas cause difficulties when they are strong and occupy non-dussthanas, while the lords of good houses cause good results when in kendras and konas. When the lord of a dussthana is weak, it is no longer capable of giving in plenty the evil results which it otherwise promises, any more than the lords of good houses can give their promised good results when they are weak or combust and are posited in dussthanas.

GAJA KESARI YOGA: Most modern books on Jyotish inaccurately define Gaja Kesari Yoga ('the Elephant-Lion Yoga') as *Jupiter in the first, fourth, seventh or tenth house (the kendra houses) from the Moon.*

Brihat Parashara Hora has a more accurate definition:

Should Jupiter be in an angle from the ascendant or from the Moon, and be conjoined with or aspected by benefics without being debilitated, combust, or in an enemy's sign, Gaja Kesari Yoga is formed. One born in Gaja Kesari Yoga will be splendorous, wealthy, intelligent, endowed with many laudable virtues, and will please the king. (36:3–4)

The lesser combination of *Moon and Jupiter in angles to each other* is in *Phaladipika* given the simpler name of *Kesari Yoga*, but even in this watered-down version of the yoga it is still important for Jupiter and the Moon to be in good houses from the ascendant. Since one full third of all horoscopes display Jupiter in a kendra from the Moon, it is wise to ensure that the combination satisfies Parashara's more stringent criteria before predicting the results promised for the yoga. A Moon in the twelfth house and a debilitated and combust Jupiter in the third house would clearly be very unlikely to produce noticeably good results.

In Chart 1 the Moon is in the fifth house and Jupiter in the second house, but, although this Jupiter is in an angle from the Moon and is exalted, it is also combust and conjoined with Rahu. In this case no Gaja Kesari Yoga is formed. A Gaja Kesari Yoga, even if in good houses from the ascendant, is also unlikely to yield beneficial effects if the Moon is depleted (i.e. if the birth was within five days either side of the new Moon). A good Gaja Kesari Yoga is said to be particularly useful for politicians.

This yoga appears almost fully formed in Chart 2, and was the cause of the following true story. On a business trip to Bombay, the owner of this horoscope was approached on the streets by a strange *sadhu* (a wandering Hindu holy man), who announced with great force that our man (let us call him K) must have a Gaja Kesari

Yoga in his chart. Knowing his own chart well, K was naturally amazed to hear this, and asked the sadhu how he could possibly know. The sadhu replied that K's strongly formed, round, vividly lustrous forehead indicated a powerful Gaja Kesari Yoga, and then forcefully suggested to K that this yoga would permit him to walk unharmed among poisonous cobras. The sadhu compellingly invited K to accompany him to a live cobra pit to prove the yoga's power, but K adroitly extricated himself from this trial by serpent. Therefore we do not yet possess the practical evidence we need to add to our list of indications of a strong Gaja Kesari Yoga: '. . . will be able to walk amongst poisonous cobras without harm'. It provides, however, strong evidence of a good jyotishi's ability to cast a horoscope simply by studying a face.

KEMADRUMA YOGA: *When there is no planet (excluding the Sun) conjoining the Moon* and *no planet in the second or twelfth houses from the Moon* and *no planet (including the Moon) in a kendra from the ascendant.* Kemadruma Yoga causes the native, even if well-born, to 'be obscure, miserable, penurious and menial', and 'be greatly reproached, be bereft of intelligence and learning, and be reduced to penury and perils'. Some say that Kemadruma is even canceled if any planet occupies a kendra as counted from the Moon.

LAKSHMI YOGA: *When the lord of the ninth house and Venus occupy their own or exalted constellations in the angular or trine houses.* Lakshmi Yoga bestows great wealth. Slight variants on this definition can be allowed; note that in Chart 2 Venus happens to be the lord of the ninth house and occupies its own rashi. It does sit in the second house, but since the second house from the ascendant happens to be the fifth house, like the ninth a trinal house, from the Moon, we can say that Lakshmi Yoga is also present in this horoscope. Yogas have both a literal dimension and interpretation and a broadly indicative function; and in a horoscope like Chart 2, in which beneficial yogas abound, such variations are worthy of consideration.

MAHA BHAGYA YOGA: *For a female, birth at night when the Sun, Moon, and Lagna all occupy even rashis; for a male, the reverse (i.e. a day birth, when the Sun, Moon and Lagna all occupy odd rashis).* Maha Bhagya means 'exceedingly auspicious'.

NEECHA BHANGA RAJA YOGA: Certain planetary combinations can modify the detrimental effects of a graha's debilitation. Canceled debility does not become equal to an exaltation or some other desirable placement, however. Debility is debility, and Neecha Bhanga is no more perfect than is a prosthesis applied to a limbless body. Giving a debilitated graha a cane with which to walk will enable the graha to exert some beneficial effects but, even if it excels at its duties, it will still never be normal. Moreover, Neecha Bhanga creates a Raja Yoga *only when* the debilitated graha occupies a kendra or a kona; otherwise the planet's debility will merely be removed.

Four of the most important ways in which debility can be canceled are: (1) if the lord of the rashi occupied by the debilitated graha is in a kendra position from the Moon or Lagna; (2) if the lord of the rashi where the debilitated graha is exalted is in a kendra position from the Moon or Lagna; (3) if the lord of the rashi occupied by the debilitated graha aspects that graha; or (4) if the planet who would be exalted in the rashi occupied by the debilitated graha is in a kendra from the Moon or from the Lagna.

As an example, take Saturn in Aries. If Mars (1 – Saturn's dispositor), Venus (2 – lord of Saturn's exaltation rashi) or the Sun (4 – who is exalted in Aries) occupies a kendra from the Moon or from the Lagna, or if Mars aspects Aries (3), Saturn's debility will be canceled. In most of the combinations which redeem a debilitated planet, its dispositor must be well placed in some way; the better the dispositor (*jiva*) is placed, the greater the relief to the debilitated planet (*deha*). The results produced by a debilitated planet will be the worst possible when its dispositor is itself debilitated, as would happen when, for example, Saturn occupies Aries and its dispositor Mars occupies Cancer.

PARIVARTANA YOGA: *When two grahas mutually occupy each other's rashis.* Parivartana Yoga (*parivartana* means 'exchange' or 'barter'), which is also known as 'mutual reception' or 'exchange of houses', exists when, for instance, Mars is in Gemini and Mercury in Aries.

An exchange between the lords of the kendra houses and of the kona houses is deemed to be very beneficial, as is the exchange between the lords of dussthanas. The latter exchange typically delivers its good effects only after first producing some stressful events; for example, some people become famous only after, and often because of, first being falsely accused and then extricating themselves from the calumny. Or, when you benefit from an inheritance, someone (probably a near and dear one) had to die in order to leave the bequest. The exchange between the lords of other houses usually produces mixed results, some good and some bad.

Parivartana Yoga can also produce evil effects. Here is one case: When the lord of the first house occupies the sixth house and the sixth lord sits in the lagna, and the lord of the sixth is conjoined with or aspected by the lord of a maraka house, the result will be penury (*Brihat Parashara Hora* 42:3).

PARVATA YOGA: A Parvata Yoga makes a person wealthy, charitable, eloquent, learned in classical subjects, fond of mirth, famous, splendiferous, and the leader of a city. Two of this yoga's several definitions appear in *Brihat Parashara Hora* and in *Phaladipika*.

Parashara defines Parvata Yoga as *benefics in kendra houses with the seventh and eighth houses empty or occupied only by benefics*. Because the seventh house is a maraka house, and the eighth house is the worst of the trik houses, any planets in those houses should be benefics in order to modify their results. Whenever a malefic occupies the seventh, it will damage the first house, while a malefic in the eighth house will create immense suffering and reduce the lifespan. A benefic in the eighth house will at least modify the negative effects of the eighth house, though much of the benefit promised by that benefic will be lost. To learn yogas thus, by analyzing their likely effects instead of merely committing them to memory, is to see how Jyotish's basic principles apply to real-life situations.

Phaladipika states that Parvata Yoga is formed *when the dispositor of the lord of the ascendant occupies its own rashi while simultaneously occupying a kendra or a kona house from the lagna*. This writer assumes, but does not mention, that the lord of the lagna should also occupy a good position in the horoscope for this yoga to be formed. If the lord of the first house is in, say, the eighth house, there will no doubt be great benefit to it if its dispositor is in its own rashi in a kendra or kona from the lagna, but the benefit will be more along the lines of a Neecha Bhanga Raja Yoga, i.e. a cancellation of a miserable position.

PUSHKALA YOGA: *When the Moon's dispositor conjoins the lord of the lagna, in a kendra, in a rashi in which it is strong, while at the same time a strong benefic aspects the lagna.* Those with Pushkala ('plenteous, abundant') Yoga, which is a fine example of the importance of the dispositor, are wealthy, honored by kings, famous, and beautifully adorned. In this case the crucial factor is the dispositor of the Moon, since the Moon is second only to the lagna in importance in the horoscope.

SARASWATI YOGA: *When Venus, Jupiter and Mercury occupy a kendra, a kona, or the second house, and all three grahas (Jupiter in particular) are strong.* This gives skill as a writer, orator or savant. The second house is included here because it indicates both speech and classical learning.

SHAKATA YOGA: *When the Moon is in the sixth, eighth or twelfth house from Jupiter.* The fortunes of those born with this yoga rise and fall again and again throughout life, just as a cartwheel (*shakata* means 'cart') turns round and round as it rolls down the road. When the Moon is in a kendra from the lagna, Shakata Yoga is not formed.

SHUBHA OR PAPA KARTARI YOGA: *When planets sit simultaneously on both sides of the first house (i.e. in houses two and twelve).* *Kartari* means 'scissors'. *Shubha Kartari Yoga* occurs when benefics unafflicted by malefics flank the first house; when malefics unaspected by benefics sit on both sides of the ascendant, the combination is known as *Papa Kartari Yoga.* The former combination is said to be highly auspicious (*shubha* means 'auspicious') and to bestow protection on the native by snipping away potential problems. The latter yoga is very inauspicious (*papa* means 'sin') and implies a lack of protection, particularly for the matters ruled by the first house, because the scissors that the planets form truncate the native's blessings.

SUNAPHA, ANAPHA AND DURUDHARA YOGAS: These three combinations are called lunar yogas because they involve positions counted from the Moon alone. When there is a planet other than the Sun, Rahu or Ketu in the second house from the Moon, it forms *Sunapha Yoga*; when the same situation exists in the twelfth house counted from the Moon, it is *Anapha Yoga*; and when the prescribed combination exists in both the second and twelfth houses from the Moon, it becomes *Durudhara Yoga*. Planets on either side of the Moon or (as for *Veshi*, *Voshi* and *Ubhayachari Yogas*, below) the Sun act as heralds for the luminaries, who are the regents of the skies. Any planet so near the Moon will be very obvious at night, enhancing thereby the Moon's splendor.

The texts list many meanings for these yogas, but our Jyotish guru taught us always to examine the nature of the grahas involved and the houses involved in them before even trying to predict their effects. Suppose that, for a Libra lagna, the Moon occupies the tenth house in Cancer and Mercury sits in the ninth house (the twelfth from the Moon) in Gemini. The Anapha Yoga thus created is substantially strengthened by the Bhadra Yoga which Mercury creates in the auspicious ninth house. We may safely assert that such a yoga will promote writing, publishing, higher studies or advanced research, for these are meanings common to both Mercury and the ninth house. If, for the same lagna, Moon tenants Aries in the seventh house and a debilitated Mercury forms Anapha Yoga in the sixth house in Pisces, the yoga will be hardly worth considering, although theoretically it is better for this enfeebled Anapha Yoga to exist than it is for Mercury simply to sit debilitated in the sixth house as lord of the ninth house of higher studies.

VASUMAT YOGA: *When the benefic planets all occupy the upachaya houses (three, six, ten and eleven) from the Moon or from the Lagna. Vasumat* means 'rich'. This combination exists in Chart 1 when counted from the Moon, but the planets involved are weak: Jupiter is combust, conjoined with and aspected by malefics; Mercury becomes malefic because of Saturn's aspect; and Venus is situated in an enemy's rashi.

VESHI, VOSHI AND UBHAYACHARI YOGAS: These solar yogas are

so called because they involve positions counted exclusively from the Sun. If planets other than the Moon, Rahu or Ketu are in the second house counted from the Sun, it forms *Veshi Yoga*; the same situation in the twelfth house from the Sun is *Voshi Yoga*; and such a combination in the second and twelfth houses from the Sun is *Ubhayachari Yoga*. Because any planet so near the Sun will appear dramatically in the sky either just before sunrise or just after sunset, these yogas enhance the Sun's splendor. If the planets involved in an Ubhayachari Yoga are exclusively benefics or exclusively malefics, the yoga is known as *Shubha Ubhayachari Yoga* or *Papa Ubhayachari Yoga* respectively. The comments made above for Sunapha, Anapha and Durudhara Yogas also apply here. Note that mixed Ubhayachari Yogas exist in both Chart 1 and Chart 2.

VIPARITA RAJA YOGA: If the lords of at least two dussthanas occupy other dussthanas without necessarily exchanging houses (which would be a case of Parivartana Yoga), a Viparita Raja Yoga is formed, which tends to cause a sudden and unexpected rise in life, often as the result of some mishap (*viparita* means 'inverted, contrary, reversed').

THE TWENTY-FOUR YOGAS

The twenty-four yogas given below are extremely helpful for those jyotishis who seek to fuse many factors when making astrological judgments. These yogas are specific to each of the twelve houses, and their results affect predominantly the matters indicated by the relevant house. Twelve of these yogas are auspicious in nature, developing the matters indicated by the relevant houses, and twelve are inauspicious, obstructing those matters in one way or another.

The twelve auspicious yogas come about when:

· a house is occupied or aspected by benefics *and*
· its lord is in a kendra, or a kona, or exalted, or in its own rashi, or in a friend's rashi, or is associated with or aspected by benefics *and*
· it is not afflicted by malefics.

The yogas, in order from the first house, are: 1 – *Chamara* ('regal fly whisk') *Yoga*; 2 – *Dhenu* ('cow') *Yoga*; 3 – *Shaurya* ('valor, prowess') *Yoga*; 4 – *Jaladhi* ('ocean') *Yoga*; 5 – *Chatra* ('regal umbrella') *Yoga*; 6 – *Astra* ('missile, arrow') *Yoga*; 7 – *Kama* ('desire') *Yoga*; 8 – *Asura* ('a demonic being') *Yoga*; 9 – *Bhagya* ('good fortune') *Yoga*; 10 – *Khyati* ('celebrity') *Yoga*; 11 – *Suparijata* ('thoroughly well-grown') *Yoga*; and 12 – *Musala* ('pestle, club, mace') *Yoga*.

The meanings for the yogas involving houses six, eight and twelve are somewhat less benevolent than those of the better houses. Benefits for these three yogas are mixed with defects, since they involve inherently evil houses, according to Principle 11. A person whose horoscope shows Astra Yoga, for example, subdues his foes but is rough and arrogant; the implications for the other two yogas are similar.

The twelve inauspicious yogas come about when:

· a house is occupied or aspected by malefics *and*
· the lord of the house is in the sixth, eighth or twelfth house, or debilitated, or in an enemy's rashi, or is aspected by or associated with malefics *and*
· it is not combined with benefics.

The yogas formed under these conditions from the first house onwards are: 1 – *Ava* ('down') *Yoga*; 2 – *Nissva* ('deprived of one's property') *Yoga*; 3 – *Mriti* ('death') *Yoga*; 4 – *Kuhu* ('New Moon') *Yoga*; 5 – *Pamara* ('rogue' or 'simpleton') *Yoga*; 6 – *Harsha* ('exhilaration') *Yoga*; 7 – *Dushkriti* ('miscreant' or 'sinner') *Yoga*; 8 – *Sarala* ('upright' or 'honest') *Yoga*; 9 – *Nirbhagya* ('luckless') *Yoga*; 10 – *Dur* ('difficult') *Yoga*; 11 – *Daridra* ('beggar') *Yoga*; and 12 – *Vimala* ('spotless') *Yoga*.

Those with Dur Yoga, for example (which differs from the more general Dur Yoga mentioned above), have their tenth-house matters obstructed. They may be 'insignificant in the eyes of the public', i.e. have no renown, a poor reputation, professional instability, or the like. Note that the yogas for the sixth, eighth and twelfth houses have positive indications; they can create benefits in much the same way that a Viparita Raja Yoga can.

KUJA DOSHA

Only two common graha yogas lack any mention in any traditional authoritative text: *Kala Sarpa Yoga* (see below) and *Kuja Dosha* ('The Blemish of Mars'). Usually referred to in North and West India as 'being Mangalik,' Kuja Dosha (as it is usually known in South India) occurs whenever Mars occupies houses one, two, four, seven, eight or twelve in a horoscope. It is unique among yogas in that it is counted not just from the ascendant but also from the Moon and from Venus, and is regarded as being particularly virulent when it recurs from all three positions.

Kuja Dosha is probably the best-known of graha yogas among India's general public, and many Indians still assiduously avoid marrying anyone with Kuja Dosha. While this yoga originally indicated the death of the spouse, it was later modified to mean marital misery. *Mangala* usually means 'auspicious'; most Indian women wear wedding necklaces called *mangala sutras* instead of wedding rings. But Mangala is also a name for Mars, a violent and argumentative graha who does not promote marital harmony when configured with one of the houses of relationship. While it is said that Mars can sometimes become auspicious for a lucky individual, some jyotishis believe that Mars is called Mangala in honor of all the penances, sacrifices and other auspicious actions a native must do to avert his evil effects.

Mars in the first house causes Kuja Dosha because of the importance of the first house as an epitome of the horoscope, and because the first house, being the seventh house from the seventh house, is a sort of derivative of the seventh house. Also, when Mars occupies the ascendant, he aspects both the seventh house (the house of marriage) and the eighth house (the *mangalya sthana*, or house of the duration of married life; the *mangala sutra* is its symbol). Mars in the second house causes Kuja Dosha because the second house both rules family life and, being the eighth from the seventh house, represents the partner's longevity, and because from the second house Mars aspects both the fifth house of progeny and the eighth house.

Mars in the fourth house causes Kuja Dosha because the fourth is the house of domestic happiness, and because from the fourth it aspects the seventh house. Mars in the seventh house disrupts married life directly, and also does so indirectly by aspecting both the first and second houses. Mars in the eighth house adversely affects the eighth by occupation and the second by aspect; and Mars in the twelfth house disturbs the positive indications of that bhava (like the pleasures of the bed) and also aspects the seventh house.

There is an alarming tendency among immature jyotishis to become unnecessarily alarmed when they discover this combination in a horoscope. Since half of all horoscopes that are counted from the lagna, half of those counted from the Moon, and half counted from Venus must possess this blemish, well over half the world's population must suffer from it. If Kuja Dosha could not be mitigated, its dire results, including the early death of the life partner, would occur in a substantial majority of the population, which is not the case. Exceptions to Kuja Dosha are therefore very important and in fact are so numerous that they could constitute a full chapter in themselves. Here are four of the most important ones:

(1) Generally speaking, anyone who has Kuja Dosha can safely marry anyone else who has a Kuja Dosha of approximately equal strength, because the two combinations will cancel each other out.

(2) One tradition says that even the strongest Kuja Dosha is over and done with once the native reaches the age of thirty, because Mars reaches maturity at age twenty-eight (see Chapter Four) and that any marital mischance which occurs after age thirty to someone whose horoscope shows a strong Kuja Dosha is probably due to other factors. Marriages contracted by such people prior to age twenty-eight usually end unhappily, though they will not necessarily end prior to age twenty-eight.

(3) Mars in its own or exaltation rashi greatly modifies any Kuja Dosha position and perhaps even cancels it ('perhaps', because the experts disagree on this point).

(4) The presence of the Moon in the house Mars occupies (which of course creates a Chandra Mangala Yoga) also cancels Kuja Dosha.

KALA SARPA YOGA

Kala Sarpa ('The Serpent of Time') *Yoga* is an admirable illustration of the many graha yogas which are not as easy to locate and comprehend as are Kuja Dosha and most of the other yogas listed above. In Kala Sarpa Yoga, all the seven planets from the Sun through to Saturn are situated in between Rahu and Ketu. The Two Nodes are described as shadow planets because they are literally shadows, the shadows which cause eclipses. Mythologically they are two portions of the same body, the body of a demon who had tried to steal the nectar of immortality. When the Sun and the Moon tattled on the rascal, Lord Vishnu beheaded the knave with His discus just as a drop of the nectar was dribbling down the fiend's throat; this made both his halves immortal. Enraged at this treachery, the Two Nodes perpetually chase and seize the Two Luminaries, who perpetually wriggle out of their grasp after a few moments of adumbration.

Kala Sarpa Yoga, which is not mentioned in any classical work on Jyotish, is probably Tantric in origin, given the Tantric fascination with shadows, with time (*kala* means both 'black' and 'time', and here refers to Ketu) and serpents (*sarpa*, which here refers to Rahu), with the occult (which the nodes rule), and with demonic beings (which they are). Kala Sarpa Yoga *is* described in Dravidian (South Indian) treatises, but even here there is no consensus as to its effect. Some texts describe it as a major flaw in a birth chart, a yoga which portends loss of everything, while others say that it bestows happiness and the goodwill of kings – provided that the child who possesses it survives.

There is not even consensus on its formation, which is not surprising, considering the confusion that is natural to the nodes. Some say that 'Rahu bites with his head', which means that Rahu must 'bite' (touch) all the grahas in his natural course (which happens to be backward from that of all the other planets). This condition occurs whenever Rahu leads all the other planets (so that they all move toward him). Others, who associate the nodal axis with the stinging scorpion, insist that 'Ketu stings with his tail', meaning that Ketu must lead all the other grahas. Yet another group considers Kala Sarpa Yoga to be formed in either way, an approach which seems to be verified by experience.

Two types of Kala Sarpa are thus distinguished: (1) *Anuloma* ('normal direction') type – all planets moving toward Rahu; this type is less likely to give trouble than is the other; and (2) *Viloma* ('reverse direction') type – all planets moving toward Ketu, which can cause prosperity but will give troubles side by side.

The Yoga is still formed even if there are planets conjoined (in the same house) with either Rahu or Ketu or both, so long as these planets are *within* the nodal axis by degree position; but a 'true' Kala Sarpa is formed only when the planets are in contiguous constellations. All five intervening rashis need not be tenanted by planets, but all the planets must clump together. The situation is worse when the planets are evenly distributed because during their transits (see Chapter Eleven) Rahu or Ketu will continuously pass over one planet after another, generating crises as they go. The texts neglect to say whether the ascendant must be included in the houses contained within the Serpent's belly (i.e. the houses which are trapped between Rahu and Ketu), or whether there is a way to cancel its effects (in the way that debility can be canceled by Neecha Bhanga Yoga).

The difficulties created by a Kala Sarpa Yoga typically focus on: (a) the houses ruled by any graha that either Rahu or Ketu conjoins, *or* (b) the houses ruled by one or both of the dispositors of Rahu and Ketu, *or* (c) the houses Rahu and Ketu occupy. This is usually an either/or situation in that one of the above houses is ordinarily a very noteworthy indicator of the problems the Yoga causes. The side of the axis that is conjoined with or aspected by malefics will usually be worse than the other or, if one of the dispositors is a malefic, the houses that it owns. A Kala Sarpa Yoga along the six/twelve axis (i.e. when one node is in the sixth house and the other in the twelfth) or the two/eight axis (the nodes in the second and eighth houses) may spell jail for its owner.

BHANGA

Most jyotishis, even in India, do not know all the many combinations which cancel or break (*bhanga*) the Raja Yogas or other beneficial yogas found in many horoscopes. These bhangas produce poverty, cause dependence and servitude, or reduce kings to beggary. Many Jyotish texts include a chapter on this subject, usually following their more extensive chapters on the many wonderful graha yogas and how they are formed. Two chapters on bhanga which stand out are *Saravali*'s Chapter 39 and *Jataka Parijata*'s Chapter 6. Parashara, in his *Brihat Parashara Hora*, follows his Chapter 41, 'Combinations for Wealth', with a Chapter 42 entitled, 'Combinations for Destitution', a juxtaposition of chapters which suggests that the author intended that beneficial graha yogas always be taught along with their cancellations, which is almost never done nowadays.

There seem to be no general rules from which these yoga breakers spring; we mention, as examples, just two of the many which are recognized:

(1) If any two of Sun, Mars, Jupiter and Saturn are debilitated, and one of these debilitated planets is simultaneously in the lagna while the Moon is in Scorpio, all Raja Yogas in the horoscope will become futile (from *Saravali* 39:2).
(2) Whoever is born in the hora (planetary hour) of Mars at a time when Saturn occupies a kendra in the horoscope and is unaspected by any benefic becomes a slave and a beggar (*Jataka Parijata* 6:4).

These two examples employ criteria which should by now be familiar to our readers. Many of the bhanga combinations however employ more unusual techniques, including the examination of birth omens: 'If a meteor, whirlwind, tornado, hurricane, thunderstorm, earthquake, comet or any other portent portending a calamity be present at the time of birth, all good Raja Yogas stand nullified' (*Saravali* 39:11). Jyotishis who were not present at the births of their clients to observe omens can often make up for that deficiency by observing the omens at the time of reading a horoscope – but that is another story entirely.

CHAPTER ELEVEN

DASHAS AND GOCHARAS

Change is all that is permanent in our world. Although many people believe that whatever is indicated in a horoscope will manifest at birth and continue in force until death, experience shows us that there is 'a time to every purpose under heaven'. Of two people whose horoscopes indicate a wonderful career with great self-fulfillment, good earnings and great accomplishments, one may find her niche early in life, while the other must first navigate difficult professional waters before finally achieving prosperity. Even Mother Theresa found her mission in life only after several years of teaching at a school for the children of wealthy Calcutta families.

Jyotish evaluates both permanence and change in life. While a *static* evaluation assesses the potentials inherent in a horoscope, a *dynamic* assessment estimates when these potentials will develop. A static interpretation can tell us whether or not a horoscope promises a successful marriage; a dynamic interpretation can predict at what age that promised marriage is likely to begin. In Jyotish, static evaluations derive from analysis of houses, their lords and their significators, while dynamic assessments are made from *dashas* and *gocharas*, the subjects of this chapter.

DASHAS

The word *dasha* means 'stage or condition of life' or 'border, hem'. Both these meanings apply to Jyotish, where dasha indicates both the conditions one will experience in life and the chronological boundaries of these stages. Jyotishis and their clients in India lay much emphasis on these dashas, often eagerly anticipating the good

changes that the commencement of a new dasha is expected to bring
or preparing for the difficulties that a bad dasha may foretell. The
dashas are indicators that particular karmas have matured (a related
word is *paka*, which means 'ripened' or 'well cooked') and are ready
to be 'enjoyed' for better or worse, according to the 'digestive'
ability of the person involved (*dasha* probably comes from a root
meaning 'to bite'). Everyone's life is composed of a succession of
dashas, an unending string of experiences created by ripening
karmas, which extends from the moment of birth to the moment of
death. Dasha also means 'wick', the 'wick of the lamp of life', and
old age, the end of one's cycle of dashas (the *dashanta*), is literally
the 'end of the wick'.

Kalachakra Dasha, Yogini Dasha, Ashtottari Dasha and Nakshatra Dasha are a few of the many types of dasha taught in Jyotish.
Each system has a unique method for allocating time over the
course of a lifetime and distinct ways of interpreting the meanings
of the dashas thus allocated. The formulas for calculating certain
types of dasha are simple, precise and invariable, while other
systems have complex, variable formulae that are sometimes open to
subjective interpretation. Dasha preference is influenced by ease of
use, and by regional preferences. The classical works promote
specific dashas, *Saravali* advocating the Moola Dasha system, and
Parashara emphasizing two types of dasha (Kalachakra and Vimshottari) from the thirty-two different dasha systems included in his
Brihat Parashara Hora.

The dasha system which has risen to pre-eminence in India after
centuries of experimentation is the Vimshottari Dasha, also occasionally known as the Nakshatra Dasha or Udu Dasha. While one
reason for its popularity may be its relatively precise, simple and
invariable formula, a more likely reason is the huge section dedicated
to it in the *Brihat Parashara Hora*. Many other classical works at least
sanction its use, even when they prefer other systems. Many 'popular-
izers' of Jyotish even introduce the Vimshottari Dasha system
to modern readers as 'the' dasha system for Jyotish, when it is only
the most widely used of Jyotish's many dasha systems. Those
who aspire to learn Jyotish fully must eventually learn some of
these other systems, since each provides a different flavor to the

interpretation of karmas. In this book, however, we will limit our discussion to the Vimshottari Dasha.

VIMSHOTTARI DASHA

Vimshottari Dasha allots varied periods of influence to each of the nine grahas in a fixed sequence, the entire cycle lasting 120 years (*vimshottari* literally means '120'). Few people live beyond 120 years, so there is little chance that a dasha will repeat in any one individual's life. The astrological rulerships of life's diverse ages will therefore tend to indicate distinct and unique results, given the wide variations in planetary positions from horoscope to horoscope.

Vimshottari Dasha is also known as Nakshatra Dasha because its years are parceled out, albeit unequally, to each of the nine nakshatras which embody the 120° of space which is one-third of the zodiac. The nine nakshatras from Ashvini to Ashlesha cover the constellations Aries to Cancer, the nine nakshatras from Magha to Jyeshtha cover the constellations Leo to Scorpio, and the nine from Mula to Revati cover Sagittarius to Pisces. In the Vimshottari system, the Vedic rulerships of the nakshatras are replaced with a system of planetary rulers, and each of the three groups of nine nakshatras has an identical sequence of rulers, beginning with Ketu and ending with Mercury (as shown in Table 11.1, below). Within each of these three cycles each nakshatra is allocated the same fixed number of years, which is the period of the dasha of that nakshatra's planetary ruler. Thus the nakshatras of Ashvini, Magha and Mula, which are all ruled by Ketu, are each allotted 7 years of the total 120 years available to one 120° segment of sky. Ketu's *Maha* (great) *Dasha* thus lasts seven years.

The remainder of the 120 years is assigned as indicated in Table 11.1. The nakshatra rulerships listed in that table are used only within the context of dashas and do not apply to most other types of prediction. For example, we cannot conclude that the nakshatras Pushya, Anuradha and Uttara Bhadrapada possess Saturnian attributes simply because Saturn owns them in this system.

Jyotish took its inspiration from the sky, but it does not limit

TABLE 11.1

Vimshottari Dasha and Nakshatras

Ruling Planet	Years	Nakshatras in Aries to Cancer	Nakshatras in Leo to Scorpio	Nakshatras in Sagittarius to Pisces
Ketu	7	1. Ashvini 00°Ar00' To 13°Ar20'	10. Magha 00°Le00' To 13°Le20'	19. Mula 00°Sa00' To 13°Sa20'
Venus	20	2. Bharani 13°Ar20' To 26°Ar40'	11. Purva Phalguni 13°Le20' To 26°Le40'	20. Purva Asadha 13°Sa20' To 26°Sa40'
Sun	6	3. Krittika 26°Ar40' To 10°Ta00'	12. Uttara Phalguni 26°Le40' To 10°Vi00'	21. Uttara Asadha 26°Sa40' To 10°Cp00'
Moon	10	4. Rohini 10°Ta00' To 23°Ta20'	13. Hasta 10°Vi00' To 23°Vi20'	22. Shravana 10°Cp00' To 23°Cp20'
Mars	7	5. Mrigashirsha 23°Ta20' To 06°Ge40'	14. Chitra 23°Vi20' To 06°Li40'	23. Dhanishtha 23°Cp20' To 06°Aq40'
Rahu	18	6. Ardra 06°Ge40' To 20°Ge00'	15. Swati 06°Li40' To 20°Li00'	24. Shatabhisha 06°Aq40' To 20°Aq00
Jupiter	16	7. Punarvasu 20°Ge00' To 03°Ca20'	16. Vishakha 20'Li00' To 03°Sc20'	25. Purva Bhadrapada 20°Aq00' To 03°Pi20'
Saturn	19	8. Pushya 03°Ca20' To 16°Ca40'	17. Anuradha 03°Sc20' To 16°Se40'	26. Uttara Bhadrapada 03°Pi20' To 16°Pi40'
Mercury	17	9. Ashlesha 16°Ca40' To 30°Ca00'	18. Jyeshtha 16°Sc40' To 30°Sc00'	27. Revati 16°Pi40' To 30°Pi00'

Total   120

itself to observational principles. Like physics, it laces the empirical data obtained by observations with the leavening of theories that have been extracted from these observations. The Vimshottari Dasha system does not seem to be directly derived from any celestial cycle or event; and, in spite of a variety of ingenious explanations, no one knows why each dasha was allocated its specific number of years, nor even why the planets were arranged in their specific order. These rules were cognized long ago, and we must simply accept them, after verifying them through experience.

While the order of Dashas in the Vimshottari Dasha is fixed, the point in the order where the sequence commences in a particular horoscope usually depends on the nakshatra position of the Moon at the moment of birth. The graha who rules that nakshatra is the first ruler of the native's life, and will continue to rule for that portion of the period allocated to it by the Vimshottari Dasha system, a portion which is proportionate to the distance the Moon has left to traverse within that nakshatra.

As an example, suppose that someone was born when the Moon sat precisely at 16° 40' of Taurus, which is within the nakshatra Rohini, which is ruled by the Moon. The Moon Maha Dasha thus began to operate at the moment of birth. Since Rohini falls between 10° 00' and 23° 20' of Taurus, when the Moon is at 16° 40' of Taurus it has traversed precisely half the 13° 20' span of that nakshatra. Therefore, one-half of the Moon's period of ten years, i.e. five years, is left at the person's birth. At the end of this five years of the Moon's period the invariable, continuous order of Vimshottari Dasha will continue to unfold, with the seven years of Mars coming next, followed by the eighteen years of Rahu, the sixteen years of Jupiter, and so on.

Suppose now that this person whose Moon at birth was at 16° 40' of Taurus was born on 15 July, 1868, and that she had extraordinary longevity. The astrological rulership of her years under one full cycle of Vimshottari Dasha would then look like Table 11.2.

DASHA ANALYSIS

Brihat Parashara Hora 47:2 provides us with Parashara's broad principle of dasha interpretation:

There are two kinds of effects of dashas – general and specific. The natural qualities of the planets cause the general effects, and the specific effects are caused by the position of the planets, etc.

The abbreviation 'etc.' here means house lordship, position in rashi

TABLE 11.2

Vimshottari Dasha
(*the dates represent the start of the various dashas*)

Moon	15 July 1868	Mercury	15 July 1933
Mars	15 July 1873	Ketu	15 July 1950
Rahu	15 July 1880	Venus	15 July 1957
Jupiter	15 July 1898	Sun	15 July 1977
Saturn	15 July 1914	Moon	15 July 1983

(a friend's or enemy's sign, exaltation or debility, vargottama, or strong or weak in many divisional charts), condition (whether or not it is combust, lying in a dead degree, or otherwise afflicted), and whether it is aspected by or conjoined with other planets.

Phaladipika 20:21 amplifies this dictum:

What has been described in this work under the sections on definitions, rulership of the planets, professions and diseases of the planets, the results of aspects and association of the planets, or the effects of the presence of the planets in the various bhavas, or the results of the lords of the various bhavas influencing each other – all this must be attributed to the planets during their dashas.

Other classical works contain verses of similar meaning. The following factors tend to be activated during a graha's dasha:

1. The yogas in which the dasha lord participates
2. The dasha lord's natural benefic or malefic nature
3. The house occupied by and the planet(s) conjoined by the dasha lord, in its capacity as a natural benefic or malefic
4. The house(s) and planet(s) aspected by the dasha lord, in its capacity as a natural benefic or malefic
5. The planets that conjoin or aspect the dasha lord, in their capacity as natural benefics or malefics
6. The houses which the dasha lord occupies or aspects and the planets which he conjoins or aspects, in its capacity as lord of certain houses

7. The houses the dasha lord owns, and the effects on these houses by virtue of the position of that dasha lord in a certain house
8. The houses owned by the planet(s) which conjoin or aspect the dasha lord
9. The houses influenced by the dispositor of the dasha lord
10. The matters signified by the dasha lord itself as a graha or bhava karaka

Whatever a planet indicates, according to static analysis, in the horoscope will be highlighted during that planet's dasha. The static analysis of the second house of Chart 2 in Chapter Nine led us to the conclusion that Venus and Mercury have an exclusively favorable influence on this house. Dynamic analysis tells us that this favorable effect will be particularly evident during the dashas of Mercury and Venus, which this man will experience from age 53 to 70 and from age 77 to 97 respectively. Likewise, the condition of the fourth house suggests that in matters of property he will experience general success throughout his life, with the odd cloud darkening his door due to the aspects of the natural malefics Mars and Saturn. These dark clouds will probably be more in evidence during the dashas of these two grahas, while Jupiter, whose influence is exclusively benefic on the fourth house, may during its dasha (ages 18 to 34) give the enjoyment of property, which has in fact been the case.

Chart 1: Jupiter Dasha

Below are some of the things Jupiter indicated for the owner of Chart 1 during his Jupiter Dasha, which he saw from the ages of 16 through 32. The bracketed references are to the eighteen principles of interpretation given in Chapter Eight.

1. *Activation of the yogas in which the dasha lord participates.* In Chart 1 Jupiter is both strong (by being exalted in Cancer – Principle 12) and very weak (by being combust within 6° 14′ of the Sun, by being associated with the malefic Rahu, and by being aspected by the malefic Mars – Principle 4). The combustion and the influence of the two malefics without the relief of any natural

benefic is a case of malefic confluence. The *Horasara*, written by Prithuyashas (who was widely assumed to be the son of Varahamihira), expresses the ephemeral nature of the good results coming from auspicious but weak planets: 'The person will experience the desirable effects of a weak planet's dasha in their dreams and thoughts. The same result will follow for yogas like the Pancha Maha Purusha Yogas' (*Horasara* 17:30).

Jupiter participates in a Kesari Yoga. Some of the results predicted for Kesari Yoga, like a propensity for 'networking', developed during Jupiter's dasha, giving him a wide network of contacts for which his friends valued him. Jupiter's weakness however caused this yoga to operate on a low level. Instead of meeting the best accountant in the city, he would meet the cheapest bookkeeper; instead of finding contacts who could make him a superlative deal on a new car, his contacts provided him good deals on used cars, and so on.

2. *Activation of the dasha lord's natural benefic or malefic nature*. Some desirable results will surely flow from Jupiter's natural beneficence and its strength through exaltation, but these results will never be unobstructed or satisfyingly benefic, because of Jupiter's confluent weakness. Both good results and dissatisfying results will be expected, because contradictory results in a horoscope are usually cumulative; they do not cancel each other out. Indeed, during Jupiter's dasha, this gentleman experienced results that were usually short of satisfying and that were typically accomplished only after surmounting many obstructions. There was a general sense of frustration throughout, which may be attributed to the fact that Jupiter is obstructed in displaying its results as a natural benefic by virtue of its confluent weakness.

3. *Activation of the house occupied by and the planet(s) conjoined by the dasha lord, in its capacity as a natural benefic or malefic*. The naturally benefic but weak Jupiter occupies the second house. As a natural benefic in the second house, Jupiter will augment the matters of that house (Principle 1) but will do so weakly and incompletely because of the malefic confluence (Principle 4). The second house represents accumulated money, of which there was

little during Jupiter's period. There was rather the constant experience of financial pressure, which, however, never developed into financial disaster, thanks to Jupiter's benefic nature and its exaltation. Likewise, familial relations (another second-house matter) were strained, but never to the point of a total break during this dasha. Other results ascribed to the second house could be interpreted similarly.

Because the Sun, the lord of the third house of short travels, is associated with the benefic but weak dasha lord Jupiter, this man had many, many short journeys throughout his Jupiter period. All this movement frustrated him by interfering with the other things he desired to accomplish. Because Rahu, which indicates foreigners, was similarly activated, thanks to its association with Jupiter, he had many dealings with foreigners during Jupiter's dasha. Jupiter also associates with Ketu, an indicator of spiritual knowledge which is sitting in the eighth house of occultism. This gave him an active interest in spirituality and occultism throughout that dasha, but he remained unfulfilled, due to Jupiter's weakness.

4. *Activation of the house(s) and planet(s) aspected by the dasha lord, in its capacity as a natural benefic or malefic.* Since Jupiter aspects the sixth, eighth and tenth houses (the last being its own house), it will activate them just as it activated the second house (Principle 1). Sixth-house matters like debt, illness and enemies, though a constant concern, never became seriously problematic because Jupiter is a benefic. Jupiter though weak maintained his longevity, and protected him against major accidents and other matters of the eighth house. Minor accidents did however occur, as did some minor surgery on his teeth (a second-house matter).

His tenth-house matters were weakly protected by Jupiter's benefic aspect, because this aspect is into its own house (Principle 1). The tenth house of career is thus doubly strong, first because it is aspected by Jupiter as a natural benefic, and secondly because it is aspected by Jupiter as its lord. The extent of this double benefit will, however, be reduced by Jupiter's weakness. Although the native was employed as a technician during much of Jupiter's dasha, there were constant delays in promotions and wage increases;

he passed skill enhancement courses but with difficulty, and so on. Although he was self-motivated, ambitious and skilled, things somehow did not work out well for him in his career during his Jupiter Dasha. He did at least remain continuously employed during this period, but he saw this simply as another case of feeble results, which left him dissatisfied.

5. *Activation of the planets that conjoin or aspect the dasha lord, in their capacity as natural benefics or malefics.* Jupiter is here conjoined with the malefic Rahu and aspected by the malefic Mars. Being a 'shadow' graha, Rahu often causes confusion, and during most of the Jupiter Dasha this man lacked direction in his life. Rahu symbolizes foreignness and, in its capacity as a malefic, Rahu made it difficult for the native to live in foreign countries. In its more malefic capacity Mars represents anger and impatience, which also characterized his Jupiter Dasha.

6. *Activation of the houses which the dasha lord occupies or aspects and the planets which he conjoins or aspects, in its capacity as lord of certain houses.* Jupiter being lord neither of a kona (Principle 8) nor of a trik house (Principle 9), its aspect by house ownership is neutral. Of all of the houses influenced by Jupiter the tenth did best, because it is the only house that Jupiter aspects as its lord.

7. *Activation of the houses the dasha lord owns, and the effects on these houses by virtue of the position of that dasha lord in a certain house.* Principle 10 tells us that because Jupiter occupies the neutral second house it will, other factors remaining equal, create average results in the matters ruled by the seventh and tenth houses, which it owns. Jupiter as tenth lord is again only neutrally placed for the tenth house of career. Neutral results are also indicated for the seventh house of marriage, and indeed he married during Jupiter's dasha. His wife was a woman from another country, and of a different religion. The marriage occurred only after he had surmounted many obstacles, in particular family opposition. Note that Rahu, which indicates foreigners and heterodoxy, is particularly influential by virtue of being conjoined with Jupiter, the lord of the seventh house.

8. *Activation of the houses owned by the planet(s)* which conjoin *with or aspect the dasha lord.* Jupiter is associated with Rahu and the Sun. Because Rahu owns no house, this principle applies only to the Sun, who owns the third house. This will cause third-house matters to be activated during Jupiter's dasha (Principle 16). The Sun occupies a friend's rashi but is influenced by the malefic Rahu and Mars. Mars here acts as a super-malefic, once in its capacity as a natural malefic and again in its capacity as ruler of the sixth house, without owning any good house (Principle 9). The short journeys promised by the Sun during Jupiter's dasha were thus frustrating journeys because of these influences.

Mars, the ruler of the sixth house (enemies, debts and disease) and the eleventh house (friendship) is the only graha that aspects Jupiter. During the Jupiter period the matters ruled by these houses will be activated proportionate to the strength of Mars. Since Mars is strong by virtue of being in its own rashi, this man was blessed with protection from the adverse effects of sixth-house matters, and benefited through friendships. However, the dasha lord is always primary when evaluating its relationship with other planets. Mars's benevolence as lord of the eleventh house could not be fully experienced, and some troubles did occur, since Jupiter is weak and influenced by malefics. Had the dasha of Mars been in operation instead, the results of the sixth and eleventh houses would perhaps have been more satisfactory.

9. *Activation of the houses influenced by the dispositor of the dasha lord.* This important (but frequently overlooked) principle of dasha interpretation caused the birth of one child, a daughter, because Jupiter's dispositor Moon, a feminine graha, occupies in this horoscope the fifth house of children.

10. *Activation of the matters signified by the dasha lord itself as a graha or bhava karaka.* Another reason for his daughter's birth during his Jupiter dasha was Jupiter's exalted (though combust) status as the significator for children. The exaltation ensured children, but the combustion and other weaknesses limited the number to one, and caused serious differences between the parents over how she should be raised.

Jupiter being an important indicator of education, Jupiter's dasha also produced mixed results in this realm. The man did not acquire formal higher education during this period, though he was fond of private, informal study throughout the dasha. He did, however, obtain a technical diploma.

Chart 1: Saturn Dasha

Now let us consider the dasha of Saturn, which began when this gentleman was 33. First we examine Saturn's house lordship, to determine whether he is a temporary benefic or malefic for this lagna. While Saturn does own the good ninth house, it is also the lord of the evil eighth house, so (according to Principles 8 and 9) these lordships will neither subtract from nor improve Saturn's aspects. But since the fundamental nature of malefics always causes them to retain a flavor of struggle and imperfection, no matter how temporarily benefic they may become, the natural malefic Saturn is bound to create some sort of havoc in every horoscope during its dasha.

To see how and where these problems will crop up, we must examine the houses that Saturn occupies, aspects, and owns in the horoscope. Saturn's seat in the first house as a natural malefic will disturb the first house of health (Principle 3), and indeed the native has experienced a number of significant health problems during Saturn's dasha. Many of these problems involved the bones, which Saturn naturally rules, with the specific involvement of some of the bones of his neck, a portion of the body ruled by Gemini, which Saturn occupies.

Saturn sits in the ascendant as a natural malefic, so its aspects on the third, seventh and tenth houses disturb those houses (Principle 3). It was during the period of Saturn that one of this man's younger sisters (third house) died. Severe marital problems (seventh house) began during this period, which were aggravated by a serious deterioration in his wife's health. This led to a brief separation, followed by his wife's death. After leaving his job (tenth house) he tried to go independent, but to date he has lost three businesses.

Saturn as lord of the eighth house (death, accidents, bankruptcies) and of the ninth house (gurus, spiritual life, higher studies, foreign travel) is in the first house in a friend's rashi. Due to the eighth-house influence, the native experienced death in the form of the tragic demise of his wife and sister; he had several vehicular accidents, and one badly broken leg; and he experienced bankruptcy (Principle 11). Yet he also traveled widely, took to the serious study of scriptures and religious practices, and was initiated by a religious preceptor on a pilgrimage to India – all ninth-house matters (Principle 10). The results indicated by Saturn owning both the eighth and ninth bhavas were thus cumulative and did not cancel. In his case, travel was particularly supported because Saturn's dispositor Mercury occupies the third house, another travel house, from which it aspects the ninth house.

Finally, while Saturn is unaspected and is not associated with any other planet, it does aspect both Mercury and Venus. Saturn as lord of the eighth bhava aspecting Mercury, who rules the first and fourth bhavas, could for example indicate the 'death' (loss) of vehicles or property (fourth house), or an accident to the native (first house). Saturn as lord of the ninth aspecting Mercury may indicate long-distance travel during Saturn's dasha, and in fact all these matters have been ongoing themes in the native's life during this dasha.

The influence of eighth and ninth lord Saturn on Venus (the fifth lord) may be interpreted as an influence on the lord of children by the lord of death and the lord of dharma. This may indicate loss of a child, or perhaps a need to fulfill one's dharma in relation to a child. Both interpretations have been accurate during the Saturn dasha: after his wife's death he agonized over making the right decision about his daughter's welfare, finally deciding to lodge her with relatives in a different country, thus becoming permanently separated from her. Here the 'death' of a child was not his daughter's physical death; it was rather her 'death' in relation to him. This is a good example of the many alternative interpretations with which an astrologer must often grapple.

Selecting the right interpretation is a job for penetrating insight. Our Jyotish guru displayed such insight when he predicted a broken leg, about three months before it transpired, for the owner of Chart 1 during his Saturn dasha. Our guru explained that the eighth house in this horoscope falls in the constellation of Capricorn, which rules the legs, and that this eighth house is afflicted by the aspect of the cruel Sun and by the occupation of the accident-causing Ketu. The accident became particularly likely during Saturn's dasha because Saturn rules the legs, is lord of the eighth house of accidents, and afflicts the first house. Our guru even predicted, correctly, that the break would be due to a fall, because falls are ruled by the tattva of Air. The afflicting planet Saturn, whose dasha was going on, is the significator for air, and Saturn is posited in the Airy rashi of Gemini.

Dasha interpretation does not always produce such dramatic results. Nor is dasha analysis always as simple and straightforward as it was for the dashas of Jupiter and Saturn in the horoscope illustrated above; however, a graha's dasha will usually correlate strikingly with the broad stream of events experienced during that period of life. Some dashas will be crisp in their meanings, and others hazier, depending on the overall tenor of individual lives. For practice, interpret in the manner described some of the dashas in the lives of people you know, and correlate your interpretations with their life experiences during these periods.

BHUKTIS

The more precisely one can time life events, the easier it will be to develop strategies to cope with them. The individual Vimshottari Dashas last too long to provide meaningful dynamic interpretation, for the shortest time allocated to a dasha is six years, and the longest time is twenty years. Suppose that the dasha of the Sun in a client's chart promises overall success in the realm of business dealings. Ups and downs are probable over that long span of six years and, if the client wishes to embark on a business trip during one particular four-month period during that six-year dasha, some way is needed to pinpoint which period during that dasha will be best for successful trips. Likewise, a prediction of marriage 'at some time' during the twenty-year dasha of Venus, for a twenty-year-old youth who is just commencing that dasha, is not likely to satisfy the questioner.

Dynamic interpretations based on the dashas help to evaluate general, broad patterns of experience likely to unfold over significant segments of a lifetime, while smaller units of time within the larger periods of the dashas permit dynamic interpretations which are usually more immediately meaningful and relevant. The dashas enable one to see the forest, and the *bhuktis* (the smaller periods of time within the dashas) enable one to focus on the trees in that forest. The bhuktis (also known as *antaras*) are minor periods or sub-periods within the major planetary period that is a dasha. Dashas are sometimes called Maha Dashas ('Major Dashas') to distinguish them from bhuktis.

Bhukti comes from the root word *bhuj*, meaning 'to enjoy, participate in, or consume', which harks back to the digestive meanings of the word *dasha*. Each major period is divided into nine minor periods which are each allotted to one graha, in the same order that characterizes the dasha. A simple way to determine the length of a bhukti is to employ the so-called Rule of Three: multiply the number of years allotted in the Vimshottari Dasha to the major period lord by the number of years allotted to the minor lord, then divide by ten and detach the remainder. The answer indicates the number of months in the minor period, and when the remainder is multiplied by three that answer indicates the number of days which must be added to the number of months to give the minor period's total length.

For example, to calculate the period of Mars within the major period of Rahu, a period usually expressed in astrological shorthand as Rahu-Mars, multiply the 18 years of the Rahu Dasha by the 7 years of the Mars Dasha to arrive at 126. Dividing by 10 gives us 12.6. The 12 indicates 12 months, and when we multiply 6, the remainder, by 3 we get 18, which means 18 days. Rahu–Mars will last, in anyone's life, for 12 months and 18 days. Jupiter–Saturn (the minor period of Saturn within the major period of Jupiter) = 16 × 19 = 304 or 30 months and (3 × 4 = 12) 12 days, so Jupiter–Saturn lasts 2 years, 6 months and 12 days. The shortest of the bhuktis is Sun–Sun (3 months and 18 days) and the longest Venus–Venus (3 years and 4 months).

The rulership of the first minor period within any major period is always that of the dasha lord itself. Therefore the first bhukti in the Maha Dasha of the Sun is that of the Sun itself (written Sun–Sun); in the major period of Mercury it is Mercury–Mercury, and so on. After the initial bhukti, the remaining eight minor periods follow the natural order of rulerships in the Vimshottari Dasha, continuing with the graha that follows the ruler of the first minor period in this natural order. The natural order of the Vimshottari Dasha, as given above, is Ketu, Venus, Sun, Moon, Mars, Rahu, Jupiter, Saturn and Mercury. The major period of the Sun thus has these nine minor periods: Sun–Sun, Sun–Moon, Sun–Mars, Sun–Rahu, Sun–Jupiter, Sun–Saturn, Sun–Mercury, Sun–Ketu and Sun–Venus.

For convenience, Table 11.3 provides the order and the duration of each bhukti within each Maha Dasha.

Bhukti division proceeds as a sort of process of extracting harmonics, so perhaps a musical analogy may make the subject a bit easier to understand. Let us first take each dasha cycle of 120 years to equal a scale which covers a full octave (imagining for a moment that each octave contained nine notes instead of the usual seven). A scale that goes from A to A will sound very different from one which goes from C to C, or from F# to F#, because the scale's initial tone (the keynote or tonic) determines the form each of the following notes will take. Likewise, to begin your life with the dasha of Ketu and end it with Mercury would generate quite a different life melody than it would if your life began with the Sun's Dasha and ended with that of Venus, or if it proceeded from the Mars Maha Dasha to the Moon Maha Dasha. Each series of dashas is like a separate musical key, with its own specific number of flats or sharps and its own peculiar flavor. Because each set of bhuktis begins with the minor period of the dasha lord, each set has a different progression and thus its own melody within the context of the major period.

The minor periods are often divided into yet smaller sub-sub-periods, by the same procedure, and these can be subdivided into yet smaller sub-sub-sub-periods. In one sense the major, minor and

TABLE 11.3 Maha Dashas

Ketu Maha Dasha – 7 years

	Ketu	Venus	Sun	Moon	Mars	Rahu	Jupiter	Saturn	Mercury	Total
Years	0	1	0	0	0	1	0	1	0	7
Months	4	2	4	7	4	0	11	1	11	0
Days	27	0	6	0	27	18	6	0	27	0

Venus Maha Dasha – 20 Years

	Venus	Sun	Moon	Mars	Rahu	Jupiter	Saturn	Mercury	Ketu	Total
Years	3	1	1	1	3	2	3	2	1	20
Months	4	0	8	2	0	8	2	10	2	0
Days	0	0	0	0	0	0	0	0	0	0

Sun Maha Dasha – 6 Years

	Sun	Moon	Mars	Rahu	Jupiter	Saturn	Mercury	Ketu	Venus	Total
Years	0	0	0	0	0	0	0	0	1	6
Months	3	6	4	10	9	11	10	4	0	0
Days	18	0	6	24	18	12	6	6	6	0

Moon Maha Dasha – 10 Years

	Moon	Mars	Rahu	Jupiter	Saturn	Mercury	Ketu	Venus	Sun	Total
Years	0	0	1	1	1	1	0	1	0	10
Months	10	7	6	4	7	5	7	8	6	0
Days	0	0	0	0	0	0	0	0	0	0

Mars Maha Dasha – 7 Years

	Mars	Rahu	Jupiter	Saturn	Mercury	Ketu	Venus	Sun	Moon	Total
Years	0	0	1	1	0	0	1	0	0	7
Months	4	11	1	1	11	4	2	4	7	0
Days	27	6	6	0	27	27	0	6	0	0

Rahu Maha Dasha – 18 Years

	Rahu	Jupiter	Saturn	Mercury	Ketu	Venus	Sun	Moon	Mars	Total
Years	2	2	2	2	1	3	0	1	1	18
Months	8	4	10	6	0	0	10	6	0	0
Days	12	24	6	18	18	0	24	0	18	0

Jupiter Maha Dasha – 16 Years

	Jupiter	Saturn	Mercury	Ketu	Venus	Sun	Moon	Mars	Rabu	Total
Years	2	2	2	0	2	0	1	0	2	16
Months	1	6	3	11	8	9	4	11	4	0
Days	18	12	6	6	0	18	0	6	24	0

Saturn Maha Dasha – 19 years

	Saturn	Mercury	Ketu	Venus	Sun	Moon	Mars	Rabu	Jupiter	Total
Years	3	2	1	3	0	1	1	2	2	19
Months	0	8	1	2	11	7	1	10	6	0
Days	3	9	9	0	12	0	9	6	12	0

Mercury Maha Dasha – 17 Years

	Mercury	Ketu	Venus	Sun	Moon	Mars	Rabu	Jupiter	Saturn	Total
Years	2	0	2	0	1	0	2	2	2	17
Months	4	11	10	10	5	11	6	3	8	0
Days	27	27	0	6	0	27	18	6	9	0

smaller periods are the macrocosmic expression of the same sort of time division which is expressed microcosmically in Svarodaya as the Five Tattvas (Earth, Water, Fire, Air and Ether). Each of the Five Tattvas can be divided into five minor periods, and each of these sub-periods into five sub-sub-periods, and so on until the subsidiary period lasts only for the space of a single breath. While, at least theoretically, a human life can thus be analyzed predictively right down to each inhalation and exhalation, only a seer can hope to achieve such perfection.

Theoretically one can use the subsidiary dasha periods for similar predictive precision, and accordingly some people nowadays use as many as five levels of dasha division in their predictions. However, this procedure activates so many factors in the horoscope that the plethora of potential interpretational choices will tend to overwhelm your interpretive ability. Or you will simply find a reason for everything you want to see, which will make everything easily explainable with hindsight and almost nothing predictable with foresight.

In India, many jyotishis confine their analysis to dasha and bhukti, and only the more seasoned usually venture into the use of sub-sub-periods. For the present, in the interest of simplicity and manageability, we will limit our dynamic interpretation to the use of major and minor planetary periods. The bhuktis are sufficiently small for most purposes, especially when they are taken in conjunction with *gochara*, the continuous movement of the planets through the zodiac. The role and method of transits in Jyotish, as well as their application to the major and minor periods, are explained in the last section of this chapter.

BHUKTI INTERPRETATION

Minor periods are used for dynamic interpretation in conjunction with their major periods by evaluating their *confluence* or *conflict*. To determine confluence or conflict between a bhukti lord and its dasha lord, analyze both separately. *When the lord of a major period and the lord of a minor period symbolically affect an area of life in the same way, either positively or negatively, it is a case of confluence, and when those two lords influence an area of life in opposite ways, one positively and the other negatively, it is a case of conflict.* Do this in three steps:

1. Find which grahas influence the relevant sector of the horoscope.
2. Determine whether these influences are positive or negative.
3. Determine whether these influences are confluent or conflicting.

For example, if the dasha lord happens to be the well-placed lord of the third house of short journeys, and the bhukti lord happens to be a natural benefic aspecting the third house, there is confluence of effect; the native is likely to enjoy pleasurable short journeys during that bhukti period. If, however, the lord of the minor period indicates success at short journeys and the major period lord promises obstruction to travel, their conflict will make confident prediction more difficult. Jupiter and Venus, which are both natural benefics, would cause a confluence of benefic factors on any house, constellation or planet which they simultaneously influence. The extent and nature of the positive influence during the bhukti of Venus within the dasha of Jupiter will depend on the strength of the two grahas.

Confluence and conflict are of course not confined to the natural qualities of the grahas, but extend also to their qualities as temporary benefics and malefics. In the case of conflict, evaluation of the relative strengths of the two grahas involved is extremely important to establish which planet's influence will predominate during their joint periods. Should Jupiter and Saturn in a horoscope both influence a factor, such as the Moon, and Jupiter be in its own rashi while Saturn occupies its friend's rashi (all other factors being equal), then the influence of Jupiter on the Moon will exceed that of Saturn.

Events during a minor period will focus on the same ten areas detailed for dasha interpretation earlier in this chapter, and one must search for confluence or conflict among all pertinent factors. For example, for a child to be born, both the major and the minor lords at the time of the birth must (with some exceptions) influence or be influenced by the fifth house, or by its lord, or by Jupiter as the significator of children, etc.

Confluence indicated the fracture of one of the legs of Chart 1's owner, an event which occurred during the Maha Dasha of Saturn in the Bhukti of Ketu (i.e. during Saturn–Ketu). It is because both Saturn (as a natural malefic and as the eighth lord) and Ketu (as a natural malefic and as a significator for accidents) already individually indicated the possibility of accident that the fall came to pass during their conjoint period.

Confluence indicated the time of death of this man's wife during Saturn–Venus: Saturn afflicts both the seventh house and the seventh-house significator Venus in its capacity as a natural malefic and as lord of the death-dealing eighth house. Venus also occupies a dussthana in an enemy's constellation. Confluence also indicated his travel during Saturn–Venus, this time the confluence of Saturn as ninth lord in a kendra house with Venus as a natural benefic aspecting the ninth house of travel, and Saturn as ninth lord aspecting Venus as twelfth lord (the twelfth being a house of relocation or immigration) in third house of journeys. The native did in fact relocate to another country during this period.

The luck of Chart 2's owner changed strongly for the better during the Moon and Mars Bhuktis of his Jupiter Maha Dasha. When we recall that in this chart the Moon forms Chandra Mangala Yoga with Mars, and that Jupiter creates Hamsa Yoga, and that all three planets are in kendras and that they mutually aspect one another, it is no surprise that these bhuktis were so rewarding. This is a sort of confluence by yogas.

Chart 2 also illustrates *conflict*, in that the twelfth house is occupied by the malefic Rahu and is aspected by the benefic Jupiter. Since Jupiter occupying its own sign is stronger than Rahu, Jupiter's influence will not allow expenses to go out of control, or stays in foreign countries to be troublesome. Rahu will act only as a bit of a spoiler by creating nagging expenses and by obstructing some foreign trips. So it happened that during Jupiter–Rahu his multiplied expenses never outstripped his growing income, and his initial business difficulties overseas were eventually resolved.

Some jyotishis use a subordinate technique for dasha–bhukti interpretation by which they rotate the horoscope so that the rashi where the dasha lord sits becomes the lagna. The bhukti lords are then said to activate the house positions in which they fall as counted from that dasha lord. For example, if we rotate Chart 2 so that Sagittarius becomes the ascendant (since Jupiter, the dasha lord, occupies Sagittarius), the Moon will then be in the seventh house to that dasha lord. This suggests that during the sub-period of the Moon during the Jupiter Maha Dasha seventh-house affairs will be activated, and it was precisely during this bhukti that he married.

One famous corollary to this principle is that any planets placed in the sixth, eighth or twelfth houses from the dasha lord will not cooperate with the dasha lord, since they will be in dussthanas to it, and so will give generally bad results during their bhuktis. This corollary, which derives from the principle that planets in dussthanas from the lagna produce bad results, appears in many texts, but it has been our experience that it does not always hold up in practice unless the bhukti lord is aspected by or conjoined with a malefic.

RAHU—KETU

Some difficulty arises when we set out to interpret the results promised by the dashas and bhuktis of Rahu and Ketu. Since they do not own houses, interpreting them only according to their positions in the horoscope would not yield much information. A verse from the *Sanketanidhi* of Ramadayalu, a mid-nineteenth-century work, reveals Jyotish's present approach to the nodes: 'The two nodes – Rahu and Ketu – produce the effect of (1) the bhavas they occupy and (2) the planets they conjoin with' (4:83b). The words 'bhava' and 'rashi' are used interchangeably here, as they often are, because usually one bhava fully covers one rashi. In Chart 1 Rahu will give the results of the bhava it occupies (the second), the rashi it occupies (Cancer), and the grahas which influence it (Jupiter, Sun and Mars). By extension, it may also give the results of the lord of the bhava and rashi in which it sits, which in this case is the Moon. While it is difficult to interpret Rahu in this horoscope because of the many planets that influence it, we can be sure that the strongest graha will throw the predominant influence. This appears to be either Mars, who is in its own sign but in a very weak Avastha – dead (Mrita), in fact – or the exalted Jupiter, who is combust and in Bala Avastha. Rahu thus afflicts the second house with the added influence of Mars or Jupiter in their own individual capacities to influence second-house matters.

In Chart 2, Jupiter aspects Rahu, and the Sun disposits that node. Because Jupiter is clearly stronger than the Sun, Jupiter's influence on Rahu will predominate, colored only somewhat by the Sun's influence. We have already discussed Jupiter's good position in this horoscope, so it should not be surprising that during the Rahu Maha Dasha, which he saw during childhood, his family's fortunes rose. If you are destined to enjoy some good luck during your childhood, it will of necessity go to your guardian (*poshaka*), since you usually will not have the legal authority, physical capability or intellectual capacity to wield that prosperity yourself. Sometimes jyotishis predict for the father, mother, siblings or other family members of a newborn child on this basis, indicating prosperity or penury for these relatives according to whether the child's horoscope shows enjoyment or misery to be its fate.

Because Jupiter's influence on Rahu in Chart 2 is modulated by that of the Sun, some of the matters promised by the Sun also transpired. Since the Sun, the lord of the evil twelfth house, sits in the good first house of health, undesirable results should be expected (based on Principle 3). Because disease is something one can experience at any age, it was he and not his guardians who suffered from fevers (the Sun being a hot graha), though the Sun did get his licks in on the family by giving them some significant expenses to cover side by side with their overall upward prosperity.

GOCHARA (TRANSITS)

One way to evaluate smaller periods during a bhukti is to subdivide it harmonically, but unless the birthtime is particularly accurate these tiny divisions will be imprecise. In practice, many jyotishis prefer instead to determine the duration of peak effects within any individual bhukti by using transits. A transit, or *gochara*, is the ongoing movement of a planet considered in relation to the birth horoscope.

Jyotish possesses several systems for gochara interpretation, including the famous and frequently used *Ashtaka Varga*, which is used not only for transits but also as an interpretational system in its own right. Other methods are based on basic principles of horoscope interpretation. The system we introduce here is extracted principally from Chapter 20 of *Phaladipika*:

When a planet whose Dasha is in progress happens to pass through (in transit) his own house, exaltation or a friendly house, he will promote the prosperity of the house it represents when counted from the ascendant, provided that the planet is endowed with full strength at the birth time as well. (20:34)

Return to Chart 2, and recall that a wave of prosperity rolled through this man's life during his Jupiter–Moon and Jupiter–Mars Bhuktis, leading to his marriage. Jupiter transited its exaltation constellation of Cancer from mid-July of 1990 to mid-August of 1991, a period which covers almost entirely the Jupiter–Moon Bhukti. Jupiter (lord of the seventh house of marriage) and the Moon mutually aspect one another, Jupiter is strong in its own sign, and at the time just preceding his marriage the transiting Jupiter posited in Gemini was conjoined with the natal Moon (the bhukti lord) and aspecting the natal Jupiter (the dasha lord). A clear confluence is thus created by this transit with the bhukti, the dasha, and the many yogas in which Jupiter and Moon participate.

A planet's influence during its transit is not limited to the house it actually transits, but includes its aspects as well. Because Jupiter is strong and benefic in this birth chart to begin with, a Jupiter transit will activate (because it is the dasha lord) and benefit (because it is both a natural and a temporary benefic) most of the houses it touches; when for example Jupiter moved into Leo, the twelfth house of expenses, his expenses came under control.

Also, whenever the dasha lord passes over or aspects its own position in the chart it is likely to activate its promised effects. When this man left his education toward the end of his Jupiter–Saturn Bhukti (mid-February 1981 to end of August 1983), transit

Jupiter was retrograde in about 8° of Scorpio, and transit Saturn sat in about 5° of Libra. By aspecting the fourth house from this position, the exalted Saturn restimulated its natal position. Since Jupiter could not support its natal position by aspect, was transiting a mild dussthana, and was in Saturn's nakshatra, Saturn's malefic influence prevailed.

The last phrase of the verse – '. . . provided that the planet is endowed with full strength at the birth time as well' – is exceedingly important. If Saturn happens to be transiting Aquarius, it is tempting to look at a chart in which Leo rises and a Saturn dasha or bhukti is ongoing, and think, 'Oh, Saturn is passing through and therefore activating the seventh house in this horoscope, which Saturn happens to own.' You then might predict marriage without pausing to consider the condition of the natal Saturn. But if at the time of birth Saturn was combust or debilitated, the activation of the seventh house in such a horoscope by transiting Saturn may promote marital disharmony, and may even cause divorce. *Transiting planets can activate results promised in the horoscope, but they cannot change the nature of those results.*

Mantreshwara goes on to say:

If the planet whose bhukti is in progress should during the course of his transit pass through his debilitation or enemy's house or become combust, there will be much misery. Should he pass through his own or exaltation house or be retrograde, the effects will then be good. (20:37)

In the case of Chart 1, Saturn transited Cancer from July 1975 to September 1977, during much of which time this man was running Saturn–Saturn. Since the Moon is Saturn's enemy, and since being a self-bhukti there was no chance for a benefic bhukti lord to monitor or moderate the situation, he had poor results in his second-house matters.

This principle can be extended to the dasha lord as well. When Jupiter transited Capricorn during most of 1985, the owner of Chart 2 experienced some difficulties in the matters of his fourth, fifth and seventh houses as he struggled to set up a new business, having left medical school a year and a half earlier. His parents (fourth house) had provided venture capital (Jupiter being a significator of money) for the business and felt somewhat insecure about doing so. His fiancée was interested in marriage then, but he felt himself to be financially too unstable for wedlock. All these stress-promoting difficulties were exacerbated by the transit of the debilitated dasha lord. All of them were manageable because his natal Jupiter is strong.

When Chart 2's owner experienced his Jupiter–Rahu Bhukti, Rahu was moving through Scorpio, its exaltation sign, and so gave him favorable results. Since Scorpio in his chart occupies the third house of younger siblings, the favorable results specifically pertained to the momentum accumulating in the prosperity of his younger sister. During his Rahu Bhukti, she and her husband acquired a house of their own. When Jupiter was retrograde in the first house of physique in Chart 2, the native engaged a personal trainer, and Jupiter's aspect on the fifth house of children at that time portended his wife's pregnancy.

'When a planet whose dasha is in progress is weak, combust, debilitated, or in an enemy's house at birth he will, during his transit through that house, cause the total destruction of that house' (20:35). In the case of Chart 1, Saturn is weak because it sits at 0° 15' of Gemini. During much of the time that Saturn transited Cancer, between July 1975 and September 1977, this man was in his Saturn–Saturn period. Since the Moon, the lord of Cancer, is Saturn's enemy, and since being a self-bhukti there was no chance for a benefic bhukti lord to monitor or modify the situation, he had poor results in his second-house matters.

'In the case of a planet whose bhukti is auspicious, the good effect will be manifested when the Sun enters the planet's exaltation constellation or when Jupiter transits that place. As regards a planet whose bhukti is inauspicious, the evil effects will be felt when the Sun in his transit passes through the bhukti lord's debilitation or inimical constellation' (20:38). This general rule is a helpful hint for tying down results to a specific month. The Jupiter–Moon Bhukti in Chart 2 began on 1 May, he was married on 3 May, and the Sun entered Taurus, the Moon's exaltation sign, twelve days later. The rule thus took him close to the event but did not actually predict it. To some extent, good effects will also arise when the Sun passes through the houses owned by the dasha lord. The Sun is important in transits because it is the sovereign of all the planets, the pivot around which they travel. The Sun's authority activates, and his brightness illumines, a house when he steps into it.

TRANSITS FROM THE CHANDRA LAGNA

Because the lagna is the factor of greatest differentiation, which therefore gives the greatest specificity of effect, many texts (such as *Phaladipika*) calculate transits from the lagna. Several treatises, however, including *Phaladipika*, say that transits can also be calculated from the Moon. Because the texts permit both, the number of jyotishis in India who reckon transits from the Moon is perhaps equal to those who reckon them from the lagna. We prefer to reckon them from the lagna. If the system of transits from the Moon is used, many other criteria must be examined. Two of the most important are:

1. *The portions of the constellations where the planets give their results* – 'Mars and Sun produce their effect during their passage when they are in the initial ten degrees (or decanate) of a constellation; Jupiter and Venus when they are in the middle third of a constellation; while the Moon and Saturn bear fruit when in the last decanate. Mercury and Rahu–Ketu produce effects throughout their passage' (*Phaladipika* 26:25).

2. *Vedha* (Cancellation of effects) – There are certain places from a transiting planet known as *Vedha* which, when occupied by planets, cancel the effect of the transiting planet. Vedha means a breach or opening, through which the transiting planet's energy is lost. As an example, consider the Sun. Vedha is created when any planet except Saturn occupies the fourth, fifth, ninth and twelfth houses from the Sun's transit position in a horoscope. In other words, if any planet other than Saturn appears in any of the above four houses, all effects expected for the Sun's transit through the house in question are nullified.

Here mythology plays a valuable role yet again, for the Sun is regarded as Saturn's father; and father and son, at least in the context of this system of transits, never counteract one another's actions. The same holds true for the Moon and Mercury, who are also father and son respectively.

SADE SATI

One special case of a transit calculated from the Moon is the *sade sati*, which is the period of approximately seven and a half years during which Saturn moves through the three constellations of the zodiac which are closest to your moon: the constellation which holds the moon, and the two constellations which flank it. If, for example, your moon occupies Aries, your *sade sati* (Hindi for 'seven and a half') will consist of those years during which Saturn wanders through the constellations Pisces, Aries and Taurus. While the origins of this principle of *sade sati* are unclear, and while it does not appear as such in the standard classical texts on Jyotish, it is recognized by all practicing jyotishis, and is superstitiously feared by millions of Indians. Like all other factors in a horoscope, *sade sati* does not act in isolation; confluence must exist to activate it, and appropriate dashas, bhuktis and transits must support it.

Most people with normal longevity experience *sade sati* on three occasions in their lives, though those who are born in *sade sati* may go through four such cycles, at intervals of $29\frac{1}{2}$ years (on the average). The specific experience of Saturn's passage over the Moon will differ from person to person according to the specific positions and interrelations of the planets in the horoscope. *Sade sati* is generally a difficult period in one's life, though the specific difficulty may need to be pinpointed in other ways. Commonly *sade sati* causes *chatra bhanga*, the 'loss of those who protected us'. People often lose their grandparents during the first *sade sati* of their lives, lose their parents during their second *sade sati*, and lose their own lives during the third, if indeed they are fated to live that long.

While in those horoscopes in which Saturn promises good results the bad results of *sade sati* are sometimes greatly modified, the effects of *sade sati* depend substantially on the Moon's rashi, and on its condition. A debilitated Moon, or a Moon posited in Saturn's debilitation constellation, or in constellations owned by Saturn's enemies, tends to intensify the consequences. Since *sade sati* is sometimes also taken to apply to the lagna, difficulties are likely to be compounded when the Moon occupies the twelfth, first or second houses in a horoscope, for then both types of *sade sati* will overlap.

In Chart 1 *sade sati* began during the summer of 1980, when Saturn entered Virgo, and ended during the end of 1987, when Saturn left Scorpio. During this time the native experienced marital and career problems, and suffered the death of his spouse. These factors were clearly supported by the dasha and bhukti then operating.

A BINARY METHOD

Sometimes the sheer force of transiting planets can indicate important life events. One relatively simple approach to *gochara* is to concentrate on the transits of the slow planets Jupiter and Saturn who, because they traverse one rashi in one year and $2\frac{1}{2}$ years respectively, can exert prolonged influences on one's experience of life. Jupiter is the *sukha karaka*, the significator of pleasure, and Saturn the *duhkha karaka*, the significator of misery. Some jyotishis predict on this binary principle, either within or outside the context of Vimshottari Dasha.

THE PROCEDURE: 1. *Find the house that the transiting Jupiter occupies, and the houses he aspects.* These houses will often be favorably activated, depending on both Jupiter's strength in the natal chart, and the strength of the transiting Jupiter. For example, an otherwise unafflicted Jupiter who occupies its own constellation in a kendra or kona in the natal chart may during its transit provide very favorable results, but a Jupiter that is afflicted natally by combustion, debilitation, residence in a trik house, or like weakness may give only feebly pleasurable results. A Jupiter who is combust, or otherwise weak, by its transit position in the natal chart also tends to give feeble results, even if it is strong in the natal chart.

2. *Find the house that the transiting Saturn occupies, and the houses he aspects.* These houses will often be unfavorably activated, depending both on Saturn's strength in the natal chart, and on the strength of the transiting Saturn. If Saturn occupies by transit its own or its exaltation constellation, it will produce relatively good results for the house it transits, and will reduce the bad results expected for the houses that it activates by aspect. A Saturn which is afflicted natally by combustion, debilitation, residence in a trik house, or like weakness may give miserable results, as may a Saturn who, even if strong in the natal chart, is weak by its transit position.

3. *Look for confluence.* When a strong natal Jupiter and a strong transiting Jupiter occupy or aspect the same house, positive results are more likely to accrue. When a malefic natal Saturn influences a house, and transit Saturn reactivates that house, negative results become more certain.

One example, in Chart 2, involves Jupiter, which transited his natal twelfth house from mid-1991 through mid-1992, from where it restimulated by aspect his strong natal Jupiter in the fourth house. During this period, Chart 2's owner acquired a new vehicle (one of the matters indicated by the fourth house). Since strong natal Jupiter aspects the twelfth house, owned by its friend Sun, through which transit Jupiter was passing, this man's foreign travels (a twelfth-house matter) accelerated noticeably.

Although this binary principle is used outside the context of dashas and bhuktis, it is best used in conjunction with Vimshottari Dasha. If desirable results are anticipated on the basis of the natal placements of the dasha and bhukti lords during long bhuktis (such as Venus–Rahu), such results are more likely to begin during a year when transit Jupiter stimulates those placements. Similarly, if undesirable results are anticipated on the basis of the natal placements of the dasha and bhukti lords during long bhuktis, such results are more likely to begin during a year when transit Saturn stimulates those placements.

CHAPTER TWELVE

EXAMPLE CHARTS

We have now reached the stage where we can synthesize the information introduced in this book into a representation of reality as it applies to an individual human being, and to the karmas which have caused that individual to take birth. A good Jyotish guru usually presents teachings to a student puzzle piece by puzzle piece, the student taking on faith that one day those seemingly unrelated pieces will suddenly coalesce into an image. When they do, it occasions a major 'Ah-ha!' in that pupil's awareness. This sort of training gradually conditions the student to approach her own analysis in a similar way, by allowing the fragments of data she gleans when reading a horoscope to accumulate and organize themselves within her mind until they spontaneously cohere into an image which is a fair representation of reality.

Broad detail and principles can give only the broadest of results. Some events will certainly occur during obvious dasha, bhukti and gochara periods, but others will be predictable only by resorting to deeper and finer levels of analysis. While we have tried hard in these examples to be consistent with the general principles of interpretation set down throughout this book, we have strenuously sought to avoid dragging in information piecemeal simply to make incidents fit the bounds imposed by these principles. None of these examples was preselected simply because it fitted snugly into the interpretive methods that we advocate. In fact, in those instances where an alternative rule fits the material in a particularly striking way, that rule has been introduced, even when it falls slightly outside this book's scope. It is our hope that such references, which demonstrate the extent of Jyotish's breadth, will neither overwhelm nor 'over-tease' the reader, but will instead inspire a desire to learn more of Jyotish.

Even though a good jyotishi rarely examines two horoscopes in precisely the same way, students of Jyotish often find it a useful exercise to examine horoscopes according to a set procedure. After you have examined many horoscopes, salient features will begin to leap out at you without your having to dig for them. At first, however, begin by looking for graha yogas. Since scanning the horoscope for planetary combinations has fallen out of favor in Western astrology, Western students of Jyotish sometimes find it difficult to get out of the habit of using general planetary symbolism and into the habit of surveying potentially significant graha yogas. While this will no doubt be a stringent intellectual exercise for many readers, it is an essential step in the development of the analytical skills which are essential to Jyotish.

Next, examine all the factors, positive and negative, which influence the ascendant, its lord, and the dispositor of the first lord. Because the ascendant is the foundation of the horoscope, a weak first house or first lord may prevent even the best of Raja Yogas from providing its promised fruit. Simultaneously examine the strength and position of the Moon, the indicator of mind. Thereafter, examine the other houses, their lords and their significators, to determine which areas in life seem most affected by Dridha Karmas, good or bad. Then scan the dashas and bhuktis, and confirm the potential by checking transits.

For didactic purposes we will analyze the examples below in this fashion: first the graha yogas, then the ascendant, its lord, and the other houses, and finally the dashas and bhuktis, and the transits of significant planets. The material developed in these examples is necessarily limited, for a whole book could easily be compiled by correlating astrological interpretations with known events in just a few well-documented lives. Since all karmas are not Dridha Karmas, every area of a natal horoscope does not perfectly mirror the native's life experience. The sectors of these horoscopes which have been analyzed were selected because they most strikingly displayed the principles to be illustrated.

PARAMAHAMSA YOGANANDA

Birth Data: 5 Jan. 1893 8:38 P.M. LMT
Gorakhpur, India

Positions		Day: Thursday
LG	6°LE 31′	Yoga: Priti
SU	23°SA 13′	
MO	3°LE 14′	Tithi: Chaturthi of Krishna
MA	13°PI 19′	Paksha
ME	00°SA 55′	
JU	23°PI 51′	Karana: Bava
VE	24°SC 44′	
SA	20°VI 13′	Nakshatra: Magha
RA	11°AR 54′	
KE	11°LI 54′	

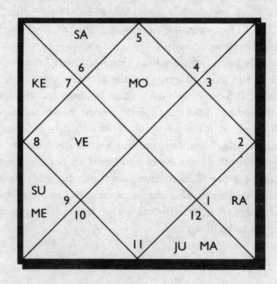

Rashi Chart

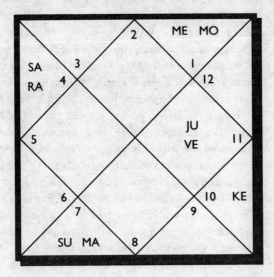

Navamsha Chart

Vimshottari Dasha

Ketu	5 Jan. 1893	Mars	25 April 1934
Venus	25 April 1898	Rahu	25 April 1941
Sun	25 April 1918	Jupiter	25 April 1959
Moon	25 April 1924		

YOGAS One should ordinarily be suspicious of most birth times, and especially those provided for births which happened a century or more ago in countries where reliable methods of timekeeping were not commonly available. In the case of Paramahamsa Yogananda, however, his guru Sri Yukteshwar was himself a jyotishi who had many years during which to rectify Yogananda's horoscope. It is therefore likely that this horoscope is accurate, particularly because of the pleasing way in which it correlates with the known events of Yogananda's life.

This birth chart of the famous renunciate yogi and founder of the Self-Realization Fellowship demonstrates convincingly the use and importance of a broad knowledge of yogas. At first glance this horoscope displays none of the prominent yogas listed in Chapter Ten: there is no Parivartana Yoga, no exalted planet and no strong Dharma Karma Adhipati Yoga; the only planet in its own rashi is Jupiter, who is seated in the eighth house conjunct with Mars and aspected by Saturn; and two flashy, sensual planets (Moon and Venus) occupy the kendras. There is a potentially detrimental Shakata Yoga, since the Moon is in the sixth house from Jupiter but, because the Moon is in a kendra from the lagna, it is cancelled.

There is however a good Budhaditya Yoga. The Sun and Mercury occupy the fifth house of discernment with the Sun as the lord of the lagna. This activates both houses (the first and the fifth) which must be activated for the yoga to give outstanding results. The effects of this yoga are enhanced because it recurs from the Moon Lagna, it is unaffected by any malefics, and it occurs in the beneficial constellation of Sagittarius, whose lord Jupiter (a graha who indicates wisdom and discernment) occupies its own rashi. Yogananda was known for his sharp mind, his powers of discernment, and his oratorical abilities (Mercury as lord of speech and of the second house involved in the Budhaditya Yoga).

The Moon, lord of the twelfth house of renunciation, seclusion and ashramas, occupies the first house (a good house), and the twelfth house is aspected only by the benefic Jupiter. This creates a Musala Yoga, which causes difficulties in mundane life but enables the native to make good spiritual progress and tends to lead him to reside in foreign countries. Since everyone whose twelfth lord occupies the lagna will not show spiritual tendencies, we must look for confluence to support this conclusion. We find it in two key combinations which exerted a crucial influence on Yogananda's life. These combinations are rarely mentioned in modern books on Jyotish, but they do appear in many of the classics, in chapters devoted to *Pravrajya Yogas* (combinations for renunciation).

The first combination, which *Phaladipika* 6:28 refers to as Srikantha Yoga, occurs when the lord of the lagna, the Sun, and the Moon occupy a kendra or a kona in their exaltation, own, or friendly rashis. Here the Sun is himself the lord of the lagna, and both he and the Moon occupy friendly rashis, the former in a kona and the latter in a kendra. The results ascribed to this yoga are listed in verse 29: the native will be a magnanimous, virtuous, powerful devotee of Lord Shiva who will refrain from belittling the religious beliefs of other people. Such a person will be 'decked with rudraksha rosaries, his body whitened by being smeared with sacred ash', both rudraksha beads and sacred ashes being symbols of renunciate yogis. These symbols should be regarded symbolically for the most part for, while Yogananda was a renunciate, he did not prominently wear either rudraksha beads or sacred ashes, nor was he a sectarian devotee of Shiva. He was, however, devoted to the Universal Soul, of which Lord Shiva is the embodiment, and was renowned for his respect for all religions.

The second Pravrajya Yoga (*Brihat Parashara Hora* 79:8) is formed by the Moon occupying a rashi of Mars and being aspected by Saturn in the navamsha chart. In Yogananda's navamsha chart the Moon sits in Aries, where it is aspected by Saturn from Cancer. It was the combination of the Budhaditya Yoga and the two Pravrajya Yogas which set the keynote for Yogananda's life and purpose, as graha yogas often do.

A Dharma Karma Adhipati Yoga does appear in the eighth house of Yogananda's chart, but it is weak because the planets involved (the fifth lord Jupiter and the fourth and ninth lord Mars) occupy a trik house. They are not completely powerless, however, since Jupiter tenants its own rashi, and Raja Yoga Karaka Mars sits in a friendly rashi. Moreover, Jupiter and Mars are friends, and are friends of the lords of the ascendant, the Moon Lagna and the Sun Lagna. This yoga recurs from all lagnas; in the Sun Lagna, Jupiter and Mars are the lords of the fourth and fifth respectively. While this Raja Yoga did not come to the forefront of his life (because it appears in the eighth house) it did play a supporting role, by making him a regal figure in America's spiritual community.

THE LAGNA AND BHAVAS Leo, the lagna here, is unafflicted by any malefic, and Leo's lord is powerful (it sits in a kona, in a friendly rashi, and is also unafflicted by any malefic). This caused the positive psychological symbolism of the Sun to shine through Yogananda's personality, producing qualities like nobility, individuality, generosity, grandeur, dignity, power, authority, leadership and creativity. Because Leo is unafflicted its symbol the lion can roar unhampered, and Yogananda did become a lion among religious people in the West. Lagna lord Sun occupies Purva Ashadha, 'the Undefeated', and Yogananda did prevail in his effort to bring Kriya Yoga to foreign lands. Because of his renunciation yogas he was not afflicted by the sexual excesses which tend to characterize this nakshatra, nor did he suffer from serious kidney or bladder disease, because his lagna and its lord are fundamentally strong.

All three of Yogananda's lagnas are strong. The Sun, lord of both the ascendant and the Moon Lagna, is strong because he occupies the fifth house in both those lagnas, sits in a friend's rashi, and is aspected by no graha (which might otherwise add malefic influence). Nor do any grahas aspect either lagna. Jupiter, the lord of the Sun Lagna, is strong because he occupies his own rashi in a kendra from the Sun.

Both Yogananda's ascendant and his Moon Lagna, the next most important of his lagnas, fall in the nakshatra of Magha, which represents a throne room. The throne may in his case have symbolized his becoming king among yogis in the West during his lifetime. Magha also represents lineages, and Yogananda emphasized to his Western disciples the importance of revering all the sages in one's spiritual lineage. Even his *Autobiography of a Yogi* is substantially the story of his mentors. The influence of the Moon, a significator of emotion, from its position in the ascendant made Yogananda a particularly emotional man, as his autobiography testifies. These emotions were directed into his spiritual pursuits by the cumulative effects of the Budhaditya Yoga, the two Pravrajya Yogas and the Musala Yoga. It was probably the Pravrajya Yogas which turned his mind away from matrimony. His guru probably also counseled him on this subject, for had he married before age twenty-eight the strong Kuja Dosha in his birth chart, which recurs from his Moon Lagna, would have strongly interfered with his marital happiness.

DASHAS AND BHUKTIS Yogananda was awarded a degree from

Calcutta University at some time during 1914, most probably during his Venus–Mercury bhukti, which began on 26 April 1914. Directional strength (*dig bala*) makes Venus in its capacity as a natural benefic powerful in the fourth house of education, and Mercury participates in the good Budhaditya Yoga in the fifth house of discernment. Venus is, however, aspected by Saturn, and in his autobiography Yogananda observes that his education was so fraught with difficulty that he despaired of ever attaining his degree. That he did squeak through was thanks only to his guru's intervention. We might predict that his guru would assist him because of the strong aspect of the benefic Jupiter (acting here in its literal capacity of guru) on the dasha lord Venus.

Yogananda left India in August 1920 during his Sun–Jupiter period, which lasted from 14 May 1920 to 2 March 1921, probably because the Sun's dispositor Jupiter aspects the twelfth house of immigration while occupying the eighth house, which is another of the houses of travel. Jupiter thus strongly indicates travel, journeys which would probably be safe because Jupiter occupies the nakshatra of Revati, which promises 'protection, shelter and hospitality while traveling'. The Sun's position in Purva Ashadha would suggest 'voyages by rivers and seas' to reach his destination.

If we now take *Phaladipika*'s advice and examine the transits of the dasha and bhukti lords, we discover that during August 1920 Jupiter would have been in the early degrees of Leo, transiting Yogananda's natal Moon (the lord of the twelfth), and aspecting both the natal Sun in the fifth house and the ninth house of long-distance travel. The dasha lord Sun himself transited the twelfth house from mid-July to mid-August, and from mid-August to mid-September transited Leo, his own rashi, which happens to be occupied by the lord of the twelfth house. When bhuktis which represent travel are thus positively supported by the transits of both the bhukti and dasha lords, travel becomes a certainty. When several trips occur over an extended period of time, the transit of the slower moving of the bhukti and dasha lords will often give some insight into their overall tenor, and the faster moving of those two planets can be used to evaluate individual trips within that larger period.

Yogananda's interest in spirituality began at an early age, but spirituality became central to his life during the dashas of the Sun, Moon and Mars, all three of which are key grahas in his Pravrajya Yogas. It was during these 23 years that he became known as a spiritual figure, and that his influence spread extensively. Yogananda left his body on 7 March 1952 during Rahu–Ketu (26 October 1951 to 12 November 1952). Rahu is disposited by Mars, who occupies the eighth house of the end of longevity, and Ketu occupies the third bhava, the other longevity house. The dasha and bhukti of two malefics connected to these two houses is not at all good for longevity. His end was sudden, which is typical of the action of the nodes. At that time transit Ketu occupied the lagna, and Rahu sat by transit in the seventh bhava, a maraka house. Seventh lord Saturn is a powerful maraka in this horoscope because it occupies the second bhava, another maraka house.

Jupiter in Yogananda's horoscope tenants his own rashi in the eighth house, which normally would suggest heightened longevity. That Yogananda died at the relatively young age of 59 is due in part to the conjunction of that Jupiter with the malefic Mars, and to the aspect of the malefic Saturn, the double maraka. This position of Jupiter *was* powerful enough to give Yogananda great posthumous fame, and may be one reason why his body did not decay for at least three weeks after he died.

FURTHERMORE While we have confined ourselves here predominantly to the principles of interpretation outlined in the chapters above, similar results could have been obtained by other methods of interpretation. For example, remember that in Jaimini Jyotish whichever planet is most advanced in any constellation is called the significator of soul (*Atma Karaka*), and whatever navamsha this planet occupies is called the *karakamsha*. In Yogananda's horoscope the Atma Karaka is Venus, who by virtue of sitting in Aquarius in the navamsha makes Aquarius the karakamsha. Chapter One, Part II, Verse 12 of the *Jaimini Sutram* tells us that such a native will perform charitable works, an interpretation which is reinforced by Jupiter's simultaneous occupation of Aquarius in the navamsha. When the Arudha Lagna, a numerological principle that Jaimini applies to the lagna, is added to this interpretation, it creates the equivalent, in Jaimini terms, of the Pravrajya Yogas.

MARILYN MONROE

Birth Data: 1 June 1926 9:30 A.M. PST
Los Angeles, California

Positions		Day: Tuesday
LG	20°CA 15'	Yoga: Indra
SU	17°TA 37'	
MO	26°CP 16'	Tithi: Shashti of Krishna
MA	27°AQ 54'	Paksha
ME	13°TA 57'	Karana: Vanija
JU	4°AQ 00'	
VE	5°AR 56'	Nakshatra: Dhanishtha
SA	28°LI 37'	
RA	25°GE 27'	
KE	25°SA 27'	

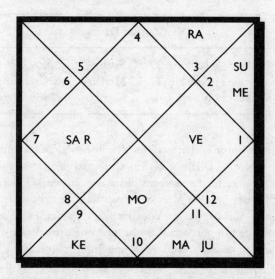

Rashi Chart

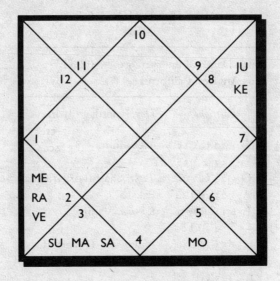

Navamsha Chart

Vimshottari Dasha

Mars	1 June 1926	Saturn	15 Nov. 1965
Rahu	15 Nov. 1931	Mercury	15 Nov. 1984
Jupiter	15 Nov. 1949	Ketu	15 Nov. 2001

YOGAS In Monroe's chart, as in Yogananda's, Mars and Jupiter together create a Dharma Karma Adhipati Yoga in the eighth house. The yoga in the actress's chart is even weaker than that in the yogi's chart because Monroe's yoga does not recur from either the Moon or Sun Lagnas, as Yogananda's yoga does, and because in her horoscope Jupiter occupies the rashi of a neutral planet, and Mars sits in an enemy's rashi. Mars and Jupiter do create a Sunapha Yoga by occupying the second house as counted from the Moon. This could strengthen the Raja Yoga, except that this Sunapha

Yoga is also rendered obscure, since the two grahas involved occupy the eighth house and are weak both by rashi and by avastha.

We cannot exclusively ascribe Monroe's fame and status to this Raja Yoga, but it did contribute to her success. This is because Saturn, the yoga's dispositor (*jiva*), is exalted and retrograde, occupies a kendra, and is aspected by two benefics and no malefics. The more significant yoga in Monroe's chart, the one which was responsible for her incredible fame, is a very powerful Parvata Yoga, as defined by *Phaladipika*. The ascendant lord Moon creates this yoga by occupying the seventh house and aspecting the ascendant. Moon's dispositor Saturn, while not in his own rashi, is, as noted above, very powerful, and is aspected by his own dispositor, who happens to be his friend.

A Parvata Yoga is said to make a person wealthy (very), charitable (she did volunteer to do charitable work), eloquent (in a sense), learned in classical subjects (she studied 'classical' method acting), fond of mirth (she was a gifted comedienne), famous (definitely), splendiferous (to most), and the leader of a city (the toast of Hollywood). While the weakness created by Saturn's position in Mrita Avastha is easily offset by his other manifold strengths, Monroe's fame might have taken on quite a different note had it not been for this deadly position of Saturn as key fame-giver in her chart.

Another major contributor to her status is Saturn's Shasha Yoga, which is particularly strong because it recurs from the Moon Lagna. Here is part of the fruit *Phaladipika* ascribes to this yoga: 'extolled by all . . . wicked in disposition . . . intrigues with women (or men) not his (or her) own . . .' Monroe was indeed 'extolled by all', and this fame was reinforced by her Parvata Yoga. The remaining two items fit her particularly well because of Saturn's rulership of the malevolent eighth house. Whether or not she was personally wicked, Monroe certainly enjoyed a scandalous reputation.

Monroe never become famous as a scholar, but the Budhaditya Yoga which aspected her fifth house helped her become known as 'Hollywood's smartest dumb blonde'. Although she was frequently taunted by reporters wanting to know if she could read and write, she joined a public library at 19, opened her first known charge account at a bookstore at age 21, attended a course entitled 'Backgrounds in Literature' at UCLA in 1951, and frequently borrowed books and discussed them with friends. She owned an impressive array of books, and her marriage with the brilliant American playwright Arthur Miller was the longest lasting of her marriages. Monroe's Budhaditya Yoga could never display its full influence in her life because her fifth house is afflicted. Contrast this yoga with the Budhaditya Yogas in the charts of Yogananda and of Einstein (see below), whose fifth houses of intelligence are strong.

Both Yogananda and Monroe have the sensual planets Moon and Venus in kendra houses, a combination which makes the native an artist and a sensualist. The sort of sensuality the individual will prefer will depend on the other yogas in the horoscope. Yogananda's Pravrajya Yogas caused his passion for art to be channeled into devotional music, while Monroe's yogas found expression through the cinema, sex and popular songs. Both also have Venus aspected by Saturn, but one became a celibate yogi, and the other the epitome of a sex goddess.

The two classic and rare renunciate yogas in Yogananda's chart which helped to guide him to his destiny are absent in Monroe's case. Two combinations which are present in her chart are:

(a) 'If the lord of the seventh house be in a constellation of Venus or Saturn and be aspected by a benefic there will be many spouses. The same results occur if the lord of the seventh house is exalted' (*Brihat Parashara Hora* 18:7). While this yoga suggests a great capacity for or interest in sex in general, both combinations do literally apply *in toto* to Monroe.

(b) When Venus, Mars and Saturn combine in some way with the seventh house of relationships and the fourth house of morals, this usually spells moral trouble, say the classics on Jyotish. Two varieties of this principle which are present in Monroe's chart are: (1) When Venus occupies a rashi of Mars and is aspected by Saturn, if either Venus or Saturn is connected to the seventh or the fourth houses, the person will be a debauchee (*Jataka Tattva*). (2) When the seventh lord occupies the fourth house and is influenced by Venus, the person becomes a profligate, particularly if that seventh lord is Mars or Saturn (*Jataka Desha Marga*).

Yogananda also had Venus in a rashi of Mars aspected by Saturn as the seventh lord, but in his case a very powerful and naturally benefic Jupiter conjoins dispositor Mars and aspects both Saturn and Venus. In Monroe's case a weaker Jupiter leaves Venus unchecked, and she lacks Yogananda's rare, powerful renunciate yogas. The result was that Monroe was prepared to play the sexpot. These parallel combinations producing different results in the charts of Monroe and Yogananda starkly illustrate the difficulties a jyotishi encounters when trying to deliver accurate judgements.

THE LAGNA AND BHAVAS Predictions about the moral character of a person require much experience and sensitivity and cannot be blindly made on the basis of a single indication in a chart. In Monroe's case, aside from the influences listed above, Rahu's presence in the twelfth house of bed pleasures strongly indicates intense sexual indulgence, for Rahu represents 'cravings that cannot be satisfied'. Fortunately Jupiter's aspect curbed this passion to some degree, for without this cover from Jupiter a twelfth-house Rahu in an otherwise afflicted chart can lead to debauchery.

Monroe's lagna is in Cancer, in Ashlesha nakshatra. The themes of tragic death and emotional thinking which are significant indications for a Cancer ascendant apply to her exceptionally well. Ashlesha's indications appeared plentifully in her life: she represented primordial sexuality, conducted secret love affairs, was subjected to and engaged in major manipulations, cast a hypnotic spell on her audiences, and was an expert at illusion. She was a frequent user of poisons (alcohol and barbiturates), and was either killed or committed suicide with poison.

One of the most important reasons for Monroe's fame was the strength of her lagna. Moon's aspect on the ascendant renders the latter strong, and the Moon is itself strong because Monroe was born less than ten days after the full Moon. Saturn, the lord of the Moon Lagna, strengthens that lagna by being in a kendra, exalted, retrograde, and aspected by two natural benefics, one of whom, Venus, is the Raja Yoga Karaka for the Moon Lagna. Two of Monroe's three lagnas are thus strong.

While Saturn's great strength when viewed from the Moon Lagna contributed significantly to Monroe's fame, that same strength caused Saturn's aspect on her ascendant to be particularly detrimental. Jupiter and Venus, the two natural benefics who aspect this retrograde, exalted natural malefic who is lord of the eighth house, greatly reduce its disruptive potential. Since, however, all results are cumulative they could not prevent this Saturn from bringing tragedy, suffering and death, all matters which are naturally ruled by Saturn, especially when he rules the eighth house, into Monroe's life.

Monroe was famed for her beauty, a first-house rulership. Her allure may be attributed to the confluence of a number of factors, including the occupation by the lagna and the Moon of even-numbered constellations. Both Moon and Venus, the other planet capable of bestowing beauty, occupy kendras, and the strong Moon aspecting its own rashi in the lagna also bestows beauty, or at least charisma. Saturn's aspect on the lagna, which should have detracted from her good looks, did not because Saturn occupies a rashi of Venus while being aspected by Venus, and disposits the Moon. These two influences cause Saturn to carry the effects of both Venus and the Moon to the ascendant.

One reason why Monroe had no full brothers or sisters is that the sibling significators, Mars and Jupiter, occupy the eighth house. The third house of younger siblings is aspected by the natural malefic Mars, the enemy of the third lord Mercury, and Mercury is combust and is aspected by Mars. The eleventh house of elder siblings is also aspected by the malefic Mars, and while the eleventh lord Venus occupies a neutral rashi in the desirable tenth house, that tenth house is twelfth to the eleventh, a position which ruins the significations of the living beings indicated by the eleventh. Venus is also aspected by the powerfully malevolent Saturn. Thus a planet, in this case Saturn, which may provide immense material benefit through participation in graha yogas can simultaneously function as a terrible malefic. Understanding this seeming paradox is one of the major hurdles that students of Jyotish must cross.

Neither can an exalted malefic be relied upon to give exclusively good results. Monroe's fourth house contains an exalted, retrograde

Saturn which is aspected by its dispositor Venus, the lord of the fourth, who is a natural benefic. It is also aspected by the other natural benefic, Jupiter, and by no malefics, and yet Monroe's domestic life was unhappy. She had a poor relationship with her mother, spent time in an orphanage, and was raised by foster-parents. Her formal education extended no further than high school. That she did enjoy luxurious vehicles and accommodations was presumably due to the presence of that exalted Saturn (a property significator) in the fourth house of property, and to the aspect on the fourth house of the fourth lord Venus (the significator for vehicles). The nature and specific indications of the grahas involved must always be considered when trying to determine which of the many indications of a particular bhava will be activated in a specific horoscope.

Mantreshwara's principles of negative house analysis help to explain why Monroe had no children. The fifth lord Mars occupies the eighth house of death in its enemy's rashi and in the deadly Mrita Avastha. Jupiter, the significator of children, also sits in the eighth house. The fifth house is flanked by malefics (Saturn and Ketu), and it is aspected by the malefic Sun, a barren planet which discourages childbirth. Finally, note the combination of three mal-efics in the proscribed fourth (Mars), eighth (Rahu) and twelfth (Saturn) houses from the fifth (see Chapter Nine). Monroe had many abortions, and it was possibly only due to Jupiter's influence as a weak benefic on the lord of the fifth that these pregnancies ever occurred in the first place.

Marilyn Monroe had three official marriages. Her seventh house is hemmed in by Ketu on the one side and Mars on the other and, though the seventh lord Saturn is very powerful, it is in Mrita Avastha. The seventh lord's strength and good position gave her powerful and successful lovers and husbands, but that lord's position in Mrita Avastha prevented those relationships from continuing for very long; they 'died'. Saturn never likes marriage anyway; and, besides, Rahu in the twelfth house usually prevents happiness in marriage. One important contributing factor is lagna lord Moon, who occupies the nakshatra of Dhanishtha, a nakshatra which promotes marital discord.

Although the yogas in her chart carried her far in life, Monroe did experience significant difficulties in her career. Mars, the lord of the tenth house of career and action, occupies the evil eighth house, and the tenth house is itself aspected by the malefic Saturn. Mars also inhabits Purva Bhadrapada, a nakshatra which is characterized by passion, impetuousness, sadness and difficulty. This in many ways describes the results of her career activities, for after a serious nervous breakdown she committed suicide, or was encouraged to do so, at the tender age of 36, after a long history of drug and alcohol abuse.

DASHAS AND BHUKTIS Because Mars, who dwells in an enemy's rashi in the eighth house, conjoins Jupiter, the sixth lord, Monroe's Mars Maha Dasha, which she experienced over the first five years of her life, was awful. She lived in foster homes, and never knew her father. Although by rulership Mars has little to do with parents in this chart, they were affected here because she was too young to experience the effects herself. In such cases, the results go to the child's protectors (*poshakas*), who are frequently his or her parents. Also, Mars as a natural malefic flanks the Moon (afflicting thereby the natural significator of mother) and aspects the Sun (the natural significator of father). Mars also afflicts Jupiter, the ruler of the ninth house (father). Some attribute her career success to the Raja Yoga in her eighth house, but if this were the case the dasha of the Raja Yoga Karaka Mars should have given her good results, not bad.

The Rahu Maha Dasha included life in an orphanage (during Rahu–Jupiter, which began in September 1935) because Rahu occupies the twelfth house (confinement) of the natal chart. During that period Rahu transited Monroe's sixth house and so aspected its own natal position. Also, the bhukti lord Jupiter, the lord of the sixth and ninth houses, inhabits the eighth house. Whenever the ninth lord being Jupiter occupies the eighth house, one's good fortune is triply detrimented, for the eighth is a dussthana both from the lagna and from the house itself (being twelfth from the ninth), and Jupiter as natural significator of good fortune is in the dungeon of the horoscope. Nor did the rest of the dasha produce success, mainly because of the general weakness of dasha lord Rahu, who sat in the twelfth disposited by a seriously combust Mercury. As Rahu is also debilitated in the navamsha, the marriage she contracted during this period did not work out.

Saturn figured prominently in Monroe's rise to fame. She vaulted into national and world prominence during her Jupiter–Saturn period, which lasted from January 1952 to July 1954. During this short span of time, she appeared in the famous nude calendar; had her first *Life* magazine cover; obtained her most famous role (as Lorelei Lee in *Gentlemen Prefer Blondes*); was grand marshal at the Miss America Pageant; had her foot- and handprints immortalized in cement outside Grauman's Chinese Theater; made her first TV appearance on the Jack Benny Show; made another successful movie (*How to Marry a Millionaire*); entertained American troops in Korea; and was signed for yet another successful movie (*The Seven Year Itch*).

Although concurrently plagued with many problems – Jupiter being after all in the eighth house as lord of the ninth and sixth conjoined with the obstreperous Mars, resulting in lawsuits and other confrontations – she never looked back. Her amazing career success during this bhukti was due less to Jupiter's participation in the weak Raja Yoga, and more so due to her sterling *dashamsha* (the one-tenth division), the divisional chart which relates to career. In this chart Monroe's Jupiter occupies the seventh house in its own rashi of Pisces, unafflicted in any manner, creating a marvelous Hamsa Yoga.

From April 1952 through April 1953 Jupiter transited her tenth house of career, from which position it fully aspected bhukti lord Saturn; then from August 1953 until the end of the Saturn bhukti Saturn transited Libra, its exaltation rashi, thereby restimulating its natal position and significations. This restimulation also influenced Saturn in its role as lord of the seventh house of marriage, and so it was then that Monroe married Joe DiMaggio on 14 January 1954, when dasha lord Jupiter was transiting the eleventh house, whence it aspected her seventh house.

Marilyn Monroe died on 5 August 1962, during Jupiter–Mars, two grahas which occupy the eighth house of death. Everyone who undergoes the conjoint period of two occupants of the eighth house will not die, of course; there are additional factors in Monroe's chart which rendered this bhukti very dangerous to her longevity. For one thing, dasha lord Jupiter inhabits Dhanishtha, which is ruled by Mars, and bhukti lord Mars inhabits Purva Bhadrapada, which is ruled by Jupiter. The major and minor period lords are thus both in the house of death, as are both of their nakshatra dispositors. Moreover, her dasha lord Jupiter had returned by transit to the eighth house, thereby restimulating its natal position.

FURTHERMORE Marilyn Monroe experienced *sade sati* twice. During the first she lost the protection of her parents (*poshakas*), and during the second she lost her own life. The same Saturn who caused her star to blaze so brightly in Hollywood also caused her great misery as it transited her Moon because Saturn, the enemy of her lagna lord Moon, was for her the eighth lord, powerful by exaltation and retrogression. These factors ensured that her *sade satis* would afflict her life intensely. Ordinarily Saturn's passage through Capricorn, its own rashi, might offer some relief; but nothing in Jyotish operates in isolation. The residence of both the dasha and bhukti lords, and both their nakshatra dispositors, in the house of death, when taken in conjunction with the *sade sati*, rendered the latter a confluent factor in her death because of Saturn's eighth-house lordship.

ADOLF HITLER

Birth Data: 20 April 1889 6:30 P.M. LMT
Braunau-am-Inn, Austria

Positions		Day: Saturday
LG	4°LI 23′	Yoga: Shiva
SU	8°AR 30′	
MO	14°SA 20′	Tithi: Shashti of Krishna
MA	24°AR 04′	Paksha
ME	3°AR 22′	Karana: Gara
JU	15°SA 56′	
VE	24°AR 23R′	Nakshatra: Purva Ashadha
SA	21°CA 09′	
RA	23°GE 45′	
KE	23°SA 45′	

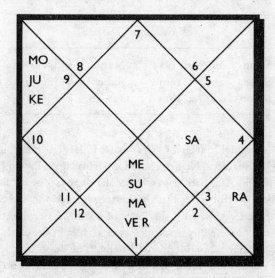

Rashi Chart

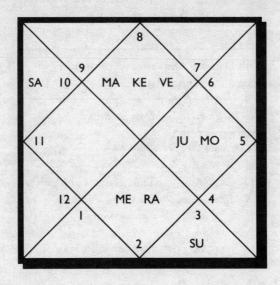

Navamsha Chart

Vimshottari Dasha

Venus	20 April 1889	Mars	23 Oct. 1923
Sun	23 Oct. 1907	Rahu	23 Oct. 1930
Moon	23 Oct. 1913	Jupiter	23 Oct. 1948

YOGAS A formidable array of yogas exists in Hitler's chart, including
Ruchaka, Budhaditya, Kesari, Hamsa, Maha Bhagya, Parvata and two
Dharma Karma Adhipati Yogas. His Maha Bhagya Yoga is classic and
supremely powerful: a day birth with ascendant, Moon and Sun all in
odd-numbered rashis, with the lords of all three ascendants in odd
rashis. This yoga literally made its owner a 'ruler of the earth', albeit a
destructive ruler who ruled only briefly. The supremely powerful
Ruchaka Yoga, which recurs from all three lagnas, gains extra strength
because Mars avoids combustion, is aspected by its friend, the powerful Jupiter, and occupies its own rashi of Scorpio in the navamsha

chart, where it creates Ruchaka Yoga again. Both *kshatriya* (warrior) planets, Sun and Mars, are strong by rashi in a kendra, aspect the ascendant, are aspected by a strong Jupiter, and conjoin the lagna lord. This is a most appropriate combination for a warlord.

The very strength of the Ruchaka Yoga made the majority of the textual indications for Ruchaka Yoga appear quite literally in Hitler's life: a long face, great enthusiasm, a very forceful personality, great luster and charisma, a love of fighting wars, lots of anger, victory over enemies (until the very end of his life), good knowledge of mantras and occult sciences (Hitler had an obsessive interest in the occult), a protector of thieves, a cruel personality, and death by weapons or fire. This is an accurate summation of Hitler, right down to the self-inflicted gunshot wound which caused his death, and the subsequent burning of his body at his request.

Mars, the dispositor of lagna lord Venus, occupies his own rashi in a kendra to form a Parvata Yoga, which is strengthened by Jupiter's powerful aspect on Mars. Because the Hamsa Yoga created by Jupiter occurs only from the Moon and Sun Lagnas, Jupiter is less powerful an influence in the chart than the belligerent Mars. The Budhaditya Yoga is configured with the lagna by aspecting it, giving Hitler the intelligence to rise to his exalted position from very humble beginnings, and the talent to have been a successful author. A Dharma Karma Adhipati Yoga is created by the conjunction of Venus and Mercury, and another by the mutual aspect of Mars and Saturn. The Kesari Yoga is created by Jupiter being in a kendra as counted from the Moon but, because neither planet sits in a strong house from the ascendant, that yoga is weak.

Hitler's chart also contains a Pravrajya Yoga, in that four or more planets occupy a single house (*Brihat Parashara Hora* 79:2–3). This yoga is not supported elsewhere in the horoscope, though, and because the warlike Mars was the strongest planet involved in the yoga, Hitler's path led him deep into the occult, instead of into spirituality, particularly because ninth lord Mercury is combust. Hitler was, however, a private person in many ways and enjoyed frequent retreats to his Valhalla in the mountains. The yoga probably also encouraged him to support the quasi-religious Aryanism which was the spiritual foundation of the Nazi Party.

THE LAGNA AND BHAVAS Hitler's lagna was very strong, particularly because lagna lord Venus, who is retrograde, occupies a kendra, and is far enough from the Sun not to be combust, aspecting his own house. The Moon Lagna is strong because Jupiter, its lord, occupies his own rashi. The Sun Lagna is similarly strong, for its lord Mars occupies his own rashi and is far enough from the Sun not to be combust. While two or three of the lagnas in the horoscopes of Yogananda, Monroe and Hitler are strong, it is only in Yogananda's chart that all three lagnas are free from the aspect of a natural malefic who is not also a Raja Yoga Karaka. Yogananda accordingly had a sterling character and a relatively smooth life. The other two, though also famous, did not because their charts have natural malefics who are not Raja Yoga Karakas afflicting the majority of the lagnas.

One of Hitler's life-long interests was architecture, perhaps because his lagna occupies Chitra, whose deity is Vishvakarma, the architect of the universe. Other meanings of Chitra which apply to Hitler include: he was very hard to defeat; he liked the arts, and was a competent sketcher and watercolorist; he was very conspicuous, ambitious and charismatic; he was a successful author; and he had a gift for oratory. His Libra ascendant gave him both a strong interest in politics and an inability to listen to good advice. This incapacity to hear contrary opinions prevented Hitler's subordinates from daring to contradict him, even when his plans were unbalanced. Libra's fashion consciousness may have influenced the stylishness of Nazi paraphernalia like uniforms and swastikas, and the theatricality of goose-stepping and staged mass events.

Saravali teaches that, as the number of planets configured with the ascendant increases, so does the individual's complexity. Here Mercury, Sun, Mars and Venus all contributed to Hitler something of their nature. Mercury made him an orator and writer, Sun a politician, Venus an artist, and Mars a self-centered military man. The Sun could also have suggested spirituality, but the afflictions to the ninth house discourage that interpretation. The aspect of the very powerful Mars also adds a propensity to injury, rashness, courage and pushiness to this equation.

One factor which made this man into a maniacal mass-murderer was the potent Martian influence on the lagna. Another is the fact that the lords of all three lagnas are in *ugra* (fierce, severe) nakshatras: Venus and Mars occupy Bharani, whose presiding deity is Yama, the lord of death, and Jupiter sits in Purva Ashadha, which is associated with declarations of war and other acts of aggression. The Moon is itself in Purva Ashadha, as is the malefic Ketu. Further, the cruel (*krura*) graha Sun aspects the lagna and conjoins the lagna lord. The Sun's influence is maximal because it sits within one degree of its maximum exaltation, in a kendra, configured with the lagna and its lord, and aspected by its powerful friend Jupiter. This puissant, cruel Sun, coupled with the influence of the violent, cruel Mars and the effect of the Ugra Nakshatras, contributed mightily to Hitler's diabolical megalomania.

The third house (courage, enterprise and adventure) in this horoscope is strong because it is occupied by its lord, Jupiter. Ketu, which also dwells in the third, acted like Mars to enhance Hitler's courage, which was undeniable: He was awarded two Iron Crosses for bravery during the First World War and, even when wounded in the leg, he begged his superior officer to be allowed to stay at the front rather than be transported to a rear-echelon hospital.

Hitler had a poor record in secular education; he failed even to obtain the usual secondary school certificate, and never resumed his formal education thereafter. Although his fourth house was aspected by its lord Saturn, the grahas which represent education (Mercury and Jupiter) influence neither the fourth house nor its lord. In the absence of their influence, other matters of the fourth house came to the fore. In Hitler's case they came in the form of property ownership, which Saturn represents. That he was actively interested in learning despite his limited secular educational attainments was due to the strength of his Budhaditya Yoga.

As with Monroe's chart, Hitler's seventh house of romantic partnerships and fourth house of morals are influenced by Venus, Mars and Saturn. In Hitler's case this is because Venus occupies a rashi of Mars in the seventh house and is conjoined with Mars as lord of the seventh, and both are aspected by Saturn as lord of the fourth. This spells moral deficiency, as is evident from what we know of Hitler's intimate relationships. For example, Hitler was almost twenty years older than Mitzi Reiter, the object of his affection who attempted suicide during the summer of 1930. There was a nineteen-year difference between Hitler and his sister's daughter Angela Maria Raubal, commonly known as Geli. Hitler courted Geli initially under the guise of the well-meaning uncle, then made her crazy with his possessive jealousy. Geli committed suicide in September 1931.

Hitler lost his bastard father at age fourteen. The ninth house of father is occupied by Rahu, and the aspect of the Moon is not very helpful on two counts: it is waning, and it carries the influence of Saturn, the only planet that occupies the Moon's constellation of Cancer. (This same principle was applied, in the reverse direction, to Saturn's carrying the influence of the Moon in Monroe's chart.) Jupiter's benefic aspect on the ninth house is not really that benefic, because it owns two dussthanas. Jupiter as a natural benefic may have made the father moral (the father's subjective reality), but Jupiter as the lord of evil houses contributed to removing him from Hitler's life early on (Hitler's objective reality). More salient than these afflictions is the fact that Mercury, the lord of the ninth house, is severely combust, is weak by being in Bala Avastha, conjoins the malefic Mars, and is fully aspected by the malefic Saturn. The Sun as significator of father also bears the baleful influence of Saturn and Mars.

DASHAS AND BHUKTIS It was predictably during the Mars Maha Dasha, which lasted from October 1923 to October 1930, that Hitler's rise began. In November 1923 he participated in the famous Beer Hall Putsch, during which he and others proclaimed a National Revolution in Munich. His efforts earned him a two-year jail term, of which he served nine months. During his incarceration he wrote the first volume of *Mein Kampf* ('My Struggle', an appropriately Martian name), which became a bestseller. The publicity from the putsch furthered his career, and by 1929 Hitler was receiving national attention and financial funding from important groups who considered him a gifted agitator.

During the Rahu Maha Dasha, Hitler became the unassailable dictator, Der Führer, who led his people into a world war which destroyed Germany and much of the rest of Europe. Hitler was thus the cause of the violent death of about fifty million humans, including himself. The period of Rahu permitted the warlord to display his full fury and barbarism because Hitler's Rahu is aspected by Moon and Jupiter, is disposited by Mercury, and occupies the Jupiter-ruled nakshatra of Punarvasu. Rahu in its own capacity as a 'shadow planet' threw by its aspect on the Moon (the significator of the mind) a shadow on Hitler's mind, for a Rahu–Moon combination is usually pernicious, and at its worst can lead to madness. This influence became emphasized during Rahu Dasha, because the aspect of Moon on Rahu enabled Rahu to give the results promised by the Moon – who also occupies an Ugra Nakshatra. Mercury, Rahu's dispositor, adds a further flavor of trauma by being seriously combust.

It is because Jupiter tenants its own rashi, and because it influences Rahu both by aspect and by nakshatra, that Rahu will predominantly give the results of Jupiter. Jupiter's involvement in the above-mentioned yogas gave Hitler his political successes, and Jupiter's position in the Ugra Nakshatra of Purva Ashadha caused him to seek and obtain these successes through war and atrocities, which led ultimately to his own destruction.

Hitler became Chancellor in January of 1933, during Rahu–Rahu. He consolidated his power during Rahu–Jupiter, which began in July 1933, by becoming first President and Chancellor and then Commander-in-Chief of the armed forces (by August 1934). In January 1933 dasha lord Rahu was transiting the fifth house (formation of government) in its own constellation of Aquarius. In 1934 bhukti lord Jupiter transited the lagna, whence it aspected the transit Rahu in the fifth house and the natal Rahu in the ninth. Being in the lagna, Jupiter also sat in the fifth house away from the natal position of the dasha lord.

Hitler died on 30 April 1945 during Rahu–Venus. During this period, dasha lord Rahu and misery significator Saturn were both transiting Gemini, Rahu's natal position. While Rahu as a dasha predominantly gave the effects of Jupiter, it also gave some of the effects of its dispositor Mercury. Rahu's restimulation of its natal position thus reinforced the influence of the combust Mercury, who occupies a maraka house. Mercury also conjoins Mars who, because he rules both maraka houses, is the primary killer for a Libra lagna. Still, the bhukti was of Venus, who rules the eighth house of length of life, no doubt, but also rules the ascendant. Why this Venus bhukti, which should not have proved dangerous to his life, ended in his death requires a more unusual explanation.

FURTHERMORE The most important influence of all the many powerful influences in Hitler's chart is probably the conjunction of Mars and Venus within the same degree, a combination known as planetary war. As we explained in Chapter Four, it is the planet with the higher latitude which wins such a fight. In this horoscope while Venus has a higher longitude than Mars (which has led most commentators to assert that it won the war) it is Mars who has the higher latitude. Mars therefore defeats Venus, which is one very important reason why Mars so dominates this horoscope.

It is also a powerful reason why Hitler suffered from a very deep psychological malaise, and why he was ultimately defeated by the Allies, for it was Venus acting as the lord of his ascendant who was vanquished by another planet. Hitler could never feel content with his many successes, nor ever felt a victory to be complete until it had been proved by conflict, for he, in the person of his vanquished lagna lord, always felt defeated by that mighty Mars. It is because a vanquished planet gives dangerous results, according to what it activates in the horoscope, that Hitler's death occurred during the Venus Bhukti of his Rahu Maha Dasha, since Venus owns and therefore activates in his chart the first house of life and the eighth house of the end of longevity. Because Venus occupies the seventh house of spouse, Hitler's romantic companion of many years, Eva Braun, also died during this bhukti.

It was in fact this defeat of Venus at the hands of Mars which caused Hitler to choose war over art. It was heart-rending for Hitler when, after living the life of a struggling artist in Vienna during his early twenties, he was twice turned down in his bid to enter the Academy of Fine Arts there, and only on volunteering for the army in the First World War did his life start to come together. As his biographer John Toland says of him then, 'He earned the respect of his comrades and officers. He belonged.' Cast away from the noble Venusian path of art, Hitler was firmly and irrevocably seized by the violent graha Mars, in whose martial grasp he finally found his terrible niche in life.

INDIRA GANDHI

Birth Data: 19 Nov. 1917 11:20 P.M. IST
Allahabad, India

	Positions	*Day:* Monday
LG	29°CA 21'	*Yoga:* Ganda
SU	4°SC 08'	
MO	5°CP 40'	*Tithi:* Shashti of Shukla
MA	16°LE 23'	Paksha
ME	13°SC 14'	*Karana:* Kaulava
JU	15°TA 00'R	
VE	21°SA 01'	*Nakshatra:* Uttara
SA	21°CA 47'	Ashadha
RA	10°SA 34'	
KE	10°GE 34'	

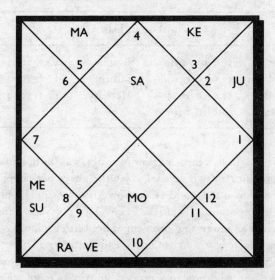

Rashi Chart

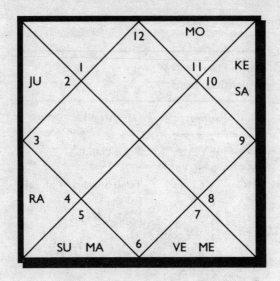

Navamsha Chart

Vimshottari Dasha

Sun	19 Nov. 1917	Jupiter	31 Oct. 1954
Moon	31 Oct. 1919	Saturn	31 Oct. 1970
Mars	31 Oct. 1929	Mercury	31 Oct. 1989
Rahu	31 Oct. 1936		

Indira Gandhi, India's former Prime Minister, was the dominant force in Indian politics for two decades. At the height of her career she was often referred to as the world's most powerful woman. Her birth time is variously reported as being between 11:15 p.m. and 11:45 p.m., which creates an interesting problem: if her birth took place prior to 11:22 p.m. her lagna would be Cancer, and if after 11:22 p.m. it would be Leo. Such situations, with which jyotishis frequently have to cope, are resolved by resorting to a process known as *rectification*, which means fitting the known personal history of the person's life with the horoscope by adjusting the birth time until they 'fit' one another.

What renders this a unique and highly instructive example is that to a considerable degree both Cancer and Leo lagnas provide a 'fit' to Gandhi's personal history, yet only one can be correct. This is unusual, since different horoscopes typically yield significantly different results. The debate among jyotishis over which lagna is correct continues in India to this day. What follows, as we wade into this controversy, is not proposed as a pro forma for rectification, but is simply a general illustration of how some of the material presented in this book can be used as an aid to rectification.

YOGAS Gandhi's birth chart brims with significant yogas, most of which recur from either the Leo or the Cancer ascendant. No fewer than three Parivartana Yogas appear in the chart, a rare occurrence. From the Leo ascendant the lords of houses 1/4, 5/10 and 6/12 mutually exchange places, while from the Cancer ascendant the exchanges involve the lords of houses 1/7, 2/5 and 6/11. Because from the Leo ascendant the exchanges are solely between two kendras, a kendra and a kona, and two dussthanas respectively, they are stronger Parivartana Yogas than those which appear from the Cancer lagna, where the exchanges involve two kendras, a neutral house with a kona, and a dussthana with a neutral house. Still, three Parivartana Yogas strengthen either lagna. The first houses of all three lagnas participate in Parivartana Yogas, which is indeed notable.

A strong Maha Bhagya Yoga occurs from the Cancer ascendant alone. This yoga is the reverse of Hitler's, since Gandhi is a woman: an even constellation rising, the Sun and Moon in even constellations, and birth at night. Even the lords of the various lagnas predominantly occupy even constellations, thereby enhancing the yoga's overall strength and impact. A strong Maha Bhagya Yoga makes one a lord of the earth (i.e. a political leader), as it did for Hitler.

The Dharma Karma Adhipati Yoga created by Sun and Jupiter which occurs in the Leo lagna is not matched in the Cancer ascendant. Budhaditya Yogas exists from both lagnas, making her perspicacious and astute, interested in the philosophy of politics, and intellectually capable. Moreover, it is activated in both lagnas:

from Leo it falls in the fourth house with the Sun owning the first house, and from Cancer it falls in the fifth house.

The desirable graha yogas in Gandhi's chart therefore correlate well with either a Cancer or a Leo lagna. Among the undesirable yogas we find a Papakartari Yoga, which exists only from the Cancer lagna by virtue of Mars and Ketu hemming in the first house. Since, except for Bhangas, graha yogas do not cancel one another out, but rather operate side by side with other combinations, the Papakartari Yoga suggests a Cancer lagna by clearly pointing to the many troubles in her life. Her father, who was born in Cancer lagna, also had a Papakartari Yoga to offset his many other greatness-producing yogas. He, like his daughter, was jailed, and he suffered many a setback to his career and life.

THE LAGNA AND BHAVAS Both the Moon and Sun Lagnas are strong, since they are aspected by their respective lords. While either a Cancer or a Leo lagna would be strong, on reviewing the meanings provided for Leo lagna, one is struck with how literally many of them apply to Gandhi's life. She was during her time the 'one lioness' in the jungle of Indian politics; formed the ministry in various governments; had no younger siblings; produced only two offspring, both of whom died tragically and violently; ruled her marriage; and had an important man (Jawaharlal Nehru, the first Prime Minister of independent India) for her father. Since a lagna in early Leo would occupy Magha nakshatra, Magha's symbol of a throne room also reflects her pre-eminent political position and impeccable family pedigree.

Cancer as lagna with Ashlesha rising provides some strong correlation as well, the most striking being that Gandhi's life was touched dramatically by highly publicized deaths. Her mother, to whom she was very close, died when Gandhi was only 18; when she was 24 Motilal Nehru, her famous grandfather in whose home she had lived most of her younger life, died; Mahatma Gandhi, who was an intimate though unrelated associate of Indira Gandhi's family, was assassinated when she was 30; her husband died, after 18 years of marriage, when she was 43; her famous father died suddenly when she was 47; her younger son, Sanjay, died in an air crash when she was 63; and she herself was assassinated at 67.

Her dynamic interest in career is typical of a Cancer ascendant. She asked to join the Congress Party, the party she was eventually to lead, at the tender age of twelve. Cancer could also account for her domestic side, which bloomed during the nearly two decades that she acted as the successful official hostess for her Prime Minister father, who was a widower.

One meaning which correlates with Ashlesha rising is secret intrigue and manipulation. Another is 'insight and wisdom, coupled with painful separations or serious troubles in life'. Indira Gandhi usually knew exactly which way the political winds were blowing, but this knowledge often required her to make unpopular decisions which came back to haunt her. One dramatic example of this was her declaration of a state of emergency, which was followed a few years later by a crushing electoral defeat which removed her from power. Another was her ordering of an army attack on a Sikh holy site to dislodge a group of Sikh militant murderers, which was revenged not long thereafter by her assassination at the hands of a trusted Sikh bodyguard.

Her life seems to correlate better with the indications of Leo and Magha, but a Cancer lagna would be slightly stronger than a Leo lagna because it receives the aspect of its lord, the Moon. Turning to the bhavas, one of the strongest memories the world has of Gandhi is the fact that she died an unnatural, premature death from an assassin's bullets. In cases of premature death, accidental or self-inflicted, the lord of the eighth house commonly influences the lagna and/or its lord. This was the case for both Monroe and Hitler, for both of whom the lord of the eighth house aspected the ascendant. The concurrent influence of Mars, the significator of violent or accidental death, on the eighth house or its lord makes even more of a case for an unnatural death. For Marilyn Monroe, Mars occupied the eighth house; and for Hitler, Mars conjoined the eighth lord. In Indira Gandhi's chart, Mars maintains a strongly inimical relationship with the eighth house for either a Cancer or a Leo lagna.

For a Leo ascendant the only relation between the lagna and its lord and the eighth house and its lord is that of the aspect between the reciprocally friendly planets Sun and Jupiter (a natural benefic), who are the lords of the first and eighth houses respectively. Only a Cancer ascendant for Indira Gandhi would create the following combinations for unnatural death: (a) the eighth lord, who happens to be the malefic Saturn, tenants the ascendant in an enemy's rashi unrelieved by the influence of any strong benefic; and (b) the same malefic lord of the eighth house aspects the lord of the ascendant, who is its enemy. This is strong testimony for the lagna being Cancer.

Gandhi had no brothers or sisters. From a Leo lagna the third house of siblings is ruled by Venus, who occupies a kona but in the house of its enemy, and is conjoined with the malefic Rahu. From Cancer the third lord is Mercury, who also occupies its enemy's constellation and who is aspected by the natural malefic Mars. It is, however, more severely afflicted than its Leo lagna counterpart, Venus, because Mercury is additionally combust. The third house from Cancer is also aspected by the malefic Saturn. Taken together, Cancer offers a greater astrological testimony for no siblings at all than does Leo.

If we take the eleventh house to rule older siblings, the Cancer lagna's eleventh house again portrays the absence of older siblings more convincingly than does its Leo counterpart. For the latter lagna, Mercury becomes the eleventh lord; while for the Cancer lagna, the eleventh lord becomes Venus. Although we have just concluded that Venus is better positioned, from the view of the third house, in a Leo lagna, in the Cancer lagna Venus occupies a dussthana (the sixth) while simultaneously residing in the eighth from the eleventh. The presence of the natural benefic Jupiter in the eleventh house may deny older siblings since, when a significator occupies the house it signifies, it creates problems for the living being that house signifies. This reinforces the idea that Cancer may be the lagna.

Gandhi believed formal education to be a waste of time. She tried to attend Oxford, but left without a degree after flunking several subjects, some for the second time. The fourth house from a Cancer lagna is unoccupied and unaspected, while its lord Venus resides in the sixth house in its enemy's rashi. Venus also conjoins the natural malefic Rahu, and is unaffiliated with the planets of education.

None of this favors success in formal secular education. For a Leo lagna, the fourth house of secular education has a Parivartana Yoga with the ascendant, both the first and fourth lords being friendly to each other and to the ascendant, and occupying kendras. This fourth house is also influenced by the two education planets, Mercury and Jupiter. Because this all augurs well for secular education, Cancer is a better choice for the lagna, since Gandhi never completed college.

This fourth-house reasoning also applies to Gandhi's tubercular mother, whose delicate health contributed to her early death. Gandhi was angered by the fact that her mother never really achieved a comfortable position of dignity and respect in the Nehru household. This again validates the Cancer ascendant, since the fourth house in a Leo ascendant would promise more in the way of dignity, health and longevity to the mother.

Gandhi had two sons and no daughters. Only from the Cancer lagna are the fifth house of children and its lord influenced predominantly by male factors: here the fifth house being occupied by Sun and aspected by Mars and Jupiter (all male planets), and the fifth lord Mars occupying a male rashi uninfluenced by any female planets (Mercury here will act like the male planets which influence it). From a Leo lagna the fifth house is influenced by Venus and Rahu, two female grahas, while the fifth lord Jupiter although aspected by the masculine Sun occupies a female rashi.

The Cancer Lagna also supports the pre-eminence her sons attained (one of them eventually became India's Prime Minister). This is attributable to the Parivartana Yoga involving houses two and five from Gandhi's lagna, which become houses one and ten when we rotate her horoscope to make her fifth house into the first house for her first-born son. While the Parivartana Yoga for the fifth house from the Leo lagna occurs between good houses (five and ten), and when the chart is rotated, the yoga now occurs between houses one and six (as counted from the fifth house), a position which is not as good as the position from Cancer.

By taking the fifth house of the Cancer ascendant as the lagna, we find that the new eighth lord is combust in the (now) first house, where it is aspected by the violent Mars. This combination, which would militate toward the violent and premature end of her children, does not work from a Leo lagna. Let us also recall that Purva Phalguni, the nakshatra which Mars occupies as ruler of the fifth house of children in a Cancer lagna, is also associated with accidents that occur through fire and heat. Since one son died in a plane crash and the other by an assassin's bomb, both causes of death can be considered to be due to fire and heat. This is not evident from a Leo lagna, where the fifth lord Jupiter occupies Rohini.

Gandhi's marriage confirms Cancer lagna from yet another dimension. Her married life, though not smooth, did continue for eighteen years, ending with her husband's untimely death from his second heart attack. In this lagna the seventh lord aspects its own house while occupying a kendra, and the seventh house is aspected by the natural benefic Jupiter. The Cancer ascendant likes to keep its married life secret, and Gandhi regularly denied allegations that her married life was troubled, claiming to be happy with her mate except for their decidedly different opinions on politics.

The marital discord that eventually did surface is partly attributable to the position of Venus, the principal significator of marriage, in the sixth house, conjoined with Rahu, in which position it sits in the twelfth from the seventh house of marriage. Also significant is the fact that the seventh house is strongly configured with Saturn, a planet who does not indicate marital happiness, all other factors being equal. The same Saturn as the seventh lord occupying a dussthana in the Leo ascendant would have more probably led to divorce or lack of marriage, especially considering the aspect of the natural malefic Mars, the seventh lord's enemy, on the seventh house.

If we are still uncertain about the seventh house, our doubt is rapidly dispelled when we consider her husband's stature as a relatively successful politician in his own right, an elected member of India's parliament. This makes sense only from the Cancer lagna, in which the seventh lord participates in a desirable Parivartana Yoga. Also, Gandhi's husband Feroze was a Parsi (a non-Hindu), which in the context of her upper-class Brahmana upbringing effectively meant she had married a foreigner. This situation is again more attributable to the Cancer ascendant horoscope, where

Saturn, one significator of foreigners, influences the seventh house by ownership and aspect while occupying the seventh house as counted from the lagna lord Moon. *Jataka Parijata* is particularly fond of this sort of reasoning, in which you examine all the combinations in the horoscope from the lord of the ascendant as well.

DASHAS AND BHUKTIS Now that our analysis of the bhavas has given us firm evidence for a Cancer lagna, let us turn to Gandhi's dashas and bhuktis. It was during the sixteen-year cycle of Jupiter and the fourteen years of Saturn's cycle that she experienced before her death that saw her rise to power. This reflects the participation of both Jupiter and Saturn in the powerful Parivartana Yogas. In a Cancer lagna Jupiter, who rules the sixth house, exchanges houses with Venus, the ruler of the eleventh. *Phaladipika* 6:32–4 classifies this as a *Parivartana Dainya Yoga*, to which Mantreshwara ascribes the following results: '. . . will be a fool, will revile others, and will commit sinful actions. He will always be tormented by his enemies, will speak woundingly and will be unsteady in mind. Interruptions will arise to all his undertakings.' Although this Parivartana Yoga raised her up, it concurrently caused problems because it belonged to the *dainya* (lowly) class.

Indira Gandhi attained power for the first time in 1966, during Jupiter–Sun, and within the remaining four years of Jupiter's main period, which were her first four years in power, she faced all sorts of major problems, including two wars. During Saturn's dasha she experienced both major advancements and major difficulties in her career, losing power once and then staging a miraculous comeback. Saturn does participate in a desirable *Parivartana Maha Yoga*, but also produces problems for the Cancer ascendant because it is a natural malefic which aspects Gandhi's tenth house into its debilitation rashi.

Indira Gandhi married on 26 March 1942, during Rahu–Saturn. Rahu is conjoined with Venus, the significator of marriage for either lagna, but only for the Cancer rising chart is Rahu in the constellation of a dispositor (Jupiter, whose results Rahu will give in either chart) who is related to the seventh house, in this case by aspecting it. Both charts would have the bhukti lord Saturn ruling the seventh house of marriage, yet marriage seems more likely for the Cancer than for the Leo lagna, since in the Leo ascendant Rahu is not connected with either the seventh house or its lord, and Saturn is very poorly placed (in the twelfth house from the lagna and the sixth house from the seventh). In the Cancer lagna, Saturn aspects the seventh as its lord. On 1 March or thereabouts, transit Saturn had aspected the exact degree of her seventh house, after which it moved into Taurus, where it aspected the natal Saturn, the seventh lord, in Cancer.

Gandhi's death took place during Saturn–Rahu on 31 October 1984. At the time she was slain, dasha lord Saturn was transiting Libra, its exaltation rashi, which rendered it very powerful as lord of the eighth. From this position it also aspected its own natal position, which further restimulated its role as eighth lord. Bhukti lord Rahu was transiting Taurus, its debilitation rashi. From the point of view of dasha, bhukti and transit, therefore, two central events of her life – marriage and death – suggest that Indira Gandhi's lagna was Cancer.

FURTHERMORE Space precludes us from describing the many other comparisons that may be done for the two possible ascendants for Gandhi's birth chart. Some of those comparisons fit better with a Leo ascendant, and others with a Cancer ascendant. One of these tools appears in *Brihad Jataka* (23:16): '. . . If the rising drekkana happens to be a Sarpa [snake] drekkana . . . and if the constellation owning the drekkana is aspected by malefics, the person will suffer imprisonment.'

The *drekkana* (one-third division) divides the 30° of a rashi into three 10° segments. Each of the drekkanas in the zodiac is named according to its innate qualities. Among the Sarpa drekkanas are two portions of Cancer: 10° to 20°, and 20° to 30°. No Sarpa drekkana or other imprisoning drekkana is to be found in Leo. With a late Cancer ascendant, Indira Gandhi would have been born in the drekkana of Pisces, who is aspected by the natural malefic Mars. This combination landed her in jail for her political activities twice during her lifetime, once at the hands of the British and once on the orders of her own countrymen. Not everyone with this combination will land in jail, of course, nor does every jailbird have this precise combination; but the Papakartari Yoga which hems in the Cancer lagna made this more likely.

In conclusion, while several of the meanings of Leo and Magha initially seemed to fit and might have led us to jump to a conclusion, analysis of the bhavas and the specifics of planetary placement and lordship from each of the ascendants yielded a picture in which Cancer emerged as the more likely ascendant. This demonstrates yet again that general interpretations, like those of the lagnas minus the planets, must always remain subordinate to specific interpretations in which the actual planetary positions in a particular chart are taken into account.

ALBERT EINSTEIN

Birth Data: 14 March 1879 11:30 A.M. LMT
Ulm, Germany

Positions		Day: Friday
LG	19°GE 34′	Yoga: Siddhi
SU	1°PI 20′	
MO	22°SC 21′	Tithi: Saptami of Krishna
MA	4°CP 44′	Paksha
ME	10°PI 58′	Karana: Bava
JU	5°AQ 19′	
VE	24°PI 49′	Nakshatra: Jyeshtha
SA	12°PI 01′	
RA	9°CP 18′	
KE	9°CA 18′	

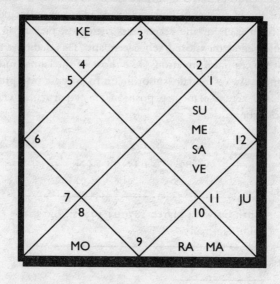

Rashi Chart

Navamsha Chart

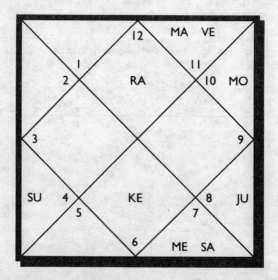

Vimshottari Dasha

Mercury	14 March 1879	Moon	12 Dec. 1921
Ketu	12 Dec. 1888	Mars	12 Dec. 1931
Venus	12 Dec. 1895	Rahu	12 Dec. 1938
Sun	12 Dec. 1915	Jupiter	12 Dec. 1956

YOGAS A Parivartana Yoga between the lords of the ninth and tenth houses, the two most powerful houses of the horoscope, graces the horoscope of Albert Einstein. This mutual exchange also constitutes a first-rate Dharma Karma Adhipati Yoga, which is rendered stronger by being an exchange of the fourth and fifth houses from the Moon Lagna. The *four* other Dharma Karma Adhipati Yogas in Einstein's birth chart consist of the conjoining of the lords of houses 1 and 5, 4 and 5, 1 and 9, and 4 and 9. All these yogas are powerful because the planets involved are friendly or neutral to each other and to the lagna lord. There is also a Budhaditya Yoga which recurs from the Moon Lagna. The Malavya Yoga, which recurs from all three ascendants, is strong because Venus is not combust. Among the many other yogas there is a Kesari Yoga and a Neecha Bhanga Raja Yoga.

The Neecha Bhanga Raja Yoga improves the significations of Mercury, which is one of two debilitated (*neecha*) planets in this chart. Mercury's debilitation is canceled because:

· Jupiter, who is Mercury's dispositor, sits in a kendra position from the Moon;
· Mercury, who is himself the lord of the rashi where he is exalted, is in a kendra from the lagna; and
· Venus, the planet who is exalted in Pisces, the rashi Mercury occupies, occupies a kendra from the lagna.

This Neecha Bhanga becomes a Raja Yoga because Mercury occupies a kendra from the lagna. Neecha Bhanga is only a prosthesis, however; as we shall see, some of the effects of Mercury's debilitation as lagna lord still made themselves evident in Einstein's life.

Einstein's Budhaditya Yoga was blemished to some extent by Mercury's debility. The Neecha Bhanga Raja Yoga was one compensating factor. Another is that the Budhaditya Yoga recurs from the Moon Lagna; and a third is that Mercury, as a participant in the Budhaditya Yoga, occupies Uttara Bhadrapada, a nakshatra which can stimulate extraordinary abilities or awareness. It is likely to do so here because Mercury is a key planet in so many of the aforementioned yogas. A fourth reason is that the Budhaditya Yoga is conjoined with Venus, the lord of the fifth house of intelligence, who is less than 1° 30′ away from its maximum exaltation in the tenth house. Moreover, the fifth house in the Moon Lagna is exceptionally well placed because it contains the Budhaditya Yoga, contains an exalted planet, and is involved in a Parivartana Yoga.

It may be that the Budhaditya Yoga is only a supportive factor, and that the prime indicator of Einstein's intelligence is this strength of the fifth houses of both the ascendant and the Moon Lagna. We find support for this idea in Mahadeva's *Jataka Tatva*, which suggests that when a benefic as lord of the fifth occupies a kendra or kona *and* is strong there in a benefic's rashi *and* is influenced by the 'thinking' planets (Jupiter and Mercury) the native will have great intelligence. This is a more insightful explanation than that set forth by those who assert that Neecha Bhanga makes a planet perform even better than it would if not debilitated.

Einstein's horoscope also contains a Pravrajya Yoga, for four or more planets occupy a single house. Because this yoga has some imperfections (i.e., two of the planets involved are combust; see *Brihat Jataka* 15:2) and is not supported elsewhere in the horoscope, he did not go the route of a full-fledged ascetic. He did, however, show many ascetic characteristics.

One final yoga to consider here is a Saraswati Yoga, a combination for knowledge. By definition this combination requires that Venus, Jupiter and Mercury all be strong in a kendra, a kona, or the second house. In Einstein's chart all are in a kendra or a kona, with Venus strong by exaltation, Jupiter strong because of the Parivartana Yoga in which it participates, and Mercury being modestly strong because of all of the yogas in which it participates, particularly the Neecha Bhanga Raja Yoga.

THE LAGNA AND BHAVAS True to his Gemini lagna, Einstein was a born colorful conversationalist and a gifted lecturer who addressed groups throughout the world. One reason why he became one of the world's archetypes for intellect is that the numerous yogas in his chart are supported by the Sun's rulership of the third house (intellect) in a Gemini lagna. Gemini being a dual rashi, with its lord in the tenth house in a dual rashi, Einstein had varied career interests. He adopted different countries as home at different stages of his life because lagna lord Mercury is also lord of the fourth house. His health, especially from age 50 onward, was delicate, and at times a serious problem, as his lagna would suggest.

His religious interest was, as is typical for Geminis, mainly an intellectual analysis of spiritual insights. Einstein himself wrote, 'I have not found a better expression than "religious" for the trust in the rational nature of reality that is, at least to a certain extent, accessible to human reason' (Clark, p. 502). Nevertheless, the strength of his ninth house caused Einstein to be more inclined to spiritual matters than are many Geminis.

Einstein's rising nakshatra was Ardra, whose meanings do not fit very well with his life experiences. If, however, we add a mere three minutes to his birthtime, his lagna point enters Punarvasu, whose descriptions seem much more appropriate to him. Punarvasu supports Einstein's tendency to frequent journeys and public involvement even while remaining substantially aloof from the world. In the last twenty years of his life he traveled very little and lived, whenever possible, a life of solitude, a tendency which was reinforced by the Pravrajya Yoga. Nakshatras can be very useful for such minor rectification of birthtimes, particularly those which we suspect may have been rounded up or down.

All three of Einstein's lagnas are rather strong. The ascendant is aspected by the benefic Jupiter, and lagna lord Mercury, who occupies a kendra, participates in many yogas. These factors more than compensate for Mercury's wide combustion, and the Neecha Bhanga Raja Yoga takes the edge off its debilitation. The Moon Lagna is free from the taint of any malefic, and its lord is exalted. The Sun Lagna contains an exalted planet, and its lord is involved in a Parivartana Yoga. While none of these lagnas is wholly clean or unobstructed, all are substantially enhanced by the wonderful array of yogas in this exceptional chart.

Einstein originally struggled with his education. Early in his life he found schools 'intimidating and boring', and left school at age 15 with poor grades and no diploma. Later he resumed his education but, though many prestigious universities bestowed honorary degrees galore on him, his own earned doctorate from the University of Zürich was a matter of 'touch and go'. Much of this is attributable to the conditions prevailing in his fourth house, and to the dashas operating in his early educational life. His fourth house is aspected by two natural malefics (Sun and Saturn) and by only a single natural benefic (Venus). Mercury will also act as a natural malefic in this regard, because it is conjoined with Sun and Saturn. Mercury, which is particularly important here because it rules the fourth house and is the significator of formal education, is also debilitated and combust. Einstein was able to muddle through because the debilitation is modified by the Neecha Bhanga *and* the combustion is wide *and* Mercury conjoins the natural benefic Venus *and* Mercury aspects its own constellation in the fourth house.

The same analysis substantially applies to other fourth-house matters, including home, the place where one lives. By extension, home represents one's country and citizenship. Einstein vacillated over his citizenship and, perhaps because he often felt himself to be a stranger wherever he lived, he ultimately harbored and encouraged notions of a world government. This attitude is attributable to the weakness of Mercury, the fourth lord and a natural dual graha, in Pisces, a dual constellation. That Einstein was welcomed with open arms by most countries throughout his life, and enjoyed the comforts of modest homes over much of his life, is due to Mercury's concurrent strengths.

'Einstein was not the kind of man for whom family feelings weighed heavily' (Clark, p. 209). The natural malefic Ketu occupies his second house (family), and the natural malefic Mars aspects it, without the relief of any benefic influences. The Moon, who rules that second house, sits debilitated in a dussthana, bereft of the influence of any benefic, its dispositor in a dussthana as well. These circumstances do not favor family matters. The same situation applies to accumulated money, another indication of the second house. Einstein never did well financially, in spite of his great success as a physicist; he even allocated to his ex-wife the cash award that accompanied the Nobel Prize several years before he actually received it.

The afflictions to his second house extended to his speech as well. The debilitation of Mercury, the natural significator of speech, contributed to this situation, as did his sequence of childhood dashas. 'The one feature of his childhood about which there appears to be no doubt is the lateness with which he learned to speak. Even at the age of nine he was not fluent' (Clark, p. 27). Yet he went on to become a prominent speaker and lecturer, predominantly because of his Saraswati Yoga, which can both make one a savant and contribute to oratorical ability. As usual, both results occurred, they did not cancel out.

We have already seen how Einstein's fifth house promoted his intelligence. The fifth house also represents children, and indeed Einstein had two sons. This is rather perplexing, since the fifth lord Venus, a female-gender graha, sits exalted in the tenth house in Pisces, a female rashi, and in the female nakshatra of Revati. Though this situation should ordinarily give daughters, it is modified by two significant factors: the aspect of the male-gender graha Jupiter on the fifth house and, more importantly, the formation of a Malavya Yoga by Venus as lord of the fifth. According to *Phaladipika*, one of the results of Malavya Yoga is that the native 'will have sons', an indication which is greatly emphasized in this chart because Venus owns the fifth house. Later in life, Einstein did gain two step-daughters through his second marriage, which confirmed the validity of both the 'female graha in female rashi and female nakshatra' principle and the 'foster care' indication of Revati nakshatra.

Einstein's sixth house is afflicted both by the presence there of the debilitated Moon and by the position of the sixth lord in the evil eighth house conjoined with the malefic Rahu. Yet the sixth lord is also strong, by virtue of being exalted. Remember that 'when a trik lord occupies a trik house some of its desirable implications will be suppressed, and some of its undesirable implications may be enhanced'. A trik lord who occupies a bad house will cause any house he owns to suffer. One of the matters ruled by the sixth house is enemies. Most people desire to have none, but when the sixth lord occupies a trik house, enemies may be enhanced. With Einstein this took the form, at least partly, of his differences with the Nazis, which occurred mainly during the planetary periods of Moon, Mars and Rahu. Because Mars is exalted, these enemies were powerful; because the sixth lord is Mars, they were bellicose.

Einstein had two marriages. The first, which lasted sixteen years, was marred by total incompatibility. The second lasted from 1919 until his wife's death in 1936. Einstein's seventh house is aspected by the malefic Saturn, who is also lord of the eighth and who conjoins Venus, the natural significator of marriage and spouse. The seventh lord, Jupiter, is hemmed by malefics, and the fourth, eighth and twelve houses from the seventh are occupied by malefics. Last but by no means least, the lord of the seventh occupies Dhanishtha nakshatra, which is known to indicate marital discord.

DASHAS AND BHUKTIS Einstein's first dasha was the nine-year remainder of the Mercury period into which he was born. We can be sure that Mercury's debility is not totally canceled in his chart for a number of reasons: he did not learn to speak clearly during these nine years, and he was intimidated by school and learning. Within a year of his birth his family moved, due to financial duress, and during this same first year his father lost his businesses to bankruptcy (Mercury rules the eighth house of bankruptcy when counted from the ninth house of father, and occupies the second house of money when counted from that ninth house). This is a good example of the value of rotating the horoscope. His family's circumstances finally did improve later in this period, because of the Neecha Bhanga Raja Yoga and the other desirable yogas in which Mercury participates. Because Einstein was too young to manage his own affairs, the results of these good combinations accrued to his protectors.

Ketu held sway in Einstein's life from age nine to age sixteen. This dasha also caused problems for his education, because Ketu as a natural malefic occupies the second house of classical education, whose dispositor Moon is debilitated in a dussthana. Ketu like

Mercury damaged his protectors' finances, and his father's business failed again.

During his Venus Maha Dasha, which extended from age 16 to age 36, Einstein's educational life finally improved, since Venus aspects the fourth house in its capacity as a natural benefic and also conjoins the fourth lord. It was during the dasha of Venus that he obtained academic credentials, by way of a scientific paper that barely earned him a doctorate at the age of 26. Because Venus creates a Malavya Yoga in the tenth house as lord of the fifth and tenth bhavas, the Venus Dasha caused him to think more about his life work, and gave him some limited recognition as a free-thinking physicist. It also brought him children and marriage.

The Sun's Maha Dasha brought Einstein more fame, since the Sun occupies the tenth bhava of fame with directional strength as the natural significator of fame and as the ruler of the third house (mind). During these six years he produced some of his most brilliant work. But only during the planetary period of the Moon did he win the Nobel Prize, during the sub-period of Mars.

The Moon's grand results are difficult to explain, since it lies debilitated in the sixth house. The Moon is subject to Neecha Bhanga, no doubt, because its dispositor is exalted, but there is no Neecha Bhanga Raja Yoga, because both the Moon and its dispositor Mars occupy trik houses from the lagna. The award of the Nobel Prize during the Moon's period is thus even more difficult to explain when we consider that it happened during the sub-period of Mars. Jyotish is merely a model of reality, which reflects many but not all aspects of reality in a neatly predictable package. Too many astrologers, on finding a certain event inexplicable through a horoscope, ignore the many events that do fit and proclaim the chart to be wrong. Not everything in life is explainable based simply on the principles used in this book.

The Moon independently gave Einstein concern over enemies, in the form of the rising specter of Nazism. This concern continued during his Mars and Rahu Maha Dashas, since all three grahas have strong associations with the sixth house of enemies in his chart. His death occurred in April 1955 during the planetary period of Rahu–Moon. Rahu, who occupies Einstein's eighth house (death), will in part give the results of Mars, since Rahu conjoins Mars, who is strong by being exalted. Bhukti lord Moon is debilitated, and is disposed by Mars, who occupies the eighth house. When the bhukti of a debilitated graha who occupies a dussthana occurs during the dasha of a malefic who also tenants a dussthana, serious trouble is very likely. This was reinforced by the fact that at the time of death Rahu had returned by transit to its natal place, thereby reactivating its death-house position.

FURTHERMORE It is precisely because people are always performing karmas that the natal chart is not always an accurate guide for everything that happens in life. Horary charts, omens and *ishta devatas* can help indicate results which the natal chart fails to provide. Since these investigations can also be performed in hindsight, we decided to check the *prashna* (horary) chart for the moment that this problem of Mars's fitness to deliver a Nobel Prize during Einstein's Moon–Mars period occurred to us. In that prashna on that Tuesday (the day of Mars) Mars occupied the lagna in Scorpio, forming a Ruchaka Yoga from all three lagnas. The Full Moon sat in the seventh house exalted, so that the Moon and Mars created a powerful Chandra–Mangala yoga. Mars and Moon were also participants in a Dharma Karma Adhipati Yoga, and both grahas influenced the Sun, the lord of the tenth house. Sun, Moon and Mars are mutual friends. Finally, and amazingly, Mars was the operating dasha lord in the prashna chart.

A prashna of this brilliance suggests (at least in hindsight) that the karma indicated at birth by the presence of both the Moon and Mars in dussthanas had been altered in some way, either by some Kriyamana Karma that Einstein had himself performed, or by grace. Had Einstein consulted a jyotishi prior to or during his Moon–Mars period, perhaps this alteration could have been detected in foresight.

RAMAKRISHNA PARAMAHAMSA

Birth Data: 18 Feb. 1836 6:23 A.M. LMT
Hooghly, India

	Positions	*Day:* Wednesday
LG	3°AQ 12'	*Yoga:* Siddha
SU	6°AQ 53'	
MO	22°AQ 04'	*Tithi:* Dvitiya of Shukla
MA	22°CP 15'	Paksha
ME	15°AQ 08'R	*Karana:* Balava
JU	14°GE 33'R	
VE	9°PI 04'	*Nakshatra:* Purva
SA	13°LI 41'R	Bhadrapada
RA	2°TA 54'	
KE	2°SC 54'	

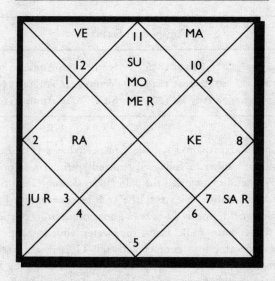

Rashi Chart

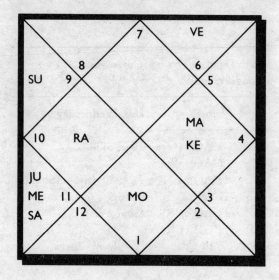

Navamsha Chart

Vimshottari Dasha

Jupiter	18 Feb. 1836	Ketu	29 August 1885
Saturn	29 August 1849	Venus	29 August 1892
Mercury	29 August 1868	Sun	29 August 1912

Ramakrishna Paramahamsa is widely respected as a genuine mystic of the highest caliber, a fully self-realized spiritual master. Indian saints are sometimes awarded the title *Paramahamsa* (Great Swan) in honor of their ability to extract the true essence of life from the dross of the world, just as a *hamsa* (a goose or swan) is purported to be able to separate milk from any water added to it. Almost everyone who came into contact with this Great Swan was struck by his simplicity, wisdom and spiritual ecstasy. His legacy lives on in the West in the form of the Vedanta Society, which has for almost a century educated people in the philosophies of India. His foremost disciple, Swami Vivekananda, is generally regarded as being the first person to bring India's spirituality to the West.

Although Ramakrishna was born in a time and culture when modern timekeeping was not common, his birthtime is probably reliable on three counts: first, the poor but traditional Brahmana family into which he was born probably used Jyotish for ritual purposes at the very least. Secondly, his horoscope has been researched by many competent jyotishis who have found no need to question its authenticity. Thirdly, Ramakrishna's life, as reflected in his birth chart, is a marvelous validation of many of the principles of Jyotish, as it should be for someone who showed such great capacity for attunement with the divine.

YOGAS Like Yogananda, the great renunciate Ramakrishna had a Pravrajya Yoga in his birthchart, for in his navamsha the Moon occupies a sign of Mars and is aspected by Saturn. This combination is particularly strong because all the participating planets occupy good houses in the navamsha. In addition, Ramakrishna's chart possesses two other almost completely formed spiritual yogas (*Shrinatha Yoga* and *Virinchi Yoga*; see *Phaladipika* 6:28–31) that in our opinion added to his spiritual success.

The Pravrajya Yogas in Ramakrishna's horoscope are complemented by an extraordinary array of other yogas. These include a Shasha Yoga, a Dharma Karma Adhipati Yoga, a Buddhaditya Yoga, a Saraswati Yoga, a Durudhara Yoga, an Ubhayachari Yoga, and a host of more common yogas, including Chamara, Dhenu and Chatra. The Shasha Yoga created by the exalted Saturn in the ninth bhava recurs, as do all the other yogas in this chart, from all three lagnas, since all three lagnas are in Aquarius. This particular Shasha Yoga is very powerful because Saturn:

(a) occupies Yuva Avastha, the best of the avasthas;
(b) is exceptionally strengthened because its dispositor Venus is also exalted;
(c) occupies Aquarius, its *mulatrikona*, in the navamsha;
(d) is supported by the aspect of the natural benefic Jupiter, who acts exclusively as a benefic in this chart because it does not own any malefic bhavas;

(e) is retrograde;
(f) is above the horizon (planets in the visible portion of the sky tend to show their results better than those in the invisible part of the celestial sphere below the horizon); and, most importantly,
(g) creates this very powerful Shasha Yoga as lord of all three lagnas.

Some suggest that an exalted but retrograde planet gives the net effect of a debilitated planet, but this chart provides ample evidence to the contrary, for the exalted but retrograde Saturn gave immensely powerful results. In this horoscope Saturn (renunciate tendencies) is the lord of the ascendant (general characteristics, including all-round success in life and renown) and of the twelfth bhava (renunciation, moksha), and it sits exalted in the ninth bhava (dharma, religion, higher knowledge). These indications combined in a potent confluence with the Pravrajya Yogas to make Ramakrishna a king among yogis.

When we contrast this yoga with Marilyn Monroe's Shasha Yoga, which also gave her fame, we see that one of the meanings quoted for the yoga in her case was 'wicked in disposition . . . intrigues with women (or men) not his (her) own . . .' This meaning did not apply to Ramakrishna's life at all, partly because of the Pravrajya Yogas, which are conspicuously absent in Monroe's chart, partly because of the different planets and houses activated in the two charts, and partly because of the condition of the grahas thus activated.

In Monroe's chart Saturn owns the seventh bhava (desire) and the eighth bhava (infamous activities, including brazen sex), and occupies the fourth bhava (morals). We choose 'desire', 'infamous activities' and 'morals' from among the many meanings of those bhavas because these choices reflect the influence of Venus, who aspects Saturn. Saturn does receive the aspect of Jupiter as well, as in Ramakrishna's chart, but Monroe's Jupiter is not as strong as it is in Ramakrishna's chart, where it is strengthened by being retrograde, by occupying Yuva Avastha, by occupying a kona, and by failing to own a dussthana. In Monroe's chart, Saturn occupies a deadly avastha, owns the nefarious eighth bhava, and is aspected by a tainted Jupiter.

The predominant influences on all three of Ramakrishna's lagnas are all Sattvic grahas: the Sun and Moon occupy all three lagnas, and a strong and unblemished Jupiter powerfully influences all three lagnas and their lord. In Monroe's chart, Saturn influences both the ascendant and the lord of her Sun Lagna, and both of the latter are without the moral influence of Jupiter. Saturn can, by its occupation of a rashi of Venus in both charts, create some concern over the native's morality. This concern in Ramakrishna's chart, already alleviated by the foregoing considerations, becomes even less of a concern when we see that Venus has become particularly benefic. Venus owns two good bhavas (being the Raja Yoga Karaka for all three of his lagnas) and occupies a rashi owned by the noble-minded Jupiter. In Monroe's chart, this same dispositor of Saturn occupies a rashi of Mars, whence it aspects Saturn reciprocally as lord of another bhava of desire (the eleventh).

Ramakrishna's Saraswati Yoga is extremely powerful and noteworthy, since the grahas who create it – Venus, Jupiter and Mercury – are all powerful in the second bhava, a kona and a kendra respectively. Mercury is strong by directional strength and by being retrograde, Jupiter is strong by retrogression, and Venus is strong by being exalted. A Saraswati Yoga suggests by its name that the goddess of learning will make herself available to the native; and Ramakrishna, although simple and humble, was sought out by the most educated pundits of his time for commentary on thorny points of philosophy. Einstein also possessed a Saraswati Yoga, but it was not quite as powerful as Ramakrishna's, due mainly to Mercury's debility.

The Durudhara and Ubhayachari Yogas, which occur frequently in horoscopes, assume importance only when they support other, more powerful combinations. In Ramakrishna's chart, the Durudhara Yoga created by Venus occupying the second house and Mars the twelfth house from the Moon is noteworthy because the exalted Venus as lord of the ninth bhava will strengthen the native's dharma, religion and higher knowledge and, as lord of the fourth bhava, will strengthen morality. Because Venus occupies the second house from the lagna, it gave Ramakrishna musical ability and the capacity to speak sweetly and kindly. It also gave him a love of classical learning, especially since it also participates in a Saraswati Yoga. Venus's involvement in other yogas causes its presence to infuse the Durudhara Yoga with greater energy, and vice versa, according to the principle that a graha gains strength as it participates in yogas.

Ubhayachari Yoga, which is formed by Venus in the second and Mars in the twelfth houses as counted from the Sun, further strengthens Venus. Although Mars's exaltation makes both this and the Durudhara Yoga valuable, Mars was less influential in Ramakrishna's life than was Venus because Mars does not participate in any other major yogas in the chart. The exalted Mars does, however, activate the twelfth bhava of moksha, thus reinforcing the effects promised by the exaltation and the Shasha Yoga of the twelfth lord (who also happens to rule the lagna, which personalizes the effect). It is because of the presence of the Pravrajya Yogas and the other strong spiritual themes in his horoscope that we do not interpret these combinations in typically mundane ways. These spiritual influences caused, for example, Venus's strength as fourth lord to appear in his life as strong moral development instead of as a Rolls Royce, and caused Mars's strength in the twelfth house to contribute to moksha and not to highly speculative investments in real estate.

Among the twenty-four Yogas referred to in Chapter Ten, the auspicious yoga for the ascendant known as *Chamara Yoga* is created because the first house is aspected by the powerfully benefic Jupiter, while its lord Saturn is strongly situated in a kona. *Phaladipika* 6:45 says of this combination, 'the person ... will every day grow in importance like the waxing moon, and will be virtuous. He becomes famous, a leader of men, long-lived, and a store-house of prosperity.' All applied literally to Ramakrishna, except that he was not long-lived, a point we address below. The Dhenu Yoga, formed in his chart by the exalted Venus in the second house and the second lord in a kona (neither of them influenced by any malefic), focuses mainly on wealth. The renunciate yogas in his chart gave him a total lack of interest in money; he could easily have had the world at his feet and amassed a fortune from his devotees, had his nature been different.

The Budhaditya Yoga may have helped Ramakrishna to live up to his title of *paramahamsa*, for it gave him an extraordinary ability to discern both pragmatic and philosophical situations accurately. While some mainly associate this yoga with parrot-like intelligence or academic ability, in Ramakrishna's chart it highlights the quality of insightful judgement which is the very function of *buddhi* (cosmic discernment). Ramakrishna's Budhaditya Yoga is influential because it occurs from both the ascendant and the Chandra lagna, with Mercury as the fifth lord being strong in both lagnas due to retrogression and to directional strength. Mercury is also vargottama and, because it owns (in addition to the fifth house) the eighth house of secrets, it causes this insight to be especially extended to hidden, occult wisdom. This yoga is strongly supported by the powerful aspect of Jupiter, the planet of wisdom, from the fifth house. While Budhaditya Yoga is not usually counted from the Sun Lagna, it is significant here because Mercury is the fifth lord for that lagna.

THE LAGNA AND BHAVAS Aquarius, the lagna in Ramakrishna's chart, represents the gathering of knowledge, which in Ramakrishna's case was spiritual knowledge. He did not place this knowledge into a materialistic or scientific framework, as Aquarians often do, because of Jupiter's influence on all three lagnas and their lords. One indication of Aquarius that did surface unmodified was his lack of interest in money. He remained aloof from material gain, even when some of his acquaintances turned him and his spiritual charisma into profitable enterprises. While this exceptional human being never cultivated friendships, clubs or societies in their prosaic sense, he certainly possessed an affinity for people. During most of his adult life he had little privacy, for he was surrounded by seekers and disciples, by the curious, and by the desperate. His behavior was highly idiosyncratic; he fell frequently and unpredictably into spiritual trances without regard to what was happening around him.

The lagna falls in that part of Aquarius which contains Dhanishtha and, like the Vasus, who are Dhanishtha's deities, Ramakrishna was 'good, superb and beneficent'. Many other characteristics also fit well with the indications of Dhanishtha. He exhibited a great capacity for charity, for he kept virtually nothing for himself. He enjoyed an innate ability to influence others. He was a temple priest who recited rhythmical incantations and prayers for much of his adult life, and so loved music that he would often movingly invoke the divine through song. Marriage can be disturbed by Dhanishtha, and his relationship with his wife was in fact unique, as we shall see.

Because Saturn, the lord of Ramakrishna's lagna, occupies Swati, many of Swati's meanings also apply to him. In particular, he was an ascetic engaged in strong devotional practices. This signification especially came to the fore because the ascetically inclined Saturn rules the lagna. The luxury-loving Venus as lagna lord in Swati would yield a quite different sort of interpretation.

All three of Ramakrishna's lagnas fall in Aquarius, which renders many of the meanings of the ascendant and the nakshatra occupied by the ascendant lord particularly strong. More significantly, all planetary placements in such a chart are totally aligned. This powerfully aligns soul, mind and body, which causes speech, thought and action always to tend to function in harmony. All three lagnas become exceptionally strong in Ramakrishna's horoscope because Saturn, the lord of all three, is exalted in the auspicious ninth bhava, where it is not hampered by the association or aspect of any malefic. Saturn's dispositor Venus is also exalted, which strengthens Saturn further, particularly because Venus is the Raja Yoga Karaka for all three lagnas. Most significantly, Saturn is aspected by the strong, benevolent Jupiter. Jupiter's aspect on all three lagnas and on their lord here redirected into the spiritual realm the typical Aquarian bent for materialistic or scientific knowledge.

While it is difficult to interpret mundane matters in the life of someone who has renounced the world, mundane karmas continue to play themselves out in every human being's life, even if the renunciate does not self-identify with those karmas. The analysis of the bhavas in Ramakrishna's chart is made even more difficult by the lack of historical fact regarding his personal history, since such information was never emphasized by those who documented his remarkable life.

We do know that Ramakrishna preferred to teach through parables. He was a gifted storyteller and an inspired singer of devotional songs because his second bhava contains a totally unafflicted exalted

Venus, who participates in many yogas. The second lord Jupiter, the planet of oratory, is also strong and unafflicted, and the Saraswati Yoga enhances these second-house strengths, which recur from all the lagnas.

Ramakrishna had little formal education and had no interest in academics, in part because the debilitated Rahu lies in his fourth bhava. While fourth lord Venus is exalted in the second house, which would suggest education, the education planets Mercury and Jupiter fail to influence the fourth bhava, and so fail to support this interpretation. This exaltation of the fourth lord is more likely to have produced exalted happiness, for example, which the fourth bhava also represents.

Ramakrishna's chart shows the beneficial fifth-house combination called *Chatra Yoga*, which is supposed to give keen wit, intelligence, an ability to give good advice, and also children (all fifth-house matters). The Pravrajya Yogas make children unlikely, an interpretation which is compounded by the presence of the significator of children in the house of children (according to Principle of Interpretation 5). Note also that the fifth bhava falls in Gemini, a barren rashi whose lord Mercury is a neuter among the grahas. In this chart Mercury occupies the semi-fruitful rashi Aquarius, and the neuter nakshatra Shatabhisha. Perhaps Shatabhisha's symbol, an empty circle, alludes here to zero children, given the other confluent factors which do not support offspring.

Students or disciples are often more appropriate fifth-house significations for a spiritual teacher than are children, and Ramakrishna did have spiritual children, whom he loved as intensely as any mother ever loved her child. The foremost among Ramakrishna's many disciples was Swami Vivekananda, who is a national hero in India for having reclaimed the dignity of Hindu philosophy in the eyes of the world. Vivekananda stole the show in 1893 at the World Parliament of Religions in Chicago. His lecture at this event propelled him to world fame almost overnight, from which vantage he used his razor-sharp mind for the rest of his short life to broadcast to the world the tenets of the Eternal Faith.

If we now examine Ramakrishna's fifth bhava from the viewpoint of disciples, the strong natural benefic Jupiter, who is literally 'the guru', occupies the fifth house, while fifth lord Mercury sits in the lagna retrograde and vargottama, with directional strength. This is precisely the combination that creates Chatra Yoga, which is also said to produce powerful disciples; in fact, another meaning for Chatra is 'pupil'. That Ramakrishna would produce a brilliant disciple is suggested by Jupiter and Mercury, the two mental and educational planets which form the Chatra Yoga. They are particularly strong for this purpose because they reinforce one another, since Jupiter occupies a rashi of Mercury while also aspecting Mercury. This sort of strong reciprocal relationship is called in Sanskrit *sambandha*.

On rotating the horoscope to make Gemini, Ramakrishna's fifth house, into the ascendant of the disciple's chart thus created, we find Mercury, lagna lord of this new chart, involved in a powerful Budhaditya Yoga in the ninth bhava. The strength of Mercury in the ninth house suggests that this disciple would travel the world, while Saturn, the lord of the ninth bhava in the student's chart, is exalted in the ninth from that ninth (see *Bhavat Bhavam* in Chapter Six). Because of all these influences we feel justified in interpreting Shatabhisha's symbol of an empty circle as a reflection of Vivekananda's dedication to the Formless Absolute, which is sometimes called *shunya* (literally, 'zero').

Despite being a life-long renunciate and celibate, Ramakrishna bowed to cultural convention sufficiently to marry. But his marriage was never consummated, and his wife treated him as her guru, not her husband. They remained 'married' in this way throughout their lives. In Ramakrishna's chart, the seventh lord aspects the seventh bhava, which is always a desirable influence, and that seventh lord is in turn aspected by the powerfully benefic Jupiter. Yet it is also aspected by the lord of the sixth house who, being the Moon, is not tempered in its malefic house rulership by simultaneously owning a beneficial house. The seventh bhava is also aspected by the powerful natural malefic Mars, and the lord of the seventh house occupies the neuter nakshatra Shatabhisha, the 'empty circle'. Moreover, in the navamsha, the subchart which represents marriage, the lagna is ruled by Venus, who occupies in the navamsha the twelfth house of seclusion in Virgo, the virginal rashi.

Mixed results in the seventh house are therefore expected, particularly because the Pravrajya Yogas make marriage unlikely from the start. Few jyotishis are likely to have foreseen the unusual circumstances surrounding his marriage, though a gifted Tantric jyotishi with some *siddhi* (superhuman ability) might in a moment of inspiration have been able to do so. No matter how perfectly we may be able to engineer Jyotish's principles, they must always be empowered by the consciousness of the jyotishi.

The spiritual bhavas of Ramakrishna's chart (the ninth and twelfth) dominated much of his life. These two houses are really houses of *potential* spirituality; they take on this meaning only when the general tenor of the horoscope suggests a spiritual theme, as for example when Pravrajya Yogas exist. Otherwise, these two houses usually represent more prosaic matters. In Ramakrishna's case, auspicious spiritual karmas of a fixed nature prevailed for a variety of reasons. Two of these are that the ninth bhava contains the exalted lagna lord Saturn, whose dispositor is also exalted; and that the twelfth house contains an exalted planet whose dispositor is also exalted in, of all places, the ninth house.

When a graha's body (*deha*) and soul (*jiva*) are both so mighty, superlative results for the matters of the houses involved become inevitable, particularly because none of the planets involved is weakened by the influence of malefics, and because Saturn is supported by the strong aspect of the exclusively benefic Jupiter. Because striking combinations like these, desirable or undesirable, display karma which is clearly fixed, we can confidently assert that Ramakrishna was born ripe to experience his spiritual insights.

Although we might also conclude that his powerful ninth house should have given Ramakrishna a great deal of foreign travel, he never left India. The main reason for this state of affairs is probably that all three of his lagnas occupy a fixed rashi (Aquarius), which gave a fixity to his life. The travel effect was felt closer to home, however, in that he made long-distance (for that era, in which travel was often difficult) pilgrimages, a variety of travel which is most appropriate both for the ninth house itself and for the overall spiritual nature of his horoscope.

DASHAS AND BHUKTIS Ramakrishna was born with some 13 years

of his Jupiter Maha Dasha remaining to be enjoyed. It was during this cycle that he began to have strong spiritual experiences, since the strong and spiritually inclined benefic Jupiter in the fifth bhava aspects all three lagnas as well as lagna lord Saturn and the ninth bhava. Even as a young child the most innocuous events in his life, like watching cranes fly through a cloudy sky, would bring on mystical experiences.

It was during the 19 years of his Saturn Maha Dasha, from age 13 to 32, that he enjoyed his peak spiritual experiences. This was to be expected, given the strong placement of Saturn for spiritual matters in the ninth bhava. He then experienced his Mercury dasha until the age of 49. Mercury as lord of the fifth bhava in the lagna for all three ascendants while retrograde and with directional strength, and as a participant in various yogas, suggests accurately that his religious experiences would continue. This chart illustrates beautifully how important it is to enjoy a beneficial dasha at the appropriate time in one's life.

One interesting verification of our conclusion that Ramakrishna was born with Dridha Karma for spiritual life occurred during his Saturn Maha Dasha. In late 1864 Ramakrishna met one of his teachers, Tota Puri, who instructed him in Advaita Vedanta and in the practice of formless ecstasy (*nirvikalpa samadhi*), a state that eludes many aspirants even after a lifetime of keen practice. Ramakrishna achieved this state in one day, for he was a spiritual prodigy, just as Mozart was a musical prodigy. The strong spiritual placement of the planet Saturn enables us to predict that such results would be enjoyed during his Saturn Maha Dasha.

Ramakrishna actually attained to *nirvikalpa samadhi* during his Saturn–Rahu period. Rahu as a bhukti lord will mainly give the effects of its dispositor Venus, the exalted lord of the ninth bhava who is the strongest of the grahas which influence Rahu. Bhukti lord Rahu was transiting dasha lord Saturn's natal position in the ninth bhava at the time of this experience, and Saturn himself had returned to its exalted natal position to reinforce by transit what he had promised natally. During the Saturn–Jupiter period Ramakrishna experienced further blissful states, to whose influence he often succumbed in swoons of spiritual ecstasy.

That these crowning achievements occurred during the dasha of a malefic proves that any graha may give superlatively good or bad results in many areas of life, depending on the particular horoscope. Yet because Saturn's nature remains unchanged it indicated, by being a natural malefic in the ninth bhava of religion, certain heterodox tendencies in Ramakrishna's life. While born a traditional Brahmana, he refused to accept Brahmanic dogma unquestioningly. Concluding that all paths lead to God, during one phase of his life he offended some of the conservative Hindus of his day by temporarily adopting Islamic and Christian mystical disciplines, to see if they would lead him to God. They did.

FURTHERMORE The eighth house in Ramakrishna's chart requires some attention. While many classical authorities aver that a strong lagna and lagna lord create longevity, they also suggest that for longevity the lagna should not be afflicted by the lord of the eighth, and that ideally the lord of the lagna and the lord of the eighth should be of equal strength. Although the lagna and its lord are very strong in this chart, all of the lagnas are simultaneously afflicted by the presence of Mercury, the eighth lord. Also the lagna lord is stronger than the eighth lord in all three lagnas. This is one of the factors that contributed to Ramakrishna's relatively early death at the age of 50.

Let us now consider, as a final contributor to the confluence of spiritual placements in his chart, that Ramakrishna was born in the soli-lunar yoga called *Siddha* ('Accomplished') *Yoga*, which gives an accommodating personality, a pleasant nature and an interest in ritual and spirituality. Although the soli-lunar Yogas are a general interpretation, in Ramakrishna's chart this general interpretation enhances those other combinations which promised great spirituality. Those who know Jyotish in its larger context of Indian spirituality know that the term *siddha* is also used to refer to a spiritual adept, and they would work this connection into the interpretation. They would not, however, try to work in the attributes of *Dvitiya Tithi*, under which Ramakrishna was born, for none of them seems to apply to him. This is presumably because all the other influences in his chart overpower this one less-than-salutary factor.

ANAÏS NIN

Birth Data: 21 Feb. 1903 8:35 P.M., L.M.T.
Neuilly-sur-Seine, France

	Positions	Day: Saturday
LG	4°VI 18′	Yoga: Vajra
SU	9°AQ 32′	
MO	7°SA 49′	Tithi: Dashami of
MA	23°VI 43′R	Krishna Paksha
ME	13°CP 32′	Karana: Vishti
JU	7°AQ 51′	
VE	29°AQ 42′	Nakshatra: Mula
SA	11°CA 19′	
RA	25°VI 55′	
KE	25°PI 55′	

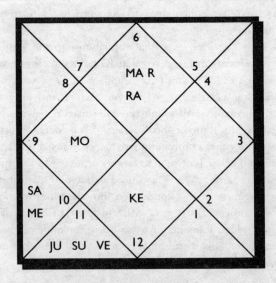

Rashi Chart

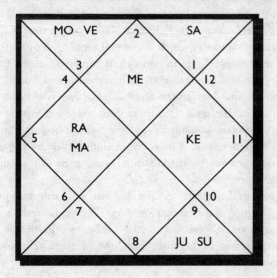

Navamsha Chart

Vimshottari Dasha

Ketu	21 Feb. 1903	Moon	14 Jan. 1932
Venus	14 Jan. 1906	Mars	14 Jan. 1942
Sun	14 Jan.1926	Rahu	14 Jan. 1949

Anaïs Nin enjoyed a certain amount of fame and notoriety by breaking taboos as a writer in the years that followed the Victorian era. She dealt primarily with issues of a sexual nature which confronted the women of her time. Kate Millett called Nin's famous and voluminous *Diary* 'the first real portrait of the artist as a woman'. Nin was world famous for her torrid love affairs and interactions with other notable personages of her day, including Henry Miller. Though vulnerable, she always remained her own person, a courageous woman who refused to conform, who followed her truth wherever it took her.

YOGAS The salient yogas in Nin's chart are Shasha Yoga, Sunapha Yoga, Voshi Yoga, *four* Dharma Karma Adhipati Yogas, a Parvata Yoga, a Vasumat Yoga, an Ashubha Mala Yoga, a near Kala Sarpa Yoga, and Kuja Dosha (which is not technically a Yoga). By being involved in multiple yogas in Nin's chart Saturn gains the same sort of prominence and strength that Mercury gains in Einstein's chart. Here Saturn is involved in the Shasha, Sunapha, Voshi and Parvata Yogas, and in the two important and strong Dharma Karma Adhipati Yogas (the combination of the lords of houses 1 and 5 and 10 and 5). Mercury, who is involved in almost as many yogas in this chart, is less influential than Saturn because Saturn occupies his own rashi.

These two grahas effectively divided Nin's life into two portions: suffering (Saturn) and writing (Mercury). Factoring in the meanings of the bhavas owned and occupied by these two grahas provides a further summation of her life: first lord Mercury (characteristics, success, position in society) who is also tenth lord (career) occupies the fifth bhava (poetry, books and authorship, which happen to be some of Mercury's indications) conjoined with fifth lord Saturn. Such a yoga logically provides a successful career in writing with a prominent position in society on this account.

The Shasha Yoga is powerful, even though it does not recur from other lagnas, because Saturn is unafflicted by any malefic and occupies Yuva Avastha, its most powerful avastha. Most importantly, though, its power comes from its simultaneous participation in powerful Sunapha and Voshi Yogas which occur in its own rashi, in good houses from the lagna. These solar and lunar yogas also strengthen Saturn's participation in the two important Dharma Karma Adhipati Yogas formed by Saturn and Mercury, particularly because both grahas are friendly to each other and to the lagna lord, and are strong by rashi and bhava. Such yogas deliver their promise.

The two other Dharma Karma Adhipati Yogas, which are formed by Jupiter and Venus as lords of bhavas 4 and 9 and 7 and 9, are only secondary in this chart because they occur in the evil sixth house and because they are not as strong by rashi as are the similar yogas formed by Saturn and Mercury. Moreover, Venus, who is in

Mrita Avastha, is the enemy of Jupiter, who is extremely combust. Had these yogas alone occurred in her chart, they would have resulted in little more than dreams or pretensions of significance.

The Parvata Yoga is, however, very strong, because lagna lord Mercury is very strong (it participates in numerous good yogas, occupies the auspicious fifth bhava, and sits in Yuva Avastha), dispositor Saturn is very strong (see above), and Mercury and Saturn are friendly to each other and to the lagna lord. Vasumat Yoga occurs when all benefics tenant upachaya houses. Both Moon (who is waning) and Mercury (who is conjoined with Saturn) become malefic in this chart, which leaves Jupiter and Venus, who both occupy the sixth bhava, as the sole benefics. This yoga recurs from the Moon Lagna, where they occupy the third bhava. Because, as we have seen, Jupiter and Venus are weak, this yoga is only a background factor, which helps to explain why she was not materially rich for most of her life, as Vasumat Yoga suggests she should be.

But Jupiter and Venus also participate in Ashubha Mala Yoga (all benefics in dussthanas), and this yoga and its undesirable meanings become very powerful precisely because of their weakness, since they are the only participants in this yoga. Ashubha Mala Yoga's implications, particularly 'great difficulties in life', became therefore greatly enhanced in Nin's life. She experienced serious family dysfunction, including incest with her father, and suffered the trauma of a stillbirth. She evinced an interest in lesbianism, bisexuality and other unconventional sexual practices during an era when these subjects could not be mentioned, much less pursued. Once again, not even a large pile of powerful yogas can cancel the results promised by the unfavorable yogas in a horoscope.

Nin's Kuja Dosha is strong because it recurs from the ascendant, the Sun Lagna, and Venus, because it is in the eighth house away from the Sun and from Venus (and therefore particularly virulent), and because Mars is already seriously afflicted by being within two degrees of Rahu. Her marriage, to Hugo Guiler, on 3 March 1923 when she was 20 (well below the Kuja Dosha upper limit of age 28 to 30) predictably produced both great unhappiness and prolonged separations which were tantamount to divorce, as is typical for this combination. Other factors, including the condition of the seventh bhava, reinforced this effect.

In Nin's chart, Mars falls outside the nodal axis by a mere 2°. This proximity allows us to count this combination as a Kala Sarpa Yoga, especially since both sides of the nodal axis are afflicted by natural malefics without the modification of benefics. This 'deemed to be' Kala Sarpa Yoga also added to her troubles, particularly in the realms of the first and seventh bhavas, where the Kala Sarpa occurs. She obsessed on her role (first bhava) in relationships (seventh bhava), probably for the good reason of her traumatic childhood (first bhava) and an unusual marriage (seventh bhava), which included numerous extra-marital liaisons. Mars, who conjoins the Kala Sarpa at one end, rules the eighth bhava of cold sexuality. The ability to relax the stringent requirements of a yoga where the context of the chart merits it comes with experience.

THE LAGNA AND BHAVAS Virgo, her lagna, is a dual sign ruled by the dual planet Mercury. Some of the salient characteristics of a Virgo lagna which applied in her life were:

- 'always thinking something unusual' – a condition enhanced because Rahu, who often causes contrary behavior (because it moves in a direction opposite to that of the other planets), occupies the lagna in the company of the truculent Mars, who is erratic because of being retrograde.
- 'skill centered around detail' – she kept a voluminous and detailed diary which had grown to 250 volumes by the time it was purchased by UCLA toward the end of her life.
- 'love of classical culture and education' – she loved classical literature.
- 'propensity for self-analysis' – a major theme in her diaries. She was psychoanalyzed by some of the most famous and progressive psychoanalysts of her day. 'Art and psychoanalysis became her religion, for it gave her knowledge, which gave her control of her life' (Fitch, p. 6).
- 'a certain lack of skill in worldly matters, even if worldly wise' – a friend, while acknowledging Nin's nymphomania, said, 'I think of her as one of the world's great innocents' (Fitch, pp. 5–6).

· 'a distinct propensity for surgery' – by the time she was ten, Nin had already suffered from appendicitis and peritonitis, both of which required surgery, as well as typhoid fever, which sometimes requires surgery.

· 'does not indicate children, is against children, or has difficulties with children' – she had no offspring and did not want any, a condition supported by the state of her fifth house. Her one pregnancy ended in a stillbirth.

Nin's lagna occupied Hasta nakshatra. One of Hasta's indications which applied most emphatically to her is 'the potential for questionable moral orientation'. This potential was actualized because Hasta is afflicted (it is occupied by Mars, and Mars is conjoined with Rahu). The indication was reinforced by the exclusive influence of the natural malefics Mars and Saturn, who also own trik houses, on her lagna and lagna lord respectively. Mars is the worst graha for a Virgo ascendant, since it is a natural malefic who owns two dussthanas, and Rahu's association worsens Mars even further. There is no modification of any benefic on the ascendant, its lord, or even on Saturn and Mars.

None of the three lagnas is even particularly strong here, since both the Moon and Sun Lagnas are afflicted to a considerable degree. Although the ascendant is afflicted by malefics, its lord does occupy a kona, and it participates in numerous yogas. Saturn as lord of the Sun Lagna also participates in several yogas, but occupies the twelfth house from this lagna. The weakness of Nin's lagnas prevented her from becoming a super-renowned writer like Emily Dickinson or Henry Miller.

The second lord occupies the evil sixth house and is as dead as a doornail, being in Mrita Avastha, since it is in the last degree of an odd rashi. This, combined with the malefic aspect of Saturn on the second house, prevented Nin from ever possessing the large quantities of money with which the good yogas in her chart might have provided her. These factors also encouraged her tendency to tell lies, since the second is also the house of speech. Toward the end of her life she began, however, to become known as a public speaker, which can be attributed partly to the involvement of Mercury, the significator of speech, in several yogas, and partly to the fact that the second lord occupies the sixth house, which is an upachaya house, where things improve.

Nin remembered her mother as domineering. The waning malefic Moon, the significator for the mother, afflicts the fourth bhava of mother. Both the Moon and the fourth bhava are aspected by the domineering and doubly malefic Mars. Jupiter, the fourth lord, is seriously combust, lies in a dussthana, and is hemmed by malefics without any sort of benefic influence. This constitutes a full Kuhu Yoga, whose principal area of affliction will be the mother, since a waning Moon in the fourth house will portend ominous results for the mother. The fourth bhava also represents formal education and the home, and the aforementioned catalog of afflictions also rendered these matters problematic. Nin left high school without a diploma, and never really felt at home in the several countries and several locales she inhabited.

The fifth house contains its lord Saturn, who occupies Shravana nakshatra, which is ruled by Saraswati, the goddess of learning and wisdom. Shravana is strong here because its lord (Moon) occupies a kendra in a friend's sign with *dig bala*. This combination gave her intelligence, which was further enhanced by the conjunction of that fifth lord with Mercury, who also occupies Shravana. Saturn does not inhibit intelligence here because it occupies its own rashi, and because it is conjoined with Mercury. This combination does not bode well for children, though, since Saturn and Mercury are eunuchs who occupy a rashi ruled by the eunuch Saturn. The fifth bhava and lord are also hemmed in by the malefic waning Moon on one side and by the Sun on the other. Jupiter, the significator for progeny, is (as noted above) severely disturbed.

Her seventh bhava is occupied by Ketu and aspected by Mars, and no benefics modify either the seventh bhava or the malefics which afflict it. Seventh lord Jupiter occupies the sixth bhava (a double detriment), is combust, and is hemmed between malefics without benefic modification. Venus, the benefic who is the marriage significator, cannot modify effectively because it is in full Mrita Avastha. Taken together with Kuja Dosha, these indications foretell fixed and unpleasant karmas in the realm of relationships, which, in fact, were numerous and filled with frustrations.

Her relationship with her father was poor. He was a cruel man who, after seducing Nin in her youth, deserted the family, then returned to resume an incestuous relationship with her when she was 30. Venus, the lord of the ninth bhava of father, occupies the sixth bhava in Mrita Avastha. The Sun, the significator for father, also occupies the sixth, where both it and Venus are hemmed by Saturn and Ketu. This is a partial Nirbhagya Yoga, since the aspect of a malefic on the ninth bhava which would complete it is missing. These afflictions to the ninth bhava account for her lack of interest in formal religion.

DASHAS AND BHUKTIS Nin's father deserted the family in 1913. This event would have happened either during the latter portion of Venus–Mars or the initial portion of Venus–Rahu. Planets in the sixth, eighth or twelfth houses from the dasha lord give bad results during their bhuktis if they are also afflicted by malefics. Because Mars and Rahu afflict one another as natural malefics, they are both destined to offer bad results during the Venus Maha Dasha.

To determine in what ninth-house matter to expect these untoward results, we consider that Venus, the ninth lord, conjoins the Sun, which is the significator for the father. When we rotate the birth chart to take as the lagna the rashi in which the dasha lord sits (to read the results of the dasha), Venus still indicates Nin's father, because Venus rules the ninth house in that chart as well. We can then read the father's life from the chart thus created. The two malefics, Mars and Rahu, now occupy the eighth house, which is the twelfth house, the house of loss, to the ninth.

Nin married on 31 March 1923 during her Venus–Mercury period. Although this event seems inexplicable in the birth chart via the series of principles which have been introduced here, it appears as a great likelihood in her navamsha chart, where Venus and Mercury participate in a Parivartana Yoga, which is vastly enhanced by Venus being the lord of the navamsha lagna and Mercury occupying the navamsha lagna. Dasha lord Venus was also exalted in the seventh bhava by transit at the time of the wedding.

Nin's only child was stillborn on 28 August 1934, during her

Moon–Rahu period. Moon sits in the rashi of Jupiter, the significa-tor of children who is combust and hemmed in a dussthana. Rahu in part will give results of its dispositor the neuter Mercury, who occupies the fifth with the neuter Saturn in Saturn's rashi. Although Saturn and Mercury cooperate to produce a good yoga, this combina-tion is not good for pregnancy. Given the previously described natal afflictions for children, the outlook is not good to begin with, and the bleak dasha-bhukti picture guarantees bad results. Moreover, Rahu was transiting Nin's fifth bhava at the time of this mishap.

FURTHERMORE Although in Chapter Four we glossed over the importance of obtaining a numerical value for a graha's strength, we did not mean to suggest that the methods which produce such quantification are valueless. Nin's chart provides an excellent ex-ample of just how valuable the system known as *Shad Bala* (The Six Strengths) can be. *Shad Bala*, which occupies Chapter 27 of the *Brihat Parashara Hora*, is a tried and true method. In Nin's *Shad Bala*, the Moon attains 9.74 *rupas* (the units used in this method), which is by far the greatest strength of any graha in her chart, the next nearest being Saturn, who has 7.49 *rupas*, and the weakest being Mars, who has 5.54 *rupas*. The Moon is therefore almost twice as strong as several of the other grahas in the chart.

This information still requires interpretation, for which we return to the Moon's traditional significations as modified by its position in the birth chart. The Moon, which is the natural significator of the emotional mind, occupies the fourth house of emotions, and is below the horizon in a night birth chart, which creates an inner focus. This made Nin a very emotional woman whose dream-like subjective experiences pack her diary. 'In keeping with the romantic temper that values the individual self as the center of all experience, her diary almost singularly focuses on her and her feelings, which she believes are unique' (Fitch, p. 22). Also, because the Moon rules the eleventh house of friends and associates, Nin went on to have many powerful and famous friends, which we might not have predicted had we simply considered the condition of her eleventh house.

ANONYMOUS

Birth Data: Birth Information
Retained for Privacy

Positions		Day: Monday
LG	7°GE 40'	Yoga: Siddha
SU	10°SA 29'	Tithi: Ekadashi of
MO	17°AR 29'	Shukla Paksha
MA	28°SC 31'	
ME	4°SA 56'R	Karana: Vishti
JU	3°VI 55'	
VE	23°CP 48'	Nakshatra:
SA	14°GE 32'R	Bharani
RA	26°GE 04'	
KE	26°SA 04'	

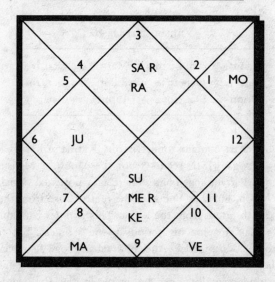

Rashi Chart

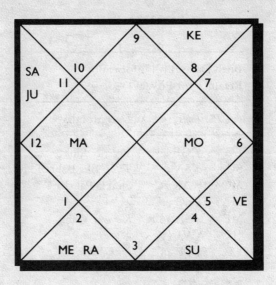

Navamsha Chart

Vimshottari Dasha

Venus	From Birth	Mars	3 Oct. 1974
Sun	3 Oct. 1958	Rahu	2 Oct. 1981
Moon	2 Oct. 1964	Jupiter	3 Oct. 1999

YOGAS This chart contains one Dharma Karma Adhipati Yoga, a
Budhaditya Yoga which recurs from the Moon, a Maha Bhagya
Yoga, and a Parivartana Yoga. There is a potential Amala Yoga
from the Moon, but that Venus in the tenth house from the Moon
is in the eighth house from the lagna. This is not a bankable yoga;
the native may imagine his actions to be stainless, but they are
unlikely to be so in practice. An Ubhayachari Yoga also occurs, but
here neither Venus nor Mars participates in other yogas and, since
both are fundamentally weak by being in the sixth and eighth
houses respectively from the lagna, this yoga is infructuous.

Even if they were strong, however, none of these good yogas would be able to deliver the goods, for a *Yoga Bhanga* also lurks in the chart. It is this: 'Whoever is born in the planetary hour of Mars at a time when Saturn occupies in the horoscope a kendra and is unaspected by any benefic becomes a slave and a beggar.' You can examine this for yourself, if you like. Sunrise at the birthplace on that day, which was a Monday, was 7:28 a.m. If you turn to the table of horas in Chapter Seven, you will clearly see that the hora of Mars would extend from 5:28 p.m. until 6:28 p.m. His birth took place at 5:48 p.m. When we now consider that all the good yogas have been negated, and we factor in the Shakata Yoga, which is caused by the Moon occupying a dussthana as counted from Jupiter, the result is great reversals of fortune in life. Indeed, this person, though born into a fabulously wealthy family, spent much of his adult life in poverty.

Bhanga is an extremely important factor to consider when examining a horoscope which is filled with good yogas, for a bhanga can swiftly bring crashing down the fragile edifice created when interpretation of a birth chart relies too heavily on yogas. But – and this is an important but – simply because the yogas are broken does not mean that the grahas lose their power to exert any kind of effect at all. The grahas will continue to exert their effects, according to the rules of interpretation that we have been outlining, but they will do so only within a limited arena. Such a person will not take the sort of bow on the world stage that is made by another person whose yogas remain unbroken. Also, bhangas are open to some interpretation; in this case, Saturn is made worse by the influence of Rahu and Mars, and no benefic aspects that Saturn, conditions which intensified the bhanga's destructive potential.

THE LAGNA AND BHAVAS The lagna here is Gemini, many of whose theoretical values apply to this man's life: he had a tendency to put his foot in his mouth, was dual-minded about most things in his life, and had very unstable health. His lagna occupied Ardra nakshatra, whose symbol is a teardrop and which is ruled by the storm deity Rudra. He did shed many tears during his misery-filled life, and his stormy mind often projected thunder-like bluster and lightning-like anger on to nearly everyone, including his near and dear ones. Many of his family members felt that he was distinctly ungrateful and malicious, and he showed on occasion a tendency to 'treachery, deception, and lawlessness' in his business and financial dealings.

Not everyone born in Ardra has these qualities; they were greatly emphasized in this case because the lagna is hammered by every malefic in the sky: Saturn and Rahu by occupation, and Mars, Sun, Ketu and Mercury by aspect. Mercury acts as a malefic here because it conjoins Ketu and is aspected by Saturn. This influence is confirmed in its malevolence because the malefics involved are completely unchecked by any benefics, either by conjunction or aspect, and is further worsened because Saturn, Mars and Sun all own dussthanas. Ardra itself is afflicted because it contains the natural malefic Saturn, who is conjoined with the natural malefic Rahu, who occupies Punarvasu. Had Rahu occupied Ardra, which he owns, Ardra would have been strengthened. This man's life experiences clearly showed the cumulative influence of natural malefics when unmitigated by benefics.

All three lagnas here are weak. The weakness of the ascendant is compounded by that of lagna lord Mercury, who is subject to the influence of all the same malefics (except for Mars) as is the lagna. Mercury should gain strength from being retrograde, but this strength is completely swallowed up by the malefic influences, by its position in Bala Avastha, and by its combustion. The Moon Lagna is weak because its lord occupies the eighth house from that lagna. Though Mars, the Moon's dispositor, is strong by virtue of being in its own rashi there, Mars is greatly weakened by being within the last 2° of his rashi. The Sun Lagna, although involved in a Parivartana Yoga, is weak because of the malefic influences of Saturn, Rahu and Ketu, which are unimpeded by any benefic. Mercury and Jupiter, the two planets who participate in the Parivartana Yoga, fail to improve the indications of the Sun Lagna because they both occupy bad avasthas.

As with Marilyn Monroe and Indira Gandhi, this man's first house is configured with the lord of the eighth house, who happens to be Saturn. All other factors being equal, this combination is not desirable for longevity, in this case particularly so since the malefics

Mars and Sun aspect that Saturn, and the malefic Rahu conjoins it. Furthermore, lagna lord Mercury is also afflicted by Saturn. These factors, coupled with the lagna's weakness, greatly reduced his lifespan. He died at the age of 43.

Mars is detrimental to the health of everyone born with a Gemini ascendant, because it rules both the sixth bhava and the sixth from the sixth, and is also the significator for the sixth. Because Mars is one of the afflictors of this weak ascendant, this man suffered through many illnesses and surgeries over his lifetime, including diabetes, four major chest operations, and a near-amputation of one leg. Another meaning of Mars as ruler of the sixth and the sixth from the sixth and karaka of the sixth is enemies. This man was plagued by enemies throughout his life, both directly (through physical violence) and indirectly (via lawsuits).

The native was married twice. His first wife died under mysterious circumstances within a year of the wedding; she may have been poisoned. The second marriage, which lasted a mere six years and ended with his death, was marred by periodic violent arguments. Both wives were from cultures which were foreign to his, which was a source of great unrest in his family. With results like these, we would expect dramatic influences on the factors of marriage in his horoscope. We find them in abundance: Saturn aspects, and Sun and Ketu occupy the seventh house; Venus, the significator for marriage, occupies the eighth house; the seventh lord, Jupiter, sits in Mrita Avastha, but in a Parivartana Yoga which involves houses four and seven. It was probably this Parivartana Yoga which permitted the marriages to occur in the first place, but all the other evil indications ensured that his married life would be hell. The influence of Saturn and Rahu in their capacity as significators for foreigners facilitated his choice of wives who were foreign to his culture.

DASHAS AND BHUKTIS His second marriage took place during his Rahu–Rahu bhukti. Besides the obvious fact that Rahu aspects the seventh house, it also gives the results of its dispositor Mercury, who aspects it from the seventh house. Moreover, Rahu occupies the nakshatra of Punarvasu, which is ruled by Jupiter, the seventh lord. At the time of the wedding, which took place during the summer of 1982, Rahu was transiting Gemini and thus restimulating its natal position.

His only child, a son, was born during his Rahu–Jupiter bhukti, in 1984. Jupiter, the natural significator for children, occupies a kendra and, although its weakness by avastha and by rashi might not have otherwise suggested the birth of a child, Jupiter also aspects Venus, the fifth lord. At the time of the birth, Jupiter was transiting Sagittarius, its own rashi, and from that position it strongly aspected the fifth house as counted both from the Moon and from the Sun Lagnas. The Rahu Maha Dasha as such was potentiated to give a child because Rahu occupies Jupiter's nakshatra.

His death occurred in 1989, during his Rahu–Saturn bhukti. Rahu and Saturn are the very two natural malefics who afflict his first house of longevity, while Saturn as the eighth lord afflicts Rahu, the dasha lord. At the time of his demise Saturn was transiting Sagittarius and afflicting thereby both the lagna and the lagna lord. Also, Sagittarius is here the seventh house, a maraka house.

FURTHERMORE Let us now consider the *Arudha Lagna*, a numerological manipulation of the various bhavas which can be calculated by two methods, one espoused by Parashara and one by Jaimini. Although both are very similar, the Parashari technique is more complex. We will consider here the simpler, Jaimini method, particularly because the same results are obtained by the Parashari method. Jaimini says: *When you count the number of rashis the lagna lord has gone from the lagna, and then count that same number again from the lagna lord, in the natural direction of the constellations, the result is the Arudha Lagna.*

We examine the Arudha Lagna as if it were another birth chart. While certain yogas are read exclusively from this chart, according to the Jaimini system of yogas, most of the standard principles of interpretation already introduced in this book can also be applied to the Arudha Lagna chart. In the horoscope above, lagna lord Mercury sits in Sagittarius, which is the seventh rashi away from the lagna, Gemini. If we now count seven rashis (always inclusive!) from Sagittarius, we return to Gemini. In this case, therefore, the lagna and the Arudha Lagna are one and the same (as it will also be when the lagna lord occupies the lagna). In this man's chart the virulent malefic combinations therefore recur even from this lagna. The lagna and Arudha Lagna were identical in the horoscopes of Hitler and Gandhi as well, which in their cases reinforced the effects of their already power-packed birth charts.

This process can then be extended to any of the bhavas of the horoscope. Take for example the eleventh house, which is Aries in the chart under consideration here. Its lord Mars occupies Scorpio, the eighth rashi from Aries. Counting eight rashis from Scorpio, we obtain Gemini, the lagna. The condition of the lagna will now act to corroborate the results we can expect in the native's eleventh-house matters, including older brothers and sisters. Since we have already seen the severe afflictions to which Gemini and its lord Mercury are subjected, it comes as no surprise that he had no elder brother.

Finally, note that this man was, like Ramakrishna Paramahamsa, born under the soli-lunar *Siddha Yoga*. While this yoga contributed to Ramakrishna's accommodating personality, pleasant nature and interest in ritual and spirituality, it did nothing of the kind for this man. Being a soli-lunar yoga, it was not destroyed by the bhanga, as the graha yogas were; it was instead submerged by the high tide of malefics which swamped his life.

AFTERWORD

Jyotish is a rich and noble pursuit. Like a surgeon's scalpel, which may be used to remove suffering while inflicting pain, Jyotish is sharp and can inflict wounds, especially on the very sensitive. A surgeon provides an anaesthetic to minimize the discomfort of the patient. Those who wield Jyotish should use the anaesthetic of great care and wisdom to avoid cutting themselves and others. Learn the tools of Jyotish. But, above all, show compassion in its use.

There is no end to Jyotish. We hope that this book will whet your appetite for more of the tasty, if hard-to-digest, morsels which await the avid connoisseur of wisdom, and that you will find this book a worthy diet to subsist on in the meanwhile. *Bon appétit!*

APPENDIX

CHART I

Birth Data: Birth Information
Retained for Privacy

Positions		Day: Saturday
LG	3°GE 52′	Yoga: Shubha
SU	21°CA 32′	
MO	7°LI 49′	Tithi: Saptami of
MA	27°AR 27′	Shukla Paksha
ME	11°LE 12′	Karana: Gara
JU	15°CA 18′	
VE	26°LE 24′	Nakshatra: Swati
SA	00°GE 15′	
RA	22°CA 51′	
KE	22°CP 51′	

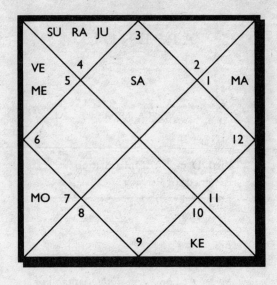

Rashi Chart

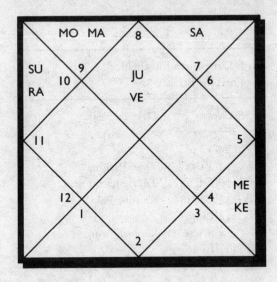

Navamsha Chart

Vimshottari Dasha

Rahu	From Birth	Mercury	17 Jan. 1995
Jupiter	17 Jan. 1960	Ketu	17 Jan. 2012
Saturn	17 Jan. 1976	Venus	17 Jan. 2019

CHART 2

Birth Data: Birth Information
Retained for Privacy

Positions		*Day:* Tuesday
LG	29°VI 05′	
SU	24°VI 25′	*Yoga:* Parigha
MO	6°GE 15′	*Tithi:* Shashti of
MA	15°GE 58′	Krishna Paksha
ME	18°LI 40′	
JU	4°SA 20′	*Karana:* Vanija
VE	23°LI 40′	
SA	19°SA 02′	*Nakshatra:* Mrigashirsha
RA	20°LE 23′	
KE	20°AQ 23′	

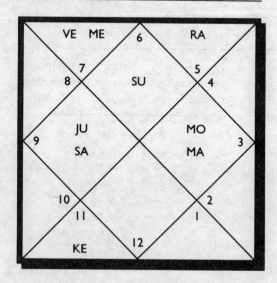

Rashi Chart

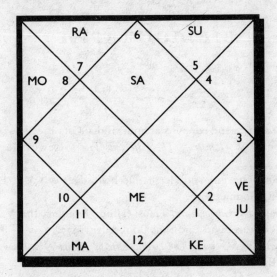

Navamsha Chart

Vimshottari Dasha

Mars	From Birth	Saturn	30 Dec. 1994
Rahu	30 Dec. 1960	Mercury	30 Dec. 2013
Jupiter	30 Dec. 1978	Venus	30 Dec. 2030

BIBLIOGRAPHY

The Bhagavadgita. 22nd edn. Gorakhpur, India: Gita Press, 1975.

Clark, Ronald W. *Einstein: The Life and Times.* New York: Avon Books, 1972.

de Santillana, Giorgio, and Hertha Dechend. *Hamlet's Mill.* Boston: David R. Godine, 1977.

Dhundhiraja. *Jatakabharanam.* Trans. (Hindi) Sitarama Jha. Varanasi, India: Thakurprasad End Sans Bookseller, 1977.

Fitch, Noel Riley. *Anaïs: The Erotic Life of Anaïs Nin.* New York: Little, Brown & Co., 1993.

Hixon, Lex. *The Great Swan: Meetings with Ramakrishna.* Boston: Shamabala, 1992.

Kalidas. *Uttarakalamrita.* Trans. V. Subrahmanya Shastri. 4th edn. Bangalore, India: Shri Mallikarjuna Press, 1981.

Kalyana. *Manasagari.* Trans. (Hindi) Sitarama Jha. Varanasi, India: Thakurprasad And Sons Bookseller, 1983.

Kalyan Varma. *Saravali: Volumes I & II.* Trans. R. Santhanam. New Delhi, India: Ranjan Publications, 1983.

Mahadeva. *Jataka Tatva.* Trans. V. Subrahmanya Shastri. 2nd edn. Bangalore, India: Sadhana Press, 1967.

Maharshi Jaimini. *Jaimini Sutram.* Trans. P. S. Shastri. New Delhi, India: Ranjan Publications, 1992.

Maharshi Parashara. *Brihat Parashara Hora: Volume I.* Trans. R. Santhanam. New Delhi, India: Ranjan Publications, 1984.

Maharshi Parashara. *Brihat Parashara Hora: Volume II.* Trans. G. S. Kapoor. New Delhi, India: Ranjan Publications, 1988.

Malhotra, Inder. *Indira Gandhi: A Personal and Political Biography.* Boston: Northeastern University Press, 1991.

Mantreshwara. *Phaladipika.* Trans. V. Subrahmanya Shastri. Bangalore, India: Yugantara Press, 1961.

Mukundavallabha. *Karmathaguruh.* (Sanskrit) Delhi, India: Motilal Banarsidas, 1986.

Narasimha. *Kalaprakashika.* Trans. N. P. Subramania Iyer. New Delhi, India: Asian Educational Services, 1982.

Neelakantha. *Tajika Neelakanthi.* Trans. (Hindi) Kedaradatta Joshi. Delhi, India: Motilal Banarsidas, 1992.

Ojha, Gopesh Kumar. *Hindu Predictive Astrology.* Bombay, India: D. B. Taraporevala Sons & Co. PvT Ltd, 1972.

Podumanai Chomadiri. *Jatakadesha Marga.* Trans. S. S. Sareen. New Delhi, India: Sagar Publications, 1992.

Prashna Marga: Volumes I, II & III. Trans. J. N. Bhasin. Delhi, India: Ranjan Publications, 1987.

Prithuyashas. *Horasara.* Trans. R. Santhanam. New Delhi, India; Ranjan Publications, 1982.

Prithuyashas. *Shatpanchasika.* Trans. V. Subrahmanya Shastri. 3rd edn. Bangalore, India: Shri Mallikarjuna Press, 1978.

Riese, Randall, and Neil Hitchens. *The Unabridged Marilyn: Her Life from A to Z.* New York: Congdon & Weed, 1987.

Sharma, Vishwanath Deva. *Astrology and Jyotir Vidya.* Calcutta, India: Vishwa Jyotirvid Samgha, 1973.

Siva Svarodaya. Trans. Ram Kumar Rai. 2nd edn. Varanasi, India: Prachya Prakashan, 1987.

Surya Siddhanta. Trans. E. Burgess and W. D. Whitney. San Diego: Wizards Bookshelf, 1978.

Toland, John. *Adolf Hitler – The Definitive Biography.* New York: Anchor Books, 1992.

Vaidyanatha Dikshita. *Jataka Parijata: Volumes I, II & III.* Trans. V. Subrahmanya Shastri. New Delhi, India: Ranjan Publications (no year given).

Varahamihira. *Brihad Jataka.* Trans. V. Subrahmanya Shastri. Bangalore, India: Sadhana Press, 1981.

Varahamihira. *Brihat Samhita: Parts I & II.* Trans. M. Ramakrishna Bhat. Delhi, India: Motilal Banarsidass, 1981.

Varahamihira. *Daivajna Vallabha.* New Delhi, India: Ranjan Publications, 1983.

van Buitenen, J. A. B. '*Dharma and Moksha*' Philosophy East and West, Vol. VII, Nos. 1 & 2, April, July 1957, pp. 33–40.

Vyankatesh Sharma. *Sarvarth Chintamani*. Trans. J. N. Bhasin. New
    Delhi, India: Sagar Publications, 1986.
Yogananda, Paramahamsa. *The Autobiography of a Yogi*. Los Angeles:
    Self-Realization Fellowship, 1987.

BIRTH DATA SOURCES

All birth data for the charts used in this book originate from the
birth records of the individuals or, in the case of Ramakrishna,
Yogananda, Hitler and Gandhi, from birth charts used and verified
by numerous prominent jyotishis.

INDEX

Figures in italics refer to tables and charts